HANDBUCH DER PISTOLEN- UND REVOLVER-PATRONEN · MANUAL OF PISTOL AND REVOLVER CARTRIDGES

HANS A. ERLMEIER · JAKOB H. BRANDT

Handbuch der Pistolen- und Revolver-Patronen

Manual of Pistol and Revolver Cartridges

BAND II
Zentralfeuer, Amerikanische und Britische Kaliber

VOLUME II
Centerfire, American and British Calibers

Journal-Verlag
Schwend GmbH
Schwäbisch Hall

Übersetzung/Translation:
D. Büttner, Wiesbaden

1. Auflage/First edition

Vorbemerkungen

Dieses Buch soll in Ergänzung des ersten Bandes ebenfalls in erster Linie ein Nachschlagewerk sein. Aus diesem Grund wurde ein katalogmäßiger Aufbau gewählt, der dem Benutzer das Auffinden der Patronen amerikanischer- oder britischer Kaliber erleichtert. Jede Patrone ist mit einer Nummer gekennzeichnet, die als „Katalognummer“ bei der Bestimmung der Patronen und zur Vermeidung von Verwechslungen nützlich sein kann.

Neben der nach Kalibern geordneten Reihenfolge der Patronen stellt das nach Kaliberbezeichnungen und alphabetisch geordnete Inhaltsverzeichnis der Synonyme im Anhang des Buches eine weitere Hilfe dar.

Wie eingangs erwähnt, befaßt sich der vorliegende Band II mit Patronen der amerikanischen- und britischen Kaliber. Er enthält Daten über Kugel- und Schrotpatronen und ihre Abarten, soweit sie serienmäßig oder auch nur in geringen Stückzahlen als Versuchspatronen kommerziell gefertigt wurden. Um die Übersichtlichkeit des Buches zu wahren, mußte auf die katalogmäßige Erfassung der großen Anzahl von Spezialpatronen (Beschuß-, Platz-, Gas-, Signal-, Zünd-, Viehbetäubungs-Patronen u. a.) verzichtet werden. Die im Anhang des Buches abgebildeten Beschuß-, Platz- und Exerzierpatronen sollen ohne Berücksichtigung des jeweiligen Kalibers nur einen allgemeinen Überblick über verschiedene gebräuchliche Kennzeichnungen sowie Formen und Arten geben. Von einer Aufnahme von sog. „wildcats“*) wurde aus berechtigten Erwägungen Abstand genommen.

*) „Wildcats“ sind Patronen, die nicht fabrikmäßig entwickelt und hergestellt wurden. Sie entstehen durch nachträgliches Abändern und beliebiges Zusammenfügen bereits existierender Patronenelemente.

Preface

This supplementary volume is also primarily a reference work. For this reason, a catalog structure has been selected, so as to help the user to trace American or British caliber cartridges. Each cartridge is allocated a number – the “catalogue number” – which should prove useful in locating cartridges and avoiding confusion. In addition to the list of cartridges, arranged by caliber, further help is given by the Appendix, which contains an Index listing all synonyms alphabetically and by caliber.

As already mentioned, Volume II covers American and British caliber cartridges. It contains data on ball and shot cartridges and their variations, insofar they have been commercially produced in quantily or in small experimental lots, to maintain clarity in this book, a large number of special cartridges (proof, blank, gas, dummy, signal, ignition, cattle-killer, etc.) had to be omitted. The proof and blank cartridges, in any case dummy cartridges illustrated in the Appendix serve to give a general view of the usual variations in marking, shapes and types, without regard for their respective calibers.

Inclusion of so-called “wildcats”*) has purposely been avoided.

*) “Wildcats” are cartridges which are not commercially developed and produced, but which are formed by modifying and assembling existing cartridge components as required.

Allgemeines

Der vorliegende Band behandelt amerikanische- und britische Zentralfeuerpatronen, d. h. Zentralfeuerpatronen im Zoll-Kaliber für Pistolen und Revolver. Es muß dazu gesagt werden, daß sich die Erfassung dieser Patronengruppe neben wenigen Patronen bei denen überwiegend Kunststoff verwandt wurde, auf Metallpatronen beschränkt.

Unter den Begriff „amerikanische- und britische Kaliber" fallen alle Patronen, die in Ländern entwickelt wurden, in denen das „Zoll-System" eingeführt ist. Von wenigen Ausnahmen abgesehen liegt der Ursprung aller dieser Patronen in Amerika und England. Die meisten dieser Patronen wurden jeweils nur während weniger Jahre hergestellt und fanden keine große Verbreitung. Einige wurden allerdings infolge der Vielzahl der für sie eingerichteten Waffen in der ganzen Welt bekannt.

Diese Patronen behielten im Gegensatz zu den Patronen europäischen Ursprungs (6,35 mm Browning = .25 ACP), auch in den Ländern mit metrischen System (Deutschland, Belgien, Italien u. a.) ihre Kaliberbezeichnung bei (.38 Smith & Wesson Special = .38 Smith & Wesson Special).

Sollten sich bei einigen Kalibern jedoch metrische Bezeichnungen ergeben, sind sie als Synonyme den Zollbezeichnungen zugeordnet.

Kaliberbezeichnung

Die Kaliberbezeichnung ist eines der kompliziertesten und undurchsichtigsten Kapitel auf diesem Gebiet und stellt nicht nur den Laien, sondern sogar Experten, die sich ständig mit dieser Materie befassen, immer wieder vor neue Probleme.

Der Grund hierfür ist in der verschiedenartigen Auffassung der Waffen- und Munutionshersteller zu suchen, die (seit der Einführung des gezogenen Laufes) bei Verwendung von in ihren Abmessungen gleichen Patronen oftmals unterschiedliche Kaliberbezeichnungen willkürlich festlegten.

Folgende Möglichkeiten waren gegeben:

1. Bezeichnung nach dem Felddurchmesser des Laufes (Abb. 1)
2. Bezeichnung nach dem Zugdurchmesser des Laufes (Abb. 2)
3. Bezeichnung nach dem Feld-Zugdurchmesser des Laufes bei einer ungeraden Anzahl von Feldern und Zügen (Abb. 3)
4. Bezeichnung nach dem Geschoßdurchmesser.
5. Frei gewählte Kaliberbezeichnung, um mögliche Verwechselungen mit bereits existierenden Patronen zu vermeiden.

General remarks

This volume covers American and British centerfire cartridges, i.e. centerfire cartridges in the inch-caliber for pistols and revolvers. This definition covers metallic cartridges only, apart from the compilation of a few cartridges manufactured above all with plastic material.

The heading "American and British calibers" includes all cartridges developed in countries using the "inch system". With few exceptions, all of these cartridges originated in America and England. Most were produced for only a few years and achieved little popularity. Some however, achieved world-wide distribution due to the large number of weapons which were adapted to them.

Contrary to the cartridges of European origin (6,35 mm Browning = .25 ACP) these cartridges did not change their calibre designation (.38 Smith & Wesson Special = .38 Smith & Wesson Special) either in the countries using the metric system (Germany, Belgium, Italy and others). However, should some calibers bear metric designations, these are listed as synonyms with the inch designations.

Caliber designations

Caliber designation is one of the most complicated and obscure subjects in this field; not only amateurs, but even experts who deal with this subject all the time, are continually confronted with new problems.

The roof of the problem lies in the diverse practices of the small arms and ammunitions manufacturers, following the introduction of rifled barrels; in denoting similar cartridges, they often fixed arbitrarily on quite different designations.

The following were possibilities:

1. Designation based on the land diameter of the barrel (Fig. 1).
2. Designation based on the groove diameter of the barrel (Fig. 2)
3. Designation based on the land/groover diameter of the barrel, where there is an uneven number of lands and grooves (Fig. 3)
4. Designation based on the bullet diameter.
5. Independent designation to avoid confusion with existing cartridges.

Kaliberbezeichnung

Caliber designations

Abb./Figure 1

Felddurchmesser
des Laufes

Land diameter
of the barrel

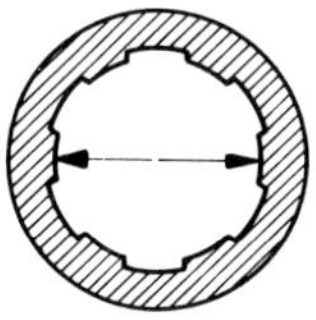

Abb./Figure 2

Zugdurchmesser
des Laufes

Groove diameter
of the barrel

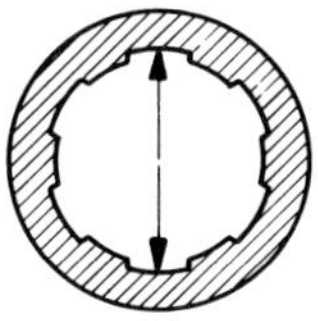

Abb./Figure 3

Feld-Zugdurchmesser
des Laufes

Land/groove diameter
of the barrel

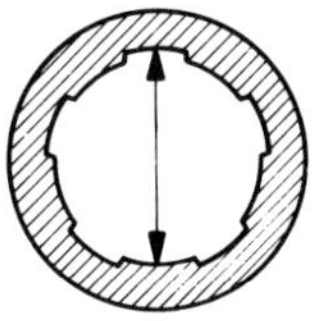

Bei Fällen vorstehend geschilderter Art (zu 5.) wurde in diesem Buch Wert darauf gelegt, die Kaliberbezeichnung jeweils in ihrer ursprünglichen Art als Hauptbegriff zu erhalten; alle anderen Bezeichnungen werden als Synonyme geführt.

In cases such as that described above (to 5.), this book gives precedence to the original designation; all other designations are listed as synonyms.

Patronenbezeichnung

Die Patronenbezeichnung setzt sich im allgemeinen zusammen aus der Kaliberbezeichnung und dem dazugehörigen Namen des Waffenkonstrukteurs bzw. Waffenherstellers (.38 Smith & Wesson, .38 Dardick, .38 Winchester C.F. u. a.).

Verschiedentlich ist auch aus der Kaliberbezeichnung und dem Verwendungszweck der Waffe die Patronenbezeichnung entstanden. (.22 C.F. Experimental, .44 S & W Amerikan., .44 S & W Russian u. a.).

Hier wurde wiederum beachtet, daß die aufgeführten Standard-Patronenbezeichnungen ihrem Ursprung entsprechen. Die Bezeichnung .32 Smith & Wesson wird daher immer die Priorität vor .32-6-85 Smith & Wesson oder 7,9 × 15,0 - S.&W. 32 haben, wenngleich letztere als Synonym mit aufgeführt ist.

Eine weitere Art der Patronenbezeichnung findet man in einigen Herstellerkatalogen auch in der Form, daß die Maße „Geschoßdurchmesser und Hülsenlänge" angegeben werden (.450 long C.F. 50/54" case oder .450 long C.F.-1-19/64 case). Andere Patronenbezeichnungen haben hinter der Kaliberangabe eine oder zwei Zahlenangaben durch Bindestrich getrennt (.44-40 Win.C.F. oder .442-20-220 long), hier bedeutet die zweite Zahl das Schwarzpulvergewicht und die dritte Zahl das Geschoßgewicht jeweils in grain.

Die Bezeichnungsart wie sie im metrischen System gelegentlich üblich ist (7,8 × 16,5R oder 9× 19) kennt man im Zollsystem nicht. Die erstere Art wird für Patronen mit Rand und die letztere Art für die Patronen ohne Rand benutzt. Die zweite Zahl bezeichnet immer die Hülsenlänge; sie wird auch gebraucht, wenn der Ursprung einer Patrone unbekannt ist und bei Patronen die einer bestimmten Waffe noch nicht zugeordnet werden konnten.

Je größer der Verbreitungsgrad einer Patrone war, desto zahlreicher waren bzw. sind die Bezeichnungen, unter denen sie von den Fabriken der einzelen Länder gefertigt wurde. Alle diese, von der Standard-Bezeichnung abweichenden Bezeichnungen sind innerhalb des Patronen-Kataloges als Synonyme aufgeführt, außerdem im Anhang, kalibermäßig und alphabetisch geordnet zu finden.

Cartridge designations

The cartridge designation generally consists of the caliber designation, together with the name of either the weapons designer of manufacturer (.38 - Smith & Wesson, .38 Dardick, .38 Winchester C. F. etc.). Occasionally it consists of the caliber designation, together with the type of weapon (.22 - C.F. Experimental, .44 S & W American, .44 S & W Russian etc.)

Again one should note here that the original, standard cartridge designation appears first. Therefore the designation .32 Smith & Wesson will always take precendence over .32-6-85 or 7,9 × 15,0 - S.&W. 32 although the latter is listed as a synonym.

Another form of cartridge designation is to be found in any manufacturers'-catalogs, in the form of "bullet diameter × case length" (.450 long C.F. 50/54" case or .450 long C.F.-1-19/64 case). Other cartridge designations show behind the caliber indication one or two numerals separated by a hyphen (.44-40 Win.C.F. or .442-20-220 long), the second figure referring to black powder weight and the third figure to the bullet weight, in grains each.

The form of cartridge designation as it is used occasionally in the metric system (7,8 × 16,5R or 9 × 19) is unknown in the inch system. The former kind is used for rimmed cartridges and the latter form for rimless cartridges. The second figure designates always the case length, it is also used when the origin of a cartridge is unknown and in case of cartridges which could not yet be classified as pertaining to a determinate weapon.

The more widely a cartridge was distributed, the greater was respectively is the number of designations under which it was manufactured by various countries. All such designations which differ from the standard cartridge designation are listed by calibre and alphabetically as synonyms in the Cartridge Catalog, as well as the Appendix.

Bodenstempel

Als Bodenstempel bezeichnet man eine auf dem Hülsenboden fabriksmäßig angebrachte sichtbare Kennzeichnung, die aus einer beliebigen Anzahl Buchstaben, Zahlen oder Zeichen, sei es in vertiefter oder in erhabener Form, besteht.

Man kann zwei Gruppen von Bodenstempeln unterscheiden,
Gruppe 1: Fertigung für den Zivilbedarf

Gruppe 2: Fertigung für polizeiliche und militärische Zwecke

In Gruppe 1 besteht der Bodenstempel in der Regel entweder aus dem vollen Namenszug des Herstellers, teilweise mit Angabe des Fertigungsortes (ELEY LONDON, SPEER, PETERS, UTENDOERFFER NUERNBERG, etc.) oder aus Initialien (DCCo, F A, REM-UMC, U.S.C.Co. etc.) und der Kaliber- oder Patronenbezeichnung bzw. deren Abkürzung.

Von dieser Regel weichen zwei Firmen ab, die „Deutsche Waffen- und Munitionsfabriken AG (DWM) und die G. Roth AG (GR)" indem sie anstelle der Kaliber- oder Patronenbezeichnung neben ihren Initialien eine sog. „Hülsen-Nummer" auf dem Hülsenboden angegeben haben.

Diese Hülsennummern dienten zugleich als Katalog- und Bestellnummern für leere Hülsen (die Bestellnummer für eine geladene Patrone setzt sich aus Hülsen- und Geschoßnummer zusammen, z. B. DWM 513A = .45 Automatic M. 1911). Dank dieser Nomenklatur wird heute oftmals die sehr schwierige Identifikation unbekannter Patronen früherer Fertigung wesentlich erleichtert, wenn nicht sogar überhaupt erst ermöglicht.

Bei Patronen der Gruppe 2 kann der Bodenstempel ganz oder teilweise bestehen aus Initialien oder Firmenzeichen des Herstellers (sowohl Privatunternehmen wie staatliche Munitionsfabriken). Jahr und Monat der Fertigung, die Fabrikationsnummer oder sonstige Kurzzeichen, die auf die Art der Patronen bzw. auf deren evtl. speziellen Verwendungszweck hinweisen.

Verschiedentlich findet man Patronen ohne Bodenstempel. Soweit beobachtet werden konnte, handelt es sich hierbei (bezogen auf gängige Patronen) meist um Erzeugnisse minderer Qualität kleiner Herstellerfirmen. Darüber hinaus kann es sich um Versuchspatronen handeln, die infolge der geringen Stückzahlen nicht mit einem Bodenstempel versehen wurden.

Schließlich sei noch erwähnt, daß es für jedermann möglich war und auch heute noch ist, bei Erteilung eines entsprechend großen Auftrages einen eigenen Bodenstempel auf der Patrone anbringen zu lassen.

Patronenabmessungen

Einen wesentlichen Punkt bei der Identifizierung von Patronen stellen die genauen Abmessungen dar. Die in diesem Buch angegebenen Maße wurden sowohl durch Vermessen von mehr als tausend Patronen verschiedener Fertigung ermittelt, als auch (mit den angegebenen Toleranzen) den Originalunterlagen einzelner Herstellerfirmen entnommen.

Headstamps

The word "headstamp" refers to a visible identification mark stamped on the cartridge base by the manufacturer, and consisting of a number of letters, figures or symbols impressed into or raised from the surface.

Two types of headstamp may be distinguished; Group 1, produced for civilian requirements, and Group 2 produced for police and military purposes.

As a rule headstamps in Group 1 consist of either the full name of the manufacturer, sometimes with an indication of the place of production (ELEY LONDON, SPEER, PETERS, UTENDOERFFER NUERNBERG etc.) or of their initials (DCCo, FA, REM-UMC, U.S.C.Co. etc.) together with an abbreviation of the caliber or cartridge designation.

Two firms form an exception to this rule, the "Deutsche Waffen- und Munutionsfabriken AG" (DWM) and "G. Roth AG (GR); in addition to their initials, these show a "case number" instead of a caliber or cartridge designation.

These case numbers served as both catalog and order numbers for empty cases (the order number for loaded cartridges consisted of the case and bullet numbers combined; for instance, DWM 513A = .45 Automatic M. 1911). Nowadays this nomenclature greatly facilitates the often extremely difficult, if not entirely impossible, identification of unknown cartridges produced during the early period.

The headstamp of cartridges in Group 2 may consist wholly or partially of: manufacturers-initials or symbols (both private companies and government factories), year and month of production, and lot number or other abbreviation, which indicate the cartridge type or its special purpose.

Occasionally, cartridges are found without any headstamp. Up to now it has been remarked that, with reference to cartridges in current production, these are usually of inferior quality produced by small manufacturers. Moreover, this may also occur with experimental cartridges which, because of their very small quantities, do not carry their own headstamp. Finally, it should be pointed out that anyone could – and still can – have his own headstamp put on cartridges when ordering a sufficient large quantity.

Cartridge dimensions

An important way of identifying cartridges is by their precise dimensions. The measurements given in this book were arrived at by measuring more than one thousand cartridges produced by various manufacturers, or else were taken (with their admitted tolerances) from the original documents of certain manufacturers.

Folgende Maße (zu messen an den bezeichneten Punkten) sind für die Identifizierung einer Patrone unerläßlich:

The following measurements (made at the points indicated) are indispensable to the identification of any cartridge:

a = Geschoß-∅
b = Hülsen-∅ Hals
c = Hülsen-∅ Boden
d = Hülsen-∅ Rand
e = Hülsenlänge
f = Patronenlänge

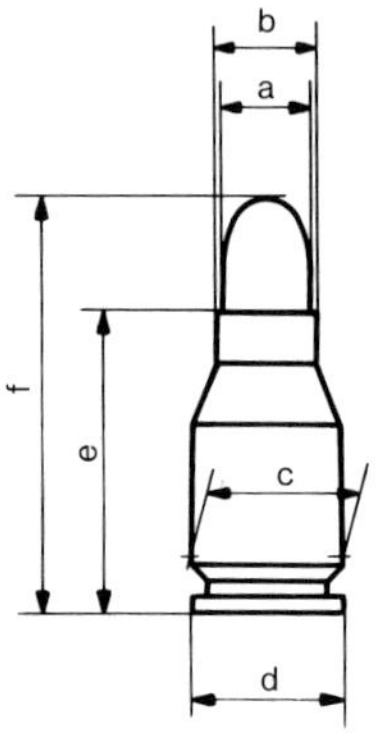

Abb./Figure 4

Meßpunkte bei einer randlosen Patrone

Points of measurement for a rimless cartridge

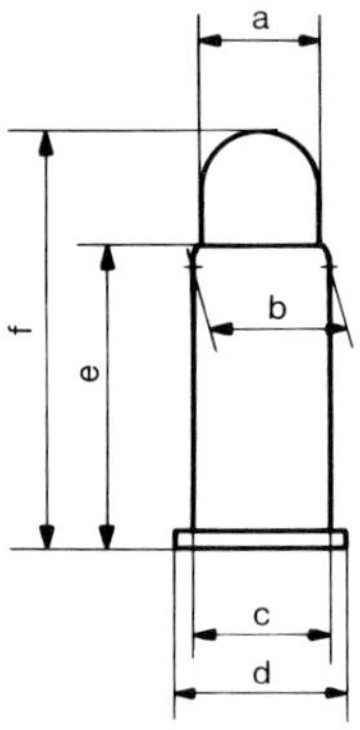

Abb./Figure 5

Meßpunkte bei einer Patrone mit Rand

Points of measurement for a rimmed cartridge

a — bullet diameter
b — case neck diameter
c — case head diameter
d — case rim diameter
e — case length
f — cartridge length

Zusätzlich zu den Maßangaben stellen die im Maßstab 1:1 abgebildeten Patronen eine weitere Hilfe bei der Identifizierung dar. Es wurde, soweit die Patronen zur Verfügung standen, bewußt das aufwendige Verfahren der maßstabsgetreuen fotografischen Reproduktion gewählt, um jede Einzelheit der Patrone aufzuzeigen, was bei zeichnerischer Darstellung nicht immer möglich gewesen wäre.

In addition to these measurements, the illustrations of cartridges to the scale 1:1 give further help for identification. Insofar as the cartridges were available, accurate scale photography was chosen to highlight every detail; this would not always have been possible with drawings.

Aufbau der Patrone

Eine Zentralfeuerpatrone setzt sich aus folgenden vier Komponenten zusammen: Hülse, Geschoß, Zündsystem und Pulver.

Cartridge construction

A centerfire cartridge consists of the following four components: case, bullet, primer and powder.

A. HÜLSE

Die Hülsen von Metallpatronen bestehen in der Regel entweder aus Kupfer oder Messing, das sich bis heute als bestes geeignetes Hülsenmaterial bewährt hat. Während des 2. Weltkrieges wurden auch Versuche mit Stahl und Aluminium durchgeführt; dabei erwies sich Stahl als ebenfalls brauchbar. Es zeigte sich allerdings, daß die Lagerfähigkeit von Patronen mit Stahlhülsen selbst bei entsprechender Oberflächenbehandlung begrenzt war. Aluminium als Hülsenmaterial wurde bei Pistolenpatronen ausschließlich in der Schweiz verwendet, jedoch bereits nach kurzer Zeit wieder durch Messing ersetzt. Verschiedene Hersteller verwenden neuerdings wieder Stahl als Hülsenmaterial, wobei unterschiedliche Oberflächenbehandlungen (Verkupfern, Lackieren u. a.) vorgenommen werden.

A. CASE

As a rule, metallic cartridge cases are made of either copper or brass, the latter having proven to be the most suitable material to date. During World War II experiments were carried out with steel and aluminium; as a result, steel also proved to be serviceable. However, it was found that steel-cased cartridges could only be stored for any length of time if they were coated with some suitable substance. Only Switzerland used aluminium as a case material for pistole cartridges, but it was soon replaced by brass. Recently a number of manufacturers have once again adopted steel as a case material, with various coatings (copper washed, lacquered etc.).

Im Zuge der technischen Entwicklung gewinnt Kunststoff als Hülsenmaterial immer größere Bedeutung. Werden heute bereits Platz-, Trainings- und Schrotpatronen aus Kunststoff (teilweise mit Metallboden) gefertigt, so ist der Zeitpunkt abzusehen, an dem die Hülsen der Kugelpatronen aus Kunststoff bestehen werden.

Seit Einführung der Metallpatronen war die Hülsenform, bedingt durch die unterschiedlichen Konstruktionen der Waffen, Wandlungen unterworfen. Allein bei Zentralfeuerpatronen sind, wie die nachfolgende Tabelle zeigt, 14 verschiedene Grundformen der Metallhülse (nur für Pistolen- und Revolverpatronen) bekannt.

As a result of its technical development, plastic is becoming increasingly important as a case material. Today we already have blank, practice and shot cartridges made of plastic (some of which have a metal base) so it is conceivable that in the foreseeable future there will be plastic cases for ball cartridges.

Ever since the introduction of metallic cartridges, the case shape has been liable to alteration on account of the various constructions of weapon. As the table below shows, all centerfire cartridges – at least, pistol and revolver cartridges – fall into 14 basic shapes.

Tabelle/Table 1

Hülsenformen *Case Shapes*	**randlos** **rimless**	**randlos** **rimless**	**unter-** **schnittener** **Rand** **rebated rim**	**Halbrand** **semi-** **rimmed**	**Rand** **rimmed**	**Gürtel** **belted**
	ohne Auszieher-Rille without extractor groove	mit Auszieher-Rille with extractor groove				
konisch **tapered**	1 2	3			6	
zylindrisch **straight**	8	10	11	12	13	14
Flaschenhals konisch **Bottle neck, tapered**	15	17				
Flaschenhals zylindrisch **Bottle neck, straight**		24			27	

Hauptbestandteil eines Geschosses ist – von wenigen Ausnahmen abgesehen – Blei. Infolge seines spezifischen Gewichtes weist Blei bei relativ kleinen Abmessungen, in entsprechende Form gebracht, gute ballistische Eigenschaften auf. Durch Zusatz von Zinn oder Antimon kann der Härtegrad des Bleis verändert werden, so daß entweder eine leichtere Verformbarkeit oder aber eine größere Durchschlagskraft des Geschosses erzielt wird.

Mit dem Aufkommen der Repetier- und Selbstladewaffen erfuhren die Geschosse in ihrer Beschaffenheit teilweise eine Veränderung. Um den störungsfreien Repetiervorgang, manuell oder automatisch, zu gewährleisten, wurde das Bleigeschoß mit einem Mantel aus dünnem Stahlblech versehen. Diese Mantelgeschosse wurden häufig nickel- oder nickelkupferplattiert, ein Verfahren, das bei der Verwendung von Flußstahl noch heute üblich ist. Neben Stahl fanden in geringem Umfang auch Kupfer und Messing Verwendung. In den USA und einigen anderen Ländern bevorzugt man zur Herstellung der Geschoßmäntel eine Kupferlegierung, die früher oft mit einer hauchdünnen Zinnschicht überzogen wurde.

Neben diesen konventionellen Grundstoffen wurden im Laufe der Zeit, teilweise in Versuchen, teils in Serienfertigung, die unterschiedlichsten Materialien (Aluminium, Sintereisen, Tombak, Holz, Kunststoff etc.) zur Fertigung von Geschossen verwendet.

Die vielfältigen, zum Teil heute noch hergestellten Geschoßformen von Pistolen- und Revolverpatronen zeigt die nachstehende Tabelle.

With few exceptions principal constituent in a bullet is lead. Because of its high specific gravity in relation to its volume, it possesses good ballistic characteristics when appropriately shaped. The hardness of the lead can be varied by the addition of tin or antimony, so that it be can made to deform more easily or to penetrate further.

With the advent of repeating and self-loading weapons, bullet construction has been somewhat modified. To avoid malfunctions in the repeating cycle, whether manual or automatic, the lead bullet was given a jacket of thin sheet-steel. These steel jacketed bullets were often plated with nickel or cupro-nickel, a process which is still generally employed for steel castings. In addition to steel, copper and brass were also employed to a limited extent. In the USA and some other countries, a copper alloy is now preferred for the manufacture of bul let jackets which used formerly to be given an extremely thin coating of tin.

Apart from these conventional materials, the most diverse materials (such as aluminium, sintered iron, pinchbeck, wood, plastic etc.) were used for bullets, either experimentally or for mass production.

The great variety of shapes of bullet for pistols and revolvers, some of which are still in production, are shown in table below.

Tabelle 2/Table 2

Geschoßformen *Bullet Shapes*

	**A** Kugel	**A** round ball		**J** Stumpfkegel	**J** blunt coned
	**B** Rundkopf	**B** round nose	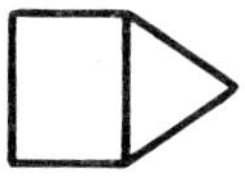	**K** Kegel	**K** coned
	**C** Rundkopf/Ferse	**C** round nose, heel	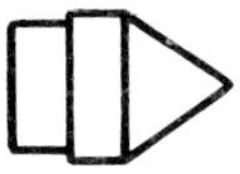	**L** Kegel/Ferse	**L** coned, heel
	**D** Rundkopf/konisch	**D** boat-tail	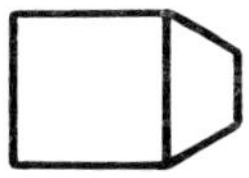	**M** Kegelstumpf	**M** truncated cone
	**E** Spitzkopf	**E** pointed	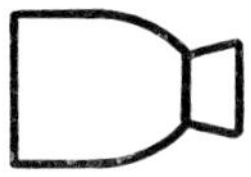	**N** Pilz	**N** Westley Richards "All range"
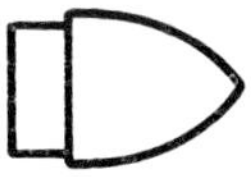	**F** Spitzkopf/Ferse	**F** pointed/heel		**P** Scharfrand	**P** wadcutter
	**G** Flachkopf	**G** flat nose	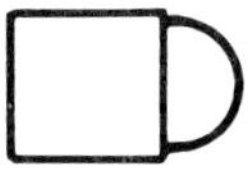	**S** Scharfrand/ Rundkopf	**S** "Mid Range"
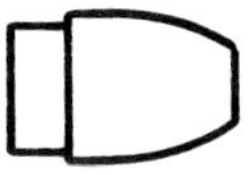	**H** Flachkopf/Ferse	**H** flat nose, heel	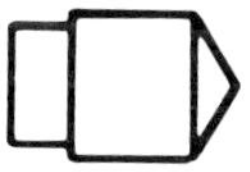	**T** Stumpfkegel Ferse	**T** blunt coned, heel
			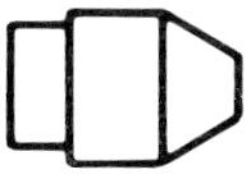	**U** Kegelstumpf/ Ferse	**U** truncated cone heel

Die meisten der in Tabelle 2 aufgeführten Geschoßformen sind bei mehreren Geschoßarten anzutreffen. Man kennt heute, soweit in mehr oder minder großen Stückzahlen jemals serienmäßig gefertigt, 39 verschiedene Geschoßarten bei metrischen Pistolen- und Revolverpatronen. Eingeteilt in 7 Klassen (A–G), sind sie im einzelnen nachfolgend kurz beschrieben und in ihrem Aufbau schematisch dargestellt.

Most of the bullet shapes shown in Table 2 are to be found with a variety of bullet types. 39 different bullet types have been used for metric pistol and revolver cartridges mass produced on either a large or a small scale. Divided into seven classes (A to G) they are briefly described below, and their construction illustrated.

Klasse A – *Voll-Geschosse*

Voll-Geschosse bestehen jeweils aus nur einem Material, wobei Geschosse aus Blei in der Regel mit einer unterschiedlichen Anzahl von Rillen versehen sind. Diese dienen zur Aufnahme von Geschoßtalg, der das Verbleien des Laufes auf ein Minimum reduzieren soll.

Class A – *Solid Bullets*

Solid bullets always consist of a single material; lead bullets are usually provided with a varying number of grooves which, when filled with a bullet lubricant, minimise leading in the barrel.

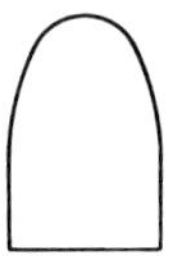

Abb./Figure 6

1 Blei
2 Stahl
3 Sintereisen
4 Aluminium
5 Graphit
6 Trolit*)
7 Kunststoff
8 Wachs
9 Hartlegierung
10 Messing, teflonbeschichtet

1 Lead
2 Steel
3 Sintered iron
4 Aluminium
5 Graphite
6 Trolit*)
7 Plastic
8 Wax
9 Hard alloy
10 Brass, teflon-coated

Eine andere, heute nicht mehr angewandte Methode, das Verbleien des Laufes weitgehend zu verhindern, war das Umwickeln der hinteren Hälfte des Bleigeschosses mit Papier.

Another, now obsolete, method of avoiding this leading of the barrel was to wrap the rear half of the lead bullet in paper.

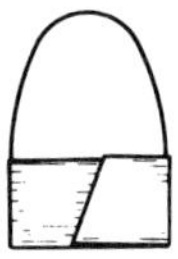

Abb./Figure 7

15 Blei/Papier

15 Lead, paper patched

Eine ebenfalls heute nicht mehr angewandte Methode, den Lauf während des Schusses zu schmieren, war ein mit Schmiermittel gefüllter Hohlraum im Geschoß. Aus dem Hohlraum führten Kanäle zur Geschoßaußenwand. Durch den Gasdruck wurde das Schmiermittel nach außen gedrückt.

Another out-of-use method to lubricate the barrel was a hollow-based bullet filled with a lubricant. Holes led from the cavity to the outer bullet surface. Thus the lubricant was pressed outward by the gas pressure when the shot was fired.

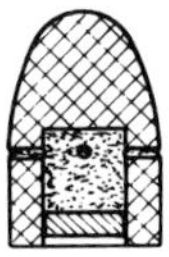

Abb./Figure 8

16 Blei, selbstschmierend

16 Lead, self-lubricating

Eine Art der Geschosse hat eine sog. „Gascheck-Kappe" am Boden. Bei der 2. Art (Stahl, Teflon-Geschosse) soll die Kappe verhindern, daß das Geschoßmaterial (Stahl) eine Laufberührung bekommt.

One bullet type has a so called "gas check cap" at the base. The second type (steel, teflon-coated) has a cap which is to prevent that the bullet material (steel) gets in touch with the barrel.

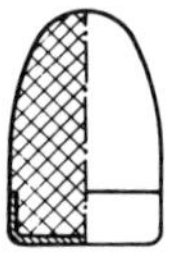

Abb./Figure 9

17 Blei/Metallboden
18 Stahl, teflonbeschichtet/Metallboden

17 Lead, metal-besed
18 Steel, teflon coated, metal-based

---

*) Erster spritzfähiger organischer Kunststoff auf Nitrozellulosebasis. Besitzt heute nur noch historischen Wert.

*) The first organic plastic with a nitrocellulose base which could be injektion moulded. Today only of historical interest.

Abb./Figure 41

c) Berdan (3- und 4-Loch)

Bei Patronen früherer Fertigung findet man verschiedentlich das Berdan-Zündsystem auch mit 3 oder 4 Zündlöchern.

c) Berdan (3 and 4 hole)

Berdan cartridges of early manufacture may also occasionally be found with three or four flash holes.

3. Amboß getrennt von Zündhütchen und Hülse

3. Anvil separate from primer and case

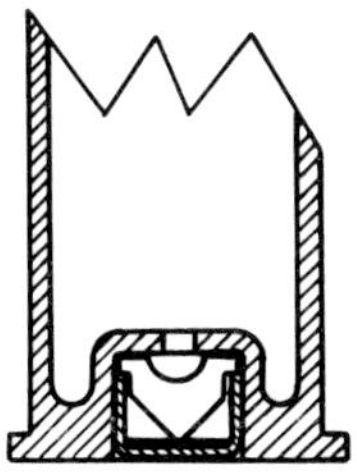

Abb./Figure 42

a) Boxer (englisch)

Diese von Oberst E. M. Boxer konstruierte Ausführung war die ursprüngliche Form des später verbesserten Zündsystems. Hauptmerkmal dieser Konstruktion ist der getrennt in die Zündglocke eingesetzte und nur durch das Zündhütchen festgehaltene Amboß.

a) Boxer (English)

This type, designed by colonel E. M. Boxer, was the forerunner of the later system (Boxer, modern), which was an improvement of it. Its special feature is the anvil, which is seated loosely in the primer pocket and is held in position by the primer alone.

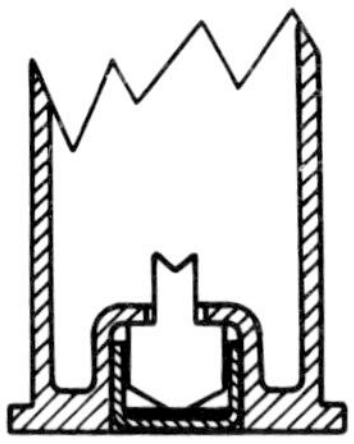

Abb./Figure 43

b) Braun & Bloem

Für eine ähnliche Konstruktion wurde der Firma Braun & Bloem, Düsseldorf, ein Patent erteilt. Alle von dieser Firma hergestellten Revolverpatronen waren mit diesem Zündsystem ausgerüstet.

b) Braun & Bloem

Braun & Bloem, of Düsseldorf, were granted a patent for a similar system. All revolver cartridges produced by this firm were furnished with this ignition system.

Das Pulver bildet die vierte Komponente der Patrone. Es besteht aus einem Gemisch verschiedener chemischer Stoffe und dient als Treibmittel. Eine Initialzündung (Stichflamme des Zündsatzes) leitet den chemischen Umsetzungsprozeß ein, wobei die freiwerdenden Gase das Geschoß mit mehr oder minder großem Druck durch den Lauf der Waffe treiben.

Man unterscheidet zwei Hauptgruppen von Pulverarten: das Schwarzpulver, benannt nach Berthold Schwarz, einem Franziskanermönch, dem die Entdeckung dieses Pulvers zu Beginn des 14. Jahrhunderts (um 1313) zugeschrieben wird, und das rauchlose (rauchschwache) Pulver auf Nitrozellulosebasis, das auf die Entdeckung der Nitrozellulose durch den deutschen Chemiker Christian Schönbein im Jahre 1846 zurückzuführen ist. Heutzutage findet im allgemeinen nur noch rauchloses Pulver Verwendung. Eine Ausnahme bilden die Ladungen von Platz- oder sonstigen Spezial-Patronen, bei denen eine entsprechende Rauchentwicklung erwünscht ist.

Rauchlose Pulversorten werden schon seit vielen Jahrzehnten in den unterschiedlichsten Zusammensetzungen, Formen und Körnungen hergestellt und können somit ihrem jeweiligen spezifischen Verwendungszweck genau angepaßt werden.

The powder is the fourth component of the cartridge. It is composed of a mixture of various chemicals, and acts as the propellant. The chemical process is initially sparked off by the flash from the primer, so that the gases which are released drive the bullet up to the barrel with a varying degree of force.

Powders can be divided into two groups: black powder, so named after Berthold Schwarz ("Black"), a Franciscan monk to whom is attributed the discovery of this powder around the beginning of the 14th century (about 1313); and smokeless (or semi-smokeless) powder based on nitrocellulose, which was developed following the discovery of nitrocellulose by the German scientist Christian Schönbein in 1846.

Nowadays smokeless powder is used almost exclusively, except in loads for black or other special cartridges where a certain amount of smoke is required.

For several decades smokeless powders have been produced in a multitude of formulars, forms and granulations to suit exactly the many different requirements.

Ballistische Daten

Die im nachfolgenden Patronen-Katalog angegebenen ballistischen Daten stellen nur Durchschnittswerte dar. Sie wurden teils durch eigene Messungen ermittelt, teils den Katalogen von Munitionsherstellern oder anderem Schrifttum entnommen.

Gewöhnlich sind ballistische Daten, insbesondere die Geschoßgeschwindigkeit (V), mit Vorbehalt zu betrachten, sofern nicht zusätzliche Angaben über die verwendete Waffe sowie über verschiedene andere Faktoren, die das Meßergebnis u. U. beeinflussen können, gemacht werden.

Folgende Faktoren haben Einfluß auf die Geschoßgeschwindigkeit (V):

1. Pulver-Sorte
2. Pulver-Gewicht
3. Lagertemperatur der Patrone
4. Lauf- bzw. Drall-Länge
5. Drall-Winkel
6. Anzahl und Tiefe der Züge
7. Lage des Schießstandes über Normalnull
8. Luftdruck
9. Lufttemperatur
10. Luftfeuchtigkeit

Findet die Messung der Geschoßgeschwindigkeit (V) außerhalb eines in sich geschlossenen Schießstandes statt, so sind außerdem Windrichtung und Windstärke zu berücksichtigen.

Wenngleich alle diese Faktoren bei der Ermittlung von ballistischen Daten heute nur noch in wenigen Fällen Berücksichtigung finden, so sei dennoch darauf hingewiesen, um vor allem die Problematik von sog. „Ballistischen Tafeln“ aufzuzeigen, deren Werte meist nur errechnet und demnach rein theoretischer Natur sind.

Ballistic data

All ballistic data given in the following Cartridge Catalog are average figures only; some were determined by actual measurement, while others were taken from ammunition manufactures' catalogs or other publications.

Ballistic data should usually be accepted with reservation, particularly the velocity (V), whenever there is no additional information about the weapon used for the test, or about any other factors which might influence the result.

The following factors affect the velocity (V):

1. Type of powder
2. Weight of powder charge
3. Storage temperature of the cartridge
4. Length of the barrel·respectively of the rifling
5. Rate of twist of the rifling
6. Number and depth of grooves
7. Height of the test range above sea level
8. Atmospheric pressure
9. Temperature
10. Humidity

When the velocity (V) is measured on an open-air range, then the direction and strength of the wind must also be taken into account.

Even all these factors are rarely taken into consideration when calculating ballistic data, they are referred to here in order to illustrate the arbitrary nature of "ballistic tables", where most of the figures are based on calculations and are therefore mainly theoretical.

Patronen-Katalog

Cartridge-Catalog

.22 C.F. Experimental

Synonyme/Synonyms:

301

Geschoß/Bullet Ausführg. Pattern	Gewicht (g)	Weight (gr.)	Katalog Catalog No.
30 C	2,60	40,12	**301-1**

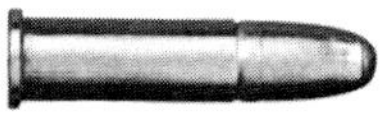

Technische und ballistische Daten

Geschoß-∅:	5,65 mm
Hülsen-∅ Hals:	5,70 mm
Boden:	5,72 mm
Rand:	6,85 mm
Hülsenlänge:	15,25 mm-15,27 mm
Hülsenmaterial:	Messing
Pulverart:	rauchlos
Zündungsart:	-
Patronenlänge:	24,80-24,85 mm

Die o. a. Patrone diente versuchsweise sowohl für Langwaffen als auch für Kurzwaffen (Revolver). Sie fand keine Verbreitung. Der Hersteller ist nicht bekannnt.

Ohne Bodenstempel

Technical and Ballistic Data

Bullet dia.	.222″
Case dia. neck:	.224″
head:	225″
rim:	.270″
Case length:	.600″-.601″
Case material:	brass
Powder type:	smokeless
Primer type:	-
Cartridge length:	.976″-.978″

This was an experimental cartridge for both rifles and handguns (revolvers). It was not distributed. The manufacturer is not known.

Without headstamp

.22 Dardick C.F.

Synonyme/Synonyms:

302

	Geschoß/Bullet Ausführg. Pattern	Gewicht (g)	Weight (gr.)	Katalog Catalog No.
siehe Sonderpatronen see special cartr. Tab./Table 5	1 E	3,2	49.38	**302–1**
siehe Sonderpatronen see special cartr. Tab./Table 5	30 E	3,2	49.38	**302–2**
siehe Sonderpatronen see special cartr. Tab./Table 5	30 B	3,2	49.38	**302–3**

Technische und ballistische Daten

Geschoß-∅:	5,7 mm
Hülsen-∅ Hals:	
Boden:	
Rand:	
Hülsenlänge:	34,20–34,25 mm
Hülsenmaterial:	Kunststoff
Pulverart:	rauchlos
Zündungsart:	Boxer
Patronenlänge:	34,20–34,25 mm
V_0	
E_0	
Lauflänge:	

Kleinstes Kaliber der „Dardick-TROUND-SERIE". Weitere Angaben und Bodenstempel unter Sondermunition.

Technical and Ballistic Data

Bullet dia.	.224″
Case dia. neck:	
head:	
rim:	
Case length:	1.347–1.349″
Case material:	Plastic
Powder type:	smokeless
Primer type:	Boxer
Cartridge length:	1.347–1.349″
V_0	
E_0	
Barrel length:	

Smallest caliber of the "Dardick-TROUND-Series". As to further details and headstamps please see special ammunition.

.22 Hornet

303

Synonyme/Synonyms:

DWM 578
.22 W.C.F. Hornet
.22 Winchester Hornet
.22 W.R.A. Hornet
.22 × 36 HO
5,6 × 35 R Hornet

	Geschoß/Bullet			Katalog Catalog No.
	Ausführg. Pattern	Gewicht (g)	Weight (gr.)	
	21 B	3,00	46,30	**303–1**
	21 E	2,30	35.50	**303–2**
	30 B	3,00	46.30	**303–3**
	41 G	2,90	44.75	**303–4**

Technische und ballistische Daten

Geschoß-∅:	5,40–5,70 mm
Hülsen-∅ Hals:	6,05– 6,20 mm
Boden:	7,45– 7,50 mm
Rand:	8,65– 8.85 mm
Hülsenlänge:	35,35–35,50 mm
Hülsenmaterial:	Messing
Pulverart:	rauchlos
Zündungsart:	Berdan
Patronenlänge:	43,58–43,85 mm
V_0	740 m/sec
E_0	837 J
Lauflänge:	250 mm

Vom Ursprung her als Langwaffen- und Jagdbüchsenpatrone konzipiert, dann jedoch auch für Revolver vorgesehen. Die Patrone hat eine große Verbreitung, da es sich um eine ausgezeichnete Schonzeitpatrone für die Jagd handelt.
Spezielle Ausführungen sind bei der US-Armee für die sog. Überlebensgewehre bestimmt.

Bodenstempel:
R.W.S. .22 HORNET,
R.W.S. H .22,
KYNOCH .22 H,
FIOCCHI .22 HORNET,
SAKO – – HORNET,
WCC 60 .22 HORNET
REM – UMC 22 HORNET,
W.R.A.Co. .22 HORNET,
S.B. .22 HORNET
NORMA Re 22 HORNET u.a.

Technical and Ballistic Data

Bullet dia.	.212–224″
Case dia. neck:	.238″ – .244″
head:	.293″ – .295″
rim:	.340″ – .348″
Case length:	1.392″–1.398″
Case material:	brass
Powder type:	smokeless
Primer type:	Berdan
Cartridge length:	1.716″–1.726″
V_0	2428 ft. per sec.
E_0	605.2 ft pounds
Barrel length:	9.842″

Originally designed as a gun and hunting rifle cartridge, subsequently however, also intended for revolver. The cartridge has found wide distribution, because it is an excellent close season cartridge for hunting purposes. Special types of this ammunition are provided with the US-Army for the so called survival guns.

Headstamps:
.22 HORNET,
R.W.S. .22 HORNET,
R.W.S. H .22,
KYNOCH .22 H,
FIOCCHI .22 HORNET,
SAKO – – HORNET,
WCC 60 .22 HORNET
REM – UMC 22 HORNET,
W.R.A.Co. .22 HORNET,
S.B. .22 HORNET
NORMA Re 22 HORNET and others

.22 Long C.F.

Synonyme/Synonyms:

.22 Long Revolver C.F.
.22-3-30 Revolver

304

	Geschoß/Bullet			
	Ausführg. Pattern	Gewicht (g)	Weight (gr.)	Katalog Catalog No.
	1 B	1,94	30.00	**304-1**
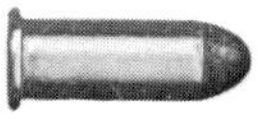	1 B			**304-2**

Technische und ballistische Daten

Geschoß-∅:	5,45- 5,50 mm
Hülsen-∅ Hals:	5,63- 5,75 mm
Boden:	5,60- 5,77 mm
Rand:	6,80- 7,07 mm
Hülsenlänge:	13,38-13,60 mm
Hülsenmaterial:	Messing
Pulverart:	Schwarz
Zündungsart:	Berdan
Patronenlänge:	16.67-18,52 mm

Sehr alte Revolverpatrone, die keine große Verbreitung gefunden hat. Sie gilt neben der Patrone .22 short C.F. als die kaliberkleinste und schwächste Revolverpatrone der Inch-Reihe. Im Katalog Fiocchi 1926 als Pistolen- u. Revolverpatronen aufgeführt.

Ohne Bodenstempel

Technical and Ballistic Data

Bullet dia.	.215"-.217"
Case dia. neck:	.222"-.226"
head:	.220"-.227"
rim:	.268"-.278"
Case length:	.527"-.535"
Case material:	brass
Powder type:	black
Primer type:	Berdan
Cartridge length:	.656"-.729"

Very old revolver cartridge that did not find a wide distribution. It is considered, besides the .22 short C.F., as the least potent revolver cartridge with the smallest caliber of the Inch series. In the 1926 Fiocchi catalog it was listed as a pistol and revolver cartridge.

Without headstamp

.22 L.R. C.F.

Synonyme/Synonyms:

.22 IfB C.F.
Einstecklauf-Patrone Marke N, Kal. .22

305

	Geschoß/Bullet Ausführg. Pattern	Gewicht (g)	Weight (gr.)	Katalog Catalog No.
	1 C	2,55	39.35	**305-1**
	40 H	2,50	38.58	**305-2**

Technische und ballistische Daten

Geschoß-Ø:	5,75 - 5,77 mm
Hülsen-Ø Hals:	5,70 - 5,72 mm
Boden:	5,70 - 5,75 mm
Rand:	7,13 - 7,25 mm
Hülsenlänge:	15.30-15,35 mm
Hülsenmaterial:	Kupfer
Pulverart:	rauchlos
Zündungsart:	verdeckt
Patronenlänge:	23,55-25,05 mm
V_0	315 m/sec
E_0	129 J
Lauflänge:	150 mm

Ursprünglich nur als Einstecklaufpatrone für Jagdwaffen hergestellt. Als die Patrone bekannter wurde, wurden auch Revolver für diese Munition konstruiert. Die Patrone hat eine verdeckte Zündung. Ein äußeres Zeichen ist die Einschnürung im hinteren Drittel der Hülse. Weitere Hersteller außer der Dynamit Nobel A.G. (heutige Bezeichnung) sind nicht bekannt.

Bodenstempel:
N im Wappen

Technical and Ballistic Data

Bullet dia.	.226"-.227"
Case dia. neck:	.224"-.225"
head:	.224"-.226"
rim:	.281"-.285"
Case length:	.602"-.604"
Case material:	copper
Powder type:	smokeless
Primer type:	inside
Cartridge length:	.927"-.986"
V_0	1033 ft. per sec.
E_0	93.3 ft. pounds
Barrel length:	5.905"

Originally only manufactured as a cartridge to be used in subcaliber barrels of sporting arms. When the cartridge became better know there were also revolvers designed for this ammunition. The cartridge has an inside primer. This can be seen by the throat in the last third of the case length. Other manufacturers apart from Dynamit Nobel A.G. (today's designation) are not known.

Headstamp:
N in coat of arms

.28 Browning Experimental

Synonyme/Synonyms:

.28 Colt Browning
.280 Colt-Browning
7 mm Colt Browning

315

	Geschoß/Bullet			Katalog Catalog No.
	Ausführg. Pattern	Gewicht (g)	Weight (gr.)	
	21 B			**315-1**

Technische und ballistische Daten

Geschoß-Ø:	7,01 - 7,11 mm
Hülsen-Ø Hals:	7,59 - 7,64 mm
Boden:	7,64 - 7,67 mm
Rand:	7,59 - 7,62 mm
Hülsenlänge:	15,59-15,62 mm
Hülsenmaterial:	Messing
Pulverart:	rauchlos
Zündungsart:	Boxer
Patronenlänge:	23,01-23,06 mm

Diese Patrone wurde in den Jahren 1908 - 1910 in den USA entwickelt und war für eine halbautomatische Selbstladepistole des Typs „Colt-Browning" gedacht, (siehe Katalog Nr. 314). Hersteller ist die Union Metallic Cartridge Co. = U M C.

Ohne Bodenstempel, (U im Zündhütchen)

Technical and Ballistic Data

Bullet dia.	.276"-.280"
Case dia. neck:	.299"-.301"
head:	.301"-.302"
rim:	.299"-.300"
Case length:	.614"-.615"
Case material:	brass
Powder type:	smokeless
Primer type:	Boxer
Cartridge length:	.906"-.908"

This cartridge was developed in the USA in the years 1908 - 1910 and was intended for a semi-automatic selfloading "Colt-Browning" pistol (see catalog No. 314). Manufacturer is the Union Metallic Cartridge Co. = U.M.C.

Without headstamp, (U in primer)

.28 B.S.A.

Synonyme/Synonyms:
.28 B.S.A. BELTED

316

Geschoß/Bullet Ausführg. Pattern	Gewicht (g)	Weight (gr.)	Katalog Catalog No.
 21 B			**316–1**

Technische und ballistische Daten

Geschoß-∅:	6,96 mm
Hülsen-∅ Hals:	7,59 mm
Boden:	7,64 mm
Gürtel:	8,20 mm
Rand:	7,62 mm
Hülsenlänge:	16,48 mm
Hülsenmaterial:	Messing
Pulverart:	rauchlos
Zündungsart:	Berdan
Patronenlänge:	23,70 mm

Kleinstes Kaliber der Versuchspatronenserie der Firma **B**irmingham **S**mall **A**rms (B.S.A.). Es handelt sich um eine neuartige Patronenserie für eine Selbstladepistole. Die Hülsen der Patronen haben einen Gürtel durch den Ladehemmungen (verursacht durch das Ineinandergreifen der Hülsenränder) verhindert werden sollten. Die Patronen dieser Serie konnten, obwohl dies vorausgesagt worden ist, keinen Erfolg erlangen. Vergleiche auch Katalog Nr. 339 und 380.

Kein Bodenstempel bekannt

Technical and Ballistic Data

Bullet dia.	.274″
Case dia. neck:	.299″
head:	.301″
belt:	.323″
rim:	.300″
Case length:	.649″
Case material:	brass
Powder type:	smokeless
Primer type:	Berdan
Cartridge length:	.933″

This is the smallest caliber of the experimental cartridge series of the firm **B**irmingham **S**mall **A**rms (B.S.A.) and by the same token a new kind of cartridge series for an automatic pistol. The cases have a belt by which jams (caused by meshing of the cartridge rims) were to be avoided. As had been predicted, the cartridges of this series did not prove successful. Compare also catalog Nos. 339 and 380.

No headstamp is know

.297 Revolver C.F.

Synonyme/Synonyms:

.297 C.F. Revolver
6,95 × 14,65 – R.N.297

317

	Geschoß/Bullet Ausführg. Pattern	Gewicht (g)	Weight (gr.)	Katalog Catalog No.
	1 C	4,54 – 4,86	70.00 – 75.00	**317–1**
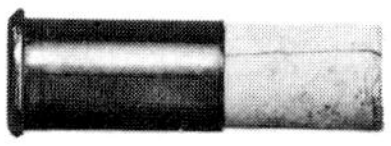	90 d	–	–	**317–2**

Technische und ballistische Daten

Geschoß-Ø:	7,14 – 7,52 mm
Hülsen-Ø Hals:	7,40 – 7,45 mm
Boden:	7,40 – 7,50 mm
Rand:	8,51 – 8,84 mm
Hülsenlänge:	14,30 – 14,70 mm
Hülsenmaterial:	Messing, Kupfer
Pulverart:	Schwarz, rauchlos
Zündungsart:	Berdan
Patronenlänge:	24,10 – 24,40 mm

Ursprungsland dieser Revolverpatrone ist England. Aus älteren Katalogen (Kynoch 1894 und R.W.S. 1898) ist lediglich zu entnehmen, daß diese Patrone für Revolver bestimmt war.

Ohne Bodenstempel

Technical and Ballistic Data

Bullet dia.	.281″–.296″
Case dia. neck:	.291″–.293″
head:	.291″–.295″
rim:	.335″–.348″
Case length:	.563″–.579″
Case material:	brass, copper
Powder type:	black, smokeless
Primer type:	Berdan
Cartridge length:	.949″–.961″

Country of origin of this revolver cartridge is England. From older catalogs (Kynoch 1894 and R.W.S. 1898) it can only be learnt that this cartridge was made for revolvers.

Without headstamp

.30 Carbine

Synonyme/Synonyms:
.30 Carbine M 1
.30 M 1 Carbine

318

	Geschoß/Bullet Ausführg. Pattern	Gewicht (g)	Weight (gr.)	Katalog Catalog No.
	21 B	7,13	110.00	**318–1**
	30 B	7,13	110.00	**318–2**
	30 B	7,13	110.00	**318–3**
	18 M	5,20	80,00	**380–4**
	7 B	0,35	5,4	**380–5**

Technische und ballistische Daten

Geschoß-∅:	7,55 – 7,80 mm
Hülsen-∅ Hals:	8,40 – 8,45 mm
Boden:	8,95 – 8,99 mm
Rand:	8,98 – 9,10 mm
Hülsenlänge:	32,60 – 32,70 mm
Hülsenmaterial:	Messing, Stahl, Kunststoff
Pulverart:	rauchlos
Zündungsart:	Boxer
Patronenlänge:	41,95 – 42,50 mm
V_0	464 m/sec
E_0	784 J
Lauflänge:	127 mm

Die Patrone wurde 1940/1941 für den US-Karabiner 30M1 von der Firma Winchester Repeating Arms Company, auf Wunsch und nach einer Spezifikation des Feldzeugamtes entwickelt. Von der Firma John W. Kimball, Detroit, Michigan wurde 1955 eine 7-schüssige Selbstladepistole für diese Patrone konstruiert.
Die Firma Sturm. Ruger & Co. Inc. stellte in den 70er Jahren den Ruger Revolver „Blackhawk" für diese Kaliber her.

Bodenstempel:
W–W 30 CARBINE,
W.R.A. 43,
E C 52,
L C 45,
P C 43
W C C 44,
norma US .30,
G.F.L. 71,
KTW 30 CARB,
G.F.L. 952 30MI,
V/E S 1–63 7,62,
u.a.

Technical and Ballistic Data

Bullet dia.	.297" – .307"
Case dia. neck:	.331" – .333"
head:	.352" – .354"
rim:	.353" – .358"
Case length:	1.283" – 1.287"
Case mateial:	brass, steel, plastic
Powder type:	smokeless
Primer type:	Boxer
Cartridge length:	1.651" – 1.673"
V_0	1524 ft. per sec.
E_0	567.0 ft. pounds
Barrel length:	5.000"

This cartridge was developed in 1940/41 for the US-carbine 30 MI by the firm Winchester Repeating Arms Company upon request and according to a specification of the ordnance department. In 1955 a 7-shot self-loading pistol was constructed for this cartridge by the firm J. W. Kimball, Detroit, Michigan USA. The firm Sturm Ruger & Co. Inc. manufactured the Ruger "Blackhawk" revolver for this calibre in the 1970ies.

Headstamp:
W–W 30 CARBINE,
W.R.A. 43,
E C 52,
L C 45,
P C 43,
W C C 44,
norma US .30,
G.F.L. 71,
KTW 30 CARB,
G.F.L. 952 30MI,
V/E S 1–63 7,62,
and others

.30 Front Loading

Synonyme/Synonyms:

319

	Geschoß/Bullet Ausführg. Pattern	Gewicht (g)	Weight (gr.)	Katalog Catalog No.
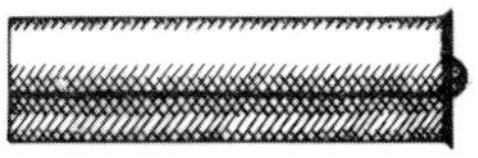	1 E			**319–1**

Technische und ballistische Daten

Geschoß-∅:	7,37 – 7,52 mm*)
Hülsen-∅ Hals:	9,14 – 9,60 mm
Boden:	8,05 – 8,18 mm
Hülsenlänge:	30,07 – 30,30 mm
Hülsenmaterial:	Kupfer
Pulverart:	Schwarz
Zündungsart:	
Patronenlänge:	30,07 – 31,32 mm

*) Innendurchmesser der Hülse

Da aus der Literatur zu entnehmen ist, daß diese Patrone in modifizierter Ausführung in den Revolvern „Wood" oder „Eagle Arms" New York benutzt worden ist, muß angenommen werden, daß der Ursprung in den USA liegt. Andere Literaturstellen meinen, es handle sich um eine Patrone mit der bei „Frankford-Arsenal" USA Geschoßfettungsversuche durchgeführt worden sind. Keine der bekannten Veröffentlichungen brachte einen Hinweis auf ein Patent. Erstmals ist die Patrone öffentlich bekanntgeworden bei Frankford Arsenal auf der Collection Ausstellung von Philadelphia 1876.
Patrone kann einen Innen- oder Außenzünder haben.

Ohne Bodenstempel

Technical and Ballistic Data

Bullet dia.	.290" – .296"*)
Case dia. neck:	.360" – .378"
head:	.317" – .322"
Case length:	1.184" – 1.193"
Case material:	copper
Powder type:	black
Primer type:	
Cartridge length:	1.184" – 1.233"

*) inside case diameter

As it may be understood from the literature that this cartridge has been used in a modified version in the "Wood" or "Eagle Arms" New York revolvers it has to be presumed that it originates from the USA. Other references say it is a cartridge that served "Frankford Arsenal" USA to carry out bullet lubricating tests. None of the know publications mentions a patent. The cartridge was made for the first time known to the public at Frankford Arsenal's on the occasion of the Exhibition of Philadelphia in 1876 were collections were shown.
The cartridge may have an inside or an outside primer.

Without headstamp

.300 Long C.F.

320

Synonyme/Synonyms:

DWM 300
.300 C.F. Long
.300 Long Revolver
.300 Rook
.300-10-80
.295-10-80
7,5 × 30,30 Revolver
7,55 × 29,25 – R.N.300 lang

	Geschoß/Bullet Ausführg. Pattern	Gewicht (g)	Weight (gr.)	Katalog Catalog No.
	1 B	5,18	80.00	**320–1**
	40 G	5,18	80.00	**320–2**
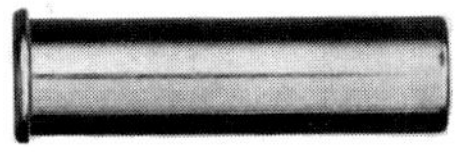	90 d	–	–	**320–3**

Technische und ballistische Daten

Geschoß-∅:	7,45 – 7,60 mm
Hülsen-∅ Hals:	8,03 – 8,06 mm
Boden:	8,08 – 8,20 mm
Rand:	9,40 – 9,50 mm
Hülsenlänge:	29,70 – 29,85 mm
Hülsenmaterial:	Messing
Pulverart:	Schwarz, rauchlos
Zündungsart:	Berdan, Boxer
Patronenlänge:	36,30 – 36,60 mm
V_0	335 m/sec
E_0	297 J

Eine Revolverpatrone die ursprünglich nur für Langwaffen vorgesehen war. Die Herkunft ist England. Als Gewehrpatrone beschrieben in den Katalogen 1894 von Kynoch und 1889 von Eley.

Ohne Bodenstempel

Technical and Ballistic Data

Bullet dia.	.293″ – .299″
Case dia. neck:	.316″ – .317″
head:	.318″ – .323″
rim:	.370″ – .374″
Case length:	1.169″ – 1.175″
Case material:	brass
Powder type:	black, smokeless
Primer type:	Berdan, Boxer
Cartridge length:	1.429″ – 1.441″
V_0	1 100 ft. per sec.
E_0	215.0 ft. pounds

A revolver cartridge which was originally intended for rifles. Country of origin is England. This ammunition is described as a rifle cartridge in the catalogs of 1894 by Kynoch and of 1889 by Eley.

Without headstamp

.300 Revolver C.F.

Synonyme/Synonyms:

.300 C.F. Revolver
.300-6-80 Revolver

321

	Geschoß/Bullet Ausführg. Pattern	Gewicht (g)	Weight (gr.)	Katalog Catalog No.
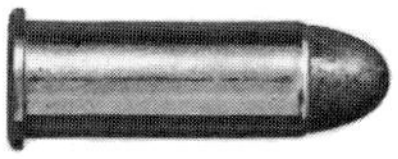	1 B	5,18	80.00	**321–1**
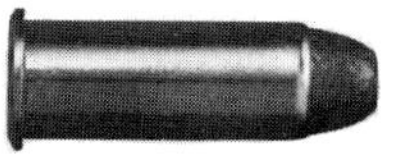	40 G	5,18	80.00	**321–2**

Technische und ballistische Daten

Geschoß-∅:	7,19– 7,49 mm
Hülsen-∅ Hals:	7,92– 8,05 mm
Boden:	8,00– 8,08 mm
Rand:	9,45– 9,60 mm
Hülsenlänge:	19,90–20,20 mm
Hülsenmaterial:	Messing
Pulverart:	Schwarz, rauchlos
Zündungsart:	Berdan
Patronenlänge:	24,70–24,73 mm
V_0	183 m/sec
E_0	88 J
Lauflänge:	102 mm

Technical and Ballistic Data

Bullet dia.	.283″–.295″
Case dia. neck:	.312″–.317″
head:	.315″–.318″
rim:	.372″–.378″
Case length:	.783″–.795″
Case material:	brass
Powder type:	black, smokeless
Primer type:	Berdan
Cartridge length:	.972″–.974″
V_0	600 ft. per sec.
E_0	64.0 ft. pounds
Barrel length:	4.000″

Ebenso wie die Patrone .300 long C.F. (Katalog Nr.320) handelt es sich um eine Patrone mit den Herkunftsland „England“. In diesem Fall handelt es sich um eine ausgesprochene Revolverpatrone für diverse Revolverarten. Enthalten in alten Eley- und Nobel-Katalogen von 1898, 1925 und 1933.

Bodenstempel:
ELEY 320 L

Just as the round .300 long C.F. (catalog No. 320) this cartridge originates from England. In this case we have to do with a specific revolver cartridge for various types of revolvers. It is listed in old ELEY and NOBEL catalogs of 1898, 1925 and 1933.

Headstamp:
ELEY 320 L

.31 Thuer

Synonyme/Synonyms:

.31 Colt, Thuer's Pat.

322

Geschoß/Bullet Ausführg. Pattern	Gewicht (g)	Weight (gr.)	Katalog Catalog No.
1 F	4,92/4,3	76,0/66,5	**322–1**

Technische und ballistische Daten

Geschoß-∅:	8,36– 8,46 mm
Hülsen-∅ Hals:	8,36– 8,46 mm
Boden:	8,87– 7,95 mm
Hülsenlänge:	21,34–22,20 mm
Hülsenmaterial:	Messing
Pulverart:	Schwarz
Zündungsart:	
Patronenlänge:	29,54–30,15 mm

Eine Patrone, die nach dem Erfinder Alexander „Thuer" benannt ist. A. Thuer hat randlose konische Zentralfeuerpatronen in den Kalibern .31, .36 und .44 in teilweise verschiedenen Ausführungen entwickelt (Katalog Nr. 345., 346, 417 und 418).
Als Angehöriger der Firma Colt ließ T. sich 1868 durch das US-Patent Nr. 82258 ein System schützen, nachdem Perkussionsrevolver in Patronenrevolver transformiert wurden. Hersteller der Patronen waren die Firmen Colt, Frankford Arsenal und Eley von 1868 – 1870. Obwohl die Patronen in Serie hergestellt wurden, hatten sie eine geringe Verbreitung.

Ohne Bodenstempel

Technical and Ballistic Data

Bullet dia.	.329"–.333"
Case dia. neck:	.329"–.333"
head:	.310"–.313"
Case length:	.840"–.874"
Case material:	brass
Powder type:	black
Primer type:	
Cartridge Length:	1.163"–1.187"

A round which is named after its inventor Alexander "Thuer". He developed rimless conical central fire cartridges of the calibers .31, .36 and .44 in partly different forms (catalog Nos. 345, 346, 417 and 418 refer). As a member of the firm COLT Thuer had a system protected for him in 1868 by the US patent No. 82258 when percussion revolvers had been transformed into cartridge revolvers. Manufacturers of the cartridges were the companies Colt, Frankford Arsenal and Eley from 1868 to 1870. Although the rounds were manufactured in series they had little success.

Without headstamp

.32 Browning Automatic

Synonyme/Synonyms:

323

Geschoß/Bullet Ausführg. Pattern	Gewicht (g)	Weight (gr.)	Katalog Catalog No.
1 B	4,78 – 4,79	73.80 – 74.00	**323–1**

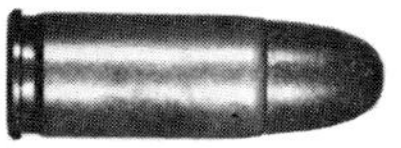

Technische und ballistische Daten

Geschoß-∅:	7,80 mm x)
	8,00 – 8,03 mm xx)
Hülsen-∅ Hals:	8,48 – 8,53 mm
Boden:	8,53 – 8,56 mm
Rand:	8,99 – 9,04 mm
Hülsenlänge:	16,97 – 17,12 mm
Hülsenmaterial:	Messing
Pulverart:	Schwarz
Zündungsart:	Boxer
Patronenlänge:	24,97 – 25,07 mm

x) am Hülsenrand
xx) maximal

Eine um 1907 entwickelte Pistolenpatrone mit Halbrand. (Aus der Literatur ist bekannt, daß auch Patronen dieses Kalibers ohne Rand existieren sollen). Die Patrone war für eine halbautomatische „Colt-Pistole“ gedacht und kann als eine Variante der Patrone Kal. 7,65 mm Browning (.32 ACP) angesehen werden. Das Mantelgeschoß hat innen im Hülsenmund einen Bleigürtel, (siehe Geschoßdurchmesserangaben). Verschiedentlich findet man einen ähnlichen Bleigürtel auch bei Patronen des Kalibers .35 Smith & Wesson Automatik, (Katalog Nr. 342). Enthalten im WINCHESTER-Katalog vom August 1899.

Bodenstempel:
W.R.A.Co. .32 B.A. u.
U.M.C. (U im Zünder)

Technical and Ballistic Data

Bullet dia.	.307″ x)
	.315″–.316″ xx)
Case dia. neck:	.334″–.336″
head:	.336″–.337″
rim:	.354″–.356″
Case length:	.668″–.674″
Case material:	brass
Powder type:	black
Primer type:	Boxer
Cartridge length:	.983″–.987″

x) at case mouth
xx) maximum

A semi-rimmed pistol cartridge developed about 1907 (we know from pertinent literature that there exist allegedly also cartridges of this caliber without a rim). The round was intended for a semi-automatic “Colt pistol” and can be considered as a variation of the cartridge cal. 7,65 mm Browning (.32 ACP). The jacketed bullet has a lead belt inside the case mouth (see bullet diameter specifications). Here and there you will find a similar lead belt also on cartridges of caliber .35 Smith & Wesson Automatic (catalog No. 342) as listed in the WINCHESTER catalog of August 1899.

Headstamps:
W.R.A. co. .32 B.A. and
U.M.C. (U in primer)

.32 Colt New Police

Synonyme/Synonyms:

.32 Colt N.P.
.32 Colt Police Positive
.32 Police

324

	Geschoß/Bullet Ausführg. Pattern	Gewicht (g)	Weight (gr.)	Katalog Catalog No.
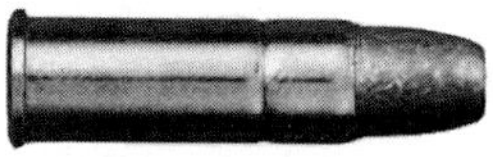	1 G	6,35–6,48	98.00–100.00	**324–1**
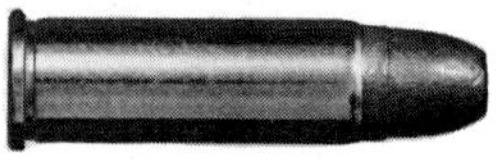	1 G	6,35–6,48	98.00–100.00	**324–2**
	60 G	6,48	100.00	**324–3**
	1 G	6,48	100.00	**324–4**
	1 G			**324–5**
	90	–	–	**324–6**

Technische und ballistische Daten

Geschoß-⌀:	7,62– 8,03 mm
Hülsen-⌀ Hals:	8,41– 8,56 mm
Boden:	8,46– 8,61 mm
Rand:	9,35– 9,65 mm
Hülsenlänge:	22,96–23,57 mm
Hülsenmaterial:	Messing
Pulverart:	Schwarz, rauchschwach, rauchlos
Zündungsart:	Boxer
Patronenlänge:	31,75–32,05 mm 24,60–25,96 mm[x])
V_0	207 m/sec
E_0	138 J
Lauflänge:	102 mm

[x]) Scheibenpatrone (mid-range)

Technical and Ballistic Data

Bullet dia.	.300″–.316″
Case dia. neck:	.331″–.337″
head:	.333″–.339″
rim:	.368″–.380″
Case length:	.904″–.928″
Case material:	brass
Powder type:	black, semi-smokeless, smokeless
Primer type:	Boxer
Cartridge length:	1.250″–1.262″ .968″–1.022″[x])
V_0	679 ft. per sec.
E_0	99.8 ft. pounds
Barrel length:	4.000″

[x]) Target cartridge (mid-range)

.32 Colt New Police

Die Patrone Kaliber .32 Colt N.P. wurde 1896 für den Colt Revolver Modell 32 New Police, später .32 Police Positive entwickelt. Sie entspricht in ihren Abmessungen der Patrone .32 S&W long (Katalog Nr. 332), hat allerdings anstelle des Rundkopfgeschosses ein Geschoß mit Flachkopf. Beide Patronen sind austauschbar.
Für Übungszwecke wurden auch Patronen mit W.C.-Geschossen hergestellt. Diese Patronen wurden in großen Stückzahlen in Serienfertigung hergestellt. Enthalten u.a. im Hartley & Graham-Katalog, August 1896.

Bodenstempel:
U.M.C. 32 COLT N.P.,
REM – UMC 32 COLT N P,
PETERS 32 COLT N P

The cartridge calibre .32 Colt N.P. was developed in 1896 for the Colt revolver 32 New Police model, later for the .32 Police Positive. Its dimensions correspond to those of the cartridge .32 S&W long (catalog No. 332), however, instead of the round nose bullet it has a projectile with a flat nose. Both rounds are interchangeable. There were also manufactured cartridges with W.C.-bullets for practice shooting. These cartridges were manufactured in series production and in great quantities. They are contained in the HARTLEY & GRAHAM catalog of August 1896, among others.

Headstamps:
U.M.C. 32 COLT N.P.,
REM – UMC 32 COLT N P,
PETERS 32 COLT N P

.32 Long C.F.

Synonyme/Synonyms:

325

Geschoß/Bullet Ausführg. Pattern	Gewicht (g)	Weight (gr.)	Katalog Catalog No.
 1 C	5,57 – 5,83	86.00–90.00	**325–1**

Technische und ballistische Daten

Geschoß-∅:	7,49 – 7,92 mm
Hülsen-∅ Hals:	7,87 – 8,05 mm
Boden:	8,00 – 8,18 mm
Rand:	9,27 – 9,65 mm
Hülsenlänge:	21,00 – 21,34 mm
Hülsenmaterial:	Messing
Pulverart:	Schwarz
Zündungsart:	Boxer
Patronenlänge:	28,40 – 32,13 mm

Bei der Patrone Kaliber .32 long C.F. handelt es sich um eine Revolverpatrone, deren Ursprung in England zu finden ist. Sie wurde in den Jahren zwischen 1865 und 1868 für Webley- und Tranter-Revolver gefertigt. Weitere Revolver wie Colt 1875 folgten. Im Jahre 1875 ist die Patrone auch in Firmenkatalog von Winchester enthalten. nach ca. 1910 ist sie in bekannten Katalogen nicht mehr zu finden.

Bodenstempel:
W.R.A.Co. .32 L,
ohne

Technical and Ballistic Data

Bullet dia.	.295″–.312″
Case dia. neck:	.310″–.317″
head:	.315″–.322″
rim:	.365″–.380″
Case length:	.827″–.840″
Case material:	brass
Powder type:	black
Primer type:	Boxer
Cartridge length:	1.118″–1.265″

The caliber .32 long C.F. cartridge is a revolver round that originates from England. It was made between the years 1865 and 1868 for Webley and Tranter revolvers. Other revolvers such as the Colt 1875 followed. In 1875 the cartridge is also listed in the firm catalog of Winchester. After 1910 it was omitted in well-known catalogs.

Headstamp:
W.R.A.Co. .32 L,
and without headstamp

.32 Long Colt (ins.lub.)

Synonyme/Synonyms:

.32 Colt (Inside Lub.)
.32 Colt – Interior Lubrication
.32 Long Centerfire (Inside Lubricated)
.32 Long Colt

326

	Geschoß/Bullet Ausführg. Pattern	Gewicht (g)	Weight (gr.)	Katalog Catalog No.
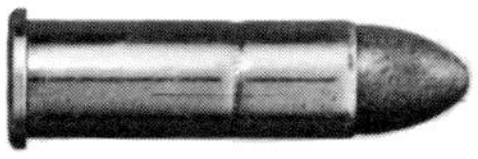	1 E	5,25 – 5,38	81.00 – 83.00	**326–1**
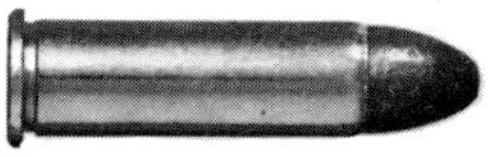	1 E	5,31	82.00	**326-2**
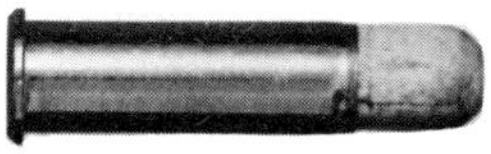	90 e	–	–	**326–3**

Technische und ballistische Daten

Geschoß-∅:	7,29 – 7,57 mm
Hülsen-∅ Hals:	7,92 – 8,05 mm
Boden:	7,95 – 8,10 mm
Rand:	9,30 – 9,70 mm
Hülsenlänge:	22,99 – 23,49 mm
Hülsenmaterial:	Messing
Pulverart:	Schwarz, rauchschwach, rauchlos
Zündungsart:	Boxer
Patronenlänge:	30,53 – 31,29 mm
V_0	230 m/sec
E_0	144 J
Lauflänge:	102 mm

Technical and Ballistic Data

Bullet dia.	.287″–,298″
Case dia. neck:	.312″–.317″
head:	.313″–.319″
rim:	.366″–.382″
Case length:	.905″–.925″
Case material:	brass
Powder type:	black, semi-smokeless smokeless
Primer type:	Boxer
Cartridge length:	1.202″–1.232″
V_0	755 ft. per sec.
E_0	104.0 ft. pounds
Barrel length:	4.000″

Es handelt sich um den Nachfolger der „außen-gefetteten"Patrone .32 long Colt (outs.lub.) – Katalog Nr.327 Sie wurde 1894/95 von der Union Metallic Cartridge Company USA, als erstem Hersteller auf den Markt gebracht und verdrängte die ältere Patrone mit Außenfettung. Von der Schwarzpulver-Treibladung über die rauchschwache- zur rauchlosen Ladung wird die Patrone heute nur noch mit rauchlosem Pulver geladen, gefertigt. Mit der Modifizierung der Patrone erhielt die Hülse ihre heutige Länge. das Geschoß hat einen tiefen hohlen Boden. Die Platzpatrone entspricht denjenigen der üblichen Revolverpatronen der damaligen Zeit.

Bodenstempel:
U M C .32 LCF,
PETERS .32 LONG,
R – P .32 LG COLT

This is the successor of the "outside lubricated" Cartridge .32 Colt – catalog No. 327 –. It was marketed in 1894/95 by the Union Metallic Cartridge Company, USA, its first manufacturer and supplanted the less potent cartridge with outside lubrication. Starting with black powder as a propellant, then changing over to semi-smokeless and smokeless charges this cartridge is manufactured nowadays only with smokeless powder. When modifying the cartridge, its case got the length it has today. The bullet has a deep hollow base. The blank corresponds to those of the usual revolver cartridges of that time.

Headstamps:
U M C .32 LCF,
PETERS .32 LONG,
R – P .32 LG COLT

.32 Long Colt (outs.lub.)

Synonyme/Synonyms:

DWM 262
.32 Colt
.32 Long
.32 Long Colt
.32 Long Colt (Outside Lubricated)
Revolver Kal. 32 lg.

327

	Geschoß/Bullet Ausführg. Pattern	Gewicht (g)	Weight (gr.)	Katalog Catalog No.
	1 C	5,51 – 5,83	85.00 – 90.00	**327–1**
	21 C			**327–2**
	1 H	5,31	82.00	**327–3**
	90	–	–	**327–4**

Technische und ballistische Daten

Geschoß-∅:	7,92– 8,13 mm
Hülsen-∅ Hals:	8,00– 8,10 mm
Boden:	8,00– 8,18 mm
Rand:	9,32– 9,65 mm
Hülsenlänge:	19,43–21,23 mm
Hülsenmaterial:	Messing
Pulverart:	Schwarz, rauchschwach, rauchlos
Zündungsart:	Boxer
Patronenlänge:	28,96–30,94 mm

Mehr dem Zufall war es zu verdanken, daß es zur Fettung des Geschosses kam, d.h. man stellte fest, daß Fett, welches beim Setzen der Geschosse benutzt wurde, die Korrosion herabsetzte und die Pulverrückstände weicher hielt. Die Geschosse mit Außenfettung wurden ursprünglich auf die notwendig erforderliche Tiefe auf die Hülse gesetzt und die Rillen wurden außerhalb der Hülsen gefettet. Als im Jahre 1865 Frankford Arsenal die Hülse seiner neuen R.F.-Patrone .50 länger machte um die Fettrillen zu überdecken, folgten andere Hersteller diesem Beispiel. Bis zum Jahre 1894/95 gab es dann neben der hier beschriebenen Patrone .32 long Colt mit Außenfettung, die Version der Patrone .32 long Colt mit Innenfettung (Katalog Nr. 326). Die Patrone .32 long Colt (outs. lub.) wurde 1875 in den USA entwickelt und ursprünglich in New Line-Colt-Revolvern verwendet. Sie löste ihrenVorgänger .32 long R.F. ab. Eine weitere Version ist die Patrone .32 short Colt (Katalog Nr. 330) mit kürzerer Hülse. Die Produktion der Patronen .32 long Colt (outs. lub.) wurde um 1895 eingestellt.

Bodenstempel:
US .32 COLT
W R A Co ,32 C
W.R.A.Co. .32 L.C.
U.S.C.Co. 32 L.C. (US im Zündhütchen)

Technical and Ballistic Data

Bullet dia.	.312″–.320″
Case dia. neck:	.315″–.319″
head:	.315″–.322″
rim:	.367″–.380″
Case length:	.765″–.836″
Case material:	brass
Powder type:	black, semi-smokeless, smokeless
Primer type:	Boxer
Cartridge length:	1.140″–1.218″

It was rather by accident that lubrication of the bullet came about, i.e. it was found that grease being used for bullet seating reduced the corrosion and softened powder residues. Outside lubricated bullets were originally seated in the required depth and the grooves were lubricated outside of the cases. When in 1865 Frankford Arsenal lengthened the case for their new R.F. cartridge in order to cover the lubricating grooves the other manufacturers followed their example. Until 1894/95 there existed, apart from the here described outside lubricated .32 long Colt cartridge the version of the inside lubricated cartridge .32 long Colt (catalog No. 326). The .32 long Colt (outs. lub.) round was developed in the USA in 1875 and originally used in New Line Colt Revolvers. It replaced its predecessor .32 long R.F. Another parent type is the .32 short Colt cartridge (catalog No. 330) with a shorter case. The production of the outside lubricated .32 long Colt cartridges was discontinued about 1895.

Headstamps:
US .32 COLT,
W R A Co .32 C
W.R.A.Co. 32 L.C.
U.S.C.Co. 32 L.C. (US in primer)

.32 Merwin, Hulbert & Co.

Synonyme/Synonyms:

.32 M.H. & Co.

328

	Geschoß/Bullet			Katalog Catalog No.
	Ausführg. Pattern	Gewicht (g)	Weight(gr.)	
	1 B	5,18 – 5,57	80.00 – 86.00	**328–1**
	1 A	3,24	50.00	**328–2**

Technische und ballistische Daten

Geschoß-∅:	8,05 – 8,10 mm
Hülsen-∅ Hals:	8,55 mm
Boden:	8,55 mm
Rand:	9,48 – 9,50 mm
Hülsenlänge:	14,90 mm
Hülsenmaterial:	Messing
Pulverart:	Schwarz
Zündungsart:	Boxer
Patronenlänge:	24,62 mm

Es handelt sich um eine modifizierte Patrone Kaliber .32 Smith & Wesson, d.h. die Patrone erhielt eine breite, tiefe und von außen sichtbare Fettrille. Das Geschoß wurde um 0,33 g reduziert. Die Patrone wurde um 1883/85 entwickelt und u. a. in einem Revolver „Merwin, Hulbert Co." mit Spannabzug benutzt.
Hersteller waren: Merwin, Hulbert Co., Smith & Wesson und US Metallic Cartridge Co. (vergl. Katalog Nr. 329). Im Munitionskatalog Merwin, Hulbert Co. 1889 zu finden. Ab ca. 1918 wurde die Patrone nicht mehr hergestellt.

Ohne Bodenstempel:

Technical and Ballistic Data

Bullet dia.	.317″ – .319″
Case dia. neck:	.337″
head:	.337″
rim:	.373″ – .374″
Case length:	.587″
Case material:	brass
Powder type:	black
Primer type:	Boxer
Cartridge length:	.969″

This is a modified cartridge of caliber .32 Smith & Wesson, i.e. the round was provided with a deep, large and outside visible lubricating groove. The bullet weight was reduced by 0,33 grammes. The cartridge was developed about 1883/85 and fired among other weapons in a double-action "Merwin, Hulbert & Co." revolver.
Manufacturers were: Merwin, Hulbert & Co., Smith & Wesson and US Metallic Cartridge Co. (see also catalog No. 329). It is metioned in the ammunition catalog of 1889 of Merwin, Hulbert & Co. as well. From about 1918 this cartridge was no longer manufactured.

Without headstamps:

.32 Merwin, Hulbert & Co. Long

Synonyme/Synonyms:

.32 H. & R.
.32 H. & R. or M. & H.
.32 Harrington & Richardson
.32 M. & H. Long
.32 M. H. & Co. Long

329

	Geschoß/Bullet Ausführg. Pattern	Gewicht (g)	Weight (gr.)	Katalog Catalog No.
	1 B	5,70	88.00	**329–1**
	1 A	3,24	50.00	**329–2**
	90 e	–	–	**329–3**

Technische und ballistische Daten

Geschoß-∅:	7,64 – 7,95 mm
Hülsen-∅ Hals:	8,46 – 8,61 mm
Boden:	8,53 – 8,61 mm
Rand:	9,47 – 9,55 mm
Hülsenlänge:	22,20 – 22,86 mm
Hülsenmaterial:	Messing
Pulverart:	Schwarz, rauchschwach
Zündungsart:	Boxer
Patronenlänge:	30,55 – 31,50 mm

Es handelt sich um eine Patrone, die der Patrone Kal. 32 S&W long sehr ähnlich sieht. Sie wurde 1883 entwickelt und ist bzw. war für einen Revolver „Merwin, Hulbert & Co Automatik mit 5 ½"-Lauf bestimmt. Weitere Revolver für diese Patronen stellte die Firma Harrington and Richardson mit den Modellen „Automatic", Police Automatic D.A. und Hammerless u. a. her. Patronenhersteller waren die Firmen Merwin, Hulbert & Co., American Metallic Co., Winchester und U.M.C.
Seit 1917/18 werden keine Patronen menr gefertigt.

Bodenstempel:
keine bekannt

Technical and Ballistic Data

Bullet dia.	.301"–.313"
Case dia. neck:	.333"–.339"
head:	.336"–.339"
rim:	.373"–.376"
Case length:	.874"–.900"
Case material:	brass
Powder type:	black, semi-smokeless
Primer type:	Boxer
Cartridge length:	1.203"–1.240"

This is a cartridge that is very similar to the .32 S&W long cartridge. It was developed in 1883 and is respectively was intended for a revolver "Merwin, Hulbert & Co." with a 5 ½" barrel. Other revolvers for this cartridge were produced by the firm Harrington and Richardson presenting their models "Automatic", Police Automatic D.A. and Hammerless, among others. The cartridges were manufactured by the firm Merwin, Hulbert & Co., American Metallic Co., Winchester and U.M.C.
Since 1917/18 no more cartridges of this kind have been made.

Headstamp:
none known

.32 Short Colt

Synonyme/Synonyms:

.32 Short C.F.
.32 Webley

330

	Geschoß/Bullet Ausführg. Pattern	Gewicht (g)	Weight (gr.)	Katalog Catalog No.
	1 C	5,31	82.00	**330-1**
	1 C	5,18	80.00	**330-2**
	90 b	–	–	**330-3**
	90 e	–	–	**330-4**

Technische und ballistische Daten

Geschoß-∅:	7,82– 8,13 mm
Hülsen-∅ Hals:	7,92– 8,13 mm
Boden:	7,97– 8,10 mm
Rand:	9,14–10,03 mm
Hülsenlänge:	15,52–16,59 mm
Hülsenmaterial:	Messing
Pulverart:	Schwarz, rauchschwach, rauchlos
Zündungsart:	Berdan, Boxer
Patronenlänge:	25,19–27,18 mm
V_0	228 m/sec
E_0	137 J
Lauflänge:	102 mm

Die Patrone Kaliber .32 short Colt (auch bekannt als Kaliber .32 short C.F.) gehört zur Munition, die für die Colt „New Line-Revolver" bestimmt war. Die Patronen wurden 1874/75 fast gleichzeitig mit den Revolvern des Kalibers .38 short und long Colt entwickelt, bzw. eingeführt. Die Treibladung bestand ursprünglich aus Schwarzpulver und das Geschoß hatte zuerst Außenfettung, dann Innenfettung (vergl. Katalog Nr. 327). In den Jahren 1875 bis 1910 wurden von den Firmen Remington, Ballard, Stevens u. a. leichte Gewehre für diese Patrone hergestellt. In England wurde in den 60 er Jahren ein Webley-Revolver und zwischen 1870 und 1910 Tranter-Revolver, sowie eine große Anzahl billiger Revolver für dieses Kaliber produziert. Ursprünglich war die Patrone mit Schwarzpulver, heute ist sie mit rauchlosem Pulver geladen. Sie ist im Handel noch erhältlich.

Bodenstempel:
REM – UMC 32 SH COLT,
U.S.C. Co. 32 S.C. (US im Zündhütchen),
DOMINION 32 S C,
W.R.A. Co. .32 S.,
U M C .32 S.C.,
PETERS .32 SHORT

Technical and Ballistic Data

Bullet dia.	.308"–.320"
Case dia. neck:	.312"–.320"
head:	.314"–.319"
rim:	.360"–.395"
Case length:	.611"–.653"
Case material:	brass
Powder type:	black, semi-smokeless, smokeless
Primer type:	Berdan, Boxer
Cartridge length:	.992"–1.070"
V_0	748 ft. per sec.
E_0	99.1 ft. pounds
Barrel length:	4.000"

The cartridge of caliber .32 short Colt (also known as .32 short C.F.) belongs to ammunition intended for the COLT "New Line Revolvers", These rounds were developed in 1874/75 almost simultaneously with the rounds of calibers .38 short and long Colt, respectively introduced at that time. The propellant was originally black powder; the bullet was at first outside lubricated, subsequently inside lubricated (compare catalog No. 327). In the years 1875 until 1910 light rifles for these cartridges were manufactured by the companies Remington, Ballard, Stevens and others. In the sixties, a Webley revolver was made in England, and from 1870 to 1910 we find the production of Tranter revolvers as well as a great number of cheap revolvers, all chambered for this cartridge. Originally a black powder cartridge, it is loaded nowadays with smokeless powder and currently commercialized.

Headstamps:
REM – UMC 32 SH COLT,
U.S.C. Co. 32 S.C. (US in primer)
DOMINION 32 S C,
W.R.A. Co. .32 S.,
U M C .32 S.C.,
PETERS .32 SHORT

.32 Smith & Wesson

331

Synonyme/Synonyms:

DWM 202
DWM 260
GR 930
GR 971
.32 S. & W.
.32 S. & W. Revolver
.32 S. & W. Short
.32-6-85 Smith & Wesson
7,9 × 15,0 – S. & W. 32
8,15 × 15,30 Smith & Wesson
8,15 × 15,80 Smith & Wesson
Revolver Smith & Wesson Kal. 32
S. & W. Cal. 32 kurz

	Geschoß/Bullet Ausführg. Pattern	Gewicht (g)	Weight (gr.)	Katalog Catalog No.
	1 B	6,48	100.00	**331–1**
	1 B	4,60 – 6,00	71.00 – 92,60	**331–2**
	16 B	5,70	88.00	**331–3**
	1 G			**331–4**
	21 B	5,31 – 5,90	82.00 – 91.00	**331–5**
	21 B	5,31 – 5,90	82.00 – 91.00	**331–6**
	60 B	5,51 – 5,70	85.00 – 88.00	**331–7**
	1 A	3,56	55.00	**331–8**
 	1 A	2,98	46.00	**331–9**
	90 b	–	–	**331–10**
	90 b	–	–	**331–11**

.32 Smith & Wesson	Geschoß/Bullet Ausführg. Pattern	Gewicht (g)	Weight (gr.)	Katalog Catalog No.
	90 c	–	–	**331–12**
	90 d	–	–	**331-13**
	90 e	–	–	**331–14**

Technische und ballistische Daten

Geschoß-∅:	7,70– 8,15 mm
Hülsen-∅ Hals:	8,30– 8,64 mm
Boden:	8,41– 8,64 mm
Rand:	9,27–10,21 mm
Hülsenlänge:	14,60–15,49 mm
Hülsenmaterial:	Messing
Pulverart:	Schwarz, rauchschwach, rauchlos
Zündungsart:	Berdan, Boxer, Braun & Bloem, verdeckt
Patronenlänge:	22,41–24,50 mm
V_0	207 m/sec
E_0	120 J
Lauflänge:	76 mm

Die Patrone Kal. .32 Smith & Wesson wurde im Jahre 1878 für den ersten .32er S.A. Kipplauf Revolver der Firma Smith & Wesson entwickelt. Es handelt sich um eine sehr verbreitete Patrone, für die im Laufe der Zeit eine große Zahl von Revolvern von den verschiedensten Firmen hergestellt worden sind. Ursprünglich war die Patrone mit Schwarzpulver, dann mit raucharmen und ca. ab 1940 mit rauchlosem Pulver geladen. Von der Firma Union Metallic Cartridge Co. wurde die Patrone mit einem selbstschmierenden Geschoß gefertigt (Katalog Nr.331–3). Die Patronen werden heute von Firmen vieler Länder hergestellt und sie ist weit verbreitet. Die Selbstladepistole „REIFGRABER", hergestellt 1907 von der Union Firearms in Toledo, Ohio, war ebenfalls für diese Patrone eingerichtet.

Bodenstempel:
W.R.A. Co. 32 S&W,
U.M.C. .32 S&W,
+ H + S&W 32,
G.F.L. Co. 32 S.W.,
C.R.B. Co. 32 S&W (W im Zündhütchen),
S O S 32 S&W,
G.G. 32 S&W (verdeckte Zündung),
PETERS 32 S&W,
R.H.A.Co. .32 S+W,
KYNOCH 32 S&W,
CCC .32 S&W,
S A CORP .32 S&W,
u. a.

Technical and Ballistic Data

Bullet dia.	.303"–.321"
Case dia. neck:	.327"–.340"
head:	.331"–.340"
rim:	.365"–.402"
Case length:	.575"–.610"
Case material:	brass
Powder type:	black, semi-smokeless smokeless
Primer type:	Berdan, Boxer, Braun & Bloem, inside
Cartridge length:	.882"–.964"
V_0	679 ft. per sec.
E_0	86.8 ft. pounds
Barrel length:	3.000"

The cartridge caliber .32 Smith & Wesson was developed in 1878 for the first .32 caliber S.A. tip-up revolver of the firm Smith & Wesson. It is a widely spread round for which in the course of time a great number of revolvers was manufactured by the various companies. Originally, this cartridge was loaded with black powder, then with a semismokeless charge and from about 1940 with smokeless powder. The firm Union Metallic Cartridge Co. manufactured the cartridge with a selflubricating bullet (catalog 331–3). The cartridges are nowadays made by factories in many countries and they are very popular. The self-loading pistol "REIFGRABER", made in 1907 by the Union Firearms Company in Toledo, Ohio, was also chambered for this round.

Headstamps:
W.R.A. Co. .32 S&W,
U.M.C. .32 S&W,
+ H + S&W 32,
G.F.L. Co. 32 S.W.,
C.R.B. Co. 32 S&W (W in primer),
S O S 32 S&W,
G.G. 32 S&W (inside primer),
PETERS 32 S&W,
R.H.A.Co. .32 S+W,
KYNOCH 32 S&W,
CCC .32 S&W,
S A CORP .32 S&W,
and others

.32 Smith & Wesson Long

Synonyme/Synonyms:

GR 931
GR 972
.32 Long, S. & W.
.32 S. & W. Long
.32 S. & W. Long Revolver
S. & W. Cal. 32 lang

332

	Geschoß/Bullet			Katalog Catalog No.
	Ausführg. Pattern	Gewicht (g)	Weight (gr.)	
	1 B	5,51 – 6,54	85.00 – 101.00	**332-1**
	1 B	5,51 – 6,54	85.00 – 101.00	**332-2**
	16 B	6,35	98.00	**332-3**
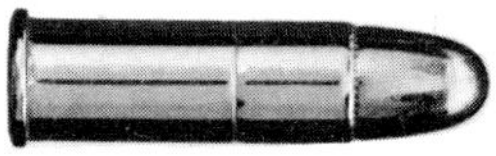	21 B	6,25	96.45	**332-4**
	21 B	6,40	98.76	**332-5**
	21 B	6,40	98,76	**332-6**
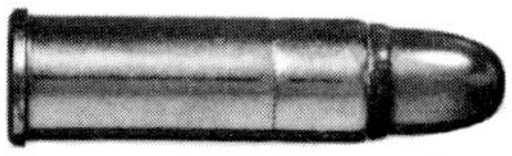	60 B	6,16 – 6,35	95.00 – 98.00	**332-7**
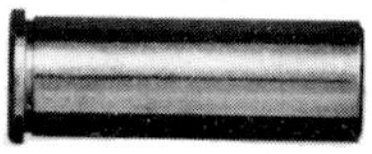	1 P	6,35	98.00	**332-8**
	1 A	2,98 – 3,24	46.00 – 50.00	**332-9**
	90 b	–	–	**332-10**
	90 d	–	–	**332-11**
	90 e	–	–	**332-12**

Technische und ballistische Daten

Geschoß-⌀:	7,62 – 8,18 mm
Hülsen-⌀ Hals:	8,36 – 8,56 mm
Boden:	8,43 – 8,58 mm
Rand:	9,24 – 9,83 mm
Hülsenlänge:	22,68 – 23,88 mm
Hülsenmaterial:	Messing, Messing vernickelt
Pulverart:	Schwarz, rauchschwach, rauchlos
Zündungsart:	Berdan, Boxer, Braun & Bloem verdeckt
Patronenlänge:	31,65 – 32,60 mm
V_0	215 m/sec
E_0	150 J
Lauflänge:	102 mm

Die Patrone Kal. .32 Smith & Wesson long stammt aus der Munitionsentwicklung der Firma Smith & Wesson. Die erste Schußwaffe für dieses Kaliber war ein Smith & Wesson Revolver „Modell 1 – Hand Ejektor" mit Schwenktrommel aus dem Jahre 1896. Weitere Revolver für dieses Kaliber wurden dann auch von den Firmen Colt, Harrington & Richardson, Iver-Johnson, Bayard, Pickert u. a. hergestellt. Mit Wad Cutter-Geschoß wird die Patrone heute auch in Selbstladepistolen zum Sportschießen benutzt. Dieselbe Patrone, allerdings mit Flachkopfgeschoß ist die Patrone Kaliber .32 Colt N.P. (vergl. Katalog Nr. 324). Ursprünglich hatte die Patrone eine Schwarzpulverladung, dann war sie mit raucharmen Pulver und heute ist sie mit rauchlosem Pulver geladen. Sie wird von vielen Firmen in vielen Ländern hergestellt.

Bodenstempel:
G.F.L. C° 32 S.W.,
Beaux S&W 32,
Geco .32 S&W Lang,
SAKO Cal. 32,
S.K.D. .32 S&W L,
U.S. 32 S.W.L. (US im Zündhütchen),
U.M.C. 32 S&W L,
REM – UMC 32 S&W L,
W R A 32 S&W LONG,
W.R.A.Co. .32 S.&W.L.

Technical and Ballistic Data

Bullet dia.	.296″ – .322″
Case dia. neck:	.329″ – .337″
head:	.332″ – .338″
rim:	.364″ – .387″
Case length:	.893″ – .940″
Case material:	brass, nickeled brass
Powder type:	black, semi-smokeless, smokeless
Primer type:	Berdan, Boxer, Braun & Bloem inside
Cartridege length:	1.246″ – 1,283″
V_0	705 ft. per sec.
E_0	108.5 ft. pounds
Barrel length:	4.000″

The cartridge caliber .32 Smith & Wesson long originates from the ammunition development of the firm Smith & Wesson. The first firearm for this caliber was a Smith & Wesson revolver "Model 1 – Hand Ejector" with a swingout cylinder coming out in 1896. Further revolvers of this caliber were subsequently also manufactured by the firms Colt, Harrington & Richardson, Iver-Johnson, Bayard, Pickert and others. Provided with a wad-cutter bullet this cartridge is currently also used in self-loading pistols for target shooting. The same cartridge, however, with flat nose bullet, is the .32 Colt N.P. cartridge (compare catalog No. 324). The round had at first a black powder charge, then it was loaded with semismokeless powder and currently it is loaded with smokeless powder. Many firms in numerous countries manufacture it.

Headstamps:
G.F.L. C° 32 S.W.,
Beaux S&W 32,
Geco .32 S&W Lang,
SAKO CAL. 32,
S.K.D. .32 S&W L,
U.S. 32 S.W.L. (US in primer),
U.M.C. 32 S&W L,
REM – UMC 32 S&W L,
W R A 32 S&W LONG,
W.R.A.Co. .32 S.&W.L.

.32 S&W Automatic

Synonyme/Synonyms:

.32 S. & W. Auto.
.32 Smith & Wesson Auto.
.32 Smith & Wesson Automatic M.1924

333

	Geschoß/Bullet			
	Ausführg. Pattern	Gewicht (g)	Weight (gr.)	Katalog Catalog No.
	60 B	4,86	75.00	**333–1**

Technische und ballistische Daten

Geschoß-∅:	7,85– 7,97 mm
Hülsen-∅ Hals:	8,46– 8,56 mm
Boden:	8,48– 8,56 mm
Rand:	8,51– 8,61 mm
Hülsenlänge:	17,19–17,27 mm
Hülsenmaterial:	Messing
Pulverart:	rauchlos
Zündungsart:	Boxer
Patronenlänge:	24,59–24,69 mm

Bei der Patrone Kaliber .32 Smith & Wesson Automatic handelt es sich um ein Kaliber, das für eine Selbstladepistole aus dem Jahre 1924 bestimmt war. Als dieses Kaliber geschaffen wurde, wurde die Waffe mit der dazugehörenden Patrone Kaliber .35 Smith & Wesson Automatic (vergl. Katalog Nr. 342) gerade aufgegeben.
Die Hülse der Patrone hat einen Halbrand und das Geschoß eine Metallkappe (Metallspitze). Die Patrone kann als Versuchspatrone bezeichnet werden, sie wurde nur in kleinen Stückzahlen, d. h. nicht in Serie gefertigt.

Bodenstempel:
U.M.C. .32 ACP (U im Zündhütchen)

Technical and Ballistic Date

Bullet dia.	.309″–.314″
Case dia. neck:	.333″–.337″
head:	.334″–.337″
rim:	.335″–.339″
Case length:	.677″–.680″
Case material:	brass
Powder type:	smokeless
Primer type:	Boxer
Catridge length:	.968″–.972″

The cartridge caliber .32 Smith & Wesson Automatic was intended for a self-loading pistol of 1924, chambered for this caliber. When this caliber was developed, the weapon and the cartridge of caliber .35 Smith & Wesson Automatic (see catalog No. 342) had just been abandoned.
The case of the round had a semi-rim and the bullet a metal cup (metal tip). The cartridge may be designated as an experimental one, because it was manufactured in small lots only and not commercially.

Headstamp:
U.M.C. .32 ACP (U in primer)

.32 S&W Browning

Synonyme/Synonyms:
.32 Smith & Wesson Browning

334

Geschoß/Bullet Ausführg. Pattern	Gewicht (g)	Weight (gr.)	Katalog Catalog No.
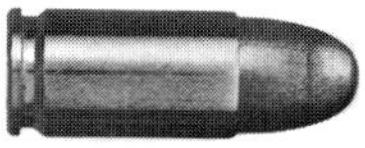 21 B			**334-1**

Technische und ballistische Daten

Geschoß-Ø:	7,80 mm
Hülsen-Ø Hals:	8,48- 8,51 mm
Boden:	8,53 mm
Rand:	8,53- 8,56 mm
Hülsenlänge:	15,19-15,34 mm
Hülsenmaterial:	Messing
Pulverart:	rauchlos
Zündungsart:	Boxer
Patronenlänge:	23,49-23,52 mm

Die Patrone Kaliber .32 Smith & Wesson Browning ist eine Versuchspatrone. Sie wurde von der Firma Winchester hergestellt und ist nicht in Serie gegangen. Sie ist mit rauchlosem Pulver geladen und hat ein verzinntes Geschoß

Bodenstempel:
W.R.A. Co. .32 S&W

Technical and Ballistic Data

Bullet dia.	.307″
Case dia. neck:	.334″-.335″
head:	.336″
rim:	.336″-.337″
Case length:	.598″-.604″
Case material:	brass
Powder type:	smokeless
Primer type:	Boxer
Cartridge length:	.925″-.926″

The cartridge caliber .32 Smith & Wesson Browning is an experimental round. It was made by the firm Winchester and not manufactured in quantity production. It has a smokeless powder charge and a tin-plated bullet.

Headstamp:
W.R.A. Co. .32 S&W

.32 Winchester C.F.

335

Synonyme/Synonyms:

GR 943
.32 C.L.M.R.
.32 Colt L.M. Rifle
.32 Colt Lightning Magazine Rifle
.32 Colt M.R.
.32 Marlin
.32 W.C.F.
.32 Winchester, Marlin & Colt
.32 (.32–20) Winchester
.32–20 Colt L.M.R.
.32–20 Hi-Power
.32–20 Marlin
.32–20 W.C.F.
.32–20 Winchester C.F.
.32–20 Winchester High Velocity
.32–20 W.H.V.
.32/20 Winchester
.32–20 (.32 Win.)
.32–20–100 Marlin Safety
.32–20–115 Winchester
8 × 33 (Cal.No.32) Winchester
8,0 × 33,0 Winchester .32
Winchester Cal. 32/20

	Geschoß/Bullet			Katalog Catalog No.
	Ausführg. Pattern	Gewicht (g)	Weight (gr.)	
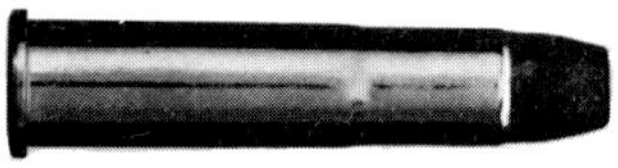	1 G	6,16 – 7,45	95.00 – 115.00	**335–1**
	17 G	7,45	115.00	**335–2**
	21 G	6,35 – 7,45	98.00 – 115.00	**335–3**
	30 G	6,35 – 7,90	98.00 – 122.00	**335–4**
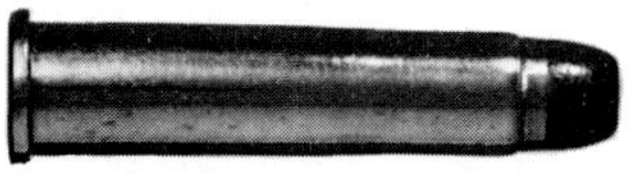	30 G	6,35 – 7,90	98.00 – 122.00	**335–5**
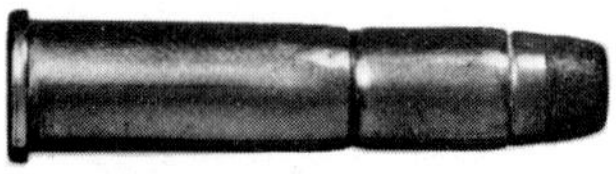	30 G	6,35 – 7,90	98.00 – 122.00	**335–6**
	30 G	6,35 – 7,90	98.00 – 122.00	**335–7**
	40 G	5,83 – 6,80	90.00 – 105.00	**335–8**
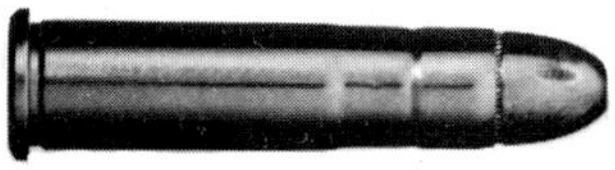	41 B	5,18	80.00	**335–9**

.32 Winchester C.F

	Geschoß/Bullet Ausführg. Pattern	Gewicht (g)	Weight (gr.)	Katalog Catalog No.
	44 G	–	–	**335-10**
	90 b	–	–	**335–11**
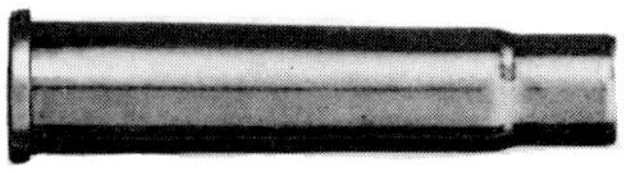	90 b	–	–	**335–12**
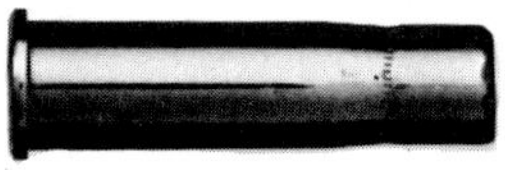	90 b	–	–	**335–13**
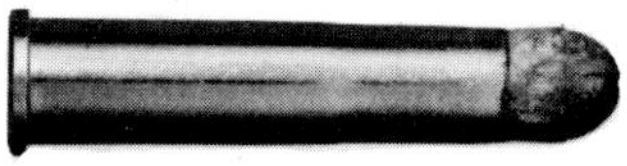	90 c	–	–	**335-14**
	90 e	–	–	**335-15**

Technische und ballistische Daten

Geschoß-⌀:	7,37 - 8,00 mm
Hülsen-⌀ Hals:	8,15 - 8,38 mm
Boden:	8,76 - 8,91 mm
Rand:	10,11 - 10,44 mm
Hülsenlänge:	31,65 - 33,78 mm
Hülsenmaterial:	Messing
Pulverart:	Schwarz, rauchschwach, rauchlos
Zündungsart:	Berdan, Boxer
Patronenlänge:	37,59 - 40,87 mm
V_0	314 m/sec
E_0	330 J
Lauflänge:	152 mm

Die Patrone Kaliber .32 Winchester C.F. ist vom Ursprung her eine Gewehrpatrone und für das „Lever-Action-Winchester Gewehr" Mod. 1873 bestimmt. Sie kam 1882 auf den Markt. Bei dem angeführten Kaliber handelt es sich um das kleinste Kaliber dieser Patronenart (vergl. Katalog Nr. 372 und 420). Um die Jahrhundertwende (1899 bis ca. 1924) wurden insbesondere folgende Revolver für diese Patronen eingerichtet: S&W Mod. 32/20, Winchester Mod. Hand Ejector, Colt S.A. – Army und daneben viele belgische- und spanische Revolver. Die Patronen werden von vielen Firmen in vielen Ländern hergestellt.

Bodenstempel:
R.W.S. W 32,
R.W.S. .32–20 C–F,
W.R.A. 32 W.C.F.,
WESTERN 32 - 20 WIN,
PETERS 32–20,
SUPER–X 32–20 WHV, (verstärkte Ladung)
REM - UMC 32 WCF,
D.C.Co. 32–20,
U.M.C. 32–20

Technical and Ballistic Data

Bullet dia:	.290" - .315"
Case dia. neck:	.321" - .330"
head:	.345" - .351"
rim:	.398" - .411"
Case length:	1.246" - 1.330"
Case material:	brass
Powder type:	black, semi-smokeless, smokeless
Primer type:	Berdan, Boxer
Cartridge length:	1.480" - 1.609"
V_0	1030 ft. per sec.
E_0	238.6 ft. pounds
Barrel length:	6.000"

The cartridge caliber .32 Winchester C.F. is originally a rifle cartridge and intended for the Lever-Action Winchester Rifle Mod. 1873. It was marketed in 1882. This is the smallest caliber of this cartridge type (see also catalog Nos. 372 and 420). About the turn of the century (1899 until ab. 1924) there were especially the following revolvers chambered for it: S&W Mod. 32/20, Winchester Mod. Hand Ejector, Colt S.A. – Army and besides these, many Belgian and Spanish revolvers. The cartridges are currently produced by many firms in numerous countries.

Headstamps:
R.W.S. W 32,
R.W.S. .32–20 C–F,
W.R.A. 32 W.C.F.,
WESTERN 32 - 20 WIN,
PETERS 32–20,
SUPER-X 32–20 WHV, (overload)
REM - UMC 32 WCF,
D.C.Co. 32–20,
U.M.C. 32–20

.32–44 Smith & Wesson

Synonyme/Synonyms:

.32–44 S. & W. Gallery
.32–44 S. & W. Target
.32–44 Smith & Wesson Gallery
.32–44 Smith & Wesson Target

336

		Geschoß/Bullet Ausführg. Pattern	Gewicht (g)	Weight (gr.)	Katalog Catalog No.
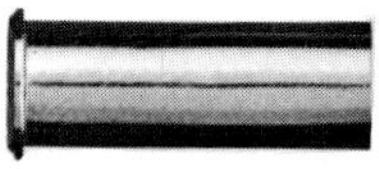		1 A	3,24 – 3,56	50.00 – 55.00	**336–1**
		1 B	5,38 – 5,51	83.00 – 85.00	**336–2**

Technische und ballistische Daten

Geschoß-∅:	8,08 – 8,23 mm	
Hülsen-∅ Hals:	8,74 – 8,81 mm	
Boden:	8,74 – 8,89 mm	
Rand:	10,31 – 10,44 mm	
Hülsenlänge:	24,56 – 24,89 mm	
Hülsenmaterial:	Messing, Stahl	
Pulverart:	Schwarz, rauchlos	
Zündungsart:	Boxer	
Patronenlänge:	24,56 – 26,00 mm	
	Gallery	Target
V_o	175 m/sec	225 m/sec
E_0	56 J	142 J
Lauflänge:	165 mm	

Technical and Ballistic Data

Bullet dia.	.318″–.324″	
Case dia. neck:	.344″–.347″	
head:	.344″–.350″	
rim:	.406″–.411″	
Case length:	.967″–.980″	
Case material:	brass, steel	
Powder type:	black, smokeless	
Primer type:	Boxer	
Cartridge length:	.967″–1.024″	
	Gallery	Target
V_0	574 ft. per sec.	738 ft. per sec.
E_0	40.5 ft. pounds	102.7 ft. pounds
Barrel length:	6.500″	

Bei der Patrone Kaliber .32–44 Smith & Wesson handelt es sich um eine Patrone, deren Entwicklung auf das Jahr 1886/87 zurückgeht. Sie wurde geschaffen, als in den 80er Jahren das Sportschießen mit Pistolen und Revolver wieder in Mode kam. Die Annahme, daß der Luftspalt beim Revolver die Präzision herabsetzen würde, wurde von einigen guten Sportschützen widerlegt. Im Dezember 1886 schoß der Meisterschütze Paine als erster mit einem Sportrevolver der Firma Smith & Wesson im Kaliber .32–44. Waffe und Munition waren in seinem Auftrag von den Firmen Smith & Wesson U.M.C. konstruiert worden. Dadurch, daß das Geschoß durch seinen Sitz in der Hülse weniger bzw. keinen Freiflug zwischen Trommel und Lauf hatte, wurde eine bessere Präzision erzielt. Die Herstellung dieser Patrone wurde 1920 eingestellt. (vergl. Katalog Nr. 373)

Bodenstempel:
U.M.C. .32–44,
W.R.A.Co. .32–44 S&W

The development of the cartridge caliber .32–44 Smith & Wesson dates back to the years 1886/87. It was designed when target shooting with pistol and revolver came again into vogue during the eighties. The assumption that the gap in revolvers reduces the precision was proved wrong by some good target shooters. In December 1886 the marksman Paine was the first to shoot with a target revolver of the firm Smith & Wesson in caliber .32–44. Weapon and ammunition had been designed upon his order by the firms Smith & Wesson respectively U.M.C. A better precision was attained on account of the fact that by the seat of the bullet in the case it had less respectively no clearance between barrel and cylinder. The production of this cartridge ceased in 1920 (see catalog No. 373)

Headstamp:
U.M.C. .32–44,
W.R.A.Co. .32–44 S&W

.320 Long C.F.

337

Synonyme/Synonyms:

DWM 219
DWM 219 A
GR 101
.320 Long
.320 Long Revolver C.F.
.320 Long (Rifle)
.320 Rook
.320–8–80 Long
7 × 19 – 320 lang
7,55 × 20,0 – 320 lang
8 × 19,5 mm – Englisch. Kal. 320
Revolver Kal. 320 lg.

	Geschoß/Bullet Ausführg. Pattern	Gewicht (g)	Weight (gr.)	Katalog Catalog No.
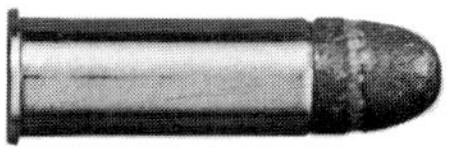	1 C	5,18	80.00	**337-1**
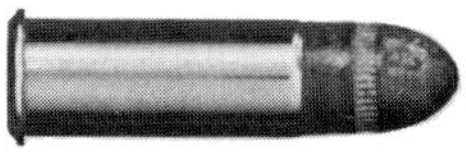	1 C	5,31	82.00	**337–2**
	1 C	5,83	90.00	**337–3**
	21 C	4,79	74.00	**337–4**
	40 C	5,18	80.00	**337–5**
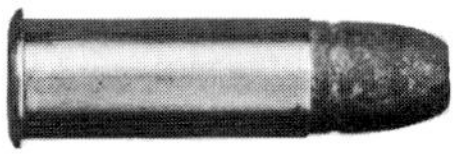	40 G	5,18	80.00	**337–6**
	90 a	–	–	**337–7**
	90 b	–	–	**337–8**
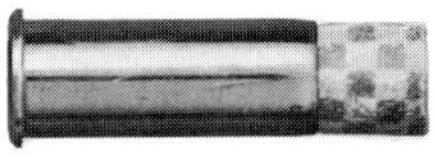	90 d	–	–	**337–9**

Technische und ballistische Daten

Geschoß-∅:	7,06 - 8,03 mm
Hülsen-∅ Hals:	7,95 - 8,10 mm
Boden:	8,00 - 8,10 mm
Rand:	9,19 - 9,65 mm
Hülsenlänge:	16,51 - 20,52 mm
Hülsenmaterial:	Messing
Pulverart:	Schwarz, rauchlos
Zündungsart:	Berdan, Boxer, verdeckt
Patronenlänge:	27,25 - 30,50 mm
V_0	215 m/sec
E_0	135 J
Lauflänge:	102 mm

Die Patrone .320 long C.F. wurde 1873 entwickelt und obwohl das Ursprungsland nicht bekannt ist, dürfte England wahrscheinlich sein. Sie ähnelt der Patrone Kaliber .32 long Colt (Katalog Nr. 327), die Hülse ist allerdings etwas kürzer. Sie fand zuerst Verwendung in Webley- und Tranter-Revolver, sowie in verschiedenenEinzelladergewehren aus der Zeit von 1873 bis 1890. Aus den U.S.A. ist für dieses Kaliber ein D.A. Revolver der Firma Harrington & Richardson Arms Company bekannt. Die Produktion der Patronen wurde um 1890 eingestellt. Im Kynoch-Katalog 1882 enthalten.

Bodenstempel:
KYNOCH .320 L,
KYNOCH .320,
W.R.A.Co. .32L,
G.F.L. .320,
FIOCCHI 320.
G. FIOCCHI LECCO 320

Technical and Ballistic Data

Bullet dia.	.278" - .316"
Case dia. neck:	313" - .319"
head:	.315" - .319"
rim:	.362" - .380"
Case length:	.650" - .808"
Case material:	brass
Powder type:	black, smokeless
Primer type:	Berdan, Boxer, inside
Cartridge length:	1.092" - 1.201"
V_0	705 ft. per sec.
E_0	97.6 ft. pounds
Barrel length:	4.000"

The cartridge caliber .320 long C.F. was developed in 1873 and although the country of origin is not known it is probably England. It resembles the cartridge caliber .32 long Colt (catalog No. 327), however, the case is somewhat shorter. It was at first used in Webley and Tranter revolvers as well as in various single shot rifles having been manufactured between 1873 and 1890. In the USA a D.A. revolver of the Harrington & Richardson Arms Company is known for this caliber. The production of the cartridges was stopped about 1890. They are contained in the Kynoch-catalog of 1882.

Headstamps:
KYNOCH .320 L,
KYNOCH .320,
W.R.A.Co. .32L,
G.F.L. .320,
FIOCCHI 320,
G. FIOCCHI LECCO 320

.320 Short C.F.

Synonyme/Synonyms:

DWM 194
DWM 233
GR 97
.320 C.F. (Revolver)
.320 Revolver
.320 Revolver C.F.
.320 Short
.320 Short Revolver
.320–6–80 Revolver
.320 (7 mm) Revolver C.F.
7 mm (.320) Revolver C. F.
7 × 16 – 320 kurz
7,5 × 16,0 – 320 kurz
8 × 16,5 mm – Englisch. Kal. 320
Revolver Cal. 320 – 7 mm
Revolver Kal. 320
Revolver Kal. 320 kz.

338

	Geschoß/Bullet			Katalog
	Ausführg. Pattern	Gewicht (g)	Weight (gr.)	Catalog No.
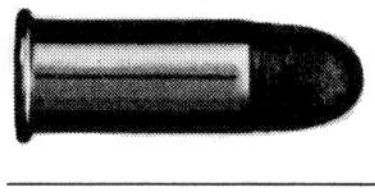	1 C	4,21	65.00	**338–1**
	1 C	5,18	80.00	**338–2**
	1 C	5,51	85.00	**338–3**
	1 C	5,51	85.00	**338–4**
	1 C	5,70	88.00	**338–5**
	1 C	5,83	90.00	**338–6**
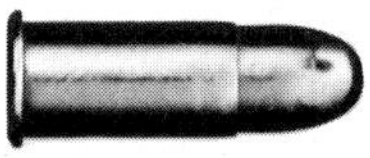	21 B	4,79	74.00	**338–7**
	21 C	4,79	74.00	**338–8**
	40 C	5,18	80.00	**338–9**
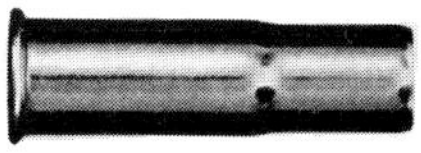	90 b	–	–	**338–10**

.320 Short C.F.	Geschoß/Bullet Ausführg. Pattern	Gewicht (g)	Weight (gr.)	Katalog Catalog No.
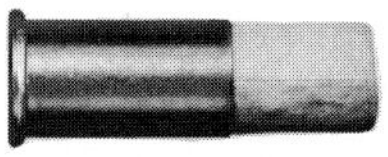	90 d	–	–	**338–11**
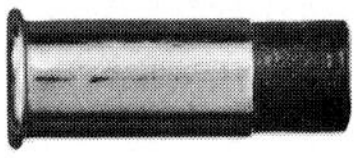	90 d	–	–	**338–12**

Technische und ballistische Daten

Geschoß-∅:	7,39 – 8,05 mm
Hülsen-∅ Hals:	7,92 – 8,15 mm
Boden:	7,64 – 8,18 mm
Rand:	8,58 – 9,68 mm
Hülsenlänge:	14,73 – 18,29 mm
Hülsenmaterial:	Messing, Stahl lackiert
Pulverart:	Schwarz, rauchlos
Zündungsart:	Berdan, Boxer, Braun & Bloem, Topf, verdeckt
Patronenlänge:	23,05 – 26,88 mm
V_0	168 m/sec
E_0	75 J
Lauflänge:	89 mm

Es handelt sich um eine weit verbreitete Patrone, deren Ursprung um 1869/70 in England zu suchen ist. Die ersten Waffen waren englische Taschenrevolver. Waffen und Munition wurden schnell in Europa bekannt, verbreitet und hergestellt. Die Patrone hat ähnliche Abmessungen wie die Patrone Kaliber .32 short Colt (Katalog Nr. 330) und ist mit dieser austauschbar. Obwohl sie in den U.S.A. nicht mehr hergestellt wird, findet man sie in Europa (insbesondere bei der italienischen Firma G. Fiocchi) in der Produktion.

Bodenstempel:
U S .32 WEBLEY,
KYNOCH .320,
L.B.C. 320,
C.B.C. 320,
GG & Cie . 320 .
320 K&C,
FIOCCHI 320,
GG (Monogramm) 320(verd. Zdg.)
R.W.S."320,"
320,
/ 320 / / H /,
8 / + / + / GR,
BRAUN & BLOEM .320,
V.F.M. & Cie LIEGE 320,
320 T 34 T,
G. FIOCCHI LECCO 320,
.320 . .PILONI . (verd. Zdg.)
G. EGESTORFF 320

Technical and Ballistic Data

Bullet dia.	.291"–.317"
Case dia. neck:	.312"–.321"
head:	.301"–.322"
rim:	.338"–.381"
Case length:	.580"–.720"
Case material:	brass, laquered steel
Powder type:	black, smokeless
Primer type:	Berdan, Boxer, Braun & Bloem, battery cup, inside
Cartridge length:	.907"–1.058"
V_0	550 ft. per sec.
E_0	54.0 ft. pounds
Barrel length:	3.500"

This is a widely distributed cartridge whose origin may be found in England about 1869/70. The first weapons for it were British pocket revolvers. Weapon and ammunation became quickly known in Europa, where they were manufactured and commercialized. The measurements of this round are similar to those of the cartridge caliber .32 short Colt (catalog No. 330); the cartridges are interchangeable. Although no longer manufactured in the USA, it is found in the production in Europa (especially the Italian firm G. Fiocchi manufactures it).

Headstamps:
U S .32 WEBLEY,
KYNOCH .320,
L.B.C. 320,
C.B.C. 320,
GG & Cie . 320 .
320 K&C,
FIOCCHI 320,
GG (Monogram) 320(inside primer)
R.W.S."320",
320,
/ 320 / / H /,
8 / + / + / GR,
BRAUN & BLOEM .320,
V.F.M. & Cie LIEGE 320,
320 T 34 T,
G. FIOCCHI LECCO 320,
.320 . .PILONI . (inside primer)
G. EGESTORFF 320

.34 B.S.A.

Synonyme/Synonyms:
.34 B.S.A. BELTED

339

Geschoß/Bullet Ausführg. Pattern	Gewicht (g)	Weight (gr.)	Katalog Catalog No.
21 B	–	–	**339–1**

Technische und ballistische Daten

Geschoß-∅:	8,38 mm
Hülsen-∅ Hals:	8,94 mm
Boden:	8,99 mm
Gürtel:	9,57 mm
Rand:	8,99 mm
Hülsenlänge:	20,12 mm
Hülsenmaterial:	Messing
Pulverart:	rauchlos
Zündungsart:	Berdan
Patronenlänge:	28,19 mm

Mittleres Kaliber der Versuchspatronenserie der Firma **B**irmingham **S**mall **A**rms (B.S.A.). Es handelt sich um eine neuartige Patronenserie für eine Selbstladepistole. Die Hülsen der Patronen haben einen Gürtel, durch den Ladehemmungen (verursacht durch das Ineinandergreifen der Hülsenränder) verhindert werden sollten. Die Patronen dieser Reihe konnten, obwohl dies vorausgesagt worden ist, keinen Erfolg erlangen. Vergleiche auch Katalog Nr. 316 und 380.

Kein Bodenstempel bekannt

Technical and Ballistic Data

Bullet dia.	.330″
Case dia. neck:	.352″
head:	.354″
belt:	.377″
rim:	.354″
Case length:	.792″
Case material:	brass
Powder type:	smokeless
Primer type:	Berdan
Cartridge length:	1,110″

Medium caliber round of the experimental series of the firm **B**irmingham **S**mall **A**rms (B.S.A.). This is a new-type cartridge series for a self-loading pistol. The cases have a belt by which jams (caused by the meshing of the cartridge rims) were to be prevented. As had been predicted, the cartridges of this series did not prove successful. Compare also catalog No. 316 and 380.

No headstamp is known.

.340 Long C.F.

Synonyme/Synonyms:

Gr 102
.340 Long Revolver
8,5 × 21,5 mm – Englisch. Kal. 340

340

	Geschoß/Bullet			
	Ausführg. Pattern	Gewicht (g)	Weight (gr.)	Katalog Catalog No.
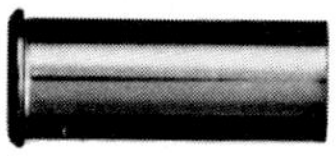	1 C	6,48	100.00	**340–1**

Technische und ballistische Daten

Geschoß-⌀:	8,51 mm
Hülsen-⌀ Hals:	8,50 mm
Boden:	8,48 mm
Rand:	9,70 mm
Hülsenlänge:	21,36–21,49 mm
Hülsenmaterial:	Messing
Pulverart:	Schwarz
Zündungsart:	Berdan

Bei der Patrone Kal. .340 long C.F. handelt es sich um eine Revolverpatrone die aus England stammt. Das Ursprungsjahr ist nicht genau festzustellen. In den Katalogen der Firmen Eley 1898 und Kynoch 1894 enthalten. Von der Firma G. Roth gefertigt, und in deren Katalog von 1913 aufgeführt.

Bodenstempel:
/ 8.5 / / /,

Technical and Ballistic Data

Bullet dia.	.335″
Case dia. neck:	.334″
head:	.333″
rim:	.382″
Case length:	.841″–.846″
Case material:	brass
Powder type:	black
Primer type:	Berdan

The cartridge caliber .340 long C.F. is a revolver cartridge originating from England. The year of its design is not exactly determinable. It is listed in the catalogs of the firms Eley 1898 and Kynoch 1894. It was manufactured by the firm G. Roth and listed in their catalog of 1913.

Headstamp:
/ 8.5 / / /

.340 Short C.F.

Synonyme/Synonyms:

GR 98
.340 Revolver C.F.
.340 Short Revolver
.340 Short Revolver C.F.
.340-8-85 Revolver
8,1 × 17,0 – .340
8,5 × 17 mm – Englisch. Kal. 340

341

	Geschoß/Bullet Ausführg. Pattern	Gewicht (g)	Weight (gr.)	Katalog Catalog No.
	1 F	5,51	85.00	**341–1**
	1 F	5,51	85.00	**341–2**
	1 F	5,51	85.00	**341–3**
	1 C	6,48	100.00	**341–4**
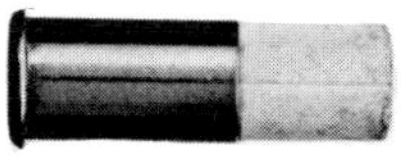	90 d	–	–	**341–5**

Technische und ballistische Daten

Geschoß-Ø:	8,38– 8,69 mm
Hülsen-Ø Hals:	8,51– 8,69 mm
Boden:	8,56– 8,74 mm
Rand:	9,70–10,24 mm
Hülsenlänge:	15,60–17,20 mm
Hülsenmaterial:	Messing, Kupfer
Pulverart:	Schwarz
Zündungsart:	Berdan, Topf
Patronenlänge:	25,32–26,72 mm

Bei dem Kaliber .340 short C.F. handelt es sich um eine weitere aus England stammende Patrone, deren Ursprungsjahr nicht genau zurückzuverfolgen ist. Sie wurde ebenfalls von der Firma G. Roth in die Fertigung aufgenommen. Im Eley-Katalog 1898 unter dem Hinweis „für Tranter- und andere Revolver" enthalten. Als Hülsenmaterial wurde Kupfer oder Messing benutzt.

ohne Bodenstempel

Technical and Ballistic Data

Bullet dia.	.330"–.342"
Case dia. neck:	.335"–.342"
head:	.337"–.344"
rim:	.382"–.403"
Case length:	.614"–.677"
Case material:	brass, copper
Powder type:	black
Primer type:	Berdan, battery cup
Cartridge length:	.997"–1.052"

The cartridge caliber .340 short C.F. is another one originating from England. The year of its design cannot be traced back exactly. It was also adopted in the production line of the firm G. Roth. It is listed in the Eley-catalog of 1898 with the remark "for Tranter- and other revolvers". Case material was copper or brass.

without headstamps

.35 S&W Automatic

Synonyme/Synonyms:

.35 S. & W.
.35 S. & W. Auto.
.35 Smith & Wesson Automatic

342

	Geschoß/Bullet Ausführg. Pattern	Gewicht (g)	Weight (gr.)	Katalog Catalog No.
	60 B	4,92	76.00	**342–1**
	60 B	4,92	76.00	**342–2**
	33 B	4,92	76.00	**342–3**
	33 B	4,92	76.00	**342–4**

Technische und ballistische Daten

Geschoß-∅:	7,70– 7,90 mm
Hülsen-∅ Hals:	8,69– 8,81 mm
Boden:	8,74– 8,86 mm
Rand:	8,74– 8,86 mm
Hülsenlänge:	16,89–17,12 mm
Hülsenmaterial:	Messing
Pulverart:	rauchlos
Zündungsart:	Boxer
Patronenlänge:	24,13–24,56 mm
V_0	260 m/sec
E_0	169 J
Lauflänge:	89 mm

Technical and Ballistic Data

Bullet dia.	.303″–.311″
Case dia. neck:	.342″–.347″
head:	.344″–.349″
rim:	.344″–.349″
Case length:	.665″–.674″
Case material:	brass
Powder type:	smokeless
Primer type:	Boxer
Cartridge length:	.950″–.967″
V_0	853 ft. per sec.
E_0	122.2 ft. pounds
Barrel length:	3.500″

Die Pistolenpatrone Kaliber .35 S&W Automatic wurde 1913 entwickelt und war für die Selbstladepistole Modell 35 bestimmt. Das Geschoß hat eine Metallkappe und Seitenschlitze, ähnlich der Patrone .26 Browning Experimental (Katalog Nr. 314). Die Patrone fand keine große Verbreitung, zumal sie der Patrone Kal. .32 ACP sehr ähnlich sieht und letztere als die bessere Patrone bekannt war. Im Katalog Rem.UMC von 1913/14 enthalten.

Bodenstempel:
W.R.A. Co. .35 S&W (teilweise W im Zündhütchen),
REM – UMC 35 S&W (teilweise U im Zündhütchen)

The pistol cartridge caliber .35 S&W Automatic was developed in 1913 and intended for the S&W self-loading pistol Model 35. The bullet had a metal cap and side-splits similar to those of the caliber .26 Browning Experimental (catalog No. 314). The cartridge was not widely distributed, since it looked very much like the cartridge .32 ACP and because the latter was known as the better cartridge. It is contained in the Rem. UMC catalog of 1913/14.

Headstamps:
W.R.A. Co. .35 S&W (partly with W in primer)
REM – UMC 35 S&W (partly with U in primer)

360 Mars

Synonyme/Synonyms:

.360 Mars Automatic Pistol

349

Geschoß/Bullet			
Ausführg. Pattern	Gewicht (g)	Weight (gr.)	Katalog Catalog No.
41 B	10,11 - 10,37	156.00 - 160.00	**349-1**

Technische und ballistische Daten

Geschoß-∅	9,15 mm
Hülsen-∅ Hals:	9.75- 9,78 mm
Boden:	12,14-12,17 mm
Rand:	11,76-11,81 mm
Hülsenlänge:	25,86-25,93 mm
Hülsenmaterial:	Messing
Pulverart:	rauchlos (Cordite)
Zündungsart:	Berdan
Patronenlänge:	35,72-36,00 mm
V_0	500 m/sec
E_0	1328 J
Lauflänge:	152 mm

Die Patrone Kaliber .360 Mars ist das kleinste und vermutlich auch das erste in Kleinserie hergestellte Kaliber der „Mars-Patronen" innerhalb der Inch-Reihe. Weitere Kaliber sind .450 Mars long- und short Case, .450 Mars Experimental I und II. Die ersten Patronen wurden um 1895 und bis zur Aufgabe des Projektes von den Firmen Eley Brothers Ltd. und Kynoch Ltd. hergestellt. H.W. Gabbett-Fairfax hat für diese Munition Selbstladepistolen entwickelt, die unter seiner Leitung bis ca. 1903 produziert wurden.

Bodenstempel:
ELEY . LONDON.

Technical and Ballistic Data

Bullet dia.	.360″
Case dia. neck:	.384- .385″
head:	.478- .479″
rim:	.463″- .465″
Case length:	1.018″-1.021″
Case material:	brass
Powder type:	smokeless (Cordite)
Primer type:	Berdan
Cartridge length:	1.406″-1.417″
V_0	1.640 ft. per. sec.
E_0	960.0 ft. pounds
Barrel length:	6.000″

The cartridge calibre .360 Mars is the smallest and presumably also the first of the "Mars cartridges" produced as a job-lot series in this caliber in the inch series. Other calibers are .450 Mars long and short cases, .450 Mars Experimental I and II. The first cartridges were produced about 1895 and until the moment the project was abandoned by the firms Eley Brothers Ltd. and Kynoch Ltd. H.W. Gabbett-Fairfaix had developed for this ammunition selfloading pistols which were manufactured under his direction until about 1903.

Headstamp:
ELEY. LONDON

360 No.5 Revolver

350

Synonyme/Synonyms:

.360 Revolver No.5
.360 No.5–18–125
9,25 × 26,5 – R.360/No.5

	Geschoß/Bullet Ausführg. Pattern	Gewicht (g)	Weight (gr.)	Katalog Catalog No.
	1 B	8,10	125.00	**350–1**
	1 A			**350–2**
	90 d	–	–	**350–3**

Technische und ballistische Daten

Geschoß-∅:	9,12– 9,50 mm
Hülsen-∅ Hals:	9,52– 9,65 mm
Boden:	9,57– 9,73 mm
Rand:	10,80–11,02 mm
Hülsenlänge:	26,08–26,67 mm
Hülsenmaterial:	Messing
Pulverart:	Schwarz, rauchlos
Zündungsart:	Berdan, Boxer
Patronenlänge:	34,62–34,65 mm 31,30 mm*)
V_0	320 m/sec
E_0	423 J
Lauflänge:	127 mm

*) Patrone mit Bleikugel

Der Ursprung der Patrone Kaliber .360 No. 5 Revolver liegt in England und geht auf die Zeit um 1878 zurück. Die erste Art dieses Kalibers (.360 No.5 Rifle) war eine Langwaffenpatrone für kleineres Wild. In späteren Firmenkatalogen wie Kynoch 1894 und Eley 1898 ist sie mit gleicher Hülse, aber mit unterschiedlicher Ladung als Langwaffen- und Revolverpatrone aufgeführt. Im Alfa-Katalog 1911 ist die Patrone als „Spezial-Revolver-Patrone" enthalten. Als Hersteller sind nur englische Firmen bekannt. Bis vor dem 2. Weltkrieg wurde diese Patrone noch angeboten (Nobel-Katalog 1925).

Bodenstempel:
ELEY . .360 № 5. ,
ELEY BROS .360 № 5,
KYNOCH .360 № 5

Technical and Ballistic Data

Bullet dia:	.359″– .374″
Case dia. neck:	,375″– .380″
head:	.377″– .383″
rim:	.425″– .434″
Case length:	1.027″–1.050″
Case material:	brass
Powder type:	black, smokeless
Primer type:	Berdan, Boxer
Cartridge length:	1.363″–1.364″ 1.232″*)
V_0	1050 ft. per sec.
E_0	306.0 ft. pounds
Barrel length:	5.000″

*) Cartridge with solid lead round ball

The origin of the cartridge caliber .360 No. Revolver lies in the England and dates back to about 1878, The first kind of this caliber (.360 No. 5 Rifle) was a rifle cartridge for varmint hunting. In later firm catalog such as those of Kynoch 1894 and Eley 1898 it is listed with the same case, but different charge as a rifle and revolver cartridge. In the ALFA Catalog of 1911 it is contained as a "Special Revolver Cartridge". Only British firms are known as manufacturers. Until the time before World War II this cartridge was still offered for sale (Nobel-Catalog 1925).

Headstamps:
ELEY . .360 № 5. ,
ELEY BROS .360 № 5,
KYNOCH .360 № 5

.360 Short C.F.

Synonyme/Synonyms:

GR 99
.360 Revolver C.F.
9,0 × 17,5 mm – Englisch. Kal. 360

351

	Geschoß/Bullet			Katalog Catalog No.
	Ausführg. Pattern	Gewicht (g)	Weight (gr.)	
	1 C	7,78 – 7,90	120.00 – 122.00	**351–1**

Technische und ballistische Daten

Geschoß-∅:	9,00– 9,03 mm
Hülsen-∅ Hals:	9,00– 9,05 mm
Boden:	9,12– 9,20 mm
Rand:	10,10–10,15 mm
Hülsenlänge:	17,50–17,91 mm
Hülsenmaterial:	Messing
Pulverart:	Schwarz
Zündungsart:	Berdan
Patronenlänge:	27,90 mm

Die Patrone Kaliber .360 short C.F. ist die kurze Ausführung der aus England kommenden Patrone Kaliber .360 (Katalog Nr. 348). Bei dieser Ausführung handelt es sich um eine ausgesprochene Revolverpatrone. Im G.Roth Katalog von 1899 ist ausgeführt, daß zur Hülse Nr. 99 das Geschoß Nr. 28 gehört. Im Kynoch-Katalog enthalten.

Bodenstempel:
KYNOCH. .360,
.360

Technical and Ballistic Data

Bullet dia.	.354"–.355"
Case dia. neck:	.354"–356"
head:	.359"–362"
rim:	.398"–.400"
Case length:	.689"–.705"
Case material:	brass
Powder type:	black
Primer type:	Berdan
Cartridge length:	1.098"

The cartridge caliber .360 short C.F. is the short version of the cartridge caliber .360 originating from England (catalog No. 348). This type is a positive revolver cartridge. The G. Roth catalog of 1899 indicates that the bullet No. 28 belongs to the case No. 99. It is listed in the Kynoch catalog of 1882.

Headstamps:
KYNOCH. .360,
.360

.38 AMU

Synonyme/Synonyms:
.38 Special AMU
.38 Special Semi-rim

352

	Geschoß/Bullet Ausführg. Pattern	Gewicht (g)	Weight (gr.)	Katalog Catalog No.
	1 P	9,52	147.00	**352–1**
	1 P	9,52	147.00	**352–2**

Technische und ballistische Daten

Geschoß-∅:	9,05 - 9,10 mm
Hülsen-∅ Hals:	9,47 - 9,55 mm
Boden:	9,47 - 9,57 mm
Rand:	10,20 - 10,25 mm
Hülsenlänge:	29,21 - 29,39 mm
Hülsenmaterial:	Messing, Messing vernickelt
Pulverart:	rauchlos
Zündungsart:	Boxer
Patronenlänge:	29,80 - 30,20 mm
V_0	235 m/sec
E_0	268 J
Lauflänge:	152 mm

Die Patrone Kaliber .38 AMU entspricht bis auf den Rand den Abmessungen der Patrone Kal. .38 S&W Spezial (Katalog Nr. 368–29). Sie wurde um 1960 für die **A**rmys **M**arksmanship **U**nit in Fort Benning für eine modifizierte Pistole Colt Super Automatic entwickelt. Im Gegensatz zur Patrone Kaliber .38 Spezial hat sie einen Halbrand. Die Patrone hat, da sie im Handel nicht erhältlich ist, nur geringe Verbreitung. Sie wird von den Firmen Remington und Western hergestellt.

Bodenstempel:
REM – UMC 38 AMU,
WESTERN 38 SPL S R

Technical and Ballistic Data

Bullet dia:	.356" - .358"
Case dia. neck:	.373" - .376"
head:	.373" - .377"
rim:	.401" - .403"
Case length:	1.150" - 1.157"
Case material:	brass, nickeled brass
Powder type:	smokeless
Primer type:	Boxer
Cartridge length:	1.173" - 1.189"
V_0	771 ft. per sec.
E_0	193.8 ft. pounds
Barrel length:	6.000"

Apart from the rim the cartridge caliber .38 AMU corresponds to the measurements of the round caliber .S&W Special (catalog No. 368–29). It was developed in 1960 for the **A**rmy **M**arkship **U**nit at Fort Benning for a modified pistol Colt Super Automatic. Unlike the cartridge caliber .38 Special it has a semi-rim. Not having been commercialized, this cartrigde finds only a limited distribution. It is manufactured by the firms Remington and Western.

Headstamps:
REM - UMC 38 AMU,
WESTERN 38 SPL S R

.38 Automatic

Synonyme/Synonyms:

DWM 582
.38 A.C.P.
.38 Automatic Colt
.38 Colt Auto.

353

	Geschoß/Bulllet Ausführg. Pattern	Gewicht (g)	Weight (gr.)	Katalog Catalog No.
	21 B	8,42	130.00	**353-1**
	21 B	8,42	130.00	**353-2**
	30 B	8,42	130.00	**353-3**
	30 B	8,42	130.00	**353-4**
	30 B	8,42	130.00	**353-3**
	30 B	8,42	130.00	**353-6**
	30 B	8,42	130.00	**353-7**
	41 G	8,42	130.00	**353-8**
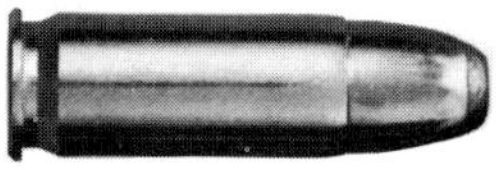	42 G	8,42	130.00	**353-9**

Technische und ballistische Daten

Geschoß-∅:	8,97 – 9,13 mm
Hülsen-∅ Hals:	9,60 – 9,80 mm
Boden:	9,63 – 9,80 mm
Rand:	10,16 – 10,34 mm
Hülsenlänge:	22,20 – 23,00 mm
Hülsenmaterial:	Messing
Pulverart:	rauchlos
Zündungsart:	Boxer, Berdan
Patronenlänge:	31,77 – 32,88 mm
V_0	317 m/sec
E_0	430 J
Lauflänge:	114 mm

Technical and Ballistic Data

Bullet dia:	.353" – .359"
Case dia. neck:	.378" – .386"
head:	.379" – .386"
rim:	.400" – .407"
Case length:	.874" – .906"
Case material:	brass
Powder type:	smokeless
Primer type:	Boxer, Berdan
Cartridge length:	1.251" – 1.294"
V_0	1040 ft. per sec.
E_0	310.9 ft. pounds
Barrel length:	4500"

Die Patrone Kaliber .38 Automatic wurde von der Firma Colt für eine J. Browning hergestellte halbautomatische Selbstladepistole „Colt Mod. 1900" gefertigt. Später wurden auch eine Pistole „Webley & Scott" und weitere spanische Pistolen wie Astra, Star u. a. hergestellt. Abgesehen von den ballistischen Daten sprechen die Abmessungen der Patrone Kaliber .38 Super Automatic (Katalog Nr. 370).

Bodenstempel:
W.R.A.Co. 38 C.A.,
U S .38 ACP,
DOMINION 38 AUTO,
PETERS 38 A.C.P.,
KYNOCH .38 A.C.
REM – UMC 38 ACP,
R – P 38 AUTO

The cartridge caliber .38 Automatic was manufactured by the firm COLT for a semi-automatic self--loading pistol "Colt Mod. 1900" made by J. Browning. Later also a pistol make "Webley & Scott" as well as other Spanish pistols like Astra, Star etc. were manufactured. Apart from the ballistic data the measurements correspond to those of the cartridge caliber .38 Super Automatic (catalog No. 370).

Headstamps:
W.R.A.Co. 38 C.A.,
U S .38 ACP,
DOMINION 38 AUTO,
PETERS 38 A.C.P.,
KYNOCH .38 A.C.
REM – UMC 38 ACP,
R – P 38 AUTO

.38 Automatic Special

Synonyme/Synonyms:

.38 Auto. Special

354

Geschoß/Bullet Ausführg. Pattern	Gewicht (g)	Weight (gr.)	Katalog Catalog No.
1 R			**354–1**

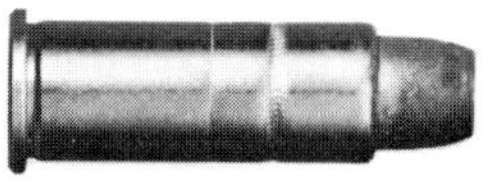

Technische und ballistische Daten

Geschoß-∅:	9,00– 9,04 mm
Hülsen-∅ Hals:	9,55– 9,60 mm
Boden:	9,55– 9,60 mm
Rand:	11,05–11,10 mm
Hülsenlänge:	24,54–24,59 mm
Hülsenmaterial:	Messing vernickelt
Pulverart:	rauchlos
Zündungsart:	Boxer
Patronenlänge:	31,29–31,47 mm

Die Patrone Kaliber .38 Automatic Special könnte ein Vorläufer der Patrone Kaliber .38 AMU (Katalog Nr. 352) sein. Sie wurde um 1955 für eine Colt .38 Super Automatic-Pistole entwickelt. Hersteller der Patrone ist die Firma Western-Winchester. In der dortigen Entwicklungsabteilung sind auch die ersten Patronen gefertigt worden.

Bodenstempel:
W.R.A. 38 SPECIAL

Technical and Ballistic Data

Bullet dia:	.354"– .356"
Case dia. neck:	.376"– .378"
head:	.376"– .378"
rim:	.435"– .437"
Case length:	.966"– .968"
Case material:	brass nickeled
Powder type:	smokeless
Primer type:	Boxer
Cartridge length:	1.232"–1.239"

The cartridge caliber .38 Automatic Special could be a precursor of the cartridge caliber .38 AMU (catalog No. 352). It was developed in 1955 for a COLT .38 Super Automatic pistol. Manufacturer of this round is the firm Western-Winchester. Their research department made the first cartridges.

Headstamp:
W.R.A. 38 SPECIAL

.38 Colt New Police

Synonyme/Synonyms:

.38 Colt N.P.
.38 Colt Police Positive Revolver

355

	Geschoß/Bullet Ausführg. Pattern	Gewicht (g)	Weight (gr.)	Katalog Catalog No.
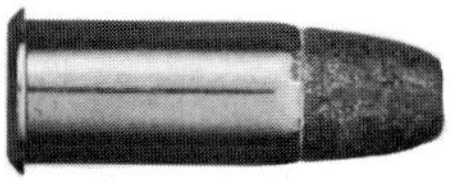	1 G	9,72	150.00	**355-1**
	1 G	9,72	150.00	**355-2**
	60 G	9,72	150.00	**355-3**
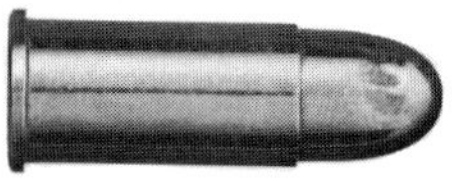	21 B	9,40	145.00	**355-4**

Technische und ballistische Daten

Geschoß-∅:	8,81 - 9,27 mm
Hülsen-∅ Hals:	9,68 - 9,75 mm
Boden:	9,69 - 9,80 mm
Rand:	10,95 - 11,23 mm
Hülsenlänge:	19,13 - 19,89 mm
Hülsenmaterial:	Messing
Pulverart:	Schwarz, rauchschwach, rauchlos
Zündungsart:	Boxer
Patronenlänge:	28,79 - 29,79 mm
V_0	210 m/sec
E_0	218 J
Lauflänge:	102 mm

Die Patrone Kaliber .36 Colt New Police wurde um 1905 für den Colt-Revolver „Police – Positive" hergestellt. In den Abmessungen entspricht die Patrone den Patronen des Kalibers .38 S&W (Katalog Nr. 364). Im Gegensatz zu der letztgenannten Patrone hat sie ein Flachkopf- und ein etwas schwereres Geschoß. Ursprünglich war die Patrone mit Schwarzpulver, dann mit raucharmen- und zuletzt mit rauchlosem Pulver geladen. Im Laufe der Zeit wurden weitere Revolver wie H.&R., Hopkins & Allen, Iver-Johnson, Enfield, S&W und Webley für diese Patrone gefertigt.

Bodenstempel:
U.M.C. .38 COLT N.P.,
REM–UMC 38 COLT N P,
R – P 38 COLT NP,
U.S.C.Co. .38 COLT NP,
W.R.A.Co. .38 COLT NP,
W C Co .38 COLT NP

Technical and Ballistic Data

Bullet dia.	.347" - .365"
Case dia. neck:	.381" - .384"
head:	.381" - .386"
rim:	.431" - .442"
Case length:	.753" - .783"
Case material:	brass
Powder type:	black, semi-smokeless, smokeless
Primer type:	Boxer
Cartridge length:	1.133" - 1.173"
V_0	689 ft. per sec.
E_0	157.9 ft. pounds
Barrel length:	4.000"

The cartridge caliber .38 Colt New Police was manufactured about 1905 for the COLT revolver "Police Positive". The measurements of the cartridge correspond to those of caliber .38 S&W (catalog No. 364). Unlike the latter cartridge is has a flat nose bullet which is somewhat heavier. Originally, the cartridge was loaded with black powder, subsequently with semi-smokeless and finally with smokeless powder. In the course of time other revolvers like Harrington & Richardson, Hopkins & Allen, Iver-Johnson, Enfield, S&W and Webley were manufactured for this cartridge.

Headstamps:
U.M.C. .38 COLT N.P.,
REM-UMC 38 COLT N P,
R – P 38 COLT NP,
U.S.C.Co. .38 COLT NP,
W.R.A.Co. .38 COLT NP,
W C Co .38 COLT NP

.38 Colt Special

Synonyme/Synonyms:

356

	Geschoß/Bullet Ausführg. Pattern	Gewicht (g)	Weight (gr.)	Katalog Catalog No.
	1 G	10,24	158.00	**356–1**
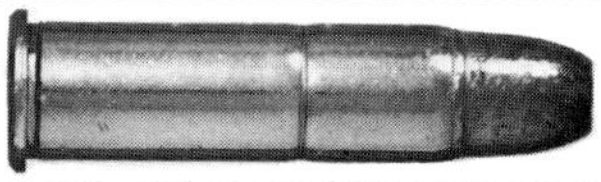	1 G	10,24	158.00	**356–2**
	1 G	10,63	164.00	**356–3**
	60 G	10,24	158.00	**356–4**

Technische und ballistische Daten

Geschoß-⌀:	8,84– 9,09 mm
Hülsen-⌀ Hals:	9,45– 9,60 mm
Boden:	9,45– 9,63 mm
Rand:	10,87–11,15 mm
Hülsenlänge:	28,96–29,59 mm
Hülsenmaterial:	Messing
Pulverart:	Schwarz, rauchschwach, rauchlos
Zündungsart:	Boxer
Patronenlänge:	38,40–38,73 mm
V_0	265 m/sec
E_0	367 J
Lauflänge:	152 mm

Die Patrone Kaliber .38 Colt Special wurde 1906 für einen Colt-Revolver „Offiziers-Modell" entwickelt. Sie entstand offensichtlich aus dem stillen Wettbewerb heraus, weil die Patrone .38 Smith & Wesson (Katalog Nr. 364) der Patrone .38 long Colt (Katalog Nr. 358) überlegen war. In den Abmessungen der Patrone Kaliber .38 Special gleich, wurde in Anlehnung an die Kaliber .32 und .38 Colt NP (Katalog Nr. 324 und 325) die Patrone mit einem Flachkopfgeschoß versehen. Im Winchester-Katalog von 1906 wurde die Patrone mit Vergleichsangaben aufgeführt. Zuletzt konnte sie im Remington-Katalog von 1955 festgestellt werden.

Bodenstempel:
PETERS .38 COLT SPL,
U.M.C. .38 Colt SPL,
U.S.C.Co. .38 COLT SPL,
REM – UMC .38 COLT SPL,
R – P 38 COLT SPL,
W.R.A.Co. .38 COLT SPL,
W.R.A. SUPER 38 SPL.

Technical and Ballistic Data

Bullet dia.	.348"– .358"
Case dia. neck:	.372"– .378"
head:	.372"– .379"
rim:	.428"– .439"
Case length:	1.140"–1.165"
Case material:	brass
Powder type:	black, semi-smokeless, smokeless
Primer type:	Boxer
Cartridge length:	1.512"–1.525"
V_0	870 ft. per sec.
E_0	265.0 ft. pounds
Barrel length:	6.000"

The cartridge caliber .38 Colt Special was developed in 1906 for a Colt revolver "Officers Model". It obviously resulted from a silent competition, because the cartridge .38 Smith & Wesson (catalog No. 364) was more than a match for the cartridge .38 long Colt (see catalog No. 358). The cartridge whose measurements are identical to those of the round .38 Special was provided with a flat nose bullet, on the model of the caliber .32 and .38 Colt NP (catalog Nos. 324 and 355). In the Winchester catalog of 1906 the cartridge was listed with comparative figures. It was ascertained for the last time in the 1955 Remington catalog.

Headstamps:

PETERS .38 COLT SPL,
U.M.C. .38 Colt SPL,
U.S.C.Co. .38 COLT SPL,
REM – UMC .38 COLT SPL,
R – P 38 COLT SPL,
W.R.A.Co. .38 COLT SPL,
W.R.A. SUPER 38 SPL.

.38 Dardick

357

Synonyme/Synonyms:

.38 Dardick "TROUND"
.38 High Velocity "TROUND"
.38 Special "TROUND"

	Geschoß/Bullet			Katalog Catalog No.
	Ausführg. Pattern	Gewicht (g)	Weight (gr.)	
siehe Sonderpatronen see special cartr. Tab./Table 5	1 B	10,2	158,0	**357-1**
siehe Sonderpatronen see special cartr. Tab./Table 5	1 B	10,2	158,0	**357-2** bis **357-9**
siehe Sonderpatronen see special cartr. Tab./Table 5	21E	10,2	158,0	**357-10** **357-11**
siehe Sonderpatronen see special cartr. Tab./Table 5	90g	–	–	**357-12**

Technische und ballistische Daten

Geschoß-⌀:	9,08- 9,10 mm
Hülsen-⌀ Hals:	
Boden:	
Rand:	
Hülsenlänge:	34,20-34,25 mm
Hülsenmaterial:	Kunststoff
Pulverart:	rauchlos
Zündungsart:	Boxer
Patronenlänge:	34,20-34,25 mm
V_0	
E_0	
Lauflänge:	

Siehe unter Sonderpatronen

Technical and Ballistic Data

Bullet dia.	0.357-0.358"
Case dia. neck:	
head:	
rim:	
Case length:	1.347-1.349"
Case material:	plastic
Powder type:	smokeless
Primer type:	Boxer
Cartridge length:	1.347-1.349"
V_0	
E_0	
Barrel length:	

see special cartridges

.38 Long Colt (ins.lub.)

Synonyme/Synonyms:

.38 L.C.F.
.38 Long Colt
.38 Long Colt Double Action
.38 Long Colt, D.A.

358

	Geschoß/Bullet Ausführg. Pattern	Gewicht (g)	Weight (gr.)	Katalog Catalog No.
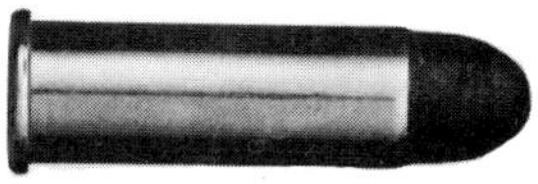	1 B	9,40 – 10,37	145.00 – 160.00	**358–1**
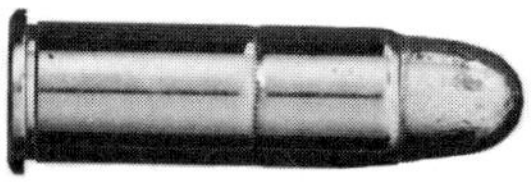	1 B	9,40 – 10,37	145.00 – 160.00	**358-2**
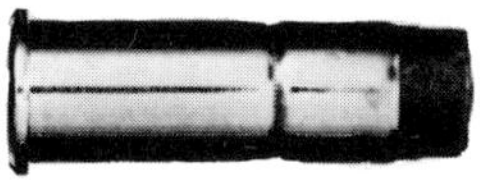	1 P	7,97	123.00	**358–3**
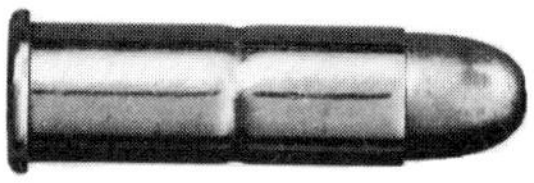	60 B	9,59	148.00	**358–4**
	90 b	–	–	**358–5**
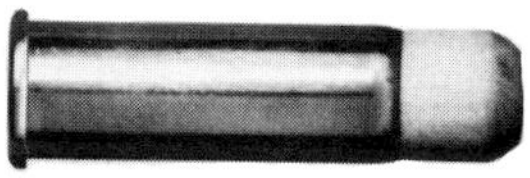	90 e	–	–	**358–6**

Technische und ballistische Daten

Geschoß-∅:	8,53 – 9,07 mm
Hülsen-∅ Hals:	9,47 – 9,70 mm
Boden:	9,47 – 9,70 mm
Rand:	10,97 – 11,30 mm
Hülsenlänge:	25,70 – 26,75 mm
Hülsenmaterial:	Messing, Messing verzinnt
Pulverart:	Schwarz, rauchschwach, rauchlos
Zündungsart:	Boxer
Patronenlänge:	33,60 – 34,92 mm
V_0	240 m/sec
E_0	276 J
Lauflänge:	152 mm

Technical and Ballistic Data

Bullet dia.	.336″ – .357″
Case dia. neck:	.373″ – .382″
head:	.373″ – .382″
rim:	.432″ – .445″
Case length:	1.012″ – 1.53″
Case material:	brass, tinned brass
Powder type:	black, semi-smokeless, smokeless
Primer type:	Boxer
Cartridge length:	1.323″ – 1,375″
V_0	787 ft. per sec.
E_0	199.5 ft. pounds
Barrel length:	6.000″

Die aus der Patrone Kal. .38 long Colt outs.lub. (Katalog Nr. 359) entwickelte Patrone Kaliber .38 long Colt mit Innenfettung hat eine etwas längere Hülse als die Patrone mit Außenfettung. Das Geschoß hat einen hohlen Boden und der Geschoßdurchmesser ist etwas kleiner. Ab 1892 war sie bei der US-Armee eingeführt und dort bis ca. 1909 in Gebrauch, d. h. sie mußte um diese Zeit dem Kaliber .45 weichen. Die erste Waffe war ein Revolver Colt D.A. Modell 1892, weitere Modelle folgten. Als Armeepatronen gab es in diesem Kaliber eine große Anzahl verschiedener Platzpatronen.

Bodenstempel:
WESTERN .38 LONG COLT,
WCCo .38 LONG,
US .38 LONG,
US .38 ARMY,
U.M.C. SH .38 LONG,
F A 11 04,
REM - UMC 18,
W.R.A. Co. 38 LONG (W im Zdh.)
PETERS .38 L,
UMC 38 LONG
U.S.C.Co. 38 LONG

The cartridge caliber .38 long Colt with inside lubrication which had developed from the cartridge .38 long Colt "outside lubricated" had a somewhat longer case than the round with outside lubrication. The bullet has a hollow base and the bullet diameter is a little smaller. From 1892 onward it was introduced in the US-Army and was in use there until about 1909, i.e. it had to give way about that time ot the caliber .45. The first weapon was a revolver Colt D.A. Model 1892, other models followed. As Army cartridges there existed a large number of different blanks.

Headstamps:
WESTERN ..38 LONG COLT,
WCCo .38 LONG,
US .38 LONG,
US .38 ARMY,
U.M.C. SH .38 LONG,
F A 11 04,
REM – UMC 18,
W.R.A. Co. .38 LONG (W in primer),
PETERS .38 L,
UMC 38 LONG
U.S.C.Co. 38 LONG

.38 Long Colt (outs.lub.)

Synonyme/Synonyms:

DWM 263
.38 Colt Navy
.38 Long C.F.
.38 Long Colt Navy
Colt-Revolver Kal. 38 lg.

359

	Geschoß/Bullet			
	Ausführg. Pattern	Gewicht (g)	Weight (gr.)	Katalog Catalog No.
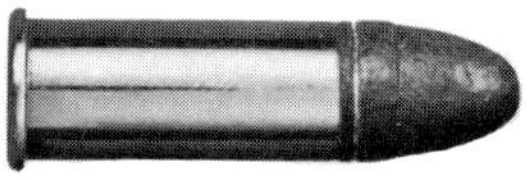	1 C	9,07 – 9,85	140.00–152.00	**359–1**
	1 C	7,19	111.00	**359–2**

Technische und ballistische Daten

Geschoß-Ø:	9,19– 9,68 mm
Hülsen-Ø Hals:	9,52– 9,63 mm
Boden:	9,52– 9,65 mm
Rand:	10,90–11,51 mm
Hülsenlänge:	21,69–22,53 mm
Hülsenmaterial:	Messing
Pulverart:	Schwarz
Zündungsart:	Berdan, Boxer
Patronenlänge:	33,93–35,41 mm

Die Patrone Kaliber .38 long Colt outs.lub. wurde 1874 entwickelt und ursprünglich .38 long C.F. oder .38 long Colt C.F. genannt. Mit verlängerter Hülse und Innenfettung entstand aus ihr die Patrone .38 long Colt ins.lub. (Katalog Nr. 358). Die Patrone war für den Colt „New Navy D.A. Self Cocking" u. a. Revolver bestimmt. Sie ist mit Schwarzpulver geladen.

Bodenstempel:
U.S. 38 COLT NAVY, und
ohne Bodenstempel

Technical and Ballistic Data

Bullet dia.	.362"– .381"
Case dia. neck:	.375"– .379"
head:	.375"– .380"
rim:	.429"– .453"
Case length:	.854"– .887"
Case material:	brass
Powder type:	black
Primer type:	Berdan, Boxer
Cartridge length:	1.336"–1.394"

The cartridge caliber .38 long Colt outside lubricated was developed in 1874 and originally designated as .38 long C.F. or .38 long Colt C.F. With a longer case and inside lubrication it was transformed into the cartridge .38 long Colt inside lubricated (catalog No. 358). The cartridge was intended for the Colt "New Navy D.A. Self Cocking" and other revolvers. It has a black powder charge.

Headstamp:

U.S. 38 COLT NAVY and
without headstamp

.38 Meigs Experimental

Synonyme/Synonyms:

360

	Geschoß/Bullet			Katalog Catalog No.
	Ausführg. Pattern	Gewicht (g)	Weight (gr.)	
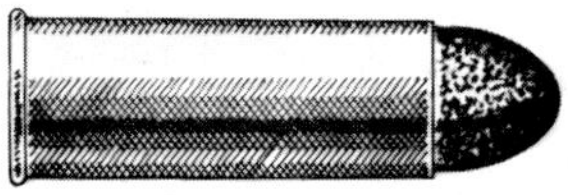	1 B			**360–1**

Technische und ballistische Daten

Geschoß-∅:	9,42 mm
Hülsen-∅ Hals:	10,21 mm
Boden:	10,36 mm
Rand:	11,48 mm
Hülsenlänge:	28,00 mm
Hülsenmaterial:	Messing
Pulverart:	Schwarz
Patronenlänge:	36,63 mm

Die Patrone Kaliber .38 Meigs Experimental ist eine Versuchspatrone mit Martin-Zündung. Bekanntgeworden sind die Patronen aus der Sammlung des Capt. J.V. Meigs. Man vermutet, daß sie bei der U.S. Cartridge Co. oder bei Frankford Arsenal hergestellt worden sind. Den Hülsen liegt ein Patent aus dem Jahre 1869 zugrunde. Wahrscheinlich waren die Patronen für frühe Versuche zu Umwandlungen von Colt- und Remington-Revolvern gedacht.

ohne Bodenstempel

Technical and Ballistic Data

Bullet dia.	.371″
Case dia. neck:	.402″
head:	.408″
rim:	.452″
Case length:	1.102″
Case material:	brass
Powder type:	black
Cartridge length:	1.442″

The cartridge caliber .38 Meigs Experimental is an experimental round with Martin primer. These cartridges have become known from the collection of Capt. J.V. Meigs. It is assumed that they were manufactured at U.S. Cartridge Co. or Frankford Arsenal. The cartridges are founded upon a patent of the year 1869. Probably they were intended for early experiments carried out with Colt and Remington revolver conversions.

Without headstamp

.38 Merwin, Hulbert & Co.

Synonyme/Synonyms:
.38 M.H.& Co.

361

	Geschoß/Bullet Ausführg. Pattern	Gewicht (g)	Weight (gr.)	Katalog Catalog No.
	1 B	9,40 – 9,46	145.00 – 146.00	**361–1**
	1 B	9,20	142.00	**361–2**
	1 A			**361–3**
	90 c	–	–	**361–4**

Technische und ballistische Daten

Geschoß-∅:	8.89 – 9,27 mm
Hülsen-∅ Hals:	9,65 – 9,78 mm
Boden:	9,65 – 9,80 mm
Rand:	10,92 – 11,23 mm
Hülsenlänge:	19,30 – 19,73 mm
Hülsenmaterial:	Messing
Pulverart:	Schwarz, rauchschwach
Zündungsart:	Boxer
Patronenlänge:	30,10 – 31,60 mm

Die Patronen Kaliber .38 Merwin,Hulbert & Co. dürften um 1881 für einen Revolver Merwin, Hulbert & Co. Automatic entstanden sein. Die Patronen haben tiefe Fettrillen über dem Hülsenmund und sie sind mit der Patrone Kaliber .38 Smith & Wesson (Katalog Nr. 364) austauschbar. Die Patronen sind mit Schwarz- oder rauchschwachen Pulver geladen.

Bodenstempel:
W.R.A.Co. .38 M&H.
U.M.C. .38 M,H&Co.
und ohne BS

Technical and Ballistic Data

Bullet dia.	.350" – .365"
Case dia. neck:	.380" – .385"
head:	.380" – .386"
rim:	.430" – .442"
Case length:	.760" – .777"
Case material:	brass
Powder type:	black, semi-smokeless
Primer type:	Boxer
Cartridge length:	1.185" – 1.244"

The cartridges caliber .38 Merwin, Hulbert & Co. are likely to have been designed about 1881 for a revolver Merwin, Hulbert & Co. Automatic. The rounds have deep lube grooves above the case mouth and they are interchangeable with the cartridge caliber .38 Smith and Wesson (catalog No. 364). The cartridges have a black powder or a semi-smokeless powder charge.

Headstamps:
W.R.A.Co. .38 M&H,
U.M.C. .38 M,H&Co.
and without headstamp

.38 Short Colt (long case)

Synonyme/Synonyms:

.38 Short
.38 Short Colt
.38 Webley
.38 Webley Revolver

362

	Geschoß/Bullet Ausführg. Pattern	Gewicht (g)	Weight (gr.)	Katalog Catalog No.
	1 C	7,84 – 8,42	121.00 – 130.00	**362–1**
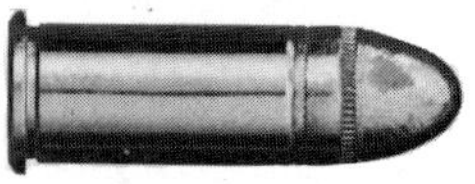	1 C	8,10	125.00	**362–2**
	90 e	–	–	**362–3**

Technische und ballistische Daten

Geschoß-∅:	9,40– 9,65 mm
Hülsen-∅ Hals:	9,47– 9,65 mm
Boden:	9,47– 9,65 mm
Rand:	10,87–11,23 mm
Hülsenlänge:	18,62–19,93 mm
Hülsenmaterial:	Messing
Pulverart:	Schwarz, rauchschwach, rauchlos
Zündungsart:	Boxer
Patronenlänge:	29,95–30,55 mm
V_0	222 m/sec
E_0	212 J
Lauflänge:	152 mm

Die Patrone Kaliber .38 short Colt (long case) wurde um 1874 entwickelt und wird als Kopie einer der englischen Revolverpatronen Kaliber .380 angenommen. Sie wurde für den Colt Revolver „Old Model Navy" und den Colt „New Line" Revolver hergestellt, paßt aber auch in verschiedene englische und andere europäische Revolver. Um 1890 wurde sie auch vorübergehend in Gewehren für die Jagd benutzt. (Vergl. Katalog Nr. 363).

Bodenstempel:
U.M.C. .38 SHORT,
PETERS .38 S,
WESTERN .38,
WESTERN 38 SHORT COLT,
SHORT COLT

Technical and Ballistic Data

Bullet dia:	.370"– .380"
Case dia. neck:	.373"– .380"
head:	.373"– .380"
rim:	.428"– .442"
Case length:	.733"– .785"
Case material:	brass
Powder type:	black, semi-smokeless, smokeless
Primer type:	Boxer
Cartridge length:	1.179"–1.203"
V_0	728 ft. per sec.
E_0	153.3 ft. pounds
Barrel length:	6.000"

The cartridge caliber .38 short Colt (long case) was developed about 1874 and it is presumed to be a copy of the British revolver cartridges caliber .380. It was manufactured for the Colt revolver "Old Model Navy" and the Colt "New Line" Revolver, but it may also be fired in various English and other European revolvers. About the year 1890 it was for some time used in hunting rifles, too. (compare catalog No. 363).

Headstamps:
U.M.C. .38 SHORT,
PETERS .38 S,
WESTERN .38,
WESTERN 38 SHORT COLT,
SHORT COLT

.38 Short Colt (short case)

Synonyme/Synonyms:
.38 S.C.F.
.38 Short C.F.

363

Geschoß/Bullet Ausführg. Pattern	Gewicht (g)	Weight (gr.)	Katalog Catalog No.
1 C	8,10	125.00	**363-1**

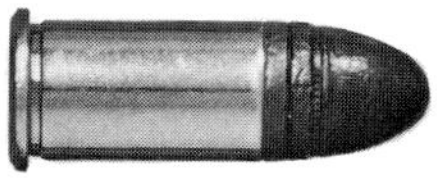

Technische und ballistische Daten

Geschoß-/ :	9,50 - 9,68 mm
Hülsen-/ Hals:	9,50 - 9,65 mm
Boden:	9,55 - 9,65 mm
Rand:	10,82 - 11,05 mm
Hülsenlänge:	16,26 - 17,27 mm
Hülsenmaterial:	Messing
Pulverart:	Schwarz, rauchschwach, rauchlos
Zündungsart:	Boxer
Patronenlänge:	27,89 - 27,99 mm
V_0	235 m/sec
E_0	228 J
Lauflänge:	152 mm

Technical and Ballistic Data

Bullet dia.	.374" - .381"
Case dia. neck:	.374" - .380"
head:	.376" - .380"
rim:	.426" - .435"
Case length:	.640" - .680"
Case material:	brass
Powder type:	black, semi-smokeless, smokeless
Primer type:	Boxer
Cartridge length:	1.098" - 1.102"
V_0	770 ft. per sec.
E_0	164.8 ft. pounds
Barrel length:	6.000"

Die Patrone Kaliber .38 short Colt (short case) ist um 1919 aus der 1874 entstandenen, gleichkalibrigen Patrone mit langer Hülse (Katalog Nr. 362) entwickelt worden. Sie konnte in Colt's New Line Police Revolver benutzt werden. Obwohl in den 20er Jahren das Kaliber veraltet war, ist nicht bekannt, warum die Hülse der Patrone gekürzt worden ist.

Bodenstempel:
WESTERN 38 SHORT COLT,
REM -UMC .38 SHORT,
R - P 38 SH COLT,
PETERS .38 SHORT

The cartridge caliber .38 short Colt (short case) was developed about 1919 out of the cartridge of the same caliber, but with a long case (catalog No. 362) that came into existence in 1874. It could be used in the Colt's New Line Police Revolver. Although the caliber became obsolete in the twenties, it is not known yet, why the case of this cartridge was shortened.

Headstamps:
WESTERN 38 SHORT COLT,
REM - UMC .38 SHORT,
R - P 38 SH COLT,
PETERS .38 SHORT

.38 Smith & Wesson

Synonyme/Synonyms:

DWM 203
DWM 261
DWM 261A
GR 932
GR 973
.38 S. & W.
.38 S. & W. Revolver
.38 S. & W. Short
.38 Short, S. & W.
.38 Super Police
.38–10–145 Smith & Wesson
9,05 × 19,80 Smith & Wesson Kal. 38
9,2 × 19,60 – S. & W.38
9,20 × 19.80 Smith & Wesson Kal. 38
9,25 × 20,30 Smith & Wesson Kal. 38
S. & W. Cal. 38 kurz

364

	Geschoß/Bullet			Katalog Catalog No.
	Ausführg. Pattern	Gewicht (g)	Weight (gr.)	
	1 B	7,39 – 9,98	114.00 – 154.00	**364–1**
	1 B	9,46	146.00	**364–2**
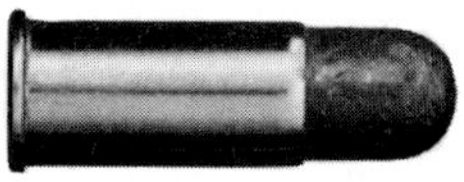	1 B	12,96	200.00	**364–3**
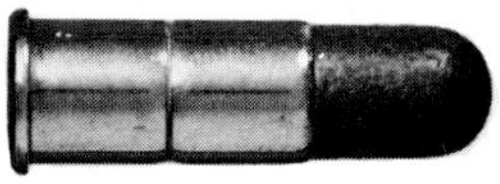	1 B	12,96	200.00	**364–4**
	1 F	7,90 – 7,91	121.90 – 122.10	**364–5**
	1 G	9,40 – 9,85	145.00 – 152.00	**364–6**
	16 B	9,46	146.00	**364–7**
	21 B	9,46	146.00	**364–8**
	21 B	9,38	144.75	**364–9**
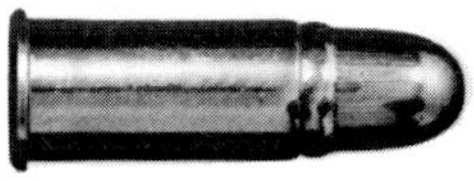	21 B	9,40	145.00	**364–10**

.38 Smith & Wesson

	Geschoß/Bullet			Katalog Catalog No.
	Ausführg. Pattern	Gewicht (g)	Weight (gr.)	
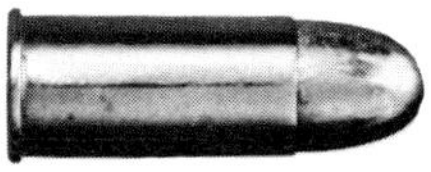	21 B	8,23 – 8,75	127.00 – 135.00	**364–11**
	30 B	9,40 – 9,41	145.00 – 145.30	**364–12**
	40 B	9,40	145.00	**364–13**
	60 B	9,27 – 9,40	143.00 – 145.00	**364–14**
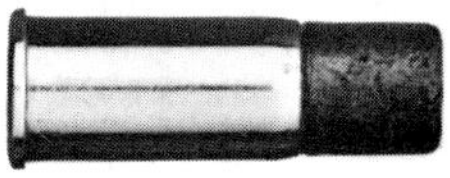	71 P	9,07 – 9,33	140.00 – 144.00	**364–15**
	1 A	4,54	70.00	**364–16**
	90 b	–	–	**364–17**
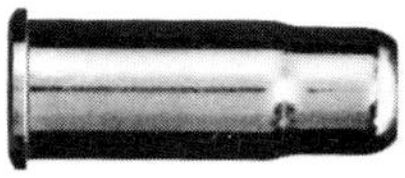	90 b	–	–	**364–18**
	90 b	–	–	**364–19**
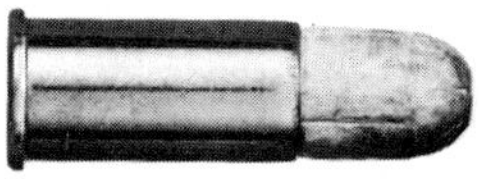	90 c	–	–	**364–20**
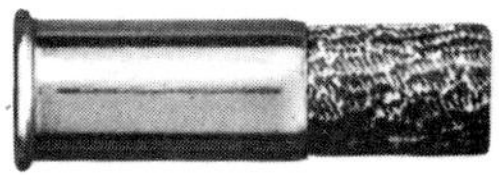	90 d	–	–	**364–21**
	90 e	–	–	**364–22**

Technische und ballistische Daten

Geschoß-⌀:	8,81 - 9,32 mm	
Hülsen-⌀ Hals:	9,45 - 9,80 mm	
Boden:	9,47 - 9,80 mm	
Rand:	10,02 - 11,20 mm	
Hülsenlänge:	18,41 - 20,17 mm	
Hülsenmaterial:	Messing, Messing vernickelt	
Pulverart:	Schwarz, rauchschwach, rauchlos	
Zündungsart:	Berdan, Boxer, Braun & Bloem, verdeckt	
Patronenlänge:	27,95 - 32,30 mm	
Geschoßgewicht:	9,40 g	12,96 g
V_0	215 m/sec	185 m/sec
E_0	221 J	226 J
Lauflänge:	102 mm	

Die Patrone Kaliber .38 Smith & Wesson ist 1876 entstanden und sie zählt heute noch zu den bekanntesten Kalibern in der Inch-Reihe. Sie wurde für den von Dan Wesson entworfenen S&W Revolver Mod. 2 „Russian Baby" in Serie gefertigt und existiert heute noch in vielen Ausführungen. Ursprünglich mit Schwarzpulver, dann mit rauchschwachem- und zuletzt mit rauchlosem Pulver geladen. Sie wird heute noch von vielen Firmen hergestellt.

Bodenstempel:
D.C.Co. 38 S&W,
U.M.C. .38 S&W,
KYNOCH .38 S&W,
L.B.C. + S&W 38 +,
BEAUX + S&W 38 +,
REM - UMC 38 S&W,
W.R.A. 38 S.&W.,
W.R.A.Co. .38 S&W (W im Zdh.)
PETERS .38 S&W,
U.M.C. SH .38 S&W,
.38 S&W . ELEY .,
GEVELOT+ .38 S&W. +,
G.F.L. 38 S&W,
F.G.L. Co. 38 S.W.
L.BEAUX & Co. 38 S&W (verdeckte Zündg.),
G G (Monogramm) 38 S&W (verdeckte Zündg.)
HP + .38 S&W +

Technical and Ballistic Data

Bullet dia.	.347" - .367"	
Case dia. neck:	.372" - .386"	
head:	.373" - .386"	
rim:	.394" - .441"	
Case length:	.725" - .794"	
Case material:	brass, nickeled brass	
Powder type:	black, semi-smokeless, smokeless	
Primer type:	Berdan, Boxer, Braun & Bloem, inside	
Cartridge length:	1.100" - 1.272"	
Bullet weight:	145.00 gr.	200.00 gr.
V_0	705 f.p.s.	607 f.p.s.
E_0	159.8 f.p.	163.4 f.p.
Barrel length:	4.000"	

The cartridge caliber .38 Smith & Wesson was developed in 1876 and is still today one of the widest known calibers of the inch series. It went into series production for the S&W revolver Mod. 2 "Russian Baby" designed by Dan Wesson und currently still exists in many versions. It originally had a black powder charge, later it was loaded with semi-smokeless powder and finally with smokeless powder. It is still being manufactured nowadays by numerous companies.

D.C.Co. 38 S&W,
U.M.C. .38 S&W,
KYNOCH .38 S&W,
L.B.C. + S&W 38 +,
BEAUX + S&W 38 +,
REM - UMC 38 S&W,
W.R.A. 38 S.&W.,
W.R.A.Co. .38 S&W (W in primer)
PETERS .38 S&W,
U.M.C. SH .38 S&W,
.38 S&W . ELEY .,
GEVELOT + .38 S&W. +,
G.F.L. 38 S&W,
F.G.L. Co. 38 S.W.
L.BEAUX & Co. 38 S&W (inside primer)
G G (Monogram) 38 S&W (inside primer)
HP + .38 S&W +

.38 Smith & Wesson Long

Synonyme/Synonyms:

.38 Long, S. & W.
.38 S. & W. Long

365

Geschoß/Bullet Ausführg. Pattern	Gewicht (g)	Weight (gr.)	Katalog Catalog No.
1 B	9,25	142.80	**365–1**
21 B	8,25	127.30	**365–2**

Technische und ballistische Daten

Geschoß-∅:	9,08 – 9,13 mm
Hülsen-∅ Hals:	9,54 – 9,56 mm
Boden:	9,54 – 9,58 mm
Rand:	10,94 – 10,98 mm
Hülsenlänge:	28,20 – 28,30 mm
Hülsenmaterial:	Messing
Pulverart:	Schwarz, rauchlos
Zündungsart:	Berdan
Patronenlänge:	38,98 – 39.00 mm

Die Patrone Kaliber .38 Smith & Wesson long ist nur in den europäischen Firmenkatalogen Guilio Fiocchi, Lecco Ital. und Alfa 1911 (unter der Rubrik „Spezielle Revolverpatronen") enthalten. Sie liegt zwischen den Patronen .38 long Colt und .38 S&W Special und es ist anzunehmen, daß hier ein Kompromiß zu diesen Patronen gefunden werden sollte. Besondere Waffenmodelle sind nicht bekannt.

Bodenstempel:
S&W 38 LONG,
M.W.S. + + 38 S&W,

Technical and Ballistic Data

Bullet dia:	.357" – .359"
Case dia. neck:	.375" – .376"
head:	.355'' – .377"
rim:	.431" – .432"
Case length:	1.110" – 1.114"
Case material:	brass
Powder type:	black, smokeless
Primer type:	Berdan
Cartridge length:	1.534" – 1.535"

The cartridge caliber .38 Smith & Wesson long is listed only in the European company catalogs of Giulio Fiocchi, Lecco/Italy and Alfa 1911 (under the headline "Special revolver cartridges"). It ranges between the cartridges .38 long Colt and .38 S&W Special and it has to be assumed that here a compromise was to be found as to those rounds. Particular gun models are not known.

Headstamps:
S&W 38 LONG,
M.W.S. + + 38 S&W,

.38 S&W Long Automatic

Synonyme/Synonyms:

.38 Smith & Wesson Auto. Long

366

Geschoß/Bullet Ausführg. Pattern	Gewicht (g)	Weight (gr.)	Katalog Catalog No.
21 B			**366–1**

Technische und ballistische Daten

Geschoß-∅:	8,64 – 8,94 mm
Hülsen-∅ Hals:	9.75 – 9,78 mm
Boden:	9,78 – 9,80 mm
Rand:	10,16 – 10,24 mm
Hülsenlänge:	22,73 – 22,78 mm
Hülsenmaterial:	Messing
Pulverart:	rauchlos
Zündungsart:	Boxer
Patronenlänge:	33,04 – 33,10 mm

Bei der Patrone Kaliber .38 S&W long Automatic handelt es sich um die längere Ausführung der S&W Patronen für Pistolen (vergleiche Katalog Nr. 367). Die Patrone gilt als Versuch für eine nicht bekannte Selbstladepistole. Das Geschoß der Patrone hat ebenso wie das der Patrone Kaliber .38 S&W short Automatic einen Bleirand über dem Mantel am Hülsenmund.

Bodenstempel:
W.R.A.Co. .38 S&W (W i. Zdh.),

Technical and Ballistic Data

Bullet dia:	.340″ – .352″
Case dia. neck:	.384″ – .385″
head:	.385″ – .386″
rim:	.400″ – .403″
Case length:	.895″ – .897″
Case material:	brass
Powder type:	smokeless
Primer type:	Boxer
Cartridge length:	1.301″ – 1.303″

The cartridge caliber .38 S&W long Automatic is the longer version of the S&W cartridges for pistols (compare catalog No. 367). It is considered as an experimental for a not further known self-loading pistol. The bullet of this round has, just like the cartridge caliber .38 S&W short Automatic, a lead rim around the jacket at the case mouth.

Headstamp:
W.R.A.Co. .38 S&W (W in primer)

.38 S&W Short Automatic

Synonyme/Synonyms:

.38 Smith & Wesson Auto. Short

367

Geschoß/Bullet Ausführg. Pattern	Gewicht (g)	Weight (gr.)	Katalog Catalog No.
21 B			**367–1**

Technische und ballistische Daten

Geschoß-⌀:	8,64– 8,94 mm
Hülsen-⌀ Hals:	9,75– 9,78 mm
Boden:	9,78– 9,80 mm
Rand:	9,73– 9,78 mm
Hülsenlänge:	19,56–19,61 mm
Hülsenmaterial:	Messing
Pulverart:	rauchlos
Zündungsart:	Boxer
Patronenlänge:	29,62–29,64 mm

Die Patrone Kaliber .38 S&W short Automatic gilt als Versuchspatrone für eine nicht bekannte Selbstladepistole. Wie viele der Patronen aus der S&W-Familie hat das Geschoß der Patrone einen Bleirand über dem Mantel am Hülsenmund. Nur der Rand und die Hülsenlänge unterscheiden die Patrone von dem Kaliber .38 long Automatic (Katalog Nr. 366).

Bodenstempel:
W.R.A.Co. .38 S&W (W i Zdh.)

Technical and Ballistic Data

Bullet dia.	.340″– .352″
Case dia. neck:	.384″– .385″
head:	.385″– .386″
rim:	.383″– .385″
Case length:	.770″– .772″
Case material:	brass
Powder type:	smokeless
Primer type:	Boxer
Cartridge length:	1.166″–1.167″

The cartridge caliber .38 S&W short Automatic is considered as an experimental round for an unknown self-loading pistol. Just like many cartridges of the S&W family the bullet of this cartridge has a lead rim around the jacket at case mouth. Only the rim and the case length make the difference between this cartridge and that of the caliber .38 long Automatic (catalog No. 366).

Headstamp:
W.R.A.Co. .38 S&W (W in primer)

.38 S & W Special

Synonyme/Synonyms:

368

GR 682
GR 933
GR 974
.38 S. & W. "Special" Revolver
.38 Smith & Wesson Special
.38 Special
.38 Special (.38-44)
.38 Special, S. & W.
.38-44 S. & W. Special
.38-44 Smith & Wesson Special
.38-44 Special
9 × 29,5 mm Revolver
S. & W. Cal. 38 Special

	Geschoß/Bullet			Katalog Catalog No.
	Ausführg. Pattern	Gewicht (g)	Weight (gr.)	
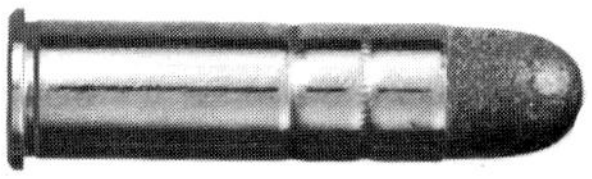	1 B	12,96	200.00	**368–1**
	1 B	12,96	200.00	**368–2**
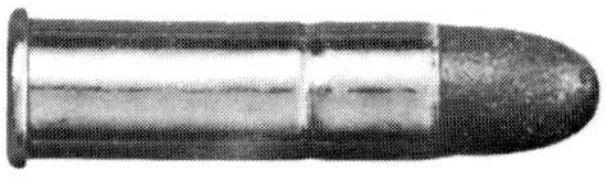	1 B	9,27 – 11,86	143.00 – 183.00	**368–3**
	1 B	9,27 – 11,86	143.00 – 183.00	**368–4**
	1 B	10,24	158.00	**368–5**
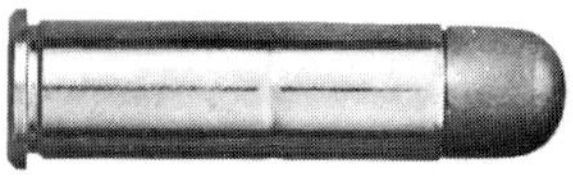	1 B	10,24	158.00	**368–6**
	1 B	10,24	158.00	**368–7**
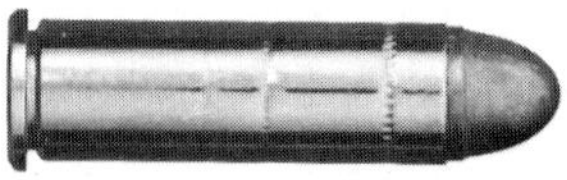	1 B	10,24	158.00	**368–8**
	1 B	7,52 / 8,42	116.00 / 130.00	**368–9**
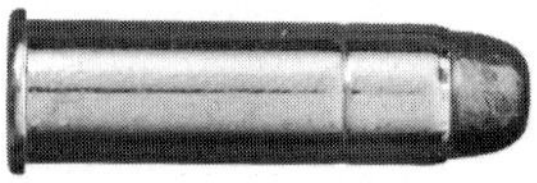	1 B	6,74 – 6,80	104.00 – 105.00	**368–10**
	16 B	9,72 – 10,24	150.00 – 158.00	**368–11**

.38 S & W Special

	Geschoß/Bullet			Katalog Catalog No.
	Ausführg. Pattern	Gewicht (g)	Weight (gr.)	
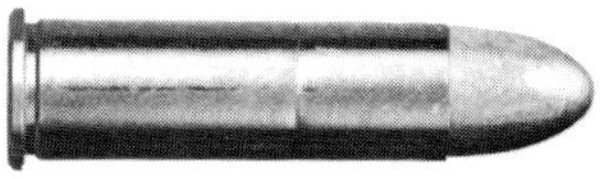	9 B	7,13	100.00	**368–12**
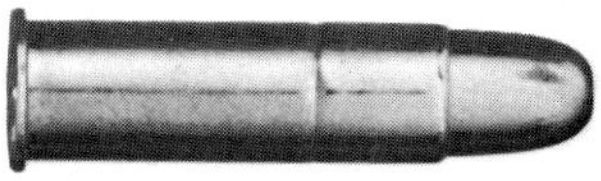	21 B	8,29 – 10,50	128.00 – 162.00	**368–13**
	21 B	10,24	158.00	**368–14**
	21 B	10,17	157.00	**368–15**
	21 B	9,00	139.00	**368–16**
	60 B	10,24	158.00	**368–17**
	60 B			**368–18**
	45 B	9,59	148.00	**368–19**
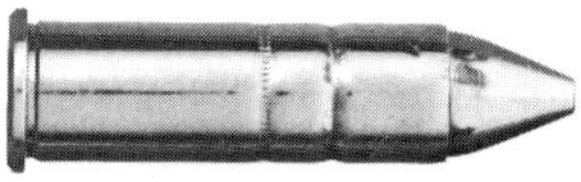	60 K	9,72	150.00	**368-20**
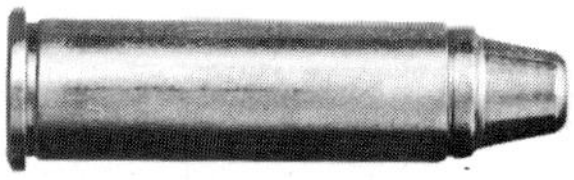	21 R	10,24	158.00	**368–21**
	18 E	12,96 (5,83)	200.00 (90.00)	**368–22**
	1 M	10,24	158.00	**368–23**
	1 R	7,52	116.00	**368–24**
	1 P	7,45	115.00	**368–25**

	Geschoß/Bullet Ausführg. Pattern	Gewicht (g)	Weight (gr.)	Katalog Catalog No.
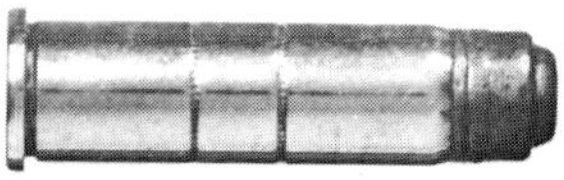	1 P			**368–26**
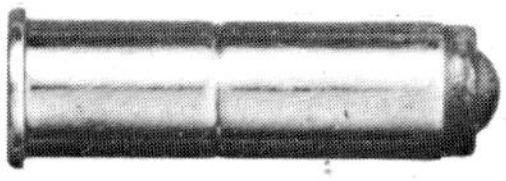	1 P	9,59	148.00	**368–27**
	1 P	9,59	148.00	**368–28**
	1 P	9,59	148.00	**368–29**
	40 R			**368–30**
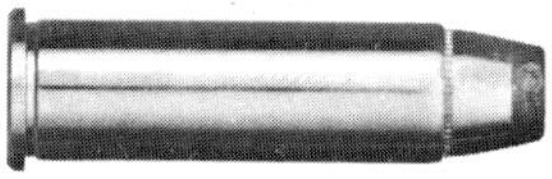	42 M	7,13	110.00	**368–31**
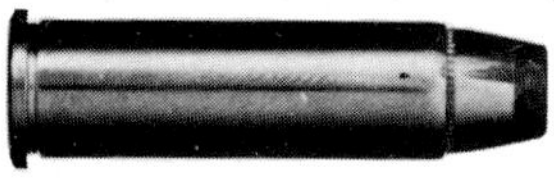	42 M	10,24	158.00	**368–32**
	42 M	10,24	158.00	**368–33**
	42 G	7,19	111.00	**368–34**
	42 G	8,10	125.00	**368–35**
	42 G	10,24	158.00	**368–36**
 	1 A	4,54	70.00	**368–37**
 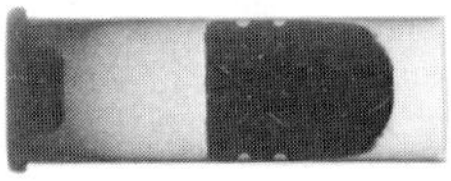	1 B			**368–38**
	8 P			**368–39**

.38 S & W Special	Geschoß/Bullet Ausführg. Pattern	Gewicht (g)	Weight (gr.)	Katalog Catalog No.
	90 b	–	–	**368–40**
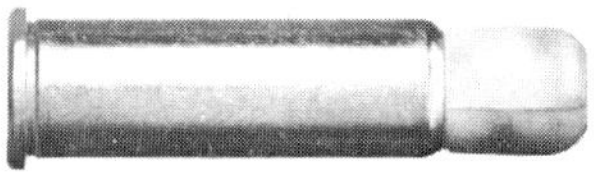	90 f	–	–	**368–41**
	90 f	–	–	**368–42**
	21 B	10,24	158.00	**368–43**
	21 B	8,4	130.00	**368–44**
	21 K	10,24	158.00	**368–45**
	21 S	8,10	125.00	**368–46**
	21 S	7,13	110.00	**368–47**
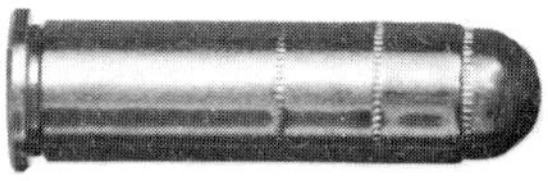	30 B	8,10	125.00	**368–48**
	1 G	10,24	158.00	**368–49**
	1 G	9,7	150.00	**368–50**
	70 M			**368–51**
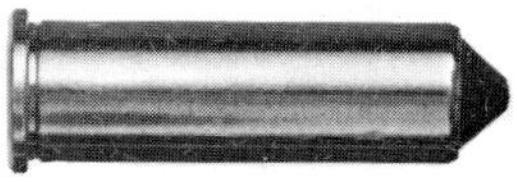	70 M			**368–52**
	32 G	8,10	125.00	**368–53**

.38 S & W Special

	Geschoß/Bullet			Katalog Catalog No.
	Ausführg. Pattern	Gewicht (g)	Weight (gr.)	
	32 G	9,7	150.00	**368–54**
	32 G	10,24	158.00	**368–55**
	4 G	2,3	35,5	**368–56**
	4 G	2,5	38,58	**368–57**
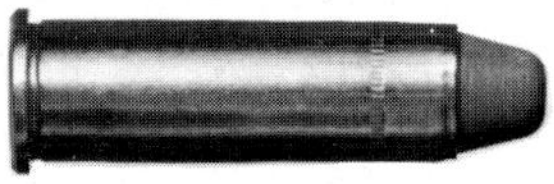	18 M	5,75	88,70	**368–58**
	90 g	4,1	63,3	**368–59**
	90 J	6,22	96.00	**368–60**

Technische und ballistische Daten

Geschoß-∅:	8,55– 9,25 mm	
Hülsen-∅ Hals:	9,30– 9,65 mm	
Boden:	9,46– 9,65 mm	
Rand:	10,79–11,82 mm	
Hülsenlänge:	28,19–29,67 mm	
Hülsenmaterial:	Messing, Messing vernickelt, Aluminium	
Pulverart:	Schwarz, rauchschwach,rauchlos	
Zündungsart:	Berdan, Boxer, Braun & Bloem,verdeckt	
Patronenlänge:	35,00–40,00 mm	
	V_0 m/sec	E_0 J
12,96 g "SUPER POLICE" (WESTERN)	222	326
10,24 g Blei, Rundkopf (Standard) (WIN)	261	354
10,24 g Blei, Rundkopf H.V. (REM)	332	579
9,72 g "SUPER-X" (WESTERN)	325	521
9,59 g Blei, "Wad Cutter" (GECO)	235	270
8,10 g Teilmantel/Hohlspitz (REM)	418	719

Technical and Ballistic Data

Bullet dia.	.337"– .364"	
Case dia. neck:	.366"– .380"	
head:	.372"– .380"	
rim:	.425"– .444"	
Case length:	1.110"–1.168"	
Case material:	brass, nickeled brass, aluminium	
Powder type:	black, semi-smokeless, smokeless	
Primer type:	Berdan, Boxer, Braun & Bloem, inside	
Cartridge length:	1.378"–1.575"	
	V_0 ft. per sec.	E_0 ft. pounds
200.00 gr. "SUPER POLICE" (WESTERN)	728	235.6
158.00 gr. Solid lead (Standard) (WIN)	856	255.9
158.00 gr. Solid lead H.V. (REM)	1090	418.6
150.00 gr. SUPER-X (WESTERN)	1066	376.7
148.00 gr. Solid lead, wad cutter (GECO)	771	195.2
125.00 gr. Soft nose, open point (REM)	1371	519.8

Technische und ballistische Daten

7,13 g Teilmantel/Hohlspitz (SUPER VEL)	418	633
7,13 g Metal-procing (REM)	402	590
Lauflänge:	152 mm	

Die Patrone Kaliber .38 S & W Special dürfte wohl zu den am weitest verbreiteten und bekanntesten Revolverpatronen der Welt gehören. Sie wird wegen ihrer Präzision sowohl als Gebrauchspatrone, wie auch zum Sportschießen in Revolvern und Pistolen benutzt. Ihr Ursprung ist, (wenn auch mit längerer Hülse) im Jahr 1899 zu suchen und wurde für den Revolver .38 Hand Ejector „Militär & Police" hergestellt. Die Patrone war zunächst mit Schwarzpulver, dann mit raucharmen- und ist heute mit rauchlosem Pulver geladen. Sie existiert in vielen Variationen für eine Vielzahl von Waffenfabrikaten und wird sehr gerne von Wiederladern laboriert (vergleiche auch Katalog Nr. 352).

Bodenstempel:
W – W 38 SPECIAL,
W – W SUPER 38 SPECIAL,
W.R.A. .38 S&W SPL,
W.R.A. SUPER .38 SPL,
W.R.A.Co. 38 S&W SPL, (W i. Zdh.),
WESTERN .38 S&W SPL,
WESTERN .38 SPL SR,
WESTERN .38 SPECIAL,
FEDERAL .38 SPECIAL,
U S .38 POLICE
U.S.C.Co. .38 SPL SPEED
U M C 38 S&W SP.L (U i. Zdh),
SUPER-X .38 SPECIAL,
U.S.C.Co. 38 S&W SP.L,
W C C 73
S&W – F 38 SPL,
RY 38 SPECIAL,
METALLVERKEN 38 SPL,
NORMA Re .38 SPECIAL,
norma .38 Special
A.R.S. 38 SPL,
L.B.C. 38 S&W,
SAKO 38 SPECIAL,
SPEER .38 SPL
REM – UMC .38 SPL
R – P .38 SPL,
REM-UMC .38 SPL HS,
Geco .38 Special,
6 7 027,
CRB + + 38 S&W,
C B C 38 SWL,
G.F.L. 38 S.W.Special
u.a.

Technical and Ballistic Data

110.00 gr. Soft nose, open point (SUPER VEL)	1371	457.6
110,00 g Metal-picering (REM)	1319	426,6
Barrel length:	6.000″	

The cartridge caliber .38 S&W Special is probably the widest distributed and known revolver cartridge of the world. Because of its accuracy it is both used as a service cartridge and for target shooting in revolvers and pistols. The year of its coming into existence (with the longer case, though) is to be sought in 1899 and it was made for revolver .38 Hand Ejector "Military & Police". At first provided with a black powder charge, then with semismokeless powder, it is currently loaded with smokeless powder. It exists in many variations for a great number of gun brands and is preferably charged by reloaders (see also catalog No. 352)

Headstamps:
W – W 38 SPECIAL,
W – W SUPER 38 SPECIAL,
W.R.A. .38 S&W SPL,
W.R.A. SUPER .38 SPL,
W.R.A.Co. 38 S&W SPL (W i. Primer),
WESTERN .38 S&W SPL,
WESTERN .38 SPL SR,
WESTERN .38 SPECIAL,
FEDERAL .38 SPECIAL,
U S .38 POLICE
U.S.C.Co. .38 SPL SPEED
U M C 38 S&W SP.L (U in Primer)
SUPER-X .38 SPECIAL,
U.S.C.Co. 38 S&W SP.L
W C C 73
S&W – F 38 SPL,
RY 38 SPECIAL,
METALLVERKEN 38 SPL,
NORMA Re .38 SPECIAL,
norma .38 Special
A.R.S. 38 SPL,
L.B.C. 38 S&W,
SAKO 38 SPECIAL,
SPEER .38 SPL,
REM – UMC .38 SPL
R – P .38 SPL,
REM–UMC .38 S&W SP.L,
Geco .38 Special,
6 7 027,
CRB + + 38 S&W,
C B C 38 SWL,
G.F.L. 38 S.W. Special
and others

.38 S&W Special Target

Synonyme/Synonyms:

.38 Smith & Wesson Special Target

369

	Geschoß/Bullet Ausführg. Pattern	Gewicht (g)	Weight (gr.)	Katalog Catalog No.
	7 C	0,50	7.72	**369-1**
	7 B	0,42	6.48	**369-2**
	7 B	0,39 - 0,41	6.02 - 6,33	**369-3**
	7 B	0,39 - 0,41	6.02 - 6.33	**369-4**
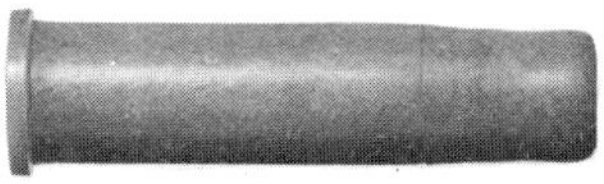	7 P	0,40	6.17	**369-5**

Technische und ballistische Daten

Geschoß-∅:	9,04 - 9,20 mm
Hülsen-∅ Hals:	9,30 - 9,60 mm
Boden:	9,52 - 9,70 mm
Rand:	11,10 - 11,18 mm
Hülsenlänge:	28,60 - 29,50 mm
Hülsenmaterial:	Kunststoff
Pulverart:	rauchlos
Zündungsart:	Boxer, Berdan
Patronenlänge:	38,30 - 38,90 mm

Die Patrone Kaliber .38 S&W Target ist eine Abart der Patrone Kaliber .38 S&W Special (Katalog Nr. 368). Sie wurde aus dem Bedürfnis heraus entwickelt, eine billige Trainingspatrone mit kurzer Reichweite zu haben. Sie wird hergestellt als Patrone zur Wiederverwendung (Hülse und Geschoß getrennt) oder als Patrone bei der das Geschoß mit der Hülse verbunden ist und das Geschoß sich beim Schuß an einer Sollbruchstelle von der Hülse trennt. Mit Metall- oder Kunststoffboden möglich.

Keine Bodenstempel bekannt.

Technical and Ballistic Data

Bullet dia.	.356" - .362"
Case dia. neck:	.366" - .378"
head:	.375" - .382"
rim:	.437" - .440"
Case length:	1.126" - 1.161"
Case material:	plastic
Powder type:	smokeless
Primer type:	Boxer, Berdan
Cartridge length:	1.508" - 1.531"

The cartridge caliber .38 S&W Target is a variation of the cartridge caliber .38 S&W Special (catalog No. 368). It was developed out of the requirement to have a cheap cartridge for practice shooting within a short range. It is manufactured as a cartridge for re-use (case and bullet separate) or as a one-piece cartridge; when fired its bullet disengages from the case at a rated break point. With metal or plastic base possible.

No headstamps known.

.38 Super Automatic

Synonyme/Synonyms:

.38 A.C.P. (Super)
.38 Automatic Super-Speed
.38 Automatic Super-X
.38 Colt Super Automatic
.38 Super Auto.

370

	Geschoß/Bullet Ausführg. Pattern	Gewicht (g)	Weight (gr.)	Katalog Catalog No.
	21 B	8,42	130.00	**370–1**
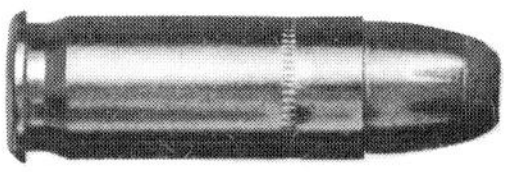	30 G	8,42	130.00	**370–2**
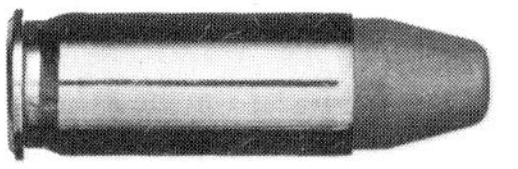	18 M	6,48	100	**370-3**

Technische und ballistische Daten

Geschoß-∅:	8,96– 9,02 mm
Hülsen-∅ Hals:	9,68– 9,72 mm
Boden:	9,63– 9,70 mm
Rand:	10.18–10,21 mm
Hülsenlänge:	22,60–22,90 mm
Hülsenmaterial:	Messing vernickelt
Pulverart:	rauchlos
Zündungsart:	Boxer
Patronenlänge:	31,95–32,25 mm
V_0	390 m/sec
E_0	657 J
Lauflänge:	127 mm

Die Pistolenpatrone Kaliber .38 Super Automatic entspricht in ihren Abmessungen der Pistolenpatrone Kaliber .38 Automatic (Katalog Nr. 353). Sie wurde 1928 für eine Colt-Selbstladepistole „Super Automatic" hergestellt. Durch ein verbessertes Pulver zur Patrone Kaliber .38 Automatic wurde eine höhere Geschwindigkeit und eine höhere Mündungsenergie erreicht. Die Hülsen sind nickelplattiert. Weiter Pistolen wurden in der Folgezeit insbesondere in Spanien von der Firma Astra, Star und Llama gefertigt.

Bodenstempel:
REM – UMC .38 AUTO,
REM – UMC .38 ACP,
SUPER-X .38 AUTO,
SUPER VEL 38 SUPER

Technical and Ballistic Data

Bullet dia.	.353″–.355″
Case dia. neck:	.381″–.383″
head:	.379″–.382″
rim:	.401″–.402″
Case length:	.890″–.902″
Case material:	nickeled brass
Powder type:	smokeless
Primer type:	Boxer
Cartridge length:	1.258″–1.270″
V_0	1280 ft. per sec.
E_0	475.0 ft. pounds
Barrel length:	5.000″

The pistol cartridge caliber .38 Super Automatic corresponds in its measurements to the pistol cartridge .38 Automatic (catalog Nr. 353). It was manufactured in 1928 for a COLT self-loading pistol "Super Automatic". By an improved powder for the cartridge caliber .38 Automatic a higher velocity and a more potent muzzle energy were achieved. The cases are nickel-plated. During the period which followed further pistols, especially in Spain, were manufactured by the firms Astra, Star and Llama.

Headstamps:
REM – UMC .38 AUTO
REM – UMC .38 ACP,
SUPER-X .38 AUTO,
SUPER VEL 38 SUPER

.38 Target

Synonyme/Synonyms:

.38 S. & W. Target
.38 Smith & Wesson Target
.38 Speer Target

371

	Geschoß/Bullet			Katalog Catalog No.
	Ausführg. Pattern	Gewicht (g)	Weight (gr.)	
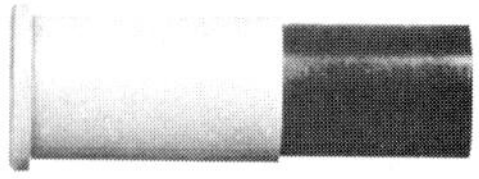	7 Q	0,95 – 1,00	14.66 – 15.43	**371-1**

Technische und ballistische Daten

Geschoß-∅:	8,76 – 8,80 mm
Hülsen-∅ Hals:	9,60 – 9,62 mm
Boden:	9,56 – 9,58 mm
Rand:	11,04 – 11,14 mm
Hülsenlänge:	17,58 – 17,64 mm
Hülsenmaterial:	Kunststoff
Zündungsart:	Boxer
Patronenlänge:	30,15 – 30,20 mm

Die Patrone Kaliber .38 Target wurde von der Firma Speer USA entwickelt. Sie ist eine billige und wiederladbare Trainingspatrone für kurze Entfernungen. Die Komponenten, Hülse, Geschoß und Zündung (ohne Treibladung) werden vor dem Schuß zusammengestellt. (Vergleiche Katalog Nr. 369 + 416)

Bodenstempel:
SPEER .38,
W-W .38 TGT.

Technical and Ballistic Data

Bullet dia.	.345"–.346"
Case dia. neck:	.378"–.379"
head:	.376"–.377"
rim:	.435"–.438"
Case length:	.692"–.694"
Case material:	plastic
Primer type:	Boxer
Cartridge length:	1.187"–1.189"

The cartridge caliber .38 Target was developed by the company Speer/USA. It is a cheap and reloadable practice cartridge for short range training. The components consisting of case, bullet and primer (without propellant) are put together before the shot is fired (compare catalog No. 369 and 416).

Headstamps:
SPEER .38,
W-W .38 TGT.

.38 Winchester C.F.

372

Synonyme/Synonyms:

.38 C.L.M.R.
.38 Colt L.M.R.
.38 Colt L.M. Rifle
.38 Colt Lightning Magazine Rifle
.38 Colt M.R.
.38 Colt N.L.M.R.
.38 Colt New L.M.R.
.38 Colt New L.M. Rifle
.38 Marlin
.38 W.C.F.
.38 Winchester, Marlin & Colt
.38 Winchester, Marlin & Remington
.38 – 40 Dominion
.38 – 40 Marlin
.38 – 40 Remington
.38 – 40 W.C.F.
.38/40 Winchester
.38 – 40 Winchester C.F.
.38 – 40 – 160 Winchester
10,1 × 33 (Cal. No. 38) Winchester
10,1 × 33,0 – Winchester. 38

	Geschoß/Bullet			Katalog Catalog No.
	Ausführg. Pattern	Gewicht (g)	Weight (gr.)	
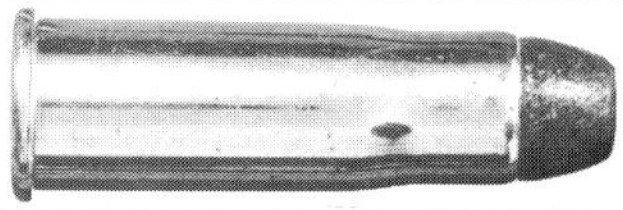	1 G	11,66	180.00	**372–1**
	1 G	10,37	160.00	**372–2**
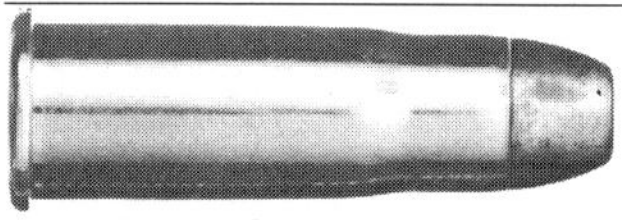	21 G	11,66	180.00	**372–3**
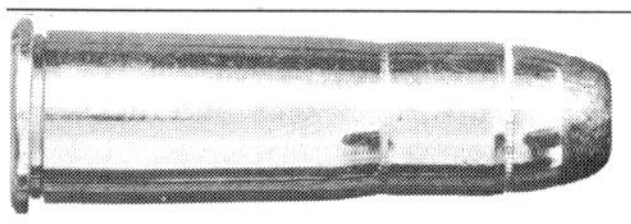	30 G	11,66	180.00	**372–4**
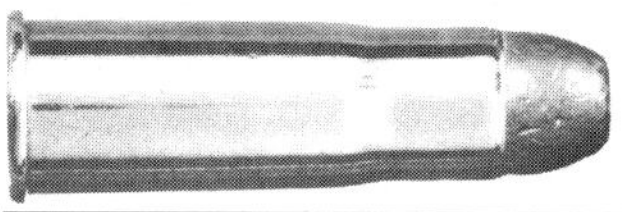	40 G	10,69	165.00	**372–5**
	40 G	9,72	150.00	**372–6**
	48 G			**372–7**
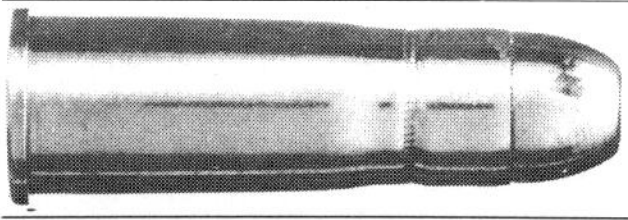	41 G			**372–8**
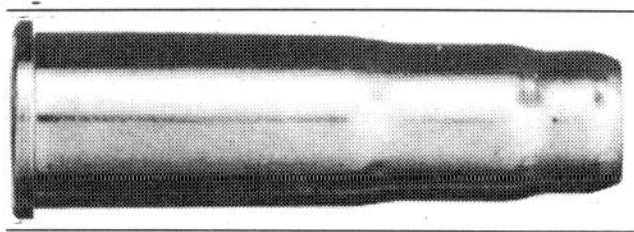	90 b	–	–	**372–9**

.38 Winchester C.F.

	Geschoß/Bullet Ausführg. Pattern	Gewicht (g)	Weight (gr.)	Katalog Catalog No.
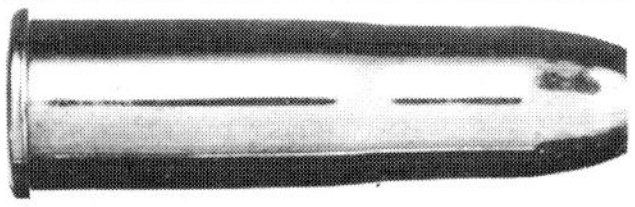	90 b	–	–	**372–10**
	90 c	–	–	**372–11**
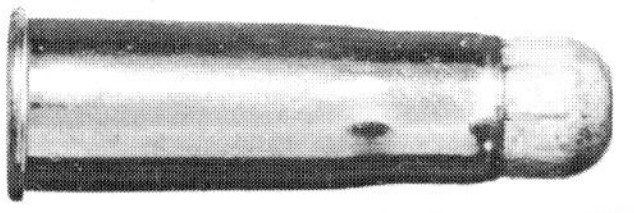	90 e	–	–	**372–12**

Technische und ballistische Daten

Geschoß-∅:	9,75–10,21 mm
Hülsen-∅ Hals:	10,41–10,79 mm
Boden:	11.75–11,94 mm
Rand:	12,88–13,33 mm
Hülsenlänge:	32,56–33,83 mm
Hülsenmaterial:	Messing
Pulverart:	Schwarz, rauchschwach, rauchlos
Zündungsart:	Berdan, Boxer
Patronenlänge:	39,88–40,55 mm
V_0	297 m/sec
E_0	526 J
Lauflänge:	127 mm

Entstanden ist die Patrone in den 70er Jahren aus den Versuchen der Firma Winchester, einen eigenen Revolver zu entwickeln. H. Borchardt der an dieser Entwicklung maßgeblich beteiligt war benutzte dabei diese „Versuchspatrone“. Obwohl Winchester die Produktion der Revolver nicht aufnahm, wurde die Patrone verbessert und als Kaliber .38 – 40 – 180 in den Handel gebracht. Obwohl diese Patrone für das „Lever-Action-Gewehr Modell 1873“ bestimmt war, wurde auch bald Smith & Wesson, Colt u. a. Revolver für diese Patrone eingerichtet (vergl. Katalog Nr. 335 und 420). Da auch weitere Firmen Lang- und Kurzwaffen (z.B. Colt, Remington u. Martin) für diese Patronen einrichteten, hatte man die gleiche Patrone für Revolver und Gewehre zur Verfügung. Heute hat man für die verschiedenen Waffenarten aucn unterschiedliche Ladungen laboriert. Außer von den bekannten Firmen wie Winchester und Remington UMC wurden die Patronen auch bald in Europa (Eley Brothers London) u. a. hergestellt. Die Patronen sind weit verbreitet.

Bodenstempel:
U.M.C. .38 C.F.W.,
CCC .38 CFW,
U S .38 WIN C F,
L H .38 WCF,
ELEY . WINCHESTER.,
REM – UMC .38 – 40 REM,
W.R.A.Co. .38 W.C.F. (W im Zündhütchen),
R – P 38 – 40 WIN,
R.W.S. .38 C.F.

Technical and Ballistic Data

Bullet dia.	.384"– .402"
Case dia. neck:	.410"– .425"
head:	.462"– .470"
rim:	.507"– .525"
Case length:	1.282"–1.332"
Case material:	brass
Powder type:	black, semi-smokeless, smokeless
Primer type:	Berdan, Boxer
Cartridge length:	1,570"–1.625"
V_0	974 ft. per sec.
E_0	380.3 ft. per pounds
Barrel length:	5.000"

The cartridge resulted from the experiments made during the seventies by Winchester to develop of revolver of their own make. H. Borchhardt who played a considerable part in this development also used thereby this "experimental". Although Winchester did not embark upon the production of this revolver, the cartridge was improved and marketed as caliber .38 – 40 – 180. Although intended for the lever action rifle "Model 1873". soon Smith & Wesson, Colt and other companies chambered revolvers for this round (compare catalog No. 335 und 420). As other firms adopted handguns and rifles (for instance Colt, Remington and Marlin) to these cartridges, the same cartridge is at hand for revolvers and rifles as well. There exist now different powder charges for different types of weapons. Besides Winchester and Remington UMC the cartridges were soon also manufactured in Europe (Eley Brothers London) and elsewhere and they prove to be a great commercial success.

Headstams:
U.M.C. .38 C.F.W.,
CCC .38 CFW,
U S .38 WIN C F,
L H .38 WCF,
ELEY . WINCHESTER.,
REM – UMC .38 – 40 REM,
W.R.A.Co. .38 W.C.F. (W in primer),
R – P 38 – 40 WIN,
R.W.S. .38C.F.

.38 – 44 Smith & Wesson

Synonyme/Synonyms:

.38 – 44 S. & W.
.38 – 44 S. & W. Gallery
.38 – 44 S. & W. Target
.38 – 44 Smith & Wesson Gallery
.38 – 44 Smith & Wesson Target

373

	Geschoß/Bullet			Katalog Catalog No.
	Ausführg. Pattern	Gewicht (g)	Weight (gr.)	
	1 A	4,54	70.00	**373-1**
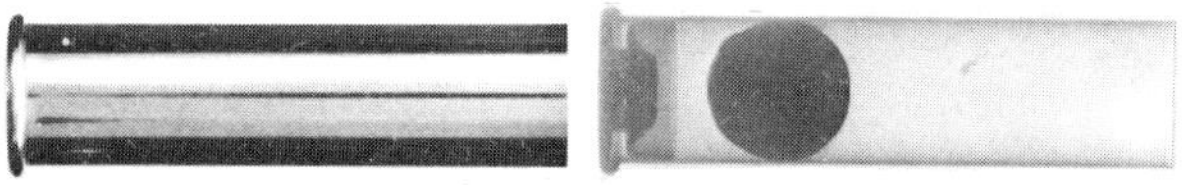	1 A	5,51	85.00	**373-2**
	1 B	9,46	146.00	**373-3**

Technische und ballistische Daten

Geschoß-∅:	9,02– 9.14 mm
Hülsen-∅ Hals:	9,70– 9,80 mm
Boden:	9,70– 9,83 mm
Rand:	11,00–11,20 mm
Hülsenlänge:	37,08–37,59 mm
Hülsenmaterial:	Messing
Pulverart:	Schwarz, rauchschwach
Zündungsart:	Boxer
Patronenlänge:	37,12–37,59 mm
V_0	240 m/sec[x])
E_0	278 J[x])
Lauflänge:	165 mm

[x]) „Target"-Patrone

Die Patrone Kaliber .38 – 44 Smith & Wesson wurde um1866 entwickelt und bis ca. 1915 in Serie gefertigt. Wie bei der Patrone Kaliber .32 – 44 wurden die Patronen im Auftrag des Meisterschützen Peine für seinen Sportrevolver „Single Action Nr. 3" hergestellt (vergl. Katalog Nr. 336). Sie wurde gleichzeitig die Munition für die Smith & Wesson-Einzelladerpistole Modell 1891.

Bodenstempel:
U.M.C. .38 – 44,
W.R.A.Co. .38 – 44

Technical and Ballistic Data

Bullet dia.	.355"– .360"
Case dia. neck:	.382"– .386"
head:	.382"– .387"
rim:	.433"– .441"
Case length:	1.460"–1.480"
Case material:	brass
Powder type:	black, semi-smokeless
Primer type:	Boxer
Cartridge length:	1.461"–1.480"
V_0	787 ft. per sec.[x])
E_0	201.0 ft pounds[x])
Barrel length:	6.500"

[x]) Target cartridge

The cartridge caliber .38 – 44 Smith & Wesson was developed about 1886 and made in series production until approximately 1915. Just like the cartridge .32 – 44 this caliber here was produced by order of the marksman Paine for his target revolver "Single Action No. 3" (compare catalog No. 336). It became at the same time the ammunition for the single shot pistol Model 1891, Smith & Wesson.

Headstamps:
U.M.C. .38 – 44,
W.R.A.Co. .38 – 44

.380 Extra Short

Synonyme/Synonyms:
.380 C.F. Extra Short

374

Geschoß/Bullet				Katalog Catalog No.
	Ausführg. Pattern	Gewicht (g)	Weight (gr.)	
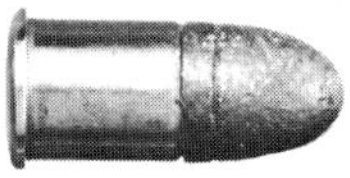	1 C			**374–1**

Technische und ballistische Daten

Geschoß-∅:	9,55 – 9,57 mm
Hülsen-∅ Hals:	9,57 – 9,60 mm
Boden:	9,65 – 9,67 mm
Rand:	10,98 – 11,02 mm
Hülsenlänge:	11,50 – 11,55 mm
Hülsenmaterial:	Messing
Pulverart:	Schwarz
Zündungsart:	Berdan
Patronenlänge:	22,64 – 22,66 mm

Die Patrone Kaliber .380 extra short könnte ihren Ursprung in England haben (vergl. Bodenstempel), obwohl sie in bekannten englischen Katalogen nicht zu finden ist. Es dürfte sich um eine Patrone für kleine Revolver oder Einzelladepistolen handeln. Über Zeitraum, Serienfertigung und Waffenmodelle kann nichts gesagt werden.

Bodenstempel:
ELEY .380.,
.380,

Technical and Ballistic Data

Bullet dia.	.376″–.377″
Case dia. neck:	.377″–.378″
head:	.380″–.381″
rim:	.432″–.434″
Case length:	.453″–.455″
Case material:	brass
Powder type:	black
Primer type:	Berdan
Cartridge length:	.891″–.892″

The cartridge caliber .380 extra short may originate from England (compare headstamp), although it cannot be traced in the renowned English catalogs. It is probably a cartridge for small revolver or single shot pistols. Nothing can be said about the period, the series production and the gun models.

Headstamps:
ELEY . 380.,
.380,

.380 Long C.F.

375

Synonyme/Synonyms:

DWM 218
DWM 218A
GR 104
.380 Long
.380 Long Revolver C.F.
.380 Long (Rifle)
.380 Long Rifle (Long Colt)
.380 Rook Rifle
.380–18–114 Long
.380–18–124 Long
.380–12–124 Long
9 × 24 – .380 lang
9,10 × 24,25 – 380 lang
9,25 × 24,50 Kal. 380 lg. Revolver
9,25 × 26,30 Kal. 380 lg. Revolver
9,5 × 24,5 mm – Englisch.Kal. 380
9,6 × 24 R Long Revolver

	Geschoß/Bullet			Katalog Catalog No.
	Ausführg. Pattern	Gewicht (g)	Weight (gr.)	
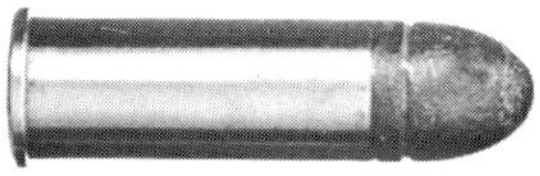	1 C	6,48 – 9,20	100.00 – 142.00	**375–1**
	1 B	8,03	124.00	**375-2**
	1 B	8,03	124.00	**375–3**
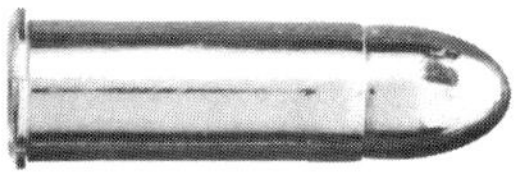	21 C	7,00 – 7,84	108.00 – 121.00	**375–4**
	21 C	7,00 – 7,84	108.00 – 121.00	**375–5**
	40 C	7,39 – 8,03	114.00 – 124.00	**375–6**
	90 a	–	–	**375–7**
	90 d	–	–	**375-8**
	90 d	–	–	**375–9**
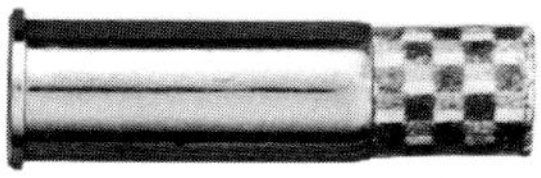	90 d	–	–	**375–10**

Technische und ballistische Daten

Geschoß-Ø:	8,69 - 9,60 mm
Hülsen-Ø Hals:	9,40 - 9,65 mm
Boden:	9,55 - 9,70 mm
Rand:	10,70 - 11,12 mm
Hülsenlänge:	23,45 - 26,30 mm
Hülsenmaterial:	Messing, Kupfer
Pulverart:	Schwarz, rauchlos
Zündungsart:	Berdan, Boxer, Topf, verdeckt
Patronenlänge:	30,65 - 35,05 mm
V_0	250 m/sec
E_0	255 J
Lauflänge:	102 mm

Die Patrone Kaliber .380 long C.F.war wie viele der aus England kommenden Patronen ursprünglich für Langwaffen zur Jagd auf kleines Raub- und anderes Kleinwild bestimmt. Sie stammt aus der Zeit zwischen 1870 und 1880. Sowohl als Gewehr- wie auch als Revolverpatrone ist sie in den Firmenkatalogen Eley 1898 und Nobel 1925 enthalten. Im Fiocchi-Katalog 1961 wird sie unter den Revolverpatronen (mit rauchlosem Pulver geladen) geführt. Laut Katalog waren die Patronen für „Webley- und Colt-Revolver bestimmt. Die von DWM gefertigten Hülsen mit der Bezeichnung DWM 218A waren etwas länger.

Bodenstempel:
KYNOCH .380L.,
KYNOCH 380,
ELEY .380 L.,
EGESTORFF.LINDEN + 380 +,
GG (Monogramm) 380.L.,
FIOCCHI 380,
G.F.L. 380

Technical and Ballistic Data

Bullet dia.	.342'' - .378''
Case dia. neck:	.376" - .380"
head:	.376" - .382"
rim:	.421" - .438"
Case length:	.923'' - 1.035''
Case material:	brass, copper
Powder type:	black, smokeless
Primer type:	Berdan, Boxer, battery cup, inside
Cartridge length:	1.207" - 1.380"
V_0	820 ft. per sec.
E_0	184.4 ft. pounds
Barrel length:	4.000"

The cartridge caliber .380 long C.F. was, as many cartridges coming from England, originally intended for shoulder arms and the hunt for varmint and other small game. It was developed between 1870 and 1880. It is contained both as rifle and revolver cartridge in the company catalog of Eley 1898 and Nobel 1925. In the Fiocchi Catalogue 1961 it is listed among the revolver cartridges (with smokeless powder charge). According to the catalog comment the cartridges were intended for "Webley and Colt Revolvers". The cases manufactured by DWM and bearing the designations DWM and DWM 218A were somewhat longer.

Headstamps:
KYNOCH .380 L.,
KYNOCH 380,
ELEY .380 L.,
EGESDORFF.LINDEN + 380 +,
GG (Monogram) 380.L.,
FIOCCHI 380,
G.F.L. 380

.380 Revolver Mk.I

Synonyme/Synonyms:

.380 Mk. I
.38. Webley Mk. I
.38 Webley & Scott Special
.38-200

376

	Geschoß/Bullet Ausführg. Pattern	Gewicht (g)	Weight (gr.)	Katalog Catalog No.
	1 B	12,83-13,09	198.00-202.00	**376-1**

Technische und ballistische Daten

Geschoß-∅:	9,00- 9,15 mm
Hülsen-∅ Hals:	9,70- 9,75 mm
Boden:	9,70- 9,75 mm
Rand:	10,90-11,00 mm
Hülsenlänge:	19,30-19,40 mm
Hülsenmaterial:	Messing
Pulverart:	rauchlos
Zündungsart:	Berdan, Boxer
Patronenlänge:	31,42-31,50 mm
V_0	183m/sec
E_0	221 J
Lauflänge:	102 mm

Die Patrone Kaliber .380 Revolver Mark I ist der Nachfolger der Revolverpatronen Kaliber .380 C.F., die um 1865 in England entwickelt wurden. Sie ist gleichzeitig der Vorläufer der Revolverpatrone Mark II und wurde im Jahre 1927 erstmals für die Armee gefertigt. Im Gegensatz zur Revolverpatrone Mk. II hat sie ein Bleigeschoß. Sie war bis 1937 im militärischen Gebrauch und wurde von der Patrone Mk. II abgelöst (vergl. Katalog Nr. 377).

Bodenstempel:
R/\L 32 .380,
US .38 WEBLEY.

Technical and Ballistic Data

Bullet dia.	.354'' - .360''
Case dia. neck:	.382'' - .384''
head:	.382'' - .384''
rim:	.429'' - .433''
Case length:	.760'' - .764''
Case material:	brass
Powder type:	smokeless
Primer type:	Berdan, Boxer
Cartridge length:	1.237'' - 1.240''
V_0	600 ft. per sec.
E_0	160.0 ft. pounds
Barrel length:	4.000''

The cartridge caliber .380 Revolver Mark I is the successor of the revolver cartridges caliber .380 C.F. which were developed in England ab. 1865. It is at the same time the predecessor of the revolver cartridge Mark II and was manufactured the first time for the Army in 1927.
Unlike the revolver cartridge Mk. II it is provided with a lead bullet. It was in military use until 1937 and was replaced by the cartridge Mk. II (compare catalog No. 377).

Headstamp:
R/\L 32 .380,
US .38 WEBLEY.

.380 Revolver Mk. II

Synonyme/Synonyms:
.380 Mk. II

377

	Geschoß/Bullet			Katalog Catalog No.
	Ausführg. Pattern	Gewicht (g)	Weight (gr.)	
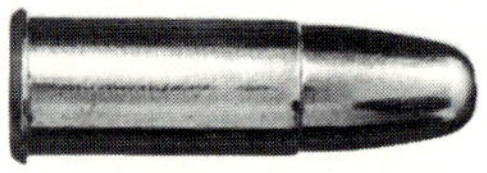	21 B	11,40 – 11,66	176.00 – 180,00	**377-1**
	21 B	11,53	178.00	**377-2**
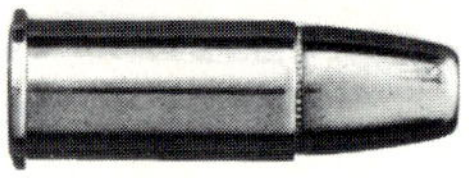	21 G			**377-3**

Technische und ballistische Daten

Geschoß-∅:	9,00 – 9,05 mm
Hülsen-∅ Hals:	9,60 – 9,70 mm
Boden:	9,70 – 9,77 mm
Rand:	10,88 – 11,10 mm
Hülsenlänge:	19,25 – 19,45 mm
Hülsenmaterial:	Messing
Pulverart:	rauchlos
Zündungsart:	Berdan, Boxer
Patronenlänge:	30,35 – 31,50 mm

Die Patrone Kaliber .380 Revolver Mark II ist der Nachfolger der militärischen Ausführung der Patrone Mk. I (vergl. Katalog Nr. 376). Sie hat ein Kupfer-Nickelmantelgeschoß und wurde ab 1937 in der englischen Armee benutzt.

Bodenstempel:
R ↑ L 43 .380 IIz,
CIS .380 2z GG,
D C 44 380,
F N 67 380 2z,
ORBEA 43 .380 II,

Technical and Ballistic Data

Bullet dia.	.354″ – .356″
Case dia. neck:	.378″ – .382″
head:	.382″ – .385″
rim:	.428″ – .437″
Case length:	.758″ – .766″
Case material:	brass
Powder type:	smokeless
Primer type:	Berdan, Boxer
Cartridge length:	1.195″ – 1.240″

The cartridge caliber .380 Revolver Mark II is the successor of the military version of the cartridge Mk. I (compare cataloge No. 376). It has a cupro-nickel jacketed bullet and was in use in the British Army from 1937 onward.

Headstamps:
R ↑ L 43 .380 IIz,
CIS .380 2z GG,
D C 44 380,
F N 67 380 2z,
ORBEA 43 .380 II,

.380 Short C.F. (long case)

Synonyme/Synonyms:

378

DWM 193
GR 100
.380 Bore, Revolver
.380 C.F.
.380 Revolver C.F.
.380 (9 mm) Revolver C.F.
.380–10–124 Revolver
8,85 x 18,40 Kal. 380 Revolver
8,9 x 17 – 380 kurz
9 mm (.380) Revolver C.F.
9,1 x 17,5 – 380 kurz E.
9,5 x 17,5 No. 380 (9 m/m)
9,5 x 18 mm – Englisch. Kal. 380
Revolver Cal. 380 – 9 mm

	Geschoß/Bullet			Katalog Catalog No.
	Ausführg. Pattern	Gewicht (g)	Weight (gr.)	
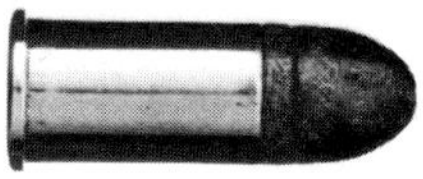	1 C	8,03	124.00	**378–1**
	1 C	4,92 – 8,29	76,00 – 128,00	**378–2**
	1 C	4,92 – 8,29	76.00 – 128,00	**378–3**
	1 B	4,92 – 8,29	76,00 – 128,00	**378–4**
	1 B	4,92 – 8,29	76,00 – 128,00	**378–5**
	1 A			**378–6**
	40 C	8,03	124.00	**378–7**
	71 P	9,07	140.00	**378–8**
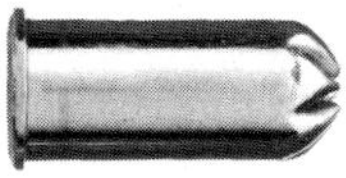	90 a	–	–	**378–9**
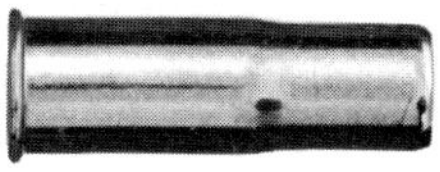	90 b	–	–	**378–10**

.380 Short C.F. (long case)

	Geschoß/Bullet Ausführg. Pattern	Gewicht (g)	Weight (gr.)	Katalog Catalog No.
	90 b	–	–	**378–11**
	90 d	–	–	**378–12**
	90 d	–	–	**378–13**
	90 d	–	–	**378–14**
	90 d	–	–	**378–15**

Technische und ballistische Daten

Geschoß-⌀:	8,95– 9,65 mm
Hülsen-⌀ Hals:	8,90– 9,68 mm
Boden:	9,49– 9,73 mm
Rand:	10,64–11,15 mm
Hülsenlänge:	16,51–18,46 mm
Hülsenmaterial:	Messing, Stahl lackiert, Stahl verkupfert
Pulverart:	Schwarz, rauchlos
Zündungsart:	Berdan, Boxer, Braun & Bloem, Topf, verdeckt
Patronenlänge:	23,27–28,40 mm
V_0	190m/sec.
E_0	148 J
Lauflänge:	76 mm

Die Patrone Kaliber .380 short C.F. (long case) wurde um 1868 in England entwickelt. Sie war insbesondere im europäischen Raum stark verbreitet und aus ihr ist die Patrone mit der kurzen Hülse entstanden (vergl. Katalog Nr. 376). Als sie entstand handelte es sich um eine Neuauflage für einen „Webley-Revolver", der im Auftrag auch in den USA hergestellt wurde. Laut Firmenkatalog Eley 1898 handelt es sich um eine ausgesprochene Patrone für Webley-, Colt-, Tranter- und andere Revolver.

Bodenstempel:
KYNOCH .380,
ELEY . 380.,
GAUPILLAT .380,
C B C ((380,
K&C. WIEN 380,
+ H + WIEN 380,
G. EGESTORFF 380,
M C & Co 380,
GG (Monogramm) .380
SB 380,
/380/ /SB/,
380 M.L.,
R.W.S. 380,
G.F.L. 380,

Technical and Ballistic Data

Bullet dia.	.352″–.380″
Case dia. neck:	.350″–.381″
head:	.372″–.383″
rim:	.419″–.439″
Case length:	.650″–.727″
Case material:	brass, laquered steel, copper washed steel
Powder type:	black, smokeless
Primer type:	Berdan, Boxer, Braun & Bloem, battery cup, inside
Cartridge length:	.916″–1.118″
V_0	625 ft. per sec.
E_0	107.0 ft. pounds
Barrel length:	3.000″

The cartridge caliber .380 short C.F. (long case) was developed in England about 1868. It was especially well distributed in the European countries and from it resulted the round with the short case. (please see also catalog No. 379). When it came out it was a re-issue for a "Webley-Revolver" and was also manufactured on commission in the USA. The firm catalog of Eley 1898 describes it as a specific cartridge for Webley, Colt, Tranter and other revolvers.

Headstamps:
KYNOCH .380,
ELEY . 380.,
GAUPILLAT .380,
C B C ((380,
K&C. WIEN 380,
+ H + WIEN 380,
G. EGESTORFF 380,
M C & Co 380,
GG (Monogram) .380
SB 380,
/380/ /SB/,
380 M.L.,
R.W.S. 380,
G.F.L. 380

.380 Short C.F. (short case)

Synonyme/Synonyms:

.380 Corto
.380 Short

379

	Geschoß/Bullet Ausführg. Pattern	Gewicht (g)	Weight (gr.)	Katalog Catalog No.
	1 B			**379-1**
	1 C			**379-2**
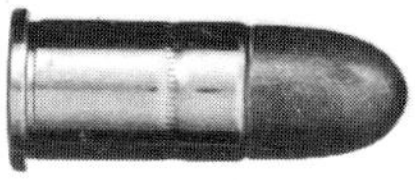	1 C	7,84	121.00	**379-3**
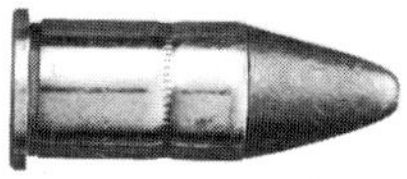	1 K			**379-4**
	21 C	7,84	121.00	**379-5**
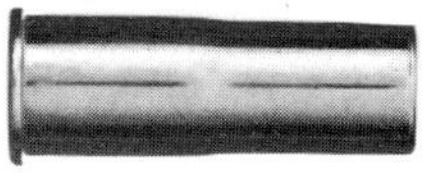	90 b	–	–	**379-6**

Technische und ballistische Daten

Geschoß-∅:	8,90– 9,30 mm
Hülsen-∅ Hals:	9,45– 9,65 mm
Boden:	9,50– 9,65 mm
Rand:	10,50–11,10 mm
Hülsenlänge:	14,25–14,85 mm
Hülsenmaterial:	Messing
Pulverart:	rauchlos
Zündungsart:	Berdan
Patronenlänge:	21,72–26,55 mm
V_0	230 m/sec
E_0	211 J
Lauflänge:	76 mm

Die Patrone Kaliber .380 short C.F. (short Case) wurde aus der Patrone mit der längeren Hülse des gleichen Kalibers entwickelt (vergl. Katalog Nr. 378). Sie war für eine Reihe von billigen Revolvern bestimmt, die zwischen 1900 und 1925 ohne Herstellerangaben (oft im Versandhandel) vertrieben worden sind.

Bodenstempel:
G. EGESTORFF 380,
R.W.S. .380
GG (Monogramm) 380,
SB 380,
G.F.L. 380

Technical and Ballistic Data

Bullet dia.	.350″– 366″
Case dia. neck:	.372″– 380″
head:	.374″– .380″
rim:	.413″– .437″
Case length:	.561″– .585″
Case material:	brass
Powder type:	smokeless
Primer type:	Berdan
Cartridge length:	.855″–1.045″
V_0	754 ft. per sec.
E_0	152.5 ft. pounds
Barrel length:	3.000″

The cartridge caliber .380 short C.F. (short case) was developed out of the cartridge of the same caliber with a longer case (compare catalog No. 378). It was destined for a number of cheap revolvers which were sold (often by mail order business) between 1900 and 1925 without indications as to the manufacturer.

Headstamps:
G. EGESTORFF 380,
R.W.S. .380
GG (Monogram) 380,
SB 380,
G.F.L. 380

.39 B.S.A.

Synonyme/Synonyms:

.40 B.S.A. BELTED
.400 B.S.A. BELTED

380

Geschoß/Bullet				Katalog Catalog No.
	Ausführg. Pattern	Gewicht (g)	Weight (gr.)	
	21 B			**380–1**

Technische und ballistische Daten

Geschoß-∅:	10,13–10,15 mm
Hülsen-∅ Hals:	10,77 mm
Boden:	10,87–10,97 mm
Gürtel:	11,38–11,42 mm
Rand:	10,82–10,92 mm
Hülsenlänge:	22,90–22,95 mm
Hülsenmaterial:	Messing
Pulverart:	rauchlos
Zündungsart:	Berdan
Patronenlänge:	31,14–31,30 mm

Größtes Kaliber der Versuchspatronenserie der **B**irmingham **S**mall **A**rms (B.S.A.). Es handelt sich um eine neuartige Patronenserie für eine Selbstladepistole. Die Hülsen der Patronen haben einen Gürtel, durch den Ladehemmungen (verursacht durch das Ineinandergreifen der Hülsenränder) verhindert werden sollen. Die Patronen dieser Serie konnten, obwohl dies vorausgesagt worden ist, keinen Erfolg erlangen. Vergleiche auch Katalog Nr. 316 und 339.

Keine Bodenstempel bekannt

Technical and Ballistic Data

Bullet dia.	.399″–.400″
Case dia. neck:	.424″
head:	.428″–.432″
belt:	.448″–.450″
rim:	.426″–.430″
Case length:	.901″– .903″
Case material:	brass
Powder type:	smokeless
Primer type:	Berdan
Cartridge length:	1.226″–1.232″

This is the biggest caliber of the experimental series of the firm **B**irmingham **S**mall **A**rms (B.S.A.) and a new-type cartridge series for a self-loading pistol. The cases have a belt by which jams (caused by the meshing of the cartridge rims) are to be prevented. As had been predicted, the cartridges of this series did not prove successful. See also catalog Nos. 316 and 339.

No headstamps known.

.400 Colt Magnum

Synonyme/Synonyms:
.400 Colt
.400 Magnum

381

Geschoß/Bullet Ausführg. Pattern	Gewicht (g)	Weight (gr.)	Katalog Catalog No.
30 G	11,61	179,20	**381-1**

Technische und ballistische Daten

Geschoß-⌀:	10,27-10,29 mm
Hülsen-⌀ Hals:	10,70-10,72 mm
Boden:	10,74-10,78 mm
Rand:	11,81-11,84 mm
Hülsenlänge:	32,30-32,64 mm
Hülsenmaterial:	Messing
Pulverart:	rauchlos
Zündungsart:	Boxer
Patronenlänge:	39,37-39,58 mm

Bei dem Kaliber .400 Colt Magnum soll es sich um eine Patrone für ein Versuchsmodell eines Colt-Revolvers handeln. Außer, daß die Patrone 1965 hergestellt worden sein soll waren keine weitere Angaben (insbesondere zur Ballistik) zu erhalten.

Bodenstempel:
W-W 400,

Technical and Ballistic Data

Bullet dia.	.404"- .405"
Case dia. neck:	.421"- .422"
head:	.423"- .424"
rim:	.465"- .466"
Case length:	1.271"-1.285"
Case material:	brass
Powder type:	smokeless
Primer type:	Boxer
Cartridge length:	1.550"-1.558"

The caliber .400 Colt Magnum is said to be a cartridge for an experimental model of a Colt revolver. Apart from the information that the cartridge was allegedly manufactured in 1965 no further details could be acquired (particularly as to ballistic data).

Headstamp:
W-W 400,

.400 Revolver C.F.

Synonyme/Synonyms:
DWM 284
11,03 × 24,90 Kal. 400 Revolver

382

Geschoß/Bullet			Katalog Catalog No.
Ausführg. Pattern	Gewicht (g)	Weight (gr.)	
1 B	15,10 – 15,30	233.03 – 236.11	**382–1**
1 B	16,50 – 16,70	254.63 – 257.72	**382–2**

Technische und ballistische Daten

Geschoß-∅:	10,85–11,00 mm
Hülsen-∅ Hals:	11,60 mm
Boden:	11,62 mm
Rand:	13,10 mm
Hülsenlänge:	24,90 mm
Hülsenmaterial:	Messing
Pulverart:	Schwarz
Zündungsart:	Berdan

Die Patrone Kaliber .400 Revolver C.F. ist nur in den Unterlagen (u.a. Katalog 1904) der Firma D.W.M. aufgeführt. Zur Hülse Nr. 284 gehören Geschosse Nr. 22 und 22A. Es handelt sich um eine Revolverpatrone, über Waffenmodelle sind keine Hinweise gegeben.

Keine Bodenstempel bekannt.

Technical and Ballistic Data

Bullet dia.	.427″–.433″
Case dia. neck:	.457″
head:	.458″
rim:	.516″
Case length:	.980″
Case material:	brass
Powder type:	black
Primer type:	Berdan

The cartridge caliber .400 Revolver C.F. is only listed in the documents (among others catalog 1904) of the firm D.W.M. The bullets Nos. 22 and 22A pertain to case No. 284. It is a revolver cartridge, no hints are to be found as to pertinent weapons.

No headstamps known.

.400 Webley Automatic

Synonyme/Synonyms:
.400 Webley Automatic Pistol

383

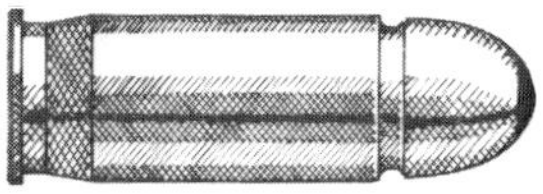

Geschoß/Bullet Ausführg. Pattern	Gewicht (g)	Weight (gr.)	Katalog Catalog No.
30 B	12,96	200.00	**383-1**

Technische und ballistische Daten

Geschoß-∅:	10,39 - 10,44 mm
Hülsen-∅ Hals:	11,00 - 11,10 mm
Boden:	11,00 - 11,10 mm
Rand:	11,68 mm
Hülsenlänge:	23,88 mm
Hülsenmaterial:	Messing
Pulverart:	rauchlos
Zündungsart:	Berdan
Patronenlänge:	34,04 mm

Die einzigen Aufzeichnungen über die Patrone Kaliber . 400 Webley Automatic sind aus den Patronenunterlagen des H.P.White-Laboratorium USA bekanntgeworden. Die technischen Aufzeichnungen stammen offensichtlich aus dem Jahre 1904. Die Patrone hat ein Teilmantel-Rundkopfgeschoß mit einer ausgeprägten Rille im Geschoß am Hülsenmund.

Bodenstempel nicht bekannt.

Technical and Ballistic Data

Bullet dia.	.409"-.411"
Case dia. neck:	.433"-.437"
head:	.433"-.437"
rim:	.460
Case length:	.940"
Case material:	brass
Powder type:	smokeless
Primer type:	Berdan
Cartridge length:	1.340"

The only record about the cartridge caliber .400 Webley Automatic has become known from the cartridge files of the H.P. White-Laboratory – USA. The technical designs evidently date back to the year 1904. The cartridge has a soft point round nose bullet with a pronounced groove in the projectile near the case mouth.

No headstamp known.

.401 Magnum

Synonyme/Synonyms:
.401 Herter's
.401 Herters's Magnum

384

	Geschoß/Bullet Ausführg. Pattern	Gewicht (g)	Weight (gr.)	Katalog Catalog No.
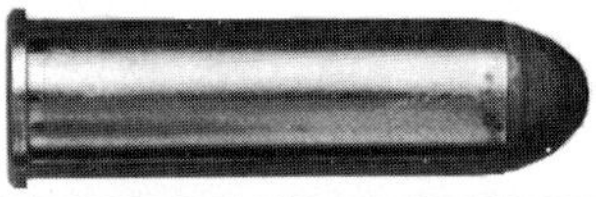	1 B	12,96	200.00	**384–1**
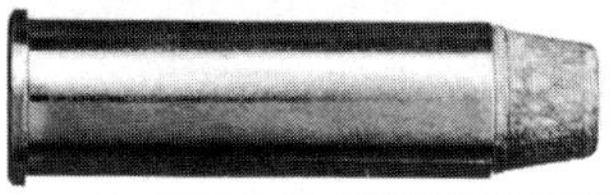	1 R	11,66	180.00	**384–2**
	21 R	11,66	180.00	**384–3**
	30 R	11,66	180.00	**384–4**
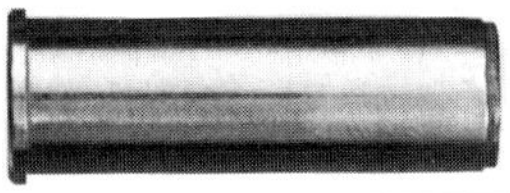	1 P	10,37	160.00	**384–5**

Technische und ballistische Daten

Geschoß-∅:	10,10–10,14 mm
Hülsen-∅ Hals:	10,70–10,80 mm
Boden:	10,80 mm
Rand:	12,05–12,10 mm
Hülsenlänge:	32,50–32,60 mm
Hülsenmaterial:	Messing
Pulverart:	rauchlos
Zündungsart:	Boxer
Patronenlänge:	39,80 mm
V_0	405 m/sec
E_0	975 J
Lauflänge:	165 mm

Die Patronen des Kalibers .401 Magnum sind u.a. bekanntgeworden, als die Firma Herter Revolver bei einer Deutschen Firma herstellen ließ. Ihre Entwicklung geht auf das Jahr 1961 zurück. Der Rückstoß dieser Patrone soll dem einer Patrone Kaliber .38 Special entsprechen. In den USA sind die Komponenten zu dieser Patrone auch für Wiederlader erhältlich, in Europa ist das Kaliber weniger bekannt. Die Waffe wird als „Herters .401 Powermag-Revolver" bezeichnet.

Bodenstempel:
HERTER'S .401 MAG.

Technical and Ballistic Data

Bullet dia.	.398"– .399"
Case dia. neck:	.421"– .425"
head:	.425"
rim:	.474"– .476"
Case length:	1.279"–1.283"
Case material:	brass
Powder type:	smokeless
Primer type:	Boxer
Cartridge length:	1.567"
V_0	1328 ft. per sec.
E_0	704.9 ft. pounds
Barrel length:	6.500"

The cartridges of caliber .401 Magnum became among others known when the company Herter had revolvers made by a German firm. Its developmental stage dates back to the year 1961. The recoil of this round is said to correspond to that of a cartridge caliber .38 Special. In the USA the components of this cartridge are also on the market for reloaders, in Europe the caliber is less known. The weapon is designated as "HERTER's .401 Powermag-Revolver".

Headstamp:
HERTER'S .401 MAG.

.41 Colt Automatic

Synonyme/Synonyms:

385

Geschoß/Bullet Ausführg. Pattern	Gewicht (g)	Weight (gr.)	Katalog Catalog No.
21 B			**385–1**

Technische und ballistische Daten

Geschoß-∅:	9,65 mm
Hülsen-∅ Hals:	10,29 mm
Boden:	10,39 mm
Rand:	10,62 mm
Hülsenlänge:	22,66 mm
Hülsenmaterial:	Messing
Pulverart:	rauchlos
Zündungsart:	Boxer
Patronenlänge:	31,98 mm

Die Patrone Kaliber .41 Colt Automatic wurde 1903 in den U.S.A. entwickelt, als insbesondere die englische Regierung nach einem größeren Kaliber als dem Kaliber .38 ACP verlangte. Die Firma Colt konstruierte daraufhin die Revolverpatrone Kaliber .41 long Colt in eine Patrone mit Halbrand für Pistolen um. Als Versuchswaffe diente ein Colt-Selbstladepistolenverschluß auf einem .38er Griffstück. Waffe und Munition fanden keine Verbreitung.

Bodenstempel:
U.M.C. 41 L.C.,
REM UMC .41 LONG

Technical and Ballistic Data

Bullet dia.	.380″
Case dia. neck:	.405″
head:	.409″
rim:	.418″
Case length:	.892″
Case material:	brass
Powder type:	smokeless
Primer type:	Boxer
Cartridge length:	1.259″

The cartridge caliber .41 Colt Automatic was developed in the USA in 1903, especially when the Britisch Government required a stronger caliber than .38 ACP. The firm Colt then transformed the revolver cartridge caliber .41 long Colt in a semi-rimmed pistol cartridge. As a test weapon served the slide of a self-loading Colt pistol mounted on a .38 receiver. Weapon and ammunition did not achieve commercial success

Headstamps:
U.M.C. 41 L.C.,
REM UMC .41 LONG

.41 Colt Special

Synonyme/Synonyms:
.41 Special

386

	Geschoß/Bullet Ausführg. Pattern	Gewicht (g)	Weight (gr.)	Katalog Catalog No.
 Typ I / Type I	1 B	13,61	210.00	**386-1**
 Typ II / Type II	1 G	13,61	210.00	**386-2**
 Typ III / Type III	1 G	13,61	210.00	**386-3**

Technische und ballistische Daten

	Typ I	**Typ II**	**Typ III**
Geschoß-∅:	9,78 mm	9,78 mm	9,78 mm
Hülsen-∅ Hals:	10,41 mm	10,41 mm	10,41 mm
Boden:	10,51 mm	10,51 mm	10,51 mm
Rand:	11,86 mm	11,94 mm	11,94 mm
Hülsenlänge:	31,50 mm	29,97 mm	32,00 mm
Hülsenmaterial:	Messing		
Pulverart:	rauchlos		
Zündungsart:	Boxer		
Patronenlänge:	38,73 mm	38,86 mm	41,40 mm
V_0 (m/sec)	287	248	350
E_0 (J)	573	425	849
Lauflänge:	152 mm		

Technical and Ballistic Data

	Type I	**Type II**	**Type III**
Bullet dia.	.385″	.385″	.385″
Case dia. neck:	.410″	.410″	.410″
head:	.414″	.414″	.414″
rim:	.467″	.470″	.470″
Case length:	1.240″	1.180″	1.260″
Case material:		brass	
Powder type:		smokeless	
Primer type:		Boxer	
Cartridge length:	1.525″	1.530″	1.630″
V_0 (ft. per sec.)	943	815	1150
E_0 (ft. pounds)	414.3	307.3	613.8
Barrel length:		6.000″	

Die Patronen Kaliber .41 Colt Special wurden 1932 in dem Gedanken entwickelt, insbesondere Polizeibeamten eine etwas stärkere Patrone für größere Entfernungen an die Hand zu geben. Das Geschoß dieser Patrone ähnelte in seiner Form dem der Patrone Kaliber .41 long Colt. Im Laufe dieser Versuche entstanden 3 Varianten. Da bei der ersten Ausführung der Rückschlag zu groß erschien, wurde u.a. die Hülse gekürzt. Die zweite Ausführung erhielt neben der kürzeren Hülse u.a. ein Flachkopfgeschoß. Bei der dritten Ausführung wurde die Hülse verlängert und das Flachkopfgeschoß beibehalten. Als Testwaffen dienten 1 Official Police- und 1 New Service Revolver. Über die abschließenden Ergebnisse wurde nichts bekannt. Die Patronen fanden keine Verbreitung.

Bodenstempel sind keine bekannt.

The cartridges caliber .41 Colt Special were developed in 1932 with the purpose to furnish particularly police officers with a more powerful cartridge for long ranges. The bullet of this cartridge resembles in its form to that of the cartridge caliber .41 long Colt. In the course of the experiments 3 variations were created.
The first version seemed to have a too rough recoil, so the case was shortened, among other modifications made. The second variation was provided, moreover, with a flat nose bullet. As test weapons served 1 Official Police Model and a new Service Revolver. Nothing became known about the concluding results. The cartridges did not achieve commercial distribution.

Headstamps are not known.

.41 Long C.F.

Synonyme/Synonyms:

.41
.41 C.F.
.41 C.F. Long
.41 Center Fire
.41. Long
.41 Long Colt (Original)

387

	Geschoß/Bullet Ausführg. Pattern	Gewicht (g)	Weight (gr.)	Katalog Catalog No.
	1 C	8,42	130.00	**387–1**

Technische und ballistische Daten

Geschoß-∅:	10,21–10,33 mm
Hülsen-∅ Hals:	10,33–10,40 mm
Boden:	10,33–10,40 mm
Rand:	11,80–11,96 mm
Hülsenlänge:	19,42–19,58 mm
Hülsenmaterial:	Messing
Pulverart:	Schwarz, rauchschwach
Zündungsart:	Boxer
Patronenlänge:	27,60–28,35 mm

Bei diesem Kaliber handelt es sich um eine Patrone die zwischen den Kalibern .41 short Colt und .410 C.F. liegt (Katalog Nr. 391 und 396). Aus der Verpackung war lediglich der Aufdruck zum Kaliber ".41 long C.F." die Anzahl der Patronen und der Hinweis „für Revolver" zu entnehmen. Ein Hersteller war nicht angegeben. Es scheint sich um eine Patrone zu handeln, die universell für viele Revolverfabrikate Verwendung finden sollte.

Kein Bodenstempel.

Technical and Ballistic Data

Bullet dia.	.402"– .406"
Case dia. neck:	.406"– .409"
head:	.406"– .409"
rim:	.465"– .471"
Case length:	.765"– .771"
Case material:	brass
Powder type:	black, semi-smokeless
Primer type:	Boxer
Cartridge length:	1.086"–1.116"

The caliber of this cartridge ranges between the calibers .41 short Colt and .410 C.F. (see catalog Nos. 391 and 396). The packing just showed the imprint as to the caliber ".41 long C.F.", the number of cartridges and the indication "for revolvers". A manufacturer was not indicated. It seems to be a cartridge which was to find the universal use for many revolver brands.

No headstamp.

.41 Long Colt (ins.lub.)

Synonyme/Synonyms:

.41 L.D.A.
.41 Long Colt
.41 Long Colt, D.A. (ins.lub.)
.41 Long Colt Double Action
.410-21-200 Extra Long
.410 Extra Long Colt

388

	Geschoß/Bullet Ausführg. Pattern	Gewicht (g)	Weight (gr.)	Katalog Catalog No.
	1 B	12,64 - 12,96	195.00 - 200.00	**388-1**
	1 B	12,96	200.00	**388-2**
	90 e	–	–	**388-3**

Technische und ballistische Daten

Geschoß-∅:	9,37-10,16 mm
Hülsen-∅ Hals:	10,24-10,39 mm
Boden:	10,26-10,41 mm
Rand:	10,82-11,07 mm
Hülsenlänge:	28,24-28,73 mm
Hülsenmaterial:	Messing
Pulverart:	Schwarz, rauchschwach,rauchlos
Zündungsart:	Boxer
Patronenlänge:	35,18-35,81 mm
V_0	222 m/sec
E_0	318 J
Lauflänge:	152 mm

Technical and Ballistic Data

Bullet dia.	.369″- .400″
Case dia. neck:	.403″- .409″
head:	.404″- .410″
rim:	.426″- .436″
Case length:	1.112″-1.131″
Case material:	brass
Powder type:	black, semi-smokeless, smokeless
Primer type:	Boxer
Cartridge lenght:	1.385″-1.410″
V_0	730 ft. per sec.
E_0	230.0 ft. pounds
Barrel length:	6.000″

Die Patronen Kaliber .41 long Colt (ins. lub.) d.h. mit Innenfettung, lösten um 1895/96 die Patronen des gleichen Kalibers mit Außenfettung ab. Sie haben auch eine längere Hülse als diese (Katalog Nr. 389). Patronen dieses Kalibers waren für Colt D.A. Revolver Navy 1889 und andere Colt Revolver bestimmt. Obwohl Waffe und Munition nicht sehr erfolgreich waren, waren sie relativ lange im Gebrauch.

Bodenstempel:
W.R.A.Co. .41 L.D.A.,
W C Co .41 LDA,
U.M.C. .41 L.C.,
REM-UMC .41 LONG,
WESTERN .41 L.D.A.,
REM-UMC 41 LG COLT,

The cartridges caliber .41 long Colt inside lubricated replaced about 1895/96 the cartridges of the same caliber with outside lubrication. They have, moreover, a longer case (see catalog No. 389). Cartridges of this caliber were intended for Colt D.A. Revolver Navy 1889 and other Colt revolvers. Although weapon and ammunition were not very successful, they had been in use for a relatively long period.

Headstamps:
W.R.A.Co. .41 L.D.A.
W C Co .41 LDA,
U.M.C. .41 L.C.,
REM-UMC .41 LONG,
WESTERN .41 L.D.A.,
REM-UMC 41 LG COLT

.41 Long Colt (outs.lub.)

Synonyme/Synonyms:

.41 Colt Double Action
.41 Double Aotion
.41 L.D.A.
.41 Long Colt
.41 Long Colt, D.A. (outs.lub.)
.41 Long Colt Double Action

389

	Geschoß/Bullet Ausführg. Pattern	Gewicht (g)	Weight (gr.)	Katalog Catalog No.
	1 C	12,64	195.00	**389-1**
	1 C	12,96	200.00	**389-2**

Technische und ballistische Daten

Geschoß-Ø:	10,26-10,46 mm
Hülsen-Ø Hals:	10,26-10,36 mm
Boden:	10,30-10,36 mm
Rand:	10,87-11,05 mm
Hülsenlänge:	23,47-24,26 mm
Hülsenmaterial:	Messing
Pulverart:	Schwarz, rauchschwach
Zündungsart:	Boxer
Patronenlänge:	35,20-35,86 mm

Die Patronen Kaliber .41 long Colt (outs.lub.) d.h. mit Außenfettung wurden um 1877 entwickelt. Sie haben eine kürzere Hülse als die gleiche Patrone mit Innenfettung (Katalog Nr. 388). Die Patronen waren für Colt Revolver „New Line" bestimmt, wurden dann aber auch in vielen anderen Colt Revolvern des Kalibers benutzt. Sie wurden von den Patronen mit Innenfettung verdrängt.

Bodenstempel:
PETERS .41 L.D.A.,
P.C.Co. 41 L.D.A.
U S .41 LONG,
U.M.C. .41 LONG
W.R.A.Co. .41 L.D.A.,
U.M.C. 41 L.C.

Technical and Ballistic Data

Bullet dia.	.404"- .412"
Case dia. neck:	.404"- .408"
head:	.405"- .408"
rim:	.428"- .435"
Case length:	.924"- .955"
Case material:	brass
Powder type:	black, semi-smokeless
Primer type:	Boxer
Cartridge length:	1.386"-1.412"

The cartridges caliber .41 long Colt outside lubricated were developed about 1877. They have a shorter case than the same cartridge with inside lubrication (see cataloge No. 388). They were intended for Colt "New Line" Revolvers, but were subsequently also used in many other Colt revolvers of this calibre. They were superseded by the inside lubricated cartridges.

Headstamps:
PETERS .41 L.D.A.,
P.C.Co. 41 L.D.A.
U S .41 LONG,
U.M.C. .41 LONG,
W.R.A.Co. .41 L.D.A.,
U.M.C. 41 L.C.

.41 Short Colt, D.A. (long case)

Synonyme/Synonyms:
.41 S.D.A.
.41 Short Colt Double Action

390

	Geschoß/Bullet Ausführg. Pattern	Gewicht (g)	Weight (gr.)	Katalog Catalog No.
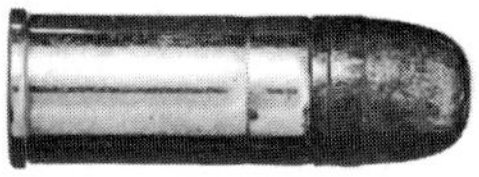	1 C	10,37 – 10,82	160.00 – 167.00	**390–1**
	1 U			**390–2**

Technische und ballistische Daten

Geschoß-∅:	10,20–10,44 mm
Hülsen-∅ Hals:	10,28–10,39 mm
Boden:	10,28–10,39 mm
Rand:	10,89–11,04 mm
Hülsenlänge:	19,58–20,15 mm
Hülsenmaterial:	Messing
Pulverart:	Schwarz, rauchschwach, rauchlos
Zündungsart:	Boxer
Patronenlänge:	29,10–30,94 mm
V_0	220 m/sec
E_0	259 J
Lauflänge:	152 mm

Die Patrone Kaliber .41 short Colt (long Case) ist eigentlich der Nachfolger der frühen Ausführung mit kurzer Hülse (Katalog Nr. 391). Der Zeitraum der Entwicklung dürfte zwischen 1884 und 1890 zu suchen sein. Diese Patrone war für den Colt D.A.-Thunder-Modell gedacht. Vor der Patrone D.A., stand die Patrone S.A. (Katalog Nr. 392).

Bodenstempel:
U.S.C.Co. .41 S.D.A. (U im Zündhütchen)
PETERS .41 S.D.A.,
REM-UMC 41 SHORT (U im Zündhütchen)

Technical and Ballistic Data

Bullet dia.	.401"– .411"
Case dia. neck:	.405"– .409"
head:	.405"– .409"
rim:	.429"– .435"
Case length:	.771"– .793"
Case material:	brass
Powder type:	black, semi-smokeless, smokeless
Primer type:	Boxer
Cartridge length:	1.146"–1.218"
V_0	721 ft. per sec.
E_0	187.2 ft. pounds
Barrel length:	6.000"

The cartridge caliber .41 short Colt (long case) is virtually the successor of the early version with short case (see catalog No. 391). Its developmental stage should be placed between 1884 and 1890. This round was intended for the Colt D.A.-Thunder-Model. Its predecessor is the cartridge S.A. (see catalog No. 392).

Headstamps:
U.S.C.Co. .41 S.D.A. (U in primer),
PETERS .41 S.D.A.,
REM-UMC 41 SHORT (U in primer)

.41 Short Colt, D.A. (short case)

Synonyme/Synonyms:
.41 S.D.A.
.41 Short C.F.
.41 Short Colt Double Action

391

	Geschoß/Bullet Ausführg. Pattern	Gewicht (g)	Weight (gr)	Katalog Catalog No.
	1 C	10,37 – 10,56	160.00 – 163.00	**391–1**
	1 C	8,42	130.00	**391–2**

Technische und ballistische Daten

Geschoß-∅:	10,16–10,44 mm
Hülsen-∅ Hals:	10,29–10,41 mm
Boden:	10,29–10,41 mm
Rand:	10,89–11,07 mm
Hülsenlänge:	15,44–16,20 mm
Hülsenmaterial:	Messing
Pulverart:	Schwarz, rauchlos
Zündungsart:	Boxer
Patronenlänge:	27,20–27,94 mm
V_0	220 m/sec
E_0	259 J
Lauflänge:	152 mm

Die Patrone Kaliber .41 short Colt D.A. (short Case) ist der Vorläufer der etwas späteren Ausführung mit langer Hülse (Katalog Nr. 390). Die Patrone ist für den Revolver Colt Navy D.A. gedacht. Listenmäßig wurde die Patrone nachweislich um 1884/85 erfaßt. Die Produktion wurde um 1950 eingestellt.

Bodenstempel:
U.S.C.Co. .41 S.D.A.,
U.M.C. .41 SHORT,
W.R.A.Co. .41 S.D.A.,
W.R.A.Co. 41 S C

Technical and Ballistic Data

Bullet dia.	.400″– .411″
Case dia. neck:	.405″– .410″
head:	.405″– .410″
rim:	.429″– .436″
Case length:	.608″– .638″
Case material:	brass
Powder type:	black, smokeless
Primer type:	Boxer
Cartridge length:	1.071″–1.100″
V_0	721 ft. per sec.
E_0	187.2 ft. pounds
Barrel length:	6.000″

The cartridge caliber .41 short Colt D.A. (short case) is the predecessor of the shortly afterwards appearing version with a longer case (compare catalog No. 390). The cartridge is intended for the Colt Revolver Navy D.A. It is traceable in lists about 1884/85. The production was discontinued about 1950.

Headstamps:
U.S.C.Co. .41 S.D.A.,
U.M.C. .41 SHORT,
W.R.A.Co. .41 S.D.A.
W.R.A.Co. 41 S C

.41 Short Colt, S.A.

Synonyme/Synonyms:

.41 Extra Short Colt
.41 Short
.41 Short Colt
.41 Short Colt Single Action

392

Geschoß/Bullet Ausführg. Pattern	Gewicht (g)		Weight (gr.)	Katalog Catalog No.
1 C	10,17	10,69	157.00 - 165.00	**392-1**

Technische und ballistische Daten

Geschoß-∅:	10,18-10,39 mm
Hülsen-∅ Hals:	10,30-10,36 mm
Boden:	10,32-10,36 mm
Rand:	11,45-11,94 mm
Hülsenlänge:	15,80-16,28 mm
Hülsenmaterial:	Messing
Pulverart:	Schwarz
Zündungsart:	Boxer
Patronenlänge:	28,04-28,07 mm

Die Patrone Kaliber .41 Colt S.A. (Single Action) wurde um 1872/73 von der Firma Colt für den Colt „New Line S.A. Revolver" hergestellt. Aus der Literatur sind 2 Arten in 3 Varianten bekannt. Im Katalog der Firma Winchester wurde die Patrone 1875 angeboten. Eine neue Herstellungsmethode brachte u.a. andere Bodenstärken an der Hülse, die damit offensichtlich zur Herstellung der D.A.-Patronen führte. Die Produktion wurde um 1920 eingestellt.

Bodenstempel:
W.R.A.Co. COLT C.F.,
und ohne Bodenstempel

Technical and Ballistic Data

Bullet dia.	.401"- .409"
Case dia. neck:	.405"- .408"
head:	.406"- .408"
rim:	.451"- .470"
Case length:	.622"- .641"
Case material:	brass
Powder type:	black
Primer type:	Boxer
Cartridge length:	1.104"-1.105"

The Colt Company manufactured this cartridge caliber .41 Colt S.A. about 1872/73 for its Revolver "Colt New Line S.A.". Literature shows two types in 3 variations. In the Winchester Catalog of 1875 this cartridge was offered for sale. A new manufacturing process lead among other things to different base diameters of the case resulting obviously in the production of Double Action cartridges. Production ceased about 1920.

Headstamps:
W.R.A.Co. COLT C.F.,
and without headstamp

.41 Smith & Wesson

Synonyme/Synonyms:
.41 S. & W.

393

Geschoß/Bullet Ausführg. Pattern	Gewicht (g)	Weight (gr.)	Katalog Catalog No.
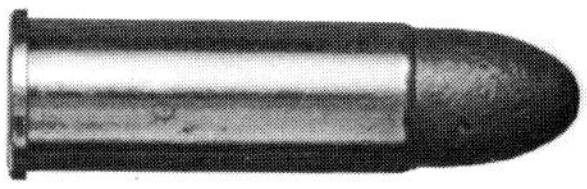 16 B			**393–1**

Technische und ballistische Daten

Geschoß-∅:	9,47 mm
Hülsen-∅ Hals:	10,31 mm
Boden:	10,31–10,36 mm
Rand:	11,56–11,60 mm
Hülsenlänge:	26,36–26,44 mm
Hülsenmaterial:	Messing
Pulverart:	
Zündungsart:	
Patronenlänge:	37,34–37,46 mm

Die Patrone Kaliber .41 Smith & Wesson stammt aus einer Versuchsserie. Angaben zu der zur Patrone gehörenden Waffe fehlen. Sie wurde in den Jahren zwischen 1890 und 1900 entwickelt und ist im Katalog der Firma Smith & Wesson aus dem Jahre 1903 enthalten. Hersteller kleiner Stückzahlen ist Firma U.M.C.Co. Die Patronen hatten geringe Verbreitung und waren für den S & W-Target-Revolver Modell 3 New Modell und den S & W-Revolver Modell 44 D.A. bestimmt.

Bodenstempel:
U.M.C. .41 S&W

Technical and Ballistic Data

Bullet dia.	.373″
Case dia. neck:	.406″
head:	.406″– .408″
rim:	.455″– .457″
Case length:	1.038″–1.041″
Case material:	brass
Powder type:	
Primer type:	
Cartridge length:	1.470″–1.475″

The cartridge caliber .41 Smith & Wesson is part of an experimental series. No details are available about the weapon pertaining to it. The cartridge was developed in the years between 1890 and 1900 and is listed in the catalog of the firm Smith & Wesson of the year 1903. Manufacturer of small lots is the firm U.M.C.Co. The cartridges were not widely distributed and intended for the S & W Target Revolver Model 3 New Model and the S & W Revolver Model 44 D.A.

Headstamp:
U.M.C. .41 S&W

.41 S & W Magnum

Synonyme/Synonyms:

.41 Magnum
.41 Remington
.41 Remington Magnum

394

	Geschoß/Bullet Ausführg. Pattern	Gewicht (g)	Weight (gr.)	Katalog Catalog No.
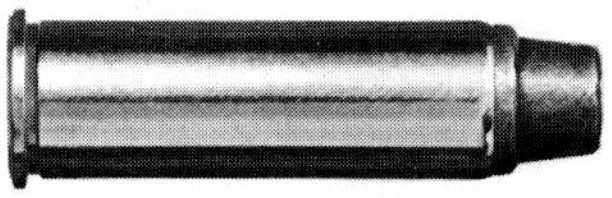	1 R	13,61	210.00	**394–1**
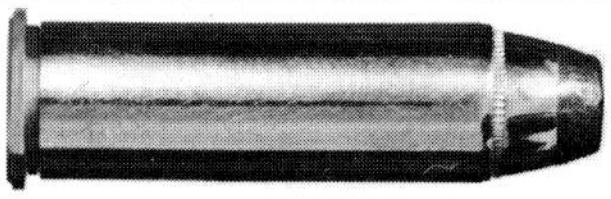	30 G	13,61	210.00	**394–2**

Technische und ballistische Daten

Geschoß-∅:	10,00–10,41 mm	
Hülsen-∅ Hals:	10,95–11,02 mm	
Boden:	10,95–11,04 mm	
Rand:	12,34–12,45 mm	
Hülsenlänge:	32,46–32,59 mm	
Hülsenmaterial:	Messing	
Pulverart:	rauchlos	
Zündungsart:	Boxer	
Patronenlänge:	39,37–40,15 mm	
V_0 (m/sec)	320[1])	457[2])
E_0 (J)	712[1])	1452[2])
Lauflänge:	213 mm	

[1]) Bleigeschoß
[2]) Teilmantel-Geschoß

Technical and Ballistic Data

Bullet dia.	.394"– .410"	
Case dia. neck:	.431"– .434"	
head:	.431"– .435"	
rim:	.486"– .490"	
Case length:	1.278"–1.283"	
Case material:	brass	
Powder type:	smokeless	
Primer type:	Boxer	
Cartridge length:	1.550"–1.581"	
V_0 (ft. per sec.)	1050[1])	1500[2])
E_0 (ft. pounds)	515[1])	1050[2])
Barrel length:	8.375"	

[1]) solid lead bullet
[2]) soft point bullet

Die Patrone Kaliber .41 S & W Magnum wurde 1964 in Zusammenarbeit der Firmen Remington Arms Co. und Smith and Wesson entwickelt. Sie ist u.a. für die Revolver S & W Modell 57 D.A. Modell 58 und Ruger S.A. Blackhawk bestimmt. Aus der Literatur ist zu entnehmen, daß bei der o.a. Patrone die „Wild-Cat-Patrone" Kaliber 400 Eimer Pate gestanden hat.

Bodenstempel:
R – P .41 MAGNUM

The cartridge caliber .41 S & W Magnum was developed in 1964 in cooperation with the firms Remington Arms Co. and Smith & Wesson. It is among other weapons destined for the revolvers S&W Model 57 D.A. Model 58 and Ruger S.A. Blackhawk. As can be learnt from pertinent literature the "Wildcat" caliber. .400 Eimer served as a model for this round.

Headstamp:
R – P .41 MAGNUM

.410 Colt Deringer C.F.

Synonyme/Synonyms:

.410 Deringer C.F.
.410 Revolver, Short
.410 Revolver (Short case)

395

	Geschoß/Bullet Ausführg. Pattern	Gewicht (g)	Weight (gr.)	Katalog Catalog No.
	1 C	9,07	140.00	**395-1**
	1 C	8,75 - 8,94	135.00 - 138.00	**395-2**

Technische und ballistische Daten

Geschoß-Ø:	10,11-10,46 mm
Hülsen-Ø Hals:	10,20-10,39 mm
Boden:	10,22-10,34 mm
Rand:	11,85-12,04"
Hülsenlänge:	11,68-12,50 mm
Hülsenmaterial:	Messing
Pulverart:	Schwarz
Zündungsart:	Boxer,Topf, verdeckt
Patronenlänge:	22,95-23,85 mm

Die Patrone Kaliber .410 Colt Deringer C.F. ist englischen Ursprungs und aus der Patrone Kaliber .41 Deringer R.F. (Derringer) entstanden. Beide Patronen wären austauschbar, wenn der Vorgänger nicht Randfeuerzündung hätte. Es handelt sich um eine Patrone für „Derringer-Pistolen" und verschiedene Revolver. Als Revolverpatrone wurde sie von der Patrone Kaliber .410 Revolver C.F. abgelöst (vergl. Katalog Nr. 396).

Bodenstempel:
GAUPILLAT PARIS (verdeckte Zündung),
.410,
ohne

Technical and Ballistic Data

Bullet dia.	.398"- .412"
Case dia. neck:	.401"- .409"
head:	.402"- .407"
rim:	.466"- .474"
Case length:	.460"- .492"
Case material:	brass
Powder type:	black
Primer type:	Boxer, battery cup, inside
Cartridge length:	.903"- .939"

The cartridge caliber .410 Colt Derringer C.F. is of British origin and developed out of the cartridge caliber .41 Derringer R.F. Both cartridges would be interchangeable, if the predecessor specimen had not been provided with rimfire ignition. It is a cartridge for "Derringer pistols" and various revolvers. As a revolver cartridge it was superseded by the cartridge caliber .410 Revolver C.F. (compare catalog No. 396).

Headstamp:
GAUPILLAT PARIS (inside primer)
.410,
without headstamp

.410 Revolver C.F.

Synonyme/Synonyms:

.410 Revolver
.410 Revolver, Long
.410 Revolver (Long case)
.410–14–160 Revolver
9,8 × 18,0 – R.N. 410

396

	Geschoß/Bullet Ausführg. Pattern	Gewicht (g)	Weight (gr.)	Katalog Catalog No.
	1 C	10,37	160.00	**396–1**
	1 C	7,13	110.00	**396–2**
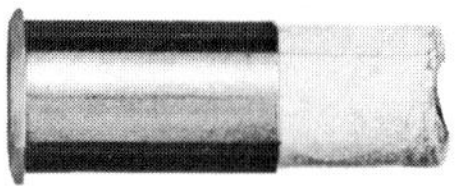	90 d	–	–	**396–3**

Technische und ballistische Daten

Geschoß-∅:	10,03–10,34 mm
Hülsen-∅ Hals:	10,29–10,34 mm
Boden:	10,31–10,41 mm
Rand:	10,90–11,78 mm
Hülsenlänge:	16,94–18,36 mm
Hülsenmaterial:	Messing
Pulverart:	Schwarz
Zündungsart:	Berdan
Patronenlänge:	28,30–29,34 mm
V_0	213 m/sec
E_0	240 J
Lauflänge:	76 mm

Die Patrone Kaliber .410 C.F. hat ihren Ursprung in England. Sie ist in den Katalogen der Firmen Kynoch 1894 und Eley 1898 unter dem Hinweis „für Colt's und andere Revolver" enthalten. Obwohl es in diesem Kaliber auch Schrotpatronen gegeben hat, ist sie noch im Katalog der Firma Nobel 1925 als ausschließliche Revolverpatrone aufgeführt.

Bodenstempel:
ELEY .410.,
ELEY 410. LONDON,
ohne

Technical and Ballistic Data

Bullet dia.	.395"– .407"
Case dia. neck:	.405"– .407"
head:	.406"– .410"
rim:	.429"– .464"
Case length:	.667"– .723"
Case material:	brass
Powder type:	black
Primer type:	Berdan
Cartridge length:	1.114"–1.155"
V_0	700 ft. per sec.
E_0	174.0 ft. pounds
Barrel length:	3.000"

The cartridge caliber .410 C.F. has its origin in England. It is contained in the catalog of the firms Kynoch 1894 and Eley 1898 in the column "for Colt's and other revolvers". Although there existed in this caliber also shot cartridges it is still listed in the 1925 catalog of the NOBEL Company exclusively as a revolver cartridge.

Headstamp:
ELEY .410.,
ELEY 410. LONDON,
without headstamp

.44 Gabbett Mock Duel

Synonyme/Synonyms:

.44 Mock Duel

405

	Geschoß/Bullet			Katalog
	Ausführg. Pattern	Gewicht (g)	Gewicht (g)	Catalog No.
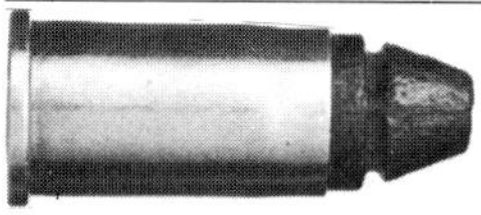	5 M	0,84	13.00	**405-1**
	5 M	0,84	13.00	**405-2**
	5 M	0,84	13.00	**405-3**

Technische und ballistische Daten

Geschoß-∅:	10,50–10,80 mm
Hülsen-∅ Hals:	11,12–11,56 mm
Boden:	11,55–11,71 mm
Rand:	12,98–13,08 mm
Hülsenlänge:	21,00–24,50 mm
Hülsenmaterial:	Messing
Pulverart:	ohne
Zündungsart:	Topf
Patronenlänge:	30,55–33,60 mm

Die Patrone Kaliber .44 Gabbett Mock Duel ist eine ausgesprochene Übungspatrone. Sie kommt aus Frankreich und sie diente auch als Vorübungspatrone zur Durchführung von Duellen. Die Teilnehmer an der Sportart „assaut au pistolet" waren am Körper, Gesicht und an den Händen durch entsprechende Bekleidung (u. a. Gesichtsmasken) geschützt. Die Patronen paßten sowohl in entsprechende Sportpistolen, wie in den französischen Ordonanzrevolver Kal. 11 mm und in den S&W Revolver Kal. .44 S&W Russian. (Vergl. Kat.-Nr. 414).

Bodenstempel sind nicht bekannt.

Technical and Ballistic Data

Bullet dia.	.413"– .425"
Case dia. neck:	.438"– .455"
head:	.454"– .461"
rim:	.511"– .515"
Case length:	.827"– .964"
Case material:	brass
Powder type:	without
Primer type:	battery cup
Cartridge length:	1.203"–1.323"

The cartridge caliber .44 Gabbett Mock Duel positively is a practice cartridge. It originates from France and also served as a training cartridge for people intending to fight a mock duel. The participants in this kind of sport, called "assaut au pistolet", protected body, face and hands by expedient clothing (protective masks, among other things). The cartridges could be fired in the corresponding target pistols as well as in the French ordnance revolver caliber 11 mm and in the .44 S&W Revolver caliber .44 S&W Russian (compare catalog No. 414).

Headstamps are not known.

.44 King's Conversion

Synonyme/Synonyms:

406

Geschoß/Bullet Ausführg. Pattern	Gewicht (g)	Weight (gr.)	Katalog Catalog No.
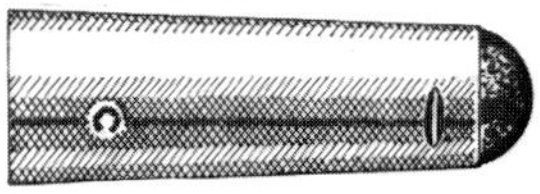 1 B			**406-1**

Technische und ballistische Daten

Geschoß-∅:	unbekannt
Hülsen-∅ Hals:	9,83- 9,88 mm
Boden:	11,89-12,01 mm
Hülsenlänge:	32,64 mm
Hülsenmaterial:	Messing
Pulverart:	Schwarz
Zündungsart:	verdeckt (Patentzündung)
Patronenlänge:	36,42 mm

Die Patrone Kaliber .44 King's Conversion gehört zu den Experimenten, die in den Jahren 1865–1880 bei Frankford Arsenal USA durchgeführt wurden. Sie soll insbesondere aus Versuchen stammen, die 1865–1869 unter Beteiligung von King bei Frankford Arsenal zur Änderung von Remington-Revolvern gemacht worden sind. Die Zündung erfolgte durch eine innensitzende und durch Körnerpunkte gehaltene Zündglocke (verdeckte Zündung).

Kein Bodenstempel

Technical and Ballistic Data

Bullet dia.	unknown
Case dia. neck:	.387"- .389"
head:	.468"- .473"
Case length:	1.285"
Case material:	brass
Powder type:	black
Primer type:	inside (patent ignition)
Cartridge length:	1.434"

The cartridge caliber .44 King's Conversion forms part of the experiments made in the years 1865 - 1880 at Frankford Arsenal's in the USA. It is said to particularly result from experiments realized between 1865 and 1869 with the participation of King at Frankford Arsenal's in connection with modified Remington revolvers. Ignition was achieved by an inside primer cup held in its position by stab crimps (inside primer).

No headstamp

.44 Magnum

Synonyme/Synonyms:

.44 Remington Magnum
.44 S. & W. Magnum

407

	Geschoß/Bullet Ausführg. Pattern	Gewicht (g)	Weight (gr.)	Katalog Catalog No.
	1 R	15,55	240.00	**407–1**
	1 R	15,55	240.00	**407–2**
	30 G	15,55	240.00	**407–3**
	30 G	15,55	240.00	**407–4**
	30 M	15,55	240.00	**407–5**
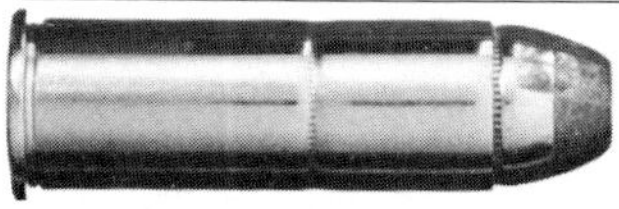	42 G	15,55	240.00	**407–6**
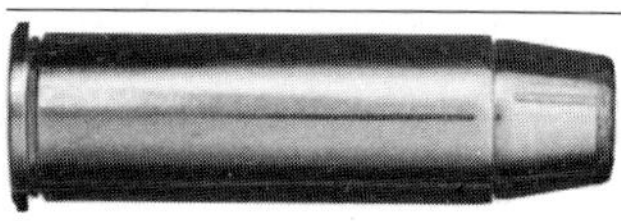	42 M	15,55	240.00	**407–7**
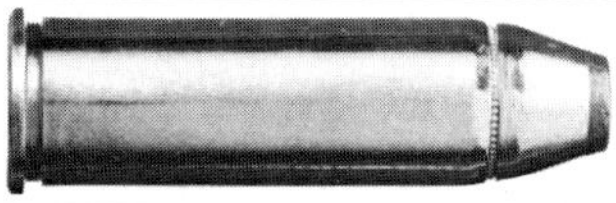	42 M	11,66	180.00	**407–8**
	90 f	–	–	**407–9**

Technische und ballistische Daten

Geschoß-Ø:	10,58–10,93 mm
Hülsen-Ø Hals:	11,40–11,57 mm
Boden:	11,50–11,60 mm
Rand:	12,75–13,05 mm
Hülsenlänge:	32,30–32,80 mm
Hülsenmaterial:	Messing
Pulverart:	rauchlos
Zündungsart:	Boxer
Patronenlänge:	40,44–41,05 mm
V_0	448 m/sec
E_0	1590 J
Lauflänge:	165 mm

Technical and Ballistic Data

Bullet dia:	.416"– .430"
Case dia. neck:	.449"– .445"
head:	.453"– .457"
rim:	.502"– .514"
Case length:	1.272"–1.291"
Case material:	brass
Powder type:	smokeless
Primer type:	Boxer
Cartridge length:	1.592"–1.616"
V_0	1470 ft. per sec.
E_0	1150.0 ft. pounds
Barrel length:	6.500"

Die Patrone Kaliber .44 Magnum wurde 1955/56 von der Firma Remington für den S&W-Revolver .44 Magnum entwickelt. Sie galt Jahre hindurch als die stärkste Revolverpatrone. Im Laufe der Zeit wurden weitere Revolver wie Ruger Blackhawk, Ruger Super Blackhawk, Great Western und Super Dakota S.A., Langwaffen von Ruger, Marlin und Winchester und auch die Pistole Contender (Katalog-Nr. 407–9) für diese Patrone eingerichtet.

Bodenstempel:
REM-UMC 44 MAGNUM,
R – P 44 REM MAG,
SUPER–X .44 MAGNUM,
NORMA Re .44 MAGNUM,
SUPER VEL .44 MAG,
SPEER .44 MAG,
DOMINION 44 MAGNUM

The cartridge caliber .44 Magnum was developed in 1955/56 by the firm Remington for the S&W Revolver .44 Magnum. It had been considered for years as the most potent revolver cartridge. In the course of time revolvers like Ruger Blackhawk, Ruger Super Blackhawk, Great Western and Super Dakota S.A., rifles of the companies Ruger, Marlin and Winchester as well as the Contender Pistol (catalog No. 407-8) were chambered for this cartridge.

Headstamps:
REM-UMC 44 MAGNUM,
R – P 44 REM MAG,
SUPER–X .44 MAGNUM,
NORMA Re .44 MAGNUM,
SUPER VEL .44 MAG,
SPEER .44 MAG,
DOMINION 44 MAGNUM

.44 Meigs Experimental

Synonyme/Synonyms:

408

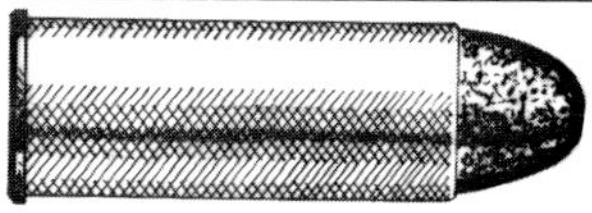

Geschoß/Bullet Ausführg. Pattern	Gewicht (g)	Weight (gr.)	Katalog Catalog No.
1 B			**408-1**

Technische und ballistische Daten

Geschoß-∅:	10,80 mm
Hülsen-∅ Hals:	11,51 mm
Boden:	11,61 mm
Rand:	12,72 mm
Hülsenlänge:	29,23 mm
Hülsenmaterial:	Messing
Pulverart:	Schwarz
Zündungsart:	–
Patronenlänge:	37,87 mm

Die Patrone Kaliber .44 Meigs Experimental war eine der vielen Versuchspatronen, die in der Zeit von 1860 bis 1870, u. a. auch von Captain J.V.Meigs entwickelt wurden. Die Patrone rechnet zu denen, die vermutlich bei Frankford Arsenal, National Armory in Springfield oder bei der United States Cartridge Company in Lowell/-Mass. U.S.A. hergestellt wurde, und die mit einer Martin-Zündung ausgestattet war.

Bodenstempel:
nicht bekannt.

Technical and Ballistic Data

Bullet dia.	.425″
Case dia. neck:	.453″
head:	.457″
rim:	.501″
Case length:	1.151″
Case material:	brass
Powder type:	black
Primer type:	–
Cartridge length:	1.491″

The cartridge caliber .44 Meigs Experimental was one of the numerous test rounds which were developed during the period of 1860 to 1870, among others also by Captain J.V.Meigs. The cartridge falls into the category of those which were presumably manufactured at Frankford Arsenal's, National Armory's in Springfield or at the United States Cartridge Company in Lowell/Mass., USA. It had a Martin primer.

Headstamps:
not known.

.44 Merwin, Hulbert & Co.

Synonyme/Synonyms:

.42 Merwin Hulbert
.42–23–352 Merwin Hulbert
.44 M. & H.
.44 M. H. & Co.

409

	Geschoß/Bullet			Katalog Catalog No.
	Ausführg. Pattern	Gewicht (g)	Weight (gr.)	
	1 B	14,26 - 16,33	220.00 -252.00	**409-1**
	1 G	14.26	220.00	**409-2**
	90 e	–	–	**409-3**
	91 c	–	–	**409-4**

Technische und ballistische Daten

Geschoß-Ø:	10,41 - 10,69 mm
Hülsen-Ø Hals:	11,10 - 11,28 mm
Boden:	11,10 - 11,23 mm
Rand:	12,42 - 12,78 mm
Hülsenlänge:	28,96 - 29,54 mm
Hülsenmaterial:	Messing
Pulverart:	Schwarz, rauchschwach
Zündungsart:	Boxer
Patronenlänge:	38,40 - 39.00 mm
V_0	200 m/sec
E_0	290 J
Lauflänge:	152 mm

Die Patrone Kaliber .44 Merwin, Hulbert & Co. wurde um 1877 für die Revolver Merwin & Hulbert .44 S.A. und D.A. entwickelt. Sie ist im Merwin & Hulbert-Katalog von 1889 enthalten. Obwohl in Serie gefertigt, fand die Patrone nur geringe Verbreitung. Die Firma U.M.C. stellte die Produktion der Patrone 1918 ein. (Vergleiche Katalog Nr. 328, 329 und 361).

Bodenstempel:
U.M.C. .44 M,H & Co.,
W.R.A.Co. .44 M, H & Co, und
ohne

Technical and Ballistic Data

Bullet dia.	.410" - .421"
Case dia. neck:	.437" - .444"
head:	.437" - .442"
rim:	.489" - .503"
Case length:	1.140" - 1.163"
Case material:	brass
Powder type:	black, semi-smokeless
Primer type:	Boxer
Cartridge length:	1.512" - 1.535"
V_0	657 ft. per sec.
E_0	209.6 ft. pounds
Barrel length:	6.000"

The cartridge caliber .44 Merwin, Hulbert & Co. was developed about 1877 for the revolvers Merwin & Hulbert .44 S.A. and D.A. It is listed in the Merwin & Hulbert Catalog of 1889. Although manufactured in series production this cartridge achieved but little commercial success. The firm U.M.C. discontinued the production of this cartridge in 1918 (compare catalog Nos. 328, 329 and 361).

Headstamps:
U.M.C. .44 M,H & Co.,
W.R.A.Co. .44 M,H & Co,
and without headstamp

.44 Nagant

Synonyme/Synonyms:

.44 Brazilian Nagant
.44 Nagant (Brazilian Model)

410

Geschoß/Bullet Ausführg. Pattern	Gewicht (g)	Weight (gr.)	Katalog Catalog No.
1 H	15,55	240.00	**410-1**

Technische und ballistische Daten

Geschoß-∅:	11,00-11,20 mm
Hülsen-∅ Hals:	11,00-11,15 mm
Boden:	11,10-11,22 mm
Rand:	12,70-13,15 mm
Hülsenlänge:	19,76-20,47 mm
Hülsenmaterial:	Messing
Pulverart:	Schwarz
Zündungsart:	Berdan
Patronenlänge:	32,95-33,75 mm
V_0	213 m/sec
E_0	361 J

Die Patrone Kaliber .44 Nagant stammt aus den europäischen Raum (Belgien) und war offensichtlich für belgische Nagant-Revolver bestimmt die wiederum für Brasilien bestimmt waren. Sie ist u. a. in den Firmenkatalogen S.F.M., Eley und Nobel bis 1925 aufgeführt.

Bodenstempel:

ELEY . .44 NAGANT.,
44 18 89 K&C,
GG (Monogramm) .44 N,

Technical and Ballistic Data

Bullet dia.	.433"- .441"
Case dia. neck:	.433"- .439"
head:	.437"- .442"
rim:	.500"- .518"
Case length:	.778"- .806"
Case material:	brass
Powder type:	black
Primer type:	Berdan
Cartridge length:	1.297"-1.329"
V_0	700 ft. per sec.
E_0	261.0 ft. pounds

The cartridge caliber .44 Nagant originates from the European Continent (Belgium) and was obviously intended for the Belgian Nagant Revolvers which were to be exported to Brazil. It is listed among other rounds in the company catalog of S.F.M., Eley and Nobel up to the year 1925.

Headstamps:
ELEY . .44 NAGANT.,
44 18 89 K&C,
GG (Monogram) .44 N,

.44 Remington

Synonyme/Synonyms:

.44 Remington Army Revolver M.1875
.44 Remington New Line Revolver
.44–28–227 Remington

411

	Geschoß/Bullet			Katalog Catalog No.
	Ausführg. Pattern	Gewicht (g)	Weight (gr.)	
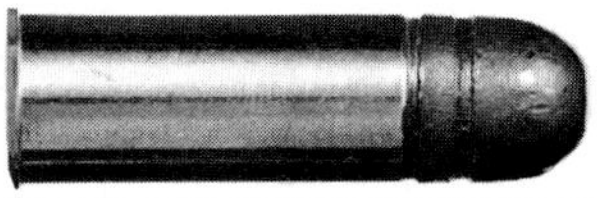	1 H	16,07	248.00	**411–1**
	1	14,68	226.60	**411–2**

Technische und ballistische Daten

Geschoß-∅:	11,12–11,43 mm
Hülsen-∅ Hals:	11,30–11,45 mm
Boden:	11,33–11,53 mm
Rand:	12,04–12,30 mm
Hülsenlänge:	26,45–27,15 mm
Hülsenmaterial:	Messing
Pulverart:	Schwarz
Zündungsart:	Boxer
Patronenlänge:	38,66–39,47 mm

Die Patrone Kaliber .44 Remington wurde 1870/71 bei der Firma Remington entwickelt. Sie wurde bis ca. 1895 hergestellt. Die Patrone war für die Remington Revolver Army und New Line bestimmt. Sie ist in Farrow's Military Encyclopedia von 1886 und in einem Werbeblatt der Firma U.S.C.Co. von 1882 enthalten.

Keine Bodenstempel bekannt

Technical and Ballistic Data

Bullet dia.	.438″– .450″
Case dia. neck:	.445″– .451″
head:	.446″– .454″
rim:	.474″– .484″
Case length:	1.041″–1.069″
Case material:	brass
Powder type:	black
Primer type:	Boxer
Cartridge length:	1.522″–1.554″

The cartridge caliber .44 Remington was developed at Remington's in 1870/71. It was manufactured until about 1895. This cartridge was intended for revolvers Remington Army and New Line. It is mentioned in Farrow's Military Encyclopedia of 1886 and in a broadsheet of the firm U.S.C. Company of 1882.

Headstamps are not known

.44 Roth

Synonyme/Synonyms:

.44 Roth Selbstlade-Pistole

412

Geschoß/Bullet Ausführg. Pattern	Gewicht (g)	Weight (gr.)	Katalog Catalog No.
21 B	16.00	247.00	**412–1**

Technische und ballistische Daten

Hülsenmaterial:	Messing
Pulverart:	rauchlos
Zündungsart:	Berdan
V_0	296 m/sec
E_0	719 J
Lauflänge:	140 mm

Im Rahmen der englischen Armeeversuche von 1900 bis 1914 legte die Firma G.Roth A.G. mehrere Selbstladepistolen vor (vergleiche Bd.1 Katalog Nr. 149 und 171). Eine dieser schon verbesserten Pistolen, mit einer Magazinkapazität von 7 Patronen, war für das Kaliber .44 bestimmt. Sie wurde 1903 der Prüfungskommision vorgelegt, aber abgelehnt. Im Gegensatz zu den von Roth angegebenen ballistischen Werten stellte die Prüfungskommision bei einer V_{27} eine Geschoßgeschwindigkeit von 252 m/s fest. Die Patrone (ebenfalls von der Roth A.G. gefertigt) kam nicht in den Handel.

Kein Bodenstempel bekannt

Technical and Ballistic Data

Case material:	brass
Powder type:	smokeless
Primer type:	Berdan
V_0	975 ft. per sec.
E_0	519.8 ft. pounds
Barrel length:	5.500″

Within the scope of British military trials from 1900 to 1914, the firm G. Roth A.G. presented several self-loading pistols (compare Volume I, catalog Nos. 149 and 171). One of these already improved pistols with a magazine capacity of 7 rounds was destined for the caliber .44. In 1903 it was presented to the board of trial, however, it was rejected. Contrary to the ballistic ratings as indicated by the firm Roth, the board of trial determined at V_{27} a bullet velocity of 252 m/s. The cartridge (likewise manufactured by the "Roth A.G.") was not distributed commercially.

No headstamps are known

.44 S&W American

413

Synonyme/Synonyms:

DWM 204
GR 959
.44 No. 3 American
.44 S. & W. (American Model)
.44 S. & W. No. 3 American
.44 S. & W. Revolver (American)
.44 Smith & Wesson American
.44 Smith & Wesson Army Revolver
.44–25–225 S.&W. Army Revolver
.44 Am.–23–220
10,40 × 23,40 Smith & Wesson Kal. 44
10,6 × 22,4 – Amerika 44.
S. & W. Cal. 44 amerikanisch
S. & W. .44–100

	Geschoß/Bullet			Katalog Catalog No.
	Ausführg. Pattern	Gewicht (g)	Weight (gr.)	
	1 C	12,31 – 14,26	190.00 – 220.00	**413–1**
	1 C	13,00	200.60	**413–2**
	1 C	14,58	225.00	**413–3**
	1 G			**413–4**
	16 C	14,13	218.00	**413–5**
	21 C	12,96	200.00	**413–6**
	60 C			**413–7**
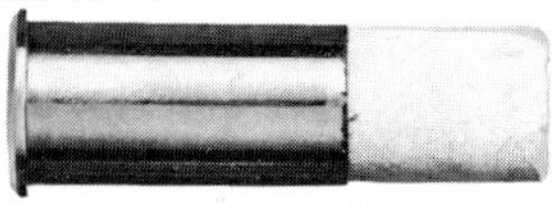	90 d	–	–	**413–8**
	90 e	–	–	**413–9**

Technische und ballistische Daten

Geschoß-∅:	10,55–11,28 mm
Hülsen-∅ Hals:	10,97–11,20 mm
Boden:	11,02–11,25 mm
Rand:	12,45–13,20 mm
Hülsenlänge:	21,31–23,49 mm
Hülsenmaterial:	Messing, Kupfer
Pulverart:	Schwarz, rauchschwach, rauchlos
Zündungsart:	Berdan, Boxer, Martin, Topf
Patronenlänge:	35,71–37,21 mm
V_0	210 m/sec
E_0	320 J
Lauflänge:	152 mm

Die Patrone Kaliber .44 S&W American wurde zwischen 1868 und 1870 für den Smith & Wesson-Kipplaufrevolver No. 3 entwickelt. Aus ihr entstand die Patrone Kaliber .44 S&W Russian (Katalog Nr. 414). Ursprünglich war die Kaliberbezeichnung S&W – .44 – 100, ab ca. 1874 wurde sie dann endgültig .44 S&W American genannt. Die Patronen für den zivilen Gebrauch wurden bis ca. 1940, die für den militärischen Gebrauch bei der Springfield Armory zwischen 1871 – 1873 hergestellt.

Bodenstempel:
U.S.C.Co. .44 S&W A,
U.M.C. .44 S&W A,
W.R.A. .44 S&W AM,
WESTERN .44 S&W A,
R.W.S. A. 44,
R W S .44 S&W A,
S&W 44,
ELEY . .44 S&W

Technical and Ballistic Data

Bullet dia.	.415"– .444"
Case dia. neck:	.432"– .441"
head:	.434"– .443"
rim:	.490"– .520"
Case length:	.839"– .925"
Case material:	brass, copper
Powder type:	black, semi-smokeless, smokeless
Primer type:	Berdan, Boxer, Martin fold, battery cup
Cartridge length:	1.406"–1.465"
V_0	689 ft. per sec.
E_0	231.7 ft. pounds
Barrel length:	6.000"

The cartridge caliber .44 S&W American was developed between 1868 and 1870 for the Smith&Wesson tip up revolver No. 3. It was the basis for the cartridge caliber .44 S&W Russian (see catalog No. 414). The original caliber designation was S&W – .44 – 100, from about 1874 it was definitely designated as .44 S&W American. The cartridges were manufactured for civil use until about 1940, those for military use at Springfield Armory's between 1871 – 1873.

Headstamps:
U.S.C.Co. .44 S&W A,
U.M.C. .44 S&W A,
W.R.A. .44 S&W AM,
WESTERN .44 S&W A,
R.W.S. A. 44,
R W S .44 S&W A,
S&W 44
ELEY . .44 S&W

.44 S&W Russian

Synonyme/Synonyms:

414

DWM 242
GR 960
.44 No.3 Russian
.44 S.&W. No. 3 Russian
.44 S.&W. Revolver (Russian)
.44 S.&W. (Russian Model)
.44 Short, S.&W. Russian
.44 Smith & Wesson Russian
.44 R.–23–255
10,9 × 23,7 – S.&W. 44
11.0 × 24,35 – S.&W. 44 Mod. Russe
11,05 × 24,80 Smith & Wesson Kal. 44 Russ. Modell
S.&W. Cal. 44 russisch

	Geschoß/Bullet			Katalog
	Ausführg. Pattern	Gewicht (g)	Weight (gr.)	Catalog No.
	1 B	16,52 – 17,82	255.00 – 275.00	**414–1**
	1 B	14,58 – 15,94	225.00 – 246.00	**414–2**
	1 B	14,58 – 15,94	225.00 – 246.00	**413–3**
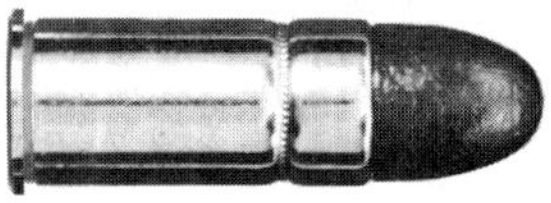	1 B	12,96	200.00	**414–4**
	16 B	15,94	246.00	**414–5**
	70 B			**414–6**
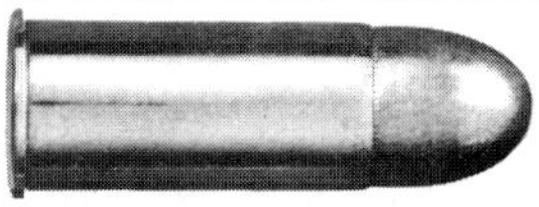	21 B	13,87 – 17,17	214.00 – 265.00	**414–7**
	21 B	13,87 – 17,17	214.00 – 265.00	**414–8**
	60 B	15,94	246.00	**414–9**
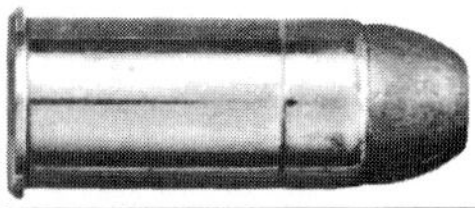	1 G			**414–10**
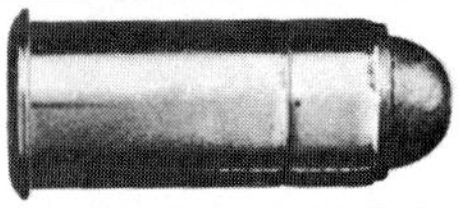	1 S	8,10	125.00	**414–11**

.44 S&W Russian

	Geschoß/Bullet			Katalog Catalog No.
	Ausführg. Pattern	Gewicht (g)	Weight (gr.)	
	1 B	8,10	125.00	**414–12**
	1 P	7,52/9,40	116.00/145.00	**414–13**
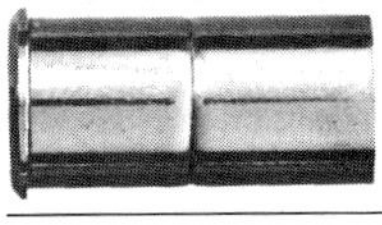 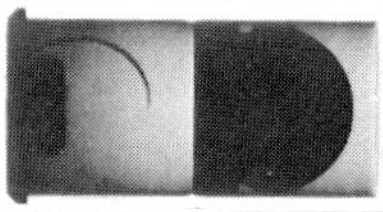	1 B	7,13	110.00	**414–14**
	1 A	7,45 – 7,65	115.00 – 118.00	**414–15**
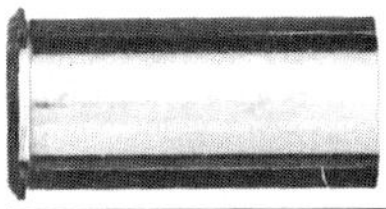 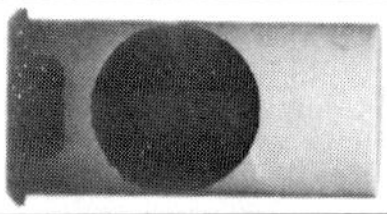	1 A	7,13	110.00	**414–16**
 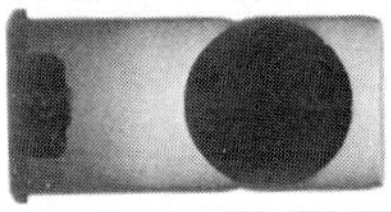	1 A	6,80	105.00	**414–17**
	8 A	0,71	11.00	**414–18**
	8 A	0,71	11.00	**414–19**
	8 A	0,71	11.00	**414–20**
	90 d	–	–	**414–21**
	90 e	–	–	**414–22**
	91 c	–	–	**414–23**

Technische und ballistische Daten

Geschoß-ø:	10,50–11,23 mm
Hülsen-ø Hals:	11,25–11,65 mm
Boden:	11,45–11,70 mm
Rand:	12,60–13,16 mm
Hülsenlänge:	23,10–24,92 mm
Hülsenmaterial:	Messing, Stahl*), Pappe mit Messingboden*)
Pulverart:	Schwarz, rauchschwach, rauchlos
Zündungsart:	Berdan, Boxer, Topf, Topf verdeckt*)
Patronenlänge:	34,40–37,00 mm 24,50–31,20 mm*)
V_0	235 m/sec
E_0	448 J
Lauflänge:	152 mm

Die Patrone Kaliber .44 S&W Russian wurde 1870/71 infolge eines Auftrages der Firma Smith & Wesson, zur Lieferung russischer Armeerevolver, entwickelt. Ursprünglich war an das American-Modell gedacht, jedoch viele Änderungen an der Waffe führten letztlich zur Änderung an der Munition und damit zur Patrone Kal. .44 S&W Russian. (Vergl. Katalog Nr. 413). Die Patrone wurde in vielen Geschoßvarianten gefertigt wie z. B. mit Aussenfettung, Innenfettung und mit selbstschmierenden Geschossen (Katalog Nr. 414–5). Mit „Gallery-Geschossen" u. a. war die Patrone für die Remington-Pistole Target 1901 und Target-Revolver vorgesehen.

Bodenstempel:
U.M.C. .44 S&W R,
REM-UMC 44 S&W R,
W.R.A.Co. 44 S&W R.,
WESTERN .44 S&W R.,
PETERS .44 S&W.R.,
D + + CAL 44,
LEON BEAUX + S&W 44 +,
L.B.&C. - S&W .44 –,
R.W.S. 44 S&W R,
GG (Monogramm) .44 S&W,
G.F.L. 44 S.W.R.
ohne

*) Diese Angaben beziehen sich auf die Devillers MOCK-DUELL-Patrone

Technical and Ballistic Data

Bullet dia.	,413"– .442"
Case dia. neck:	.443"– .459"
head:	.451"– .461"
rim:	.496"– .518"
Case length:	.909"– .981"
Case material:	brass, steel*),
Powder type:	black, semi-smokeless, smokeless
Primer type:	Berdan, Boxer, battery cup, battery cup inside*)
Cartridge length:	1.354"–1.427" .964"–1.228"*)
V_0	770 ft. per sec.
E_0	324.4 ft. pounds
Barrel length:	6.000"

The cartridge .44 S&W Russian was developed in 1870/71 on account of an order of the firm Smith & Wesson in connection with the delivery of Russian Army revolvers. It was at first thought of the American model, however, many modifications of the weapon led at last to the modification of the ammunition and thus to the cartridge existing in many variations, for instance with inside and outside lubrication and selflubricating bullets No. 414–5); with gallery bullets and others the cartridge was intended for the Remington Target Pistol 1901 and Target revolvers.

U.M.C. .44 S&W R,
REM-UMC 44 S&W R,
W.R.A.Co. 44 S&W R.,
WESTERN .44 S&W R,
PETERS .44 S&W.R.,
D + + CAL 44,
LEON BEAUX + S&W 44 +,
L.B.&C. - S&W .44 –,
R.W.S. 44 S&W R,
GG (Monogram) .44 S&W,
G.F.L. 44 S.W.R.
without headstamp

*) This type refers to the Devillers Mock-Duel cartridge

.44 S&W Special

Synonyme/Synonyms:

GR 964
.44 Smith & Wesson Special
.44 Special
S. & W. Cal. 44 Spezial

415

	Geschoß/Bullet Ausführg. Pattern	Gewicht (g)	Weight (gr.)	Katalog Catalog No.
	1 B	15,88 – 15,94	245.00 – 246.00	**415–1**
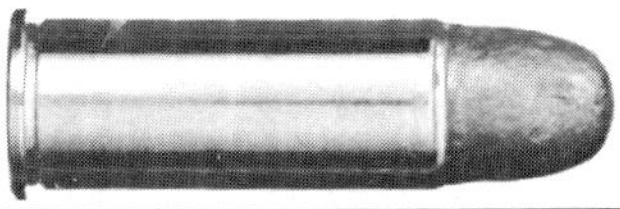	1 B	15,94	246.00	**415–2**
	21 B	15,94	246.00	**415–3**
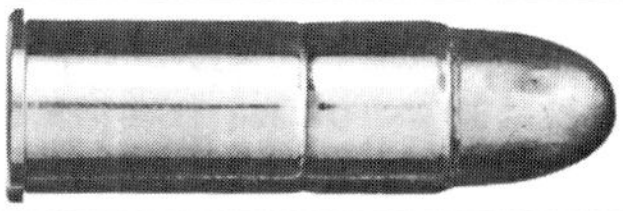	60 B	15,94	246.00	**415–4**
	1 S	8,10	125.00	**415–5**
	1 B	8,10	125.00	**415–6**
	1 P	13,67	211.00	**415–7**
	1 P	7,52/9,40	116.00/145.00	**415–8**
	1 A	4,54	70.00	**415–9**
	90 b	–	–	**415–10**

Technische und ballistische Daten

Geschoß-∅:	10,51–11,00 mm
Hülsen-∅ Hals:	11,48–11,61 mm
Boden:	11,51–11,75 mm
Rand:	12,80–13,11 mm
Hülsenlänge:	28,29–29,62 mm
Hülsenmaterial:	Messing
Pulverart:	Schwarz, rauchschwach, rauchlos
Zündungsart:	Boxer
Patronenlänge:	38,80–40,50 mm
V_0	235 m/sec
E_0	448 J
Lauflänge:	171 mm

Die Patrone Kaliber .44 S&W Special wurde auf der Basis der Patrone Kaliber .44 S&W-Russian 1907 für den S&W-Revolver New Century – Hand Ejector entwickelt (vergleiche Katalog Nr. 414). Es folgten dann weitere Revolver von Colt und anderen (auch Europäischen) Firmen. Die Patronen wurden in Serie gefertigt, waren ursprünglich mit Schwarzpulver geladen und sind heute nur noch mit rauchlosem Pulver erhältlich.

Bodenstempel:
REM-UMC 44 S&W SPL,
U S C Co .44 S&W SPL,
U.M.C. .44 S.&W. SPL. (U im Zündhütchen),
W.R.A. .44 S&W SPL,
W.R.A.Co. .44 S&W SPL, (W im Zündhütchen),
PETERS .44 S&W SPL,
Geco .44 S&W SPL,
R.W.S. 44. S&W SPL,

Technical and Ballistic Data

Bullet dia.	.414″– .433″
Case dia. neck:	.452″– .457″
head:	.453″– .462″
rim:	.504″– .516″
Case length:	1.114″–1.166″
Case material:	brass
Powder type:	black, semi-smokeless, smokeless
Primer type:	Boxer
Cartridge length:	1.527″–1.594″
V_0	770 ft. per sec.
E_0	323.9 ft. pounds
Barrel length:	6.750″

The cartridge caliber .44 S&W Special was developed on the basis of the cartridge calibre .44 S&W Russian 1907 for the S&W Revolver New Century – Hand Ejector (compare catalog No. 414). There followed other revolvers made by Colt and other (also European) companies. The rounds were series produced, originally loaded with black powder and they are currently sold with smokeless powder.

Headstamps:
REM-UMC 44 S&W SPL,
U S C Co .44 S&W SPL,
U.M.C. .44 S.&W. SPL. (U in primer)
W.R.A. .44 S&W SPL,
W.R.A.Co. .44 S&W SPL, (U in primer),
PETERS .44 S&W SPL,
Geco .44 S&W SPL,
R.W.S. 44. S&W SPL,

.44 Target

Synonyme/Synonyms:
.44 Speer Target

416

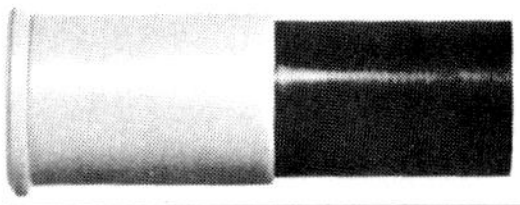

Geschoß/Bullet Ausführg. Pattern	Gewicht (g)	Weight (gr.)	Katalog Catalog No.
7 Q	1,28 – 1,30	19,75 – 20,06	**416–1**

Technische und ballistische Daten

Geschoß-∅:	10,57 – 10,60 mm
Hülsen-∅ Hals:	11,55 – 11,60 mm
Boden:	11,55 – 11,60 mm
Rand:	12,98 – 13,00 mm
Hülsenlänge:	17,55 mm
Hülsenmaterial:	Kunststoff
Pulverart:	ohne
Zünungsart:	Boxer
Patronenlänge:	33,20 mm

Die Patrone Kaliber .44 Target ist das mittlere Kaliber in dieser Patronenreihe. Sie wurde ebenso wie das Kaliber .38 Target und .45 Target in den USA bei der Firma SPEER entwickelt (vergleiche Katalog Nr. 371 und 438A). Es handelt sich um eine billige wiederladbare Trainingspatrone für kurze Entfernungen. Die Komponenten (Hülse, Geschoß und Zündung – ohne Treibladung) werden vor dem Schuß zusammengestellt.

Bodenstempel:
SPEER .44

Technical and Ballistic Data

Bullet dia.	.416″ – .417″
Case dia. neck:	.455″ – .457″
head:	.455″ – .457″
rim:	.511″ – .512″
Case length:	.691″
Case material:	plastic
Powder type:	without
Primer type:	Boxer
Cartridge length:	1.307″

The cartridge caliber .44 Target is the medium caliber of this cartridge series. It was developed by SPEER Company (compare catalog Nos. 371 and 348A) just like the calibers .38 Target and .45 Target, in the USA. It is a cheap, reloadable practice ammunition for short ranges. The components (case, bullet and primer without propellant) are put thogether before firing the shot.

Headstamp:
SPEER .44

.44 Thuer

Synonyme/Synonyms:
.44 Colt, Thuer's Pat.

417

Geschoß/Bullet Ausführg. Pattern	Gewicht (g)	Weight (gr.)	Katalog Catalog No.
1 F	13,7 (13,4)	212 (208)	**417-1**

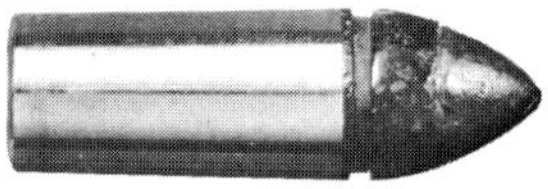

Technische und ballistische Daten

Geschoß-Ø:	11,71-11,73 mm
Hülsen-Ø Hals:	11,71-11,73 mm
Boden:	10,87-10,95 mm
Hülsenlänge:	22,22-22,45 mm
Hülsenmaterial:	Messing
Pulverart:	Schwarz
Zündungsart:	-
Patronenlänge:	35,73-36,04 mm

Die Patrone Kaliber .44 Thuer ist das größte Kaliber in dieser Patronenreihe. (Vergl. Katalog Nr. 322, 345, 346 und 418). Es handelt sich um eine 1868 entwickelte randlose, konische Zentralfeuerpatrone. Sie war für Perkussionsrevolver, welche in Patronenrevolver transformiert wurden bestimmt.

Keine Bodenstempel

Technical and Ballistic Data

Bullet dia.	.461"- .462"
Case dia. neck:	.461"- .462"
head:	.428"- .431"
Case length:	.875"- .884"
Case material:	brass
Powder type:	black
Primer type:	-
Cartridge length:	1.407"-1.419"

The cartridge caliber .44 Thuer is the bigbore caliber in this cartridge series (compare catalog Nos. 322, 345, 346 and 418). It is a rimless, conical central fire cartridge developed about 1868. It was intended for percussion revolvers which were transformed into cartridge revolvers.

No headstamps

.44 Thuer Experimental

Synonyme/Synonyms:

418

	Geschoß/Bullet Ausführg. Pattern	Gewicht (g)	Weight (gr.)	Katalog Catalog No.
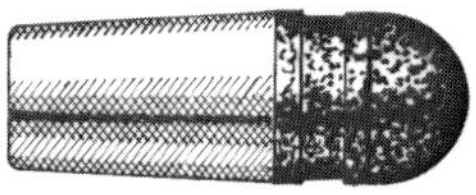	1 C			**418–1**

Technische und ballistische Daten

Geschoß-∅:	11,23 mm
Hülsen-∅ Hals:	11,15 mm
Boden:	9.32 mm
Hülsenlänge:	17,53 mm
Hülsenmaterial:	Messing
Pulverart:	Schwarz
Zündungsart:	–
Patronenlänge:	30,30 mm

Bei der Patrone Kaliber .44 Thuer Experimental handelt es sich um den Vorläufer der Patronen Kaliber .31, .36 und .44 Thuer. Als Betriebsleiter der Firma Colt erhielt Alexander Thuer am 15. Sept. 1868 das US-Patent Nr. 82258 für sein System, Perkussionsrevolver in Patronenrevolver umzubauen. Er verwendete dazu Patronen mit randlosen, konischen Hülsen. Die ersten Patronen wurden von Frankford Arsenal hergestellt.

Kein Bodenstempel

Technical and Ballistic Data

Bullet dia.	.442″
Case dia. neck:	.439″
head:	.367″
Case length:	.690″
Case material:	brass
Powder type:	black
Primer type:	–
Cartridge length:	1.193″

The cartridge caliber .44 Thuer Experimental is the predecessor of the cartridges calibres .31, .36 and .44 Thuer. As the manager of the firm Colt, Alexander Thuer obtained on 15 September 1868 the US-Patent No. 82258 for his system to transform percussion revolvers into cartridge revolvers. For this purpose he used rimless conical cases. The first cartridges were manufactured by Frankford Arsenal.

No headstamps

.44 Webley

Synonyme/Synonyms:

.44 Webley Revolver
.44–18–200 Webley

419

Geschoß/Bullet Ausführg. Pattern	Gewicht (g)	Weight (gr.)	Katalog Catalog No.
1 C	12,96	200.00	**419–1**
90 d	–	–	**419–2**

Technische und ballistische Daten

Geschoß-∅:	11,13–11,23 mm
Hülsen-∅ Hals:	11,30–11,35 mm
Boden:	11,51–11,53 mm
Rand:	12,70–12,80 mm
Hülsenlänge:	17,15–17,30 mm
Hülsenmaterial:	Messing
Pulverart:	Schwarz
Zündungsart:	Berdan, Boxer
Patronenlänge:	28,30–28,35 mm

Die Patrone Kaliber .44 Webley wurde um 1868 in England entwickelt und war für den „Webley's Royal Irish Constabulary – Revolver" bestimmt. Weitere Revolver folgten. In den USA stellte die Firma Harrington und Richardson Arms Co. einen Revolver für dieses Kaliber her. 1875 folgte in den USA auch die Patronenfertigung. Die Patronen wurden bis 1939/40 hergestellt.

Bodenstempel:
U.M.C. .44 WEBLEY.,
U.S.C.Co. .44 WEBLEY,
PETERS .44 WEBLEY,
ohne

Technical and Ballistic Data

Bullet dia.	.438"– .442"
Case dia. neck:	.445"– .447"
head:	.453"– .454"
rim:	.500"– .504"
Case length:	.675"– .681"
Case material:	brass
Powder type:	black
Primer type:	Berdan, Boxer
Cartridge length:	1.114"–1.116"

The cartridge caliber .44 Webley was developed in England about the year 1868 and it was intended for the "Webley's Royal Irish Constabulary Revolver". Other revolvers followed. In the USA it was the Harrington and Richardson Arms Co. which manufactured a revolver for this caliber .In 1875 the ammunition production began in the USA. The cartridges were manufactured until about 1939/40.

Headstamps:
U.M.C. .44 WEBLEY.,
U.S.C.Co. .44 WEBLEY,
PETERS .44 WEBLEY,
without headstamp

.442 Tranter

Synonyme/Synonyms:

DWM 221
GR 909
.442 British Tranter
.442 Revolver C.F.
.442 Tranter Revolver
.442 Webley
.442-13-220 Tranter
10,5 × 17 – 442 kurz
10,85 × 18,80 Kal. 442 Revolver
10,9 × 17,5 – R.N. 442 kurz
Revolver Cal. 442

425

	Geschoß/Bullet Ausführg. Pattern	Gewicht (g)	Weight (gr.)	Katalog Catalog No.
	1 C	16,20	250.00	**425–1**
	1 C	13,61 – 14,80	210.00 – 228.40	**425–2**
	1 C	13,61 – 14,80	210.00 – 228.40	**425–3**
	1 C	13,61 – 14,80	210.00 – 228.40	**425–4**
	1 C	13,61 – 14,80	210.00 – 228.40	**425–5**
	1 E	11,85 – 13,61	182.87 – 210.00	**425–6**
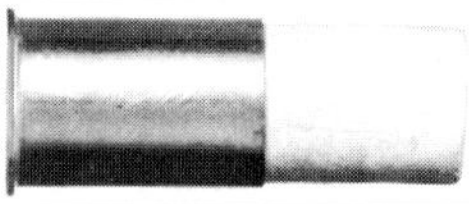	90 d	–	–	**425–7**
	90 d	–	–	**425–8**

Technische und ballistische Daten

Geschoß-Ø:	10,83 – 11,35 mm
Hülsen-Ø Hals:	11,25 – 11,48 mm
Boden:	11,33 – 11,47 mm
Rand:	12,39 – 12,90 mm
Hülsenlänge:	16,41 – 17,50 mm
Hülsenmaterial:	Messing
Pulverart:	Schwarz, rauchlos
Zündungsart:	Berdan, Boxer, Topf
Patronenlänge:	27,30 – 30,28 mm
V_0	213 m/sec
E_0	330 J
Lauflänge:	102 mm

Technical and Ballistic Data

Bullet dia.	.426″ – .447″
Case dia. neck:	.443″ – .452″
head:	.446″ – .451″
rim:	.488″ – .508″
Case length:	.646″ – .689″
Case material:	brass
Powder type:	black, smokeless
Primer type:	Berdan, Boxer, battery cup
Cartridge length:	1.075″ – 1.192″
V_0	700 ft. per sec.
E_0	239.0 ft. pounds
Barrel length:	4.000″

Die Patrone Kaliber .442 Tranter ist im Gegensatz zur Patrone Kaliber .442 long C.F. eine ausgesprochene Revolverpatrone für Waffen der Firma Enfield, Webley und Tranter (vergl. Katalog Nr. 424). Die „Royal Irish Constabulary" war nach 1868 mit einem Webley-Revolver in diesem Kaliber ausgerüstet. Offensichtlich war der Vorgänger die Patrone Kaliber .442 R.F. In den USA wurde die Patrone unter der Bezeichnung .44 Webley von ca. 1875 bis 1939 hergestellt. Die Munition war in Europa sehr verbreitet.

Bodenstempel:
ELEY BROS,
ELEY BROS . LONDON.,
ELEY .442.,
R.W.S. .442.,
G.F.L. 442,
.442.

The cartridge caliber .442 Tranter, contrary to the cartridge caliber .442 long C.F., is a pronounced revolver cartridge for weapons of the firms Enfield, Webley and Tranter (compare catalog No. 424). After 1868, the "Royal Irish Constabulary" was equipped with a Webley revolver of this caliber. Evidently the predecessor was the cartridge caliber .442 R.F. In the USA the cartridge was manufactured from about 1875 until 1939 with the designation .44 Webley. The ammunition was widely known in Europe.

Headstamps:
ELEY BROS,
ELEY BROS . LONDON.,
ELEY .442.,
R.W.S. .442.,
G.F.L. 442,
.442.

.45 Automatic Colt

426

DWM 513A
GR 941
.45 A.C.P.
.45 Auto.
.45 Auto. Colt M.11
.45 Automatic Colt, Government Model
.45 Automatic M.1911
.45 Automatic Pistol
.45 Colt Auto. U.S.A. Govt.
.45 Colt Automatic
.45 Colt Automatic, Model 1911
Autom. Colt-Pistole Kal. 11,43 mm (.45)
Colt autom. Cal. 45

	Geschoß/Bullet			Katalog Catalog No.
	Ausführg. Pattern	Gewicht (g)	Weight (gr.)	
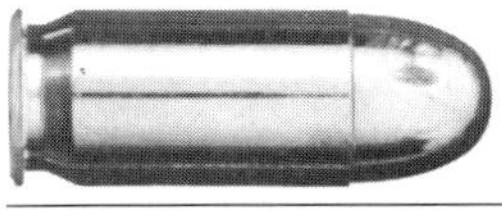	21 B	14,90	230.00	**426–1**
	21 B	14,90	230,00	**426–2**
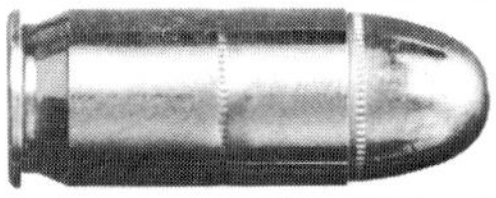	21 B	14,90	230.00	**426–3**
	21 B	14,90	230.00	**426–4**
	21 B	14,90	230.00	**426–5**
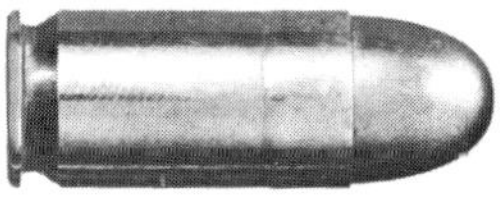	21 B	12,96	200.00	**426–6**
	9 B	11,21	173.00	**426–7**
	3 B	10,82	167.00	**426–8**
	9 B	9,52	147.00	**426–9**
	22 B	4,08	63.00	**426–10**
	50 B	2,27	35.00	**426–11**

.45 Automatic Colt

	Geschoß/Bullet Ausführg. Pattern	Gewicht (g)	Weight (gr.)	Katalog Catalog No.
	1 B	11,73	181.00	**426–12**
	24 E	14,90	230.00	**426–13**
	24 E	14,90	230.00	**426–14**
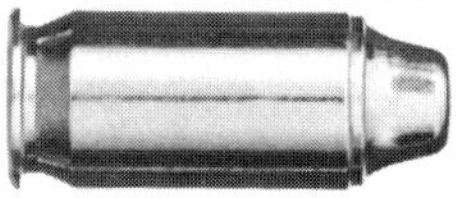	21 S	11,99	185.00	**426–15**
	21 S	11,99	185.00	**426–16**
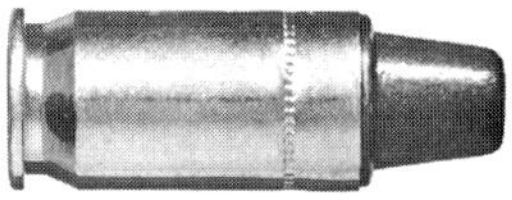	1 S	13,61	210.00	**426–17**
	1 G	12,31/12,96	190.00/200.00	**426–18**
	1 G	11,18/11,73	172.50/181.10	**426–19**
	41 M	12,31	190.00	**426–20**
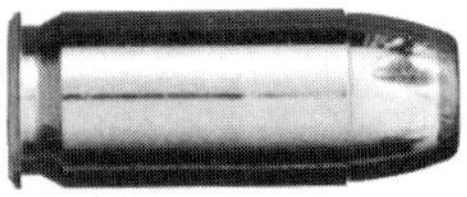	42 G	14,90	230.00	**426–21**
	42 G	14,90	230.00	**426–22**
 	70 B	13,22	204.00	**426–23**
	90 a	–	–	**426–24**
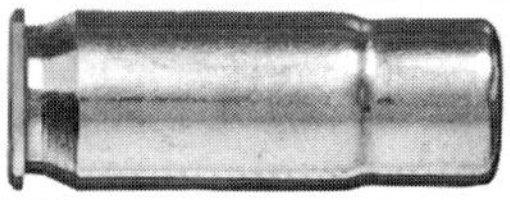	90 b	–	–	**426–25**

.45 Automatic Colt

	Geschoß/Bullet Ausführg. Pattern	Gewicht (g)	Weight (gr.)	Katalog Catalog No.
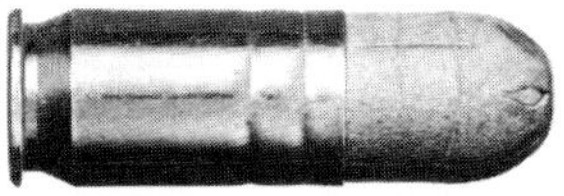	90 c	–	–	**426-26**
	90 c	–	–	**426-27**
	90	–	–	**426-28**
	90 e	–	–	**426-29**
	90 e	–	–	**426-30**
	90 f	–	–	**426-31**

Technische und ballistische Daten

Geschoß-∅:	11,12–11,45 mm	
Hülsen-∅ Hals:	11,84–12,05 mm	
Boden:	11,90–12,09 mm	
Rand:	11,84–12,19 mm	
Hülsenlänge:	22,45–23,01 mm	
Hülsenmaterial:	Messing, Messing vernickelt, Stahl lackiert, Stahl vermessingt, Stahl verkupfert, Stahl verbleit, Stahl verzinkt, Stahl phosphatiert, Aluminium	
Pulverart:	rauchlos	
Zündungsart:	Berdan, Boxer	
Patronenlänge:	29,00–32,50 mm	
	V_0 m/sec	E^0 J
14,90 g Ganzmantel/ Rundkopf (REM)	259	510
13,61 g "SUPER MATCH" Clean Cutting (WESTERN)	216	325
12,96 g Ganzmantel/ Rundkopf (WIN)	277	509
12,31 g Ganzmantel/ Hohlspitz (SUPER VEL)	323	1027
11,99 g Wad Cutter "TARGETMASTER" (REM)	236	339
Lauflänge:	127 mm	

Technical and Ballistic Data

Bullet dia.	.438"–.451"	
Case dia. neck:	.466"–.474"	
head:	.468"–.476"	
rim:	.466"–.480"	
Case length:	.884"–.906"	
Case material:	brass, nickeled brass, lacquered steel, brass plated steel, copper washed steel, lead plated steel, zinc plated steel, phosphate coated steel, aluminium	
Powder type:	smokeless	
Primer type:	Berdan, Boxer	
Cartridge length:	1.142"–1.279"	
	V_0 ft. per sec.	E^0 ft. pounds
230.00 gr. Metal cased "Ball, M.1911" (REM)	850	369.0
210.00 gr. SUPER MATCH Clean Cutting (WESTERN)	710	235.0
200.00 gr. Metal cased (WIN)	910	368.0
190.00 gr. Jacketed Hollow Point (SUPER VEL)	1060	743.0
185.00 gr. Wad Cutter TARGETMASTER (REM)	775	245.0
Barrel length:	5.000"	

Die Patrone Kaliber .45 Automatic Colt u.a. auch als Kaliber .45 Automatic M 1911 in den Synonymen bezeichnet, könnte auch die Modellbezeichnung 1905 tragen, denn in diesem Jahre begann die Entwicklung dieser Patrone. Sie wurde jedoch erst 1911 offiziell in die US-Armee eingeführt. In der Folgezeit wurde sie in vielen Geschoßausführungen hergestellt. (Weitere Patronen aus dieser Zeit 1905–1911 siehe unter Katalog Nr. 427 und 428). Die Verwendung dieser Patrone unter der Benutzung von Clips in Revolvern führte um 1920 zur Herstellung der Patrone Kaliber .45 Automatic Rim (Katalog Nr. 429). Die Patrone wird in Norwegen u.a. in der Armeepistole 1914 unter der Bezeichnung 11,25 mm Norwegen geführt (Band I Katalog Nr. 165).

Bodenstempel:
E C 43,
E C S 44,
F A 45,
F A 4 14,
F C 60,
F.M.F.L.E. 66–11,25
M.M.C. 4–17,
MAXIM U.S.A.,
MAXIM 5–17,
P C C Co 18,
PETERS 27,
REM-UMC 18,
PETERS 45 AC,
REM-UMC 45 ACP,
REM-UMC 45 AUTO,
REM-UMC 45 TMG,
R-P 45 AUTO,
RHACo 45 AUTO,
SUPER VEL 45 ACP,
SUPER-X 45 AUTO,
U.M.C. .45 ACP,
U S C Co 45 ACP,
WESTERN 45 AUTO,
W.R.A.Co. 45 AC,
W-W 45 AUTO,
R–A 42,
T W 55,
WESTERN 30,
W C C 61,
USCCo 17,
W.R.A.Co. 3–13,
W 18,
W.R.A. 54,
BROWNING 45 AUTO,
FEDERAL 45 AUTO,
Geco 45 ACP,
norma 45 ACP,
KYNOCH .45 ACP,
F de M 45 AUTO Mexico,
FNC 45 1934,
D W M 513
R.W.S. 45 ACP,
GFL
SYI 55,
NORMA 45 ACP,
PPU 62 Kal. .45,
DAM MM 45 ACP,
DOMINION 45 AUTO,
SFM + CAL + 45,
ORBEA 45 AC,
CBC 45 ACP,

The cartridge caliber .45 Automatic Colt, also listed among the synonyms as caliber .45 Automatic M 1911, might as well bear the model designation 1905, for in that year began the development of this round. However, it was only in 1911 officially adopted by the US-Army. During the following period it was manufactured with many bullet forms (more cartridges from the time between 1905 and 1911 appear under catalog Nos. 427 and 428). The use of this cartridge by means of clips in revolvers resulted in 1920 in the production of the cartridge caliber. 45 Automatic Rim (catalog No. 429). The cartridge is used in Norway among others in the Army pistol 1914 under the designation 11,26 mm Norway (Volume I, catalog No. 165).

Headstamps:
E C 43,
E C S 44,
F A 45,
F A 4 14,
F C 60,
F.M.F.L.E. 66–11,25,
M.M.C. 4–17,
MAXIM U.S.A.,
MAXIM 5–17,
P C C Co 18,
PETERS 27,
REM-UMC 18,
PETERS 45 AC,
REM-UMC 45 ACP,
REM-UMC 45 AUTO,
REM-UMC 45 TMG,
R-P 45 AUTO,
RHACo 45 AUTO,
SUPER VEL 45,
SUPER-X 45 AUTO,
U.M.C. .45 ACP,
U S C Co 45 ACP,
WESTERN 45 AUTO,
W.R.A.Co. 45 AC,
W-W 45 AUTO,
R–A 42,
T W 55,
WESTERN 30,
W C C 61,
USCCo 17,
W.R.A.Co. 3–13,
W 18,
W.R.A. 54,
BROWNING 45 AUTO,
FEDERAL 45 AUTO,
Geco 45 ACP,
norma 45 ACP,
KYNOCH .45 ACP,
F de M 45 AUTO Mexico
FNC 45 1934,
D W M 513,
R.W.S. 45 ACP,
GFL 45 M 11,
SYI 55,
NORMA 45 ACP,
PPU 62 Kal. .45,
DAM MM 45 ACP,
DOMINION 45 AUTO,
SFM + CAL + 45,
ORBEA 45 AC,
CBC 45 ACP,

.45 Automatic M.1906

Synonyme/Synonyms:

DWM 513
.45 Automatic Pistol, M.1906
Autom. Colt-Pistole Kal. 11,43 mm (.45) – Amerikan. Armee Modell

427

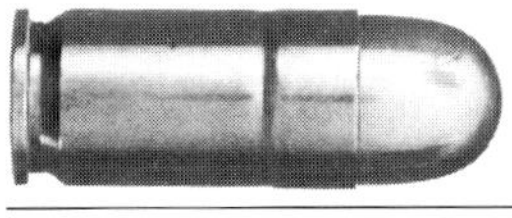

Geschoß/Bullet Ausführg. Pattern	Gewicht (g)	Weight (gr.)	Katalog Catalog No.
21 B	14,90	230.00	**427-1**

Technische und ballistische Daten

Geschoß-Ø:	11,43 – 11,50 mm
Hülsen-Ø Hals:	11,94 – 12,05 mm
Boden:	11,94 – 12,05 mm
Rand:	11,94 – 12,00 mm
Hülsenlänge:	23,14 – 23,32 mm
Hülsenmaterial:	Messing
Pulverart:	rauchlos
Zündungsart:	Boxer
Patronenlänge:	32,94 – 33,02 mm
V_0	245 m/sec
E_0	456 J
Lauflänge:	127 mm

Die Patrone Kaliber .45 Automatic 1906 ist eine der Versuchspatronen die im Auftrag der Regierung von Frankford Arsenal 1905/06 durchgeführt wurden (vergl. Katalog Nr. 428). Bei den Versuchen wurden 2 Arten dieser 45er Patronen hergestellt, eine randlose für Pistolen und eine mit Rand für Revolver (vergl. Katalog Nr. 432). Die Versuche führten, obwohl keine der Versuchswaffen übenommen wurden, zur späteren Übernahme des Modells 1911 mit der Munition.

Bodenstempel:
F A 4 06,

Technical and Ballistic Data

Bullet dia.	.450" – .453"
Case dia. neck:	.470" – .474"
head:	.470" – .474"
rim:	.470" – .472"
Case length:	.911" – .918"
Case material:	brass
Powder type:	smokeless
Primer type:	Boxer
Cartridge length:	1.297" – 1.300"
V_0	804 ft. per sec.
E_0	329.7 ft. pounds
Barrel length:	5.000"

The cartridge caliber .45 Automatic 1906 is one of the experimental cartridges used in the tests carried out by order of the Government at Frankford Arsenal's in 1905/06 (compare catalog No. 428). Two kinds of cartridges were manufactured for the tests, a rimless .45 cartridge for pistols and a rimmed one for revolvers (compare catalog No. 432). Although none of the test weapons was adopted, they led to a later adoption of the Modell 1911 and the ammunition (catalog No. 426).

Headstamp: F A 4 06

.45 Automatic, 1908

Synonyme/Synonyms:
.45 Automatic Pistol, 1908

428

Geschoß/Bullet Ausführg. Pattern	Gewicht (g)	Weight (gr.)	Katalog Catalog No.
21 B	14,90	230.00	**428–1**

Technische und ballistische Daten

Geschoß-∅:	11,48 mm
Hülsen-∅ Hals:	11,99 mm
Boden:	11,99 mm
Rand:	11,96 mm
Hülsenlänge:	23,44 mm
Hülsenmaterial:	Messing
Pulverart:	rauchlos
Zündungsart:	Boxer
Patronenlänge:	33.02 mm

Die Patrone Kaliber .45 Automatic 1908 ist ähnlich wie die Patrone Kaliber .45 Automatic M.1906 eine Patrone der Entwicklungs- und Versuchszeit, die zur späteren Annahme der Patrone Kaliber .45 Automatic Colt geführt hat (vergl. Katalog Nr. 426 und 427). Sie war eigentlich die erste Gebrauchspatrone für die frühen Colt-Pistolenmodelle 1911 und sie ist nur durch den Bodenstempel eindeutig zuzuordnen.

Bodenstempel:
F A 11 08,

Technical and Ballistic Data

Bullet dia.	.452″
Case dia. neck:	.472″
head:	.472″
rim:	.471″
Case length:	.923″
Case material:	brass
Powder type:	smokeless
Primer type:	Boxer
Cartridge length:	1.300″

Similar to the cartridge caliber .45 Automatic M. 1906, the cartridge caliber .45 Automatic 1908 is a round of the developmental and experimental stages resulting in the later adoption of the cartridge caliber .45 Automatic Colt (compare catalog Nos. 426 and 427). It was virtually the first service cartridge for the early Colt pistol models 1911 and can be classified unmistakably only by its headstamp.

Headstamp:
F A 11 08,

.45 Automatic Rim

Synonyme/Synonyms:
.45 Auto. Rim

429

	Geschoß/Bullet Ausführg. Pattern	Gewicht (g)	Weight (gr.)	Katalog Catalog No.
	21 B	14,90	230.00	**429-1**
	1 B	14,90	230.00	**429-2**
	1 B	14,90	230.00	**429-3**
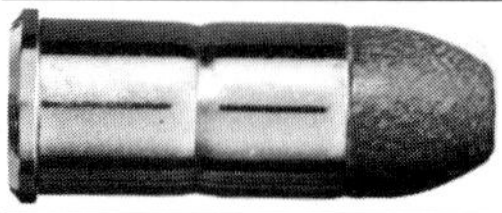	1 G	16,52	255.00	**429-4**

Technische und ballistische Daten

Geschoß-ø:	11,15-11,70 mm
Hülsen-ø Hals:	11,84-12,01 mm
Boden:	11,86-12,01 mm
Rand:	12,90-13,20 mm
Hülsenlänge:	22,50-22,96 mm
Hülsenmaterial:	Messing, Messing venickelt
Pulverart:	rauchlos
Zündungsart:	Boxer
Patronenlänge:	31,95-32,82 mm
V_0	250 m/sec
E_0	475 J
Lauflänge:	152 mm

Die Patrone Kaliber .45 Automatic Rim wurde 1920 in den USA entwickelt. Sie entstand aus dem Bedürfnis heraus, den Clip abzuschaffen, mit dem es möglich war, Patronen Kaliber .45 Automatic Colt aus S&W- und Colt-Revolvern zu verschießen. (Vergl. Katalog Nr. 426). Erster Hersteller war die Firma Peters Cartridge Company, andere Firmen folgten.

Bodenstempel:
PETERS .45 AUTO RIM,
REM-UMC 45 AUTO RIM,
REM-UMC 45 A R,
U.S.C.Co. 45 A.R. (US im Zündhütchen),
W.R.A. .45 A.R.,
C B C M G 45 AR

Technical and Ballistic Data

Bullet dia.	.439"-.461"
Case dia. neck:	.466"-.473"
head:	.467"-.473"
rim:	.508"-.520"
Case length:	.886"-.904"
Case material:	brass,
Powder type:	smokeless
Primer type:	Boxer
Cartridge length:	1.258"-1.292"
V_0	820 ft. per sec.
E_0	343.4 ft. pounds
Barrel length:	6.000"

The cartridge caliber .45 Automatic Rim was developed in 1920 in the USA. It was a consequence of the wish to dispose of the clip by which it had been possible to fire cartridges caliber .45 Automatic Colt in S&W and Colt revolvers (see catalog No. 426). The first manufacturer was Peters Cartridge Company, other firms followed.

Headstamps:
PETERS .45 AUTO RIM,
REM-UMC 45 AUTO RIM,
REM-UMC 45 A R,
U.S.C.Co. 45 A.R. (US in primer),
W.R.A. .45 A.R.,
C B C M G 45 AR

.45 Colt

Synonyme/Synonyms:
.45 Colt, Army & Double Action
.45 Colt Long
.45 Colt U.S.A.
.45 Long Colt
.45–40–250 Colt Revolver

430

	Geschoß/Bullet			Katalog Catalog No.
	Ausführg. Pattern	Gewicht (g)	Weight (gr.)	
	1 G	16,20	250.00	**430–1**
	1 G	16,20–16,85	250.00–260.00	**430–2**
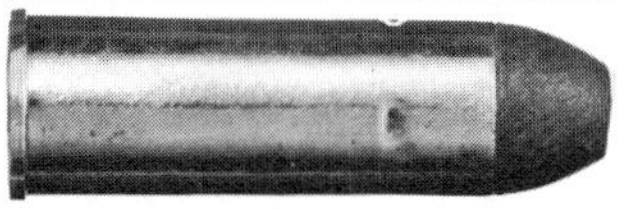	1 G	16,20–16,85	250.00–260.00	**430–3**
	21 B			**430–4**
	60 B	16,20	250.00	**430–5**
	1 P	12,83	198.00	**430–6**
	1 A	8,94	138.00	**430–7**
	90 a	–	–	**430–8**
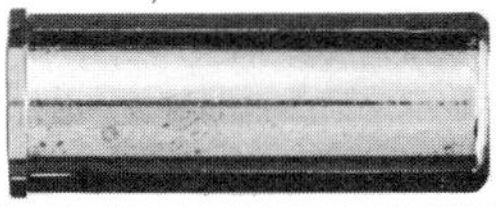	90 b	–	–	**430–9**
	90 c	–	–	**430–10**
	90 e	–	–	**430–11**
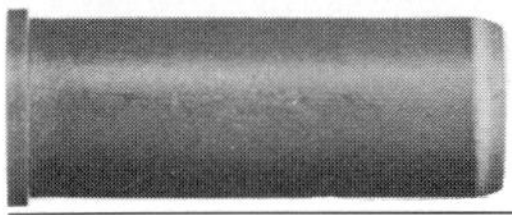	90 g	–	–	**430–12**

Technische und ballistische Daten

Geschoß-Ø:	11.18 – 11,60 mm
Hülsen-Ø Hals:	11,84 – 12,19 mm
Boden:	11,98 – 12,26 mm
Rand:	12,67 – 13,30 mm
Hülsenlänge:	31,75 – 33,00 mm
Hülsenmaterial:	Messing, Messing vernickelt, Kupfer, Kunststoff
Pulverart:	Schwarz, rauchschwach, rauchlos
Zündungsart:	Boxer, Benet
Patronenlänge:	39,80 – 41,76 mm
V_0	265 m/sec
E_0	580 J
Lauflänge:	152 mm

Die Patrone Kaliber .45 Colt wurde 1873 von der Firma Colt für den Colt S.A.-Revolver "Army" entwickelt, weitere Revolver folgten. Die Treibladung für die Armee bestand aus 1,8 g Schwarzpulver bei einem Bleigeschoß von 15 g. Für zivile Zwecke hatten die Patronen 0,7 g Schwarzpulver mehr Treibladung. Die Patronen wurden in vielen Varianten von verschiedenen Firmen hergestellt.

Bodenstempel:
U S C Co .45 COLT,
U.M.C. .45 COLT,
REM–UMC .45 COLT,
DC 44 .45 COLT,
DOMINION .45 COLT,
W.R.A.Co. .45 COLT,
D.C.Co. .45 COLT,
ELEY . LONDON .,
ohne

Technical and Ballistic Data

Bullet dia.	.440" – .457"
Case dia. neck:	.466" – .480"
head:	.472" – .483"
rim:	.499" – .524"
Case length:	1.250" – 1.299"
Case material:	brass, nickeled brass, copper, plastic
Powder type:	black, semi-smokeless, smokeless
Primer type:	Boxer, Benet cup
Cartridge length:	1.567" – 1.644"
V_0	870 ft. per sec.
E_0	419.3 ft. pounds
Barrel length:	6.000"

The cartridge caliber .45 Colt was developed in 1873 by the Colt Company for the Colt S.A. Revolver "Army", other revolvers followed. The propellant for the "Army" consisted of 1.8 grams black powder with a lead bullet of 15 grams. For civil purposes these cartridges had a by 0.7 grams stronger black powder load. Many firms manufactured the cartridges in numerous variations.

Headstamps:
U S C Co .45 COLT
U.M.C. .45 COLT,
REM-UMC .45 COLT,
DC 44 .45 COLT,
DOMINION .45 COLT,
W.R.A.Co. .45 COLT,
D.C.Co. .45 COLT,
ELEY . LONDON .,
without headstamp

.45 Colt Government

Synonyme/Synonyms:
.45 Colt Gov't. (.45 S. & W.)

431

Geschoß/Bullet Ausführg. Pattern	Gewicht (g)	Weight (gr.)	Katalog Catalog No.
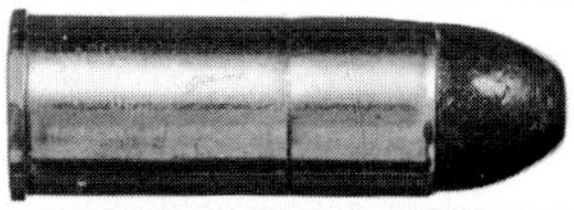 1 G	16,20	250.00	**431-1**
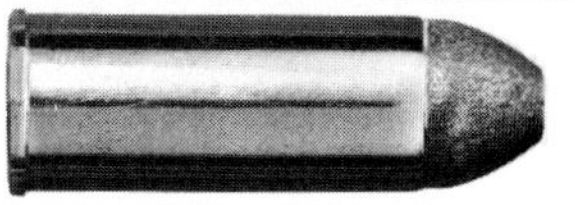 1 G	16,20	250.00	**431-2**

Technische und ballistische Daten

Geschoß-⌀:	11,45–11,61 mm
Hülsen-⌀ Hals:	12,06–12,17 mm
Boden:	12,06–12,19 mm
Rand:	12,78–12,90 mm
Hülsenlänge:	27,74–28,10 mm
Hülsenmaterial:	Messing
Pulverart:	Schwarz, rauchschwach, rauchlos
Zündungsart:	Boxer
Patronenlänge:	36,28–36,90 mm
V_0	235 m/sec
E_0	456 J
Lauflänge:	190 mm

Technical and Ballistic Data

Bullet dia.	.451"– .457"
Case dia. neck:	.475"– .479"
head:	.475"– .480"
rim:	.503"– .508"
Case length:	1.092"–1.106"
Case material:	brass
Powder type:	black, semi-smokeless,smokeless
Primer type:	Boxer
Cartridge length:	1.428"–1.453"
v_0	770 ft. per sec.
E_0	329.7 ft. pounds
Barrel length:	7.500"

Bei der Patrone Kaliber .45 Colt Government handelt es sich um die Armeeausführung der Patrone Kaliber .45 S&W Schofield (Katalog Nr. 438). Sie wurde 1874/75 in den USA entwickelt und wurde bei Frankford Arsenal bis ca. 1892 hergestellt.

Bodenstempel:
R F 2 83,
L F 5 87,
F 5 87,
F 11 91,
ohne

The cartridge caliber .45 Colt Government is the Army version of the cartridge caliber .45 S&W Schofield (catalog No. 438). It was developed in the USA in 1874/75 and manufactured by Frankford Arsenal until about 1892.

Headstamps:
R F 2 83,
L F 5 87,
F 5 87,
F 11 91,
without headstamp

.45 Colt M.1906

Synonyme/Synonyms:

.45 Revolver M.1906
.45 U.S. Gov't., M.1906
.45 U.S. Gov't. Revolver M.1906

432

	Geschoß/Bullet Ausführg. Pattern	Gewicht (g)	Weight (gr.)	Katalog Catalog No.
	21 B	14,90	230.00	**432-1**

Technische und ballistische Daten

Geschoß-∅:	11,38 - 11,45 mm
Hülsen-∅ Hals:	11,89 - 12,01 mm
Boden:	11,89 - 12,01 mm
Rand:	13,33 - 13,44 mm
Hülsenlänge:	23,24 - 23,49 mm
Hülsenmaterial:	Messing
Pulverart:	rauchlos
Zündungsart:	Boxer
Patronenlänge:	32,88 - 32,99 mm
V_0	245 m/sec
E_0	456 J
Lauflänge:	127 mm

Die Patrone Kaliber .45 Colt M.1906 gehört zu den 2 Arten der Versuchspatronen, die aus einem Auftrag der US-Regierung bei Frankford Arsenal entstanden, und ausschließlich dort hergestellt worden sind. Außer diesem Kaliber wurde eine randlose Pistolenpatrone entwickelt (vergl. Katalog Nr. 427). Sie fand keine Verbreitung, da mit der Entstehung der Patrone Kaliber .45 Colt M.1909 (Katalog Nr. 433) diese Patrone uninteressant wurde. Als Testwaffen dienten Colt-Revolver D.A.

Bodenstempel:
F A 4 06

Technical and Ballistic Data

Bullet dia.	.448" - .451"
Case dia. neck:	.468" - .473"
head:	.468" - .473"
rim:	.525" - .529"
Case length:	.915" - .925"
Case material:	brass
Powder type:	smokeless
Primer type:	Boxer
Cartridge length:	1.294" - 1.299"
V_0	804 ft. per sec.
E_0	329.7 ft. pounds
Barrel length:	5.000"

The cartridge caliber .45 Colt M 1906 pertains to the 2 types of experimental cartridges which developed out of an order of the US-Government to Frankford Arsenal and they were manufactured exclusively there. Apart from this caliber a rimless pistol cartridge was designed (compare catalog No. 427). It did not become popular, because the cartridge caliber .45 Colt M 1909 (catalog No. 433) rendered it uninteresting. Test weapons used were Colt Double Action revolvers.

Headstamp:
F A 4 06

.45 Colt M. 1909

Synonyme/Synonyms:

.45 Colt, U.S. Government Model 1909

433

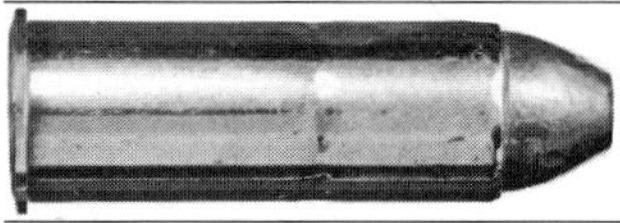

Geschoß/Bullet Ausführg. Pattern	Gewicht (g)	Weight (gr.)	Katalog Catalog No.
1 G	16,20	250.00	**433–1**
1 A			**433–2**

Technische und ballistische Daten

Geschoß-∅:	11,27–11,30 mm
Hülsen-∅ Hals:	12,06–12,15 mm
Boden:	12,06–12,20 mm
Rand:	13,61–13,72 mm
Hülsenlänge:	32,23–32,64 mm
Hülsenmaterial:	Messing
Pulverart:	rauchlos
Zündungsart:	Boxer
Patronenlänge:	40,11–40,13 mm
V_0	225 m/sec
E_0	418 J
Lauflänge:	140 mm

Die Patrone Kaliber .45 Colt M.1909 wurde im Jahre 1909 für einen neuen Dienstrevolver D.A. geschaffen, da sich in den Jahren zwischen 1899 – 1905/06 herausstellte, daß die bisherigen Kaliber zu schwach waren. Obwohl sie der Patrone Kaliber .45 Colt Government sehr ähnlich sieht, hat sie doch andere Abmessungen als diese. Insbesondere ist dies an der Hülsenlänge, der Patronenlänge und am Randdurchmesser erkennbar. Aus wirtschaftlichen Gründen wurde die Patrone nach dem Übungsschießen häufig wiedergeladen. Erste Kurzwaffe war ein Colt-Revolver Army Modell 1909. Die Munition wurde nur bei Frankford Arsenal zwischen 1909 und 1915 hergestellt.

Bodenstempel:
F A 11 09,
F A 6 10,
F A 2 11,

Technical and Ballistic Data

Bullet dia.	.444″ – .445″
Case dia. neck:	.475″ – .478″
head:	.475″ – .480″
rim:	.536″ – .540″
Case length:	1.269″ – 1.285″
Case material:	brass
Powder type:	smokeless
Primer type:	Boxer
Cartridge length:	1.579″ – 1.580″
V_0	728 ft. per sec.
E_0	302.3 ft. pounds
Barrel length:	5.500″

The cartridge caliber .45 Colt M. 1909 was designed in 1909 for a new double action service revolver because it was found in the years between 1899 – 1905/06 that the previous calibers had been too low-powered. Although resembling very much the cartridge .45 Colt Government its measurements differ from those of that cartridge which is identifiable by comparison of the case length, the cartridge length and the rim diameter. The cartridge was frequently reloaded after practice shooting for economic reasons. The first handgun was a Colt Revolver Army Model 1909. The ammunition was manufactured at Frankford Arsenal's between 1909 and 1915.

Headstamps:
F A 11 09,
F A 6 10,
F A 2 11,

.45 Enfield

Synonyme/Synonyms:

.45 Enfield Revolver

434

	Geschoß/Bullet			Katalog Catalog No.
	Ausführg. Pattern	Gewicht (g)	Weight (gr.)	
	1 G	17,17	265.00	**434–1**

Technische und ballistische Daten

Geschoß-∅:	11,35–11,37 mm
Hülsen-∅ Hals:	12,10 mm
Boden:	12,15 mm
Rand:	13,50 mm
Hülsenlänge:	21,75–21,80 mm
Hülsenmaterial:	Messing
Pulverart:	Schwarz
Zündungsart:	Boxer
Patronenlänge:	30,82 mm

Die Patrone Kaliber .45 Enfield kann als Variante zu den Patronen Kaliber .455 Webley Mk.I und .455 Enfield Mk.I und II angesehen werden, war jedoch für einen eigenen Revolver bestimmt (vergleiche Katalog Nr. 457, 458 und 460). Sie weicht in der Hülsenlänge und im Geschoßgewicht von der vergleichbaren Patrone Kaliber .455 Colt geringfügig ab (vergl. Katalog Nr. 456–5) und muß als eigenes Kaliber behandelt werden. Als Unterschiedsmerkmal kann äußerlich der Bodenstempel angesehen werden.

Bodenstempel:
D.C.Co. 45. ENFIELD

Technical and Ballistic Data

Bullet dia.	.447″ – .448″
Case dia. neck:	.476″
head:	.478″
rim:	.531″
Case length:	.856″ – .858″
Case material:	brass
Powder type:	black
Primer type:	Boxer
Cartridge length:	1.213″

The cartridge caliber .45 Enfield may be considered as a variation of the cartridges caliber .455 Webley Mk.I and .455 Enfield Mk.I and II, however, it was intended for a particular revolver (compare catalog Nos 457, 458 and 460). Its case length and bullet weight slightly differ from these dimensions of the comparable cartridge caliber .455 Colt (compare catalog No. 456–5) and has to be treated as a caliber of its own. As an outer distinguishing mark can be considered its headstamp.

Headstamp:
D.C.Co. 45. ENFIELD

45 M.P.

Synonyme/Synonyms:

.45 Mauser Pistol
.45-25-225

435

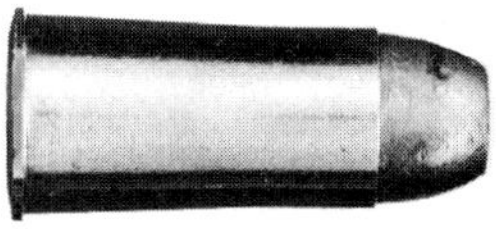

Geschoß/Bullet Ausführg. Pattern	Gewicht (g)	Weight (gr.)	Katalog Catalog No.
1 G	14,55 – 14,63	224.50–225.80	**435-1**

Technische und ballistische Daten

Geschoß-∅:	11,40–11,43 mm
Hülsen-∅ Hals:	12,09–12,14 mm
Boden:	13,31–13,33 mm
Rand:	14,60–14,65 mm
Hülsenlänge:	24,48–24,59 mm
Hülsenmaterial:	Messing
Pulverart:	Schwarz
Zündungsart:	Boxer
Patronenlänge:	31,90–32,10 mm

Die Herkunft dieser Patrone ist unbekannt, wird jedoch England zugeschrieben. Dem Schachteletikett ist lediglich die Bezeichnung .45 M.P. (ohne weiteren Hinweis) zu entnehmen. Aus der Schachtelaufschrift werden 2 Deutungen abgeleitet, a) Metropolitan Police und b) Mauser Pistole. Keine dieser Deutungen ist jedoch belegt. Der Ursprung dieser Patrone dürfte in der Patrone Kaliber .450 Rifle Nr. 1 zu suchen sein, deren Hülse gekürzt worden ist. (Firmen-Katalog Eley 1898). Eine Mauser-Pistole in diesem Kaliber ist nicht bekannt.

Bodenstempel:
ELEY . LONDON .

Technical and Ballistic Data

Bullet dia.	.449″ – .450″
Case dia. neck:	.476″ – .478″
head:	.524″ – .525″
rim:	.575″ – .577″
Case length:	.964″ – .968″
Case material:	brass
Powder type:	black
Primer type:	Boxer
Cartridge length:	1.256″ – 1.264″

The origin of this cartridge is unknown, however, it is attributed to England. The designation on the box lable just reads .45 M.P. (without any further hint). Two meanings might be derived from this inscription: a/ Metropolitan Police and b/ Mauser Pistol, however, neither of them has been proved so far. This cartridge probably originates from the cartridge caliber .450 Rifle No. 1, whose case has been shortened. (Company Catalog Eley 1898 refers). A Mauser pistol in this caliber is not known.

Headstamp:
ELEY . LONDON .

.45 Remington

Synonyme/Synonyms:

.45 Remington Rolling Block
.45 Remington SS Pistol
.45–50 Remington

436

Geschoß/Bullet Ausführg. Pattern	Gewicht (g)	Weight (gr.)	Katalog Catalog No.
1 G			**436–1**

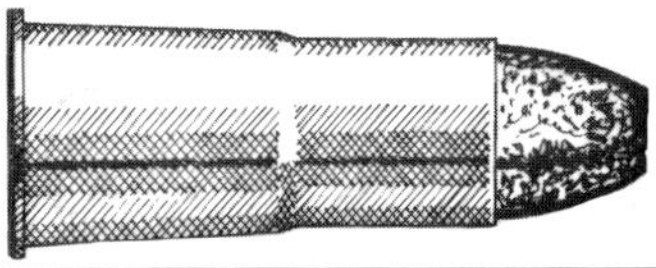

Technische und ballistische Daten

Geschoß-Ø:	11,15–11,38 mm
Hülsen-Ø Hals:	12,32–12,40 mm
Boden:	14,12–14,73 mm
Rand:	16,74–16,89 mm
Hülsenlänge:	30,48–31,57 mm
Hülsenmaterial:	Messing
Pulverart:	Schwarz
Zündungsart:	unbekannt
Patronenlänge:	41,27–41,66 mm

Der Ursprung der Patrone Kaliber .45 Remington ist nicht eindeutig festzulegen. Patrone und Waffen (eine Remington Pistole mit Blockverschluß) wurden auf der internationalen Ausstellung 1873 in Wien gezeigt. In dem Werk „Remington-Handguns 1960 – 4. Ausgabe" von Charles Lee Karr jr. und Caroll Robbins Karr sind zwei Einzelladepistolen der Firma Remington abgebildet, die für eine kurze Zentralfeuerpatrone mit Flaschenhals eingerichtet sein sollen. Es ist nicht auszuschließen, daß es sich bei der Patrone um eine gekürzte und am Hals eingezogene Langwaffenpatrone Kaliber .50 gehandelt hat.

Bodenstempel:
nicht bekannt,

Technical and Ballistic Data

Bullet dia.	.439" – .448"
Case dia. neck:	.485" – .488"
head:	.556" – .580"
rim:	.659" – .665"
Case length:	1.200" – 1.243"
Case material:	brass
Powder type:	black
Primer type:	unknown
Cartridge length:	1.625" – 1.640"

The origin of the cartridge caliber .45 Remington is not clearly determinable. Cartridge and weapon (a REMINGTON pistol with falling-block action) were shown at the international Exposition 1873 in Vienna. In the volume "Remington-Handguns 1960 – 4th Edition" by Charles Lee Karr jr. and Caroll Robbins Karr there are two single shot pistols of the Remington Company illustrated which are said to be chambered for a short center fire cartridge with bottleneck. It cannot be excluded that the cartridge is a shortened and necked down rifle cartridge caliber .50.

Headstamp:
not known

.45 Ross

Synonyme/Synonyms:
.45 Ross Automatic Pistol

437

Geschoß/Bullet Ausführg. Pattern	Gewicht (g)	Weight (gr.)	Katalog Catalog No.
21 B	16,20	250.00	**437–1**

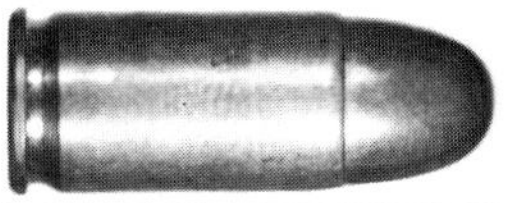

Technische und ballistische Daten

Geschoß-∅:	11,56–11,58 mm
Hülsen-∅ Hals:	12,19–12,32 mm
Boden:	12,47 mm
Rand:	12,88 mm
Hülsenlänge:	22,15–22,22 mm
Hülsenmaterial:	Messing
Pulverart:	rauchlos
Zündungsart:	Boxer
Patronenlänge:	32,33–33,02 mm

Die Patrone Kaliber .45 Ross soll nur in 50 Exemplaren existieren, die 1903 aufgetaucht sind. Es wird angenommen, daß die Patronen dazu dienen sollten, die Funktionseigenschaften des von Ch. Ross angemeldeten englischen Patents Nr. 21.668 vom 24.10.1905 zu erklären.

Bodenstempel:
nicht bekannt

Technical and Ballistic Data

Bullet dia.	.455″ – .456″
Case dia. neck:	.480″ – .485″
head:	.490″
rim:	.507″
Case length:	.872″ – .875″
Case material:	brass
Powder type:	smokeless
Primer type:	Boxer
Cartridge length:	1.273″ – 1.300″

The cartridge caliber .45 Ross reportedly exists in 50 specimens only which were discovered in 1903. It is supposed that these cartridges were to explain the functional caracteristics of British patent No. 21.668 filed by Ch. Ross on 24–10–1905.

Headstamp:
not known

.45 S&W Schofield

Synonyme/Synonyms:

.45 S. & W.
.45 S. & W. Army Revolver
.45 Smith & Wesson Schofield

438

	Geschoß/Bullet Ausführg. Pattern	Gewicht (g)	Weight (gr.)	Katalog Catalog No.
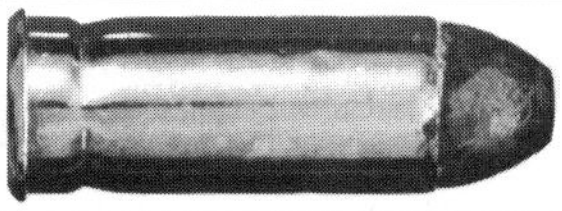	1 G	14,90	230.00	**438–1**
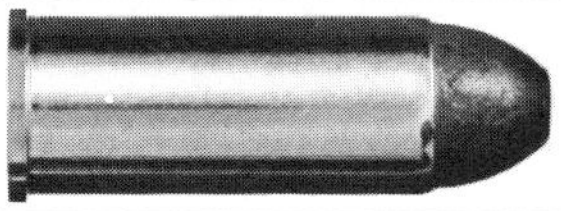	1 G	16,20 — 16,52	250.00 - 255.00	**438–2**
	70 G			**438–3**
	90 e	–	–	**438–4**

Technische und ballistische Daten

Geschoß-Ø:	11,23–11,40 mm
Hülsen-Ø Hals:	12,12–12,15 mm
Boden:	12,17–12,20 mm
Rand:	13,00–13,33 mm
Hülsenlänge:	28,20–28,45 mm
Hülsenmaterial:	Messing, Messing verzinnt, Kupfer
Pulverart:	Schwarz, rauchschwach, rauchlos
Zündungsart:	Boxer, Benet
Patronenlänge:	36,17–36,28 mm
V_0	235 m/sec
E_0	456 J
Lauflänge:	178 mm

Die Patrone Kaliber .45 S&W Schofield wurde ursprünglich (bis 1874) von Frankford Arsenal mit Benet-Zündung hergestellt. (Vergl. Abb. 36). Ab 1875 bekam die Patrone Boxerzündung. Sie war für den S&W-Revolver Nr. 3 Schofield's Patent bestimmt, weitere Revolver folgten. (Vergl. Katalog Nr. 431)

Bodenstempel:
ohne und
REM–UMC 45 S&W,

Technical and Ballistic Data

Bullet dia.	.442'' - .449''
Case dia. neck:	.477'' - .478''
head:	.479'' - .480''
rim:	.512'' - .525''
Case length:	1.110'' - 1.120''
Case material:	brass, tinned brass, copper
Powder type:	black, semi-smokeless, smokeless
Primer type:	Boxer, Benet cup
Cartridge length:	1.424'' - 1.428''
V_0	770 ft. per sec.
E_0	329.7 ft. pounds
Barrel length:	7.000''

The cartridge caliber .45 S&W Schofield was originally (until 1874) manufactured by Frankford Arsenal with Benet primer (compare ill.36). From 1875 onward the cartridge was provided with a Boxer primer. It was destined for S&W Revolver No. 3 Schofield's Patent, other revolvers followed (compare catalog No. 431).

Headstamps:
without and
REM–UMC 45 S&W

.45 Target

Synonyme/Synonyms:
.45 Speer Target
.45/44 Speer Target

438 A

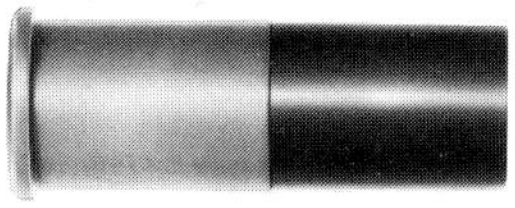

Geschoß/Bullet Ausführg. Pattern	Gewicht (g)	Weight (gr.)	Katalog Catalog No.
51 Q	1,38 – 1,48	21.30 – 22.84	**438A-1**

Technische und ballistische Daten

Geschoß-∅:	11,25–11,35 mm
Hülsen-∅ Hals:	11,55–11,60 mm
Boden:	11,55–11,60 mm
Rand:	12,98–13,00 mm
Hülsenlänge:	17,55 mm
Hülsenmaterial:	Kunststoff
Pulverart:	ohne
Zündungsart:	Boxer
Patronenlänge:	33,20 mm

Die Patrone Kaliber .45 Target ist neben der Patrone Kaliber .44 Target das größte Kaliber in dieser Serie (vergl. Katalog Nr. 371 und 416). Die Firma Speer USA hat für dieses Kaliber die Hülse der Patrone .44 Target vorgesehen, jedoch ein Geschoß im Kaliber .45. Die Komponenten (Hülse, Geschoß und Zündung – ohne Treibladung) werden vor der Benutzung zusammengestellt.

Bodenstempel:
SPEER .44 ,

Technical and Ballistic Data

Bullet dia.	.443″ – .447″
Case dia. neck:	.455″ – .457″
head:	.455″ – .457″
rim:	.511″ – .512″
Case length:	.691″
Case material:	plastic
Powder type:	without
Primer type:	Boxer
Cartridge length:	1.307″

Besides the cartridge caliber .44 Target this round caliber .45 Target is the biggest caliber of the series (compare catalog Nos. 371 and 416). The Company SPEER/USA has provided for this caliber the case of the cartridge caliber .44 Target, however, a bullet in caliber .45. The components (case, bullet and primer – without propellant) are put together before firing the shot.

Headstamp:
SPEER .44,

.45 Webley

Synonyme/Synonyms:
.45 Webley Revolver

439

	Geschoß/Bullet Ausführg. Pattern	Gewicht (g)	Weight (gr.)	Katalog Catalog No.
	1 B	14,90	230.00	**439-1**
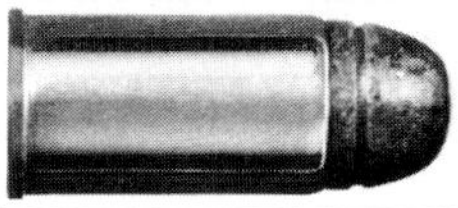	1 B	14,90	230.00	**439-2**

Technische und ballistische Daten

Geschoß-∅:	11,25–11,86 mm
Hülsen-∅ Hals:	11,81–12,14 mm
Boden:	11,99–12,19 mm
Rand:	12,70–12,98 mm
Hülsenlänge:	20,57–21,34 mm
Hülsenmaterial:	Messing
Pulverart:	Schwarz, rauchschwach
Zündungsart:	Boxer
Patroenlänge:	29,05–29,63 mm

Die Patrone Kaliber .45 Webley ist als USA-Herstellung aus der aus England stammenden Patrone Kaliber .450 short C.F. entstanden (vergl. Katalog Nr. 454). Sie war für die gleichen Revolverarten gedacht und wurde in den USA bis ca. 1939 von verschiedenen Firmen hergestellt. Die Firma Winchester hatte sie 1875 in ihrem Katalog.

Bodenstempel:
W.R.A.Co. 45 WEB (W im Zündhütchen),
REM-UMC 45 WEB,

Technical and Ballistic Data

Bullet dia.	.443" – .467"
Case dia. neck:	.465" – .478"
head:	.472" – .480"
rim:	.500" – .511"
Case length:	.810" – .840"
Case material:	brass
Powder type:	black, semi-smokeless
Primer type:	Boxer
Cartridge length:	1.144" – 1.166"

The American version of the cartridge caliber .45 Webley resulted from the cartridge caliber .450 short C.F. originating from England (compare catalog No. 454). It was intended for the same revolver brands and manufactured in the USA by various companies until about 1939. The Winchester Companie had it in their catalog in 1875.

Headstamps:
W.R.A.Co. 45 WEB (W in primer)
REM-UMC 45 WEB,

.45 Winchester Magnum

Synonyme/Synonyms:
.45 Magnum

440

Geschoß/Bullet Ausführg. Pattern	Gewicht (g)	Weight (gr.)	Katalog Catalog No.
21 B	14,90	230.00	**440–1**

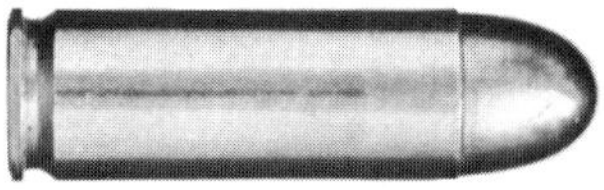

Technische und ballistische Daten

Geschoß-∅:	11,40 mm
Hülsen-∅ Hals:	11,95–11,98 mm
Boden:	11,95 mm
Rand:	12,00 mm
Hülsenlänge:	30,25–30,42 mm
Hülsenmaterial:	Messing
Pulverart:	rauchlos
Zündungsart:	Boxer
Patronenlänge:	40,01 mm
V_0	427 m/sec
E_0	1385 J
Lauflänge:	127 mm

Die Patrone Kaliber .45 Winchester Magnum wurde 1979 in den USA für eine Selbstladepistole Wildey (Firma Firearms Company, Colt Spring N.Y.) hergestellt. Die Patrone ist das derzeit zweitstärkste Pistolenkaliber neben der Patrone Kaliber .44 Auto Magnum in der Inch-Reihe (vergl. Katalog Nr. 400). Das Geschoß bringt eine ca. 72% höhere Geschwindigkeit im Verhältnis zur Patrone Kaliber .45 Automatic Colt (Katalog Nr. 426). Gleichzeitig wurde im Kaliber 9 mm Winchester Magnum für eine gleiche Waffe, eine neue starke 9 mm Patrone geschaffen (vergl. Nachtrag zu Band 1). Erstmalig sind beide Patronen im Firmenkatalog Winchester 1979 enthalten.

Bodenstempel:
W – W SUPER 45 WIN MAG

Technical and Ballistic Data

Bullet dia.	.435″
Case dia. neck:	.471″ – .472″
head:	.471″
rim:	.473″
Case length:	1.192″ – 1.19
Case material:	brass
Powder type:	smokeless
Primer type:	Boxer
Cartridge length:	1.575″
V_0	1400 ft. per sek.
E_0	1001 ft. – lbs.
Barrel length:	5.00″

The cartridge caliber .45 Winchester Magnum was manufactured in 1979 in the USA for the self-loading pistol WILDEY (Wildey Firearms Company, Cold Spring N.Y.). At the present time, this cartridge represents the second-heaviest pistol caliber of the inch series besides the cartridge caliber .44 Auto Magnum (compare catalog No. 400). The bullet achieves an about 72% higher velocity in comparison to the cartridge caliber .45 Automatic Colt (catalog No. 426). At the same time, there was designed in the caliber 9 mm Winchester Magnum (for an analogous weapon) a new, potent 9 mm cartridge (compare Appendix to Volume I). The two cartridges were listed the first time in the 1979 Winchester Company Catalog.

Headstamp:
W – W SUPER 45 WIN MAG

.45/38 Salvo Squeeze Bore

Synonyme/Synonyms:

.45 ACP Salvo squeeze bore
.45 ACP SSB
.45 SSB
.45/38 SSB

440 A

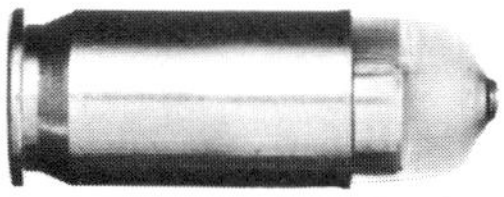

Geschoß/Bullet Ausführg. Pattern	Gewicht (g)	Weight (gr.)	Katalog Catalog No.
70 J	3,55 10,65 gesamt	54.78 164.35 entire	**440A-1**

Technische und ballistische Daten

Geschoß-∅: •	11,43 mm*) 10,40 mm**) 9,65 mm***)
Hülsen-∅ Hals:	12,00–12,05 mm
Boden:	12,00–12,02 mm
Rand:	12,10–12,12 mm
Hülsenlänge:	22,45–22,80 mm
Hülsenmaterial:	Messing vernickelt
Pulverart:	rauchlos
Zündungsart:	Boxer
Patronenlänge:	32,25–33,75 mm
V_0	1. Geschoß: 340 m/sek 2. Geschoß: 320 m/sek 3. Geschoß: 315 m/sek
E_0	1. Geschoß: 205 J 2. Geschoß: 182 J 3. Geschoß: 178 J

*) mit Kunststoffhülle
**) ohne Kunststoffhülle (vor d. Schuß)
***) nach dem Schuß

siehe Sonderpatronen

Technical and Ballistic Data

Bullet dia.	.450''*) .409''**) .380''***)
Case dia. neck:	.473''–.475''
head:	.473''–.474''
rim:	.477''–.478''
Case length:	.885''–.898''
Case material:	nickeled brass
Powder type:	smokeless
Primer type:	Boxer
Cartridge length:	1.271''–1.330''
V_0	1st bullet: 1115 ft/sec 2nd bullet: 1050 ft/sec 3rd bullet: 1033 ft/sec
E_0	1st bullet: 148,2 ft/pds 2nd bullet: 131,6 ft/pds 3rd bullet: 128,7 ft/pds

*) with plastic
**) without plastic (before firing)
***) after firing

see special cartridges

.450 Adams Mk.I

Synonyme/Synonyms:
.450 Adams Revolver Mk.I

441

Geschoß/Bullet				
	Ausführg. Pattern	Gewicht (g)	Weight (gr.)	Katalog Catalog No.
	1 G	14,58	225.00	**441-1**

Technische und ballistische Daten

Geschoß-⌀:	11,48 - 11,63 mm
Hülsen-⌀ Hals:	12,14 - 12,19 mm
Boden:	12,09 - 12,19 mm
Rand:	12,80 - 12,98 mm
Hülsenlänge:	17,98 - 18,46 mm
Hülsenmaterial:	Messinghülse mit Stahlboden
Pulverart:	Schwarz
Zündungsart:	Topf
Patronenlänge:	29,23 mm
V_0	198 m/sec
E_0	291 J
Lauflänge:	152 mm

Technical and Ballistic Data

Bullet dia.	.452″ - .458″
Case dia. neck:	.478″ - .480″
head:	.476″ - .480″
rim:	.504″ - .511″
Case length:	.708″ - .727″
Case material:	brass tube with steel base
Powder type:	black
Primer type:	battery cup
Cartridge length:	1.151″
V_0	650 ft. pe sec.
E_0	210.6 ft. pounds
Barrel length:	6.000″

Die Patrone Kaliber .450 Adams Mk.I ist die älteste und erste Patrone diese Serie, die ihren Ursprung in England hat. Sie war für den Adams-Armeerevolver bestimmt und wurde 1868 eingeführt. Diese erste Patrone hat eine Messinghülse mit Eisenboden und ist ausschließlich mit Schwarzpulver geladen (vergl. Katalog Nr. 442 und 443).

Ohne Bodenstempel:

The cartridge caliber .450 Adams Mk.I is the oldest and first cartridge of this series having its origin in England. It was intended for the Adams Army Revolver and was adopted in 1868. This first round had a brass case with a steel head and is exclusively loaded with black powder (compare catalog Nos.442 and 443).

without headstamp:

.450 Adams Mk.II

Synonyme/Synonyms:
.450 Adams Revolver Mk.II

442

	Geschoß/Bullet Ausführg. Pattern	Gewicht (g)	Weight (gr.)	Katalog Catalog No.
	1 B	14,58	225.00	**442-1**
	1 B	14,58	225.00	**442-2**

Technische und ballistische Daten

Geschoß-∅:	11,45-11,50 mm
Hülsen-∅ Hals:	12,05 mm
Boden:	12,10-12,15 mm
Rand:	12,70-12,75 mm
Hülsenlänge:	16,90-17,00 mm
Hülsenmaterial:	Messing
Pulverart:	Schwarz
Zündungsart:	Topf
Patronenlänge:	27,85 - 29,23 mm
V_0	198 m/sec
E_0	291 J
Lauflänge:	152 mm

Technical and Ballistic Data

Bullet dia.	.451"-.453"
Case dia. neck:	.474"
head:	.476"-.478"
rim:	.500"-.502"
Case length:	.665"-.669"
Case material:	brass
Powder type:	black
Primer type:	battery cup
Cartridge length:	1.096" - 1.151"
V_0	650 ft. per sec.
E_0	210.6 ft. pounds
Barrel length:	6.000"

Die Patrone Kaliber .450 Adams Mark II ist der Nachfolger der Patrone Mk.I und damit die zweite Patrone dieser Serie (vergl. Katalog Nr. 441 und 443). 1877 wurde die Patrone dergestalt verbessert, indem man den Eisenboden durch einen Messingboden ersetzte. Sie ist wie die Mk.I Patrone mit Schwarzpulver geladen und hat die gleiche Geschoßart. Außer ihrer militärischen Verwendung war sie später im freien Handel erhältlich.

Bodenstempel:
ELEY BROS,
ELEY BROS),

The cartridge caliber .450 Adams Mark II is the successor of the cartridge Mk.I and consequently the second round of this series (compare catalog Nos. 441 and 443). In 1877 the cartridge was improved inasmuch as the steel head was replaced by a brass head. Just like the Mk.I cartridge it has a black powder charge and the same bullet type. Apart from its military use it was later commercialized for everybody to purchase it.

Headstamps:
ELEY BROS,
ELEY BROS),

.450 Adams Mk.III

Synonyme/Synonyms:
.450 Adams Revolver Mk.III

443

	Geschoß/Bullet Ausführg. Pattern	Gewicht (g)	Weight (gr.)	Katalog Catalog No.
	1 B	14,58	225.00	**443–1**

Technische und ballistische Daten

Geschoß-∅:	11,30–11,32 mm
Hülsen-∅ Hals:	12,10–12,14 mm
Boden:	12,10–12,12 mm
Rand:	12,78–12,82 mm
Hülsenlänge:	17,35–17,40 mm
Hülsenmaterial:	Messing
Pulverart:	rauchlos
Zündungsart:	Berdan
Patronenlänge:	27,10 mm
V_0	220 m/sec
E_0	360 J
Lauflänge:	152 mm

Technical and Ballistic Data

Bullet dia.	.445″–.446″
Case dia. neck:	.476″–.478″
head:	.476″–.477″
rim:	.503″–.505″
Case length:	.683″–.685″
Case material:	brass
Powder type:	smokeless
Primer type:	Berdan
Cartridge length:	1.067″
V_0	722 ft. per sec.
E_0	260.3 ft. pounds
Barrel length:	6.000″

Die Patrone Kaliber .450 Adams Mk.III ist die dritte Patrone in dieser Patronenreihe (vergl. Katalog Nr. 441 und 442). Sie unterscheidet sich insbesondere von der Patrone Kaliber Mk.II durch eine einteilige Messinghülse, Berdanzündung und rauchlosem Pulver als Treibladung. Neben ihrem Ursprungsland wurde sie auch von US-Firmen bis ca. 1939 geladen. Am Anfang des 1. Weltkrieges wurden in England infolge Waffenmangels alte Adamsrevolver mit dieser Patrone benutzt. Aus dieser Patrone ist letztlich die Kaliberart .450 short C.F. entstanden (Vergl. Katalog Nr. 451).

Bodenstempel:
ELEY ⩚ 450.

The cartridge caliber .450 Adams Mk.III is the third cartridge of this series (compare catalog Nos. 441 and 442). It differs particularly from the cartridge caliber .450 Mk.II by its one-piece brass case, Berdan primer and semi-smokeless powder as a propellant. Apart from its country of origin it was also loaded by US firms until about 1939. At the beginning of World War I old Adams revolvers firing this cartridge were employed in England, due to a lack of weapons. Out of this cartridge developed finally the caliber .450 short C.F. (compare catalog No. 454).

Headstamp:
ELEY ⩚ 450.

.450 Long C.F. (50/64'' case)

Synonyme/Synonyms:

.450 Long (Rifle)
.450-18-225 Long

444

Geschoß/Bullet Ausführg. Pattern	Gewicht (g)	Weight (gr.)	Katalog Catalog No.
1 B	14,58	225.00	**444-1**

Technische und ballistische Daten

Geschoß-Ø:	11,45 mm
Hülsen-Ø Hals:	11,80-11,90 mm
Boden:	12,15-12,20 mm
Rand:	13,00 mm
Hülsenlänge:	19,90-19,95 mm
Hülsenmaterial:	Messing
Pulverart:	Schwarz
Zündungsart:	Topf
Patronenlänge:	30,80 mm

Die Patrone Kaliber .450 long C.F. (50/64" Case) wird in alten Firmenkatalogen wie Eley 1898 und Nobel 1925 noch als ausschließliche Gewehrpatrone geführt. Als in Europa später Revolver für dieses Kaliber angeboten wurden, wurde sie als „Spezial-Revolverpatrone" angeboten. Die Patrone kann in die Reihe der nachfolgenden Kaliber (Katalog Nr. 445-448) eingefügt werden.

Bodenstempel:
450 und
ohne

Technical and Ballistic Data

Bullet dia.	.451"
Case dia. neck:	,464"-.468"
head:	.478"-.480"
rim:	.512"
Case length:	.783"-.785"
Case material:	brass
Powder type:	black
Primer type:	battery cup
Cartridge length:	1.212"

The cartridge caliber .450 long C.F. (50/64" case) is listed in old company catalogs such as Eley 1898 and Nobel 1925 exclusively as a rifle cartridge. When later in Europe revolvers for this caliber were offered it was designated as a "Special Revolver Cartridge". The cartridge can be classified in the series of the calibers that follow (catalog Nos. 445 - 448).

Headstamp:
450 and
without headstamp

.450 Long C.F. (55/64" case)

Synonyme/Synonyms:
.450 Long Revolver

445

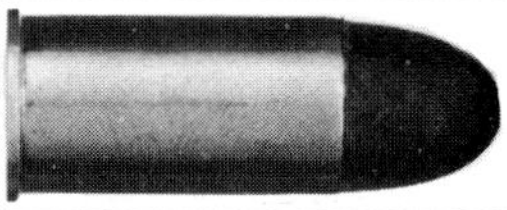

Geschoß/Bullet Ausführg. Pattern	Gewicht (g)	Weight (gr.)	Katalog Catalog No.
1 B	14,58	225.00	**445-1**

Technische und ballistische Daten

Geschoß-∅:	11,52-11,60 mm
Hülsen-∅ Hals:	11,95-12,01 mm
Boden:	11,95-12,09 mm
Rand:	12,83-13,05 mm
Hülsenlänge:	21,87-22,20 mm
Hülsenmaterial: Messing	
Pulverart:	Schwarz
Zündungsart:	Berdan, Braun & Bloem
Patronenlänge:	33,00 mm

Die Patrone Kaliber .450 long C.F. (55/64" Case) hat ihren Ursprung in England und es dürfte sich bei der Hülse dieser Patrone um die gleiche wie bei der Patrone Kaliber .455 Webley Mark I handeln (vergl. Katalog Nr. 460). Sie wurde auch in Deutschland von der Firma Braun & Bloem gefertigt. Nach 1939 sind keine Patronen englischer Herstellung mehr bekanntgeworden. Weitere Varianten siehe Katalog Nr. 444, 446 - 448.

Bodenstempel:
BRAUN & BLOEM . 450 .,
ohne

Technical and Ballistic Data

Bullet dia.	.453"-.457"
Bullet dia. neck:	.470"-.473"
head:	.470"-.476"
rim:	.505"-.514"
Case length:	.861"-.874"
Case material: brass	
Powder type:	black
Primer type:	Berdan, Braun & Bloem
Cartridge length:	1.299"

The cartridge caliber .450 long C.F. (55/64" case) has its origin in England and the case of this cartridge is very probably the same as used for the cartridge caliber .455 Webley Mark I (compare catalog No. 460). It was also manufactured in Germany by the firm Braun & Bloem. After 1939 no cartridges of British make have become known.
As to other variations see catalog Nos. 444, 446 - 448.

Headstamp:
BRAUN & BLOEM . 450 .,
and without headstamp

.450 Long C.F. (60/64″ case)

Synonyme/Synonyms:

.450 Long (Revolver)

446

	Geschoß/Bullet Ausführg. Pattern	Gewicht (g)	Weight (gr.)	Katalog Catalog No.
	1 B	14,25	220.00	**446-1**
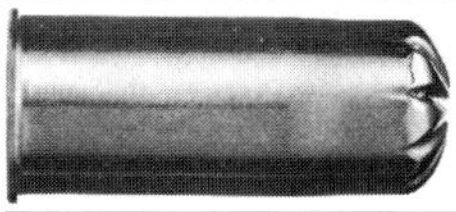	90 a	–	–	**446-2**

Technische und ballistische Daten

Geschoß-⌀:	11,43–11,45 mm
Hülsen-⌀ Hals:	11,88–11,95 mm
Boden:	12,02–12,05 mm
Rand:	12,90 mm
Hülsenlänge:	23,70–23,75 mm
Hülsenmaterial:	Messing
Pulverart:	Schwarz, rauchlos
Zündungsart:	Berdan, verdeckt
Patronenlänge:	35,35 mm

Die Patrone Kaliber .450 long C.F. (60/64″ Case) dürfte erstmalig um 1926 bei der italienischen Firma G. Fiocchi, Lecco hergestellt worden sein. Sie ist im Firmenkatalog 1926 dieser Firma enthalten. Die Patrone wurde auch von der deutschen Firma Braun & Bloem gefertigt. Sie ist für Revolver bestimmt und sollte als Variante zu den Patronen Katalog Nr. 444, 445, 447 und 448 angesehen werden.

Bodenstempel:
FIOCCHI 450 L,
BRAUN & BLOEM .450 .,

Technical and Ballistic Data

Bullet dia.	.450″–.451″
Case dia. neck:	.468″–.470″
head:	.473″–.474″
rim:	.508″
Case length:	.933″–.935″
Case material:	brass
Powder type:	black, smokeless
Primer type:	Berdan, inside
Cartridge length:	1.392″

The cartridge caliber .450 long C.F. (60/64″ case) was probably manufactured the first time about 1926 by the Italian company G. Fiocchi, Lecco. It was listed in this company's catalog of 1926. The cartridge was also produced by the German firm Braun & Bloem. It is intended for revolvers and should be considered as a variation of the cartridges listed under catalog Nos. 444, 445, 447 and 448.

Headstamps:
FIOCCHI 450 L,
BRAUN & BLOEM .450 .,

.450 Long C.F. (1–2/64″ case)

Synonyme/Synonyms:
.450 Long Revolver
11,1 × 26 – 450 lang

447

	Geschoß/Bullet Ausführg. Pattern	Gewicht (g)	Weight (gr.)	Katalog Catalog No.
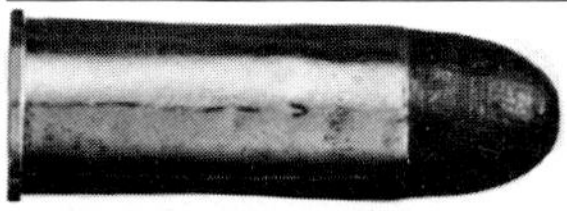	1 B			**447–1**
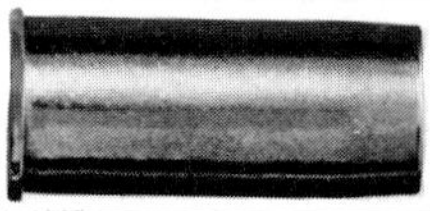	90 b	–	–	**447–2**

Technische und ballistische Daten

Geschoß-∅:	11,45 mm
Hülsen-∅ Hals:	11,95–12,00 mm
Boden:	11,95–12,00 mm
Rand:	12,83–13,10 mm
Hülsenlänge:	26,47–26,70 mm
Hülsenmaterial:	Messing
Pulverart:	Schwarz
Zündungsart:	Berdan, Braun & Bloem
Patronenlänge:	37,23 mm

Die Patrone Kaliber .450 long C.F. (1–2/64″ Case) wurde über den Firmenkatalog der deutschen Herstellerfirma Rheinisch-Westfälische Sprengstoff A.G. (RWS) von 1898 bekannt. Sie wurde auch von der Firma Braun & Bloem hergestellt. Die Patrone ist für Revolver bestimmt und kann als Variante zu den Patronen der Katalog Nr. 444 – 446 und 448 angesehen werden.

Bodenstempel:
R.W.S. .450.,
BRAUN & BLOEM .450.

Technical and Ballistic Data

Bullet dia.	.451″
Case dia. neck:	470″– .472″
head:	.470″– .472″
rim:	.505″– .516″
Case length:	1.042″–1.051″
Case material:	brass
Powder type:	black
Primer type:	Berdan, Braun & Bloem
Cartridge length:	1.466″

The cartridge caliber .450 long C.F. (1–2/64″ case) became known by its publication in the company catalog of the German firm Rheinisch-Westfälische Sprengstoff A.G. (RWS) of 1898. It was also manufactured by the firm Braun & Bloem. The cartridge is intended for revolvers and can be considered as a variation of the cartridges under catalog Nos. 444 – 446 and 448.

Headstamps:
R.W.S. .450.,
BRAUN & BLOEM .450.

.450 Long C.F. (1–19/64″ case)

Synonyme/Synonyms:

DWM 231
.450 Long Revolver
11,50 × 32,80 Kal. 450 lg.

448

Geschoß/Bullet Ausführg. Pattern	Gewicht (g)	Weight (gr.)	Katalog Catalog No.
1 B	14,58	225.00	**448–1**
1 B	14,06 – 14,25	217.00 – 220.00	**448–2**
1 B	12,00	185.00	**448–3**
21 B	14,25	220.00	**448–4**
90 a	–	–	**448–5**

Technische und ballistische Daten

Geschoß-∅:	11,02–11,48 mm
Hülsen-∅ Hals:	12,01–12,11 mm
Boden:	12,04–12,14 mm
Rand:	12,80–12,90 mm
Hülsenlänge:	32,13–32,80 mm
Hülsenmaterial:	Messing
Pulverart:	Schwarz, rauchlos
Zündungsart:	Berdan
Patronenlänge:	41,05–41,10 mm
V_0	220 m/sec*)
E_0	360 J*)

*) Schwarzpulver

Technical and Ballistic Data

Bullet dia.	.434″– .452″
Case dia. neck:	.473″– .477″
head:	.474″– .478″
rim:	.504″– .508″
Case length:	1.265″–1.291″
Case material:	brass
Powder type:	black, smokeless
Primer type:	Berdan
Cartridge length:	1.616″–1.618″
V_0	722 ft. per sec.*)
E_0	260.3 ft. pounds*)

*) black powder

Die Patrone Kaliber .450 long C.F. (1–19/64″ Case) wurde fast gleichzeitig in den deutschen und französischen Firmenkatalogen der Deutschen Waffen und Munitionsfabriken Karlsruhe (DWM) und Société Francaise des Munitions (SFM) bekanntgemacht. Weitere Hersteller sind nicht bekanntgeworden. Die Hülse könnte der der Patrone Kaliber .45 Colt entsprechen (vergl. Katalog Nr. 430). Es handelt sich um eine Revolverpatrone, die als Variante zu den Patronen der Katalog Nr. 444 – 447 angesehen werden kann.

Bodenstempel sind nicht bekannt.

The cartridge caliber .450 long C.F. (1 – 19/64″ case) was made public almost simultaneously in the German and French companies' catalogs of the Deutschen Waffen- und Munitionsfabriken (DWM) and the Société Française des Munitions (SFM). Other manufacturers have not become known. The case might correspond to that of the cartridge caliber .45 Colt (compare catalog No. 430). It is a revolver cartridge which can be considered as a variation of the cartridges of catalog Nos. 444 – 447.

Headstamps are not known.

.450 Mars (long case)

Synonyme/Synonyms:

.45 Gabbett-Fairfax
.450 Mars Long

449

Geschoß/Bullet Ausführg. Pattern	Gewicht (g)	Weight (gr.)	Katalog Catalog No.
21 B	14,00 – 14,38	216.00 – 222.00	**449-1**

Technische und ballistische Daten

Geschoß-∅:	11,40–11,43 mm
Hülsen-∅ Hals:	11,99–12,06 mm
Boden:	12,67–12,70 mm
Rand:	12,62–12,67 mm
Hülsenlänge:	27,60–27,69 mm
Hülsenmaterial:	Messing
Pulverart:	rauchlos
Zündungsart:	Berdan
Patronenlänge:	35,56–35,71 mm
V_0	365 m/sec
E_0	1507 J
Lauflänge:	222 mm

Bei diesem Kaliber handelt es sich um das größte und stärkste Kaliber der „Mars-Patronen“ innerhalb der Inch-Reihe. Weitere Kaliber: .360 Mars, .450 Mars short Case und .450 Mars Experimental I und II (vergl. Katalog Nr. 349 und 450 bis 452). Die Patronen wurden von dem Engländer H. W. Gabbett-Fairfax für eine Mars-Selbstladepistole in der Zeit von 1895 bis 1903 entwickelt. Das Kaliber .45 war insbesondere für militärische Zwecke gedacht. Die Produktion der Patronen blieb auf England beschränkt.

Keine Bodenstempel bekannt

Technical and Ballistic Data

Bullet dia.	.449″– .450″
Case dia. neck:	.472″– .475″
head:	.499″– .500″
rim:	.497″– .499″
Case length:	1.087″–1.090″
Case material:	brass
Powder type:	smokeless
Primer type:	Berdan
Cartridge length:	1.400″–1.406″
V_0	1197 ft. per sec.
E_0	1089.6 ft. pounds
Barrel length:	8.750″

This is the largest and heaviest caliber of the “Mars cartridges” within the inch series. Further calibers are: .360 Mars, .450 Mars short case and .450 Mars Experimental I and II (compare catalog Nos. 349 and 450 to 452). The cartridges were developed by the English citizen H. W. Gabbett-Fairfax for a Mars self-loading pistol between 1895 and 1903. The caliber .45 was above all intended for military purposes. The production of the cartridge remained limited to England.

No headstamps known

.450 Mars (short case)

Synonyme/Synonyms:

.45 Gabbett-Fairfax
.450 Mars Short

450

Geschoß/Bullet Ausführg. Pattern	Gewicht (g)	Weight (gr.)	Katalog Catalog No.
21 B	14,26	220.00	**450-1**

Technische und ballistische Daten

Geschoß-∅:	11,35–11,40 mm
Hülsen-∅ Hals:	12,04–12,10 mm
Boden:	12,47–12,67 mm
Rand:	12,57–12,65 mm
Hülsenlänge:	20,20–20,25 mm
Hülsenmaterial:	Messing
Pulverart:	rauchlos
Zündungsart:	Berdan
Patronenlänge:	27,90 mm
V_0	290 m/sec
E_0	611 J
Lauflänge:	222 mm

Technical and Ballistic Data

Bullet dia.	.447"–.449"
Case dia. neck:	.474"–.476"
head:	.491"–.499"
rim:	.495"–.498"
Case length:	.795"–.797"
Case material:	brass
Powder type:	smokeless
Primer type:	Berdan
Cartridge length:	1.098"
V_0	950 ft. per sec.
E_0	442.0 ft. pounds
Barrel length:	8.750"

Neben der Patrone Kaliber .450 Mars long Case das größte – jedoch nicht stärkste Kaliber der „Mars-Patronen" aus der Inch-Reihe. Weitere Kaliber: .360 Mars, .450 Mars long Case und .450 Mars Experimental I und II (vergl. Katalog Nr. 349, 449, 451 und 452). Entwickelt um 1895 in England von H. W. Gabbett-Fairfax für eine Selbstladepistole. Nachdem festgestellt war, daß die Waffe nicht den Bedingungen der englischen Kriegs-Prüfungskommission entsprach, kamen Waffe und Munition in den freien Handel, fanden jedoch kaum Verbreitung. Die Produktion der Patrone blieb auf England beschränkt und wurde nach kurzer Zeit eingestellt (Siehe Band I).

Kein Bodenstempel bekannt

Besides the cartridge caliber .450 long case this round is the largest, however, not the most potent caliber of the "Mars Cartridges" within the inch series. Further calibers are: .360 Mars long case and .450 Mars Experimental I and II (compare catalog No. 349, 449, 451 and 452). It was developed about 1895 in England by H. W. Gabbett-Fairfax for a self-loading pistol. When it had been established that the weapon did not come up to the standards as required by the British board of trial, gun and ammunition were made available for free sale, however, they achieved little commercial success. The production remained limited to England and was discontinued after a short period (see Volume I).

No headstamp known

.450 Mars Experimental I

Synonyme/Synonyme:

451

Geschoß/Bullet Ausführg. Pattern	Gewicht (g)	Weight (gr.)	Katalog Catalog No.
21 E	16,81 – 16,82	259.42 – 259.57	**451–1**

Technische und ballistische Daten

Geschoß-∅:	11,50 mm
Hülsen-∅ Hals:	12,00–12,10 mm
Boden:	12,90 mm
Rand:	12,80 mm
Hülsenlänge:	33,10 mm
Hülsenmaterial:	Messing
Pulverart:	rauchlos
Zündungsart:	Berdan
Patronenlänge:	45,25 mm

Versuchspatrone der „Mars-Serie" in der Inch-Reihe. Pistole und Patrone um 1895 von H. W. Gabbett-Fairfax entwickelt, wurden nur für Versuche im Rahmen der englischen Armee-Versuche hergestellt. Keine kommerzielle Fertigung.
Siehe: 8,5 mm Mars, 9 mm Mars und 10 mm Mars – Band I und .360 Mars, .450 Mars long- und short Case (Katalog Nr. 349, 449 und 450).

ohne Bodenstempel

Technical and Ballistic Data

Bullet dia.	.453"
Case dia. neck:	.472"–.476"
head:	.508"
rim:	.504"
Case length:	1.303"
Case material:	brass
Powder type:	smokeless
Primer type:	Berdan
Cartridge length:	1.781"

Experimental cartridge of the "Mars Series" within the inch line. Pistol and cartridge were developed about 1895 by H. W. Gabbett-Fairfax and were manufactured for experiments only within the scope of tests of the British Army. No commercial production.
See also: 8.5 mm Mars, 9 mm Mars and 10 mm Mars – Volume I and .360 Mars long and short case (catalog Nos. 349, 449 and 450).

Without headstamp:

.450 Mars Experimental II

Synonyme/Synonyms:

.450 Mars, Intermediate case

452

Geschoß/Bullet Ausführg. Pattern	Gewicht (g)	Weight (gr.)	Katalog Catalog No.
21 B			**452–1**

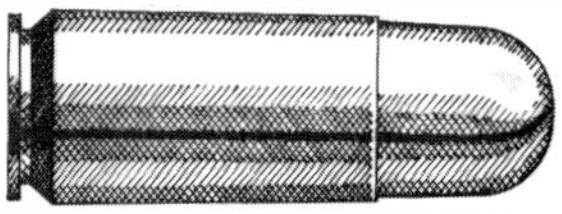

Technische und ballistische Daten

Geschoß-∅:	11,43 mm
Hülsen-∅ Hals:	12,01 mm
Boden:	12,65 mm
Rand:	12,19 mm
Hülsenlänge:	24,13 mm
Hülsenmaterial:	Messing
Pulverart:	rauchlos
Zündungsart:	Berdan
Patronenlänge:	35,81 mm

Es handelt sich um eine Versuchspatrone aus der „Mars-Serie“ der Inch-Kaliber, deren Hülsenlänge zwischen denen der Kaliber .450 short Case und .450 Mars long Case liegt (vergleiche Katalog Nr. 449 und 450).
Mars Patronen wurden um 1895 von H. W. Gabbett-Fairfax in England für eine Selbstladepistole entwickelt. Die Waffe wurde auf ihre Eignung als Armeepistole getestet, aber nicht angenommen. Keine kommerzielle Fertigung.
Siehe: 8,5 mm Mars, 9 mm Mars und 10 mm Mars – Band I – und .360 Mars, .450 Mars long und short Case (Katalog Nr. 349, 449 und 450).

ohne Bodenstempel

Technical and Ballistic Data

Bullet dia.	.450″
Case dia. neck:	.473″
head:	.498″
rim.	.480″
Case length:	.950″
Case material:	brass
Powder type:	smokeless
Primer type:	Berdan
Cartridge length:	1.410″

This is an experimental cartridge of the “Mars Series” in the inch line, whose cartridge length ranges between the calibers .450 Mars short case and .450 Mars long case (compare catalog Nos. 449 and 450).
Mars cartridges were developed about 1895 by H. W. Gabbett-Fairfax in England for a self-loading pistol. The weapon was tested as to its suitability as an Army pistol, but was not adopted. No commercial production.
See also: 8.5 mm Mars, 9mm Mars and 10 mm Mars – Volume I – and .360 Mars, .450 Mars long and short case (catalog Nos. 349, 449 and 450).

Without headstamp

.450 No. 1 Bland

Synonyme/Synonyms:
.450 Bland No. 1
.450 No. 1 Bland Revolver

453

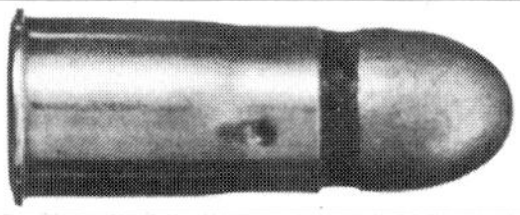

Geschoß/Bullet Ausführg. Pattern	Gewicht (g)	Weight (gr.)	Katalog Catalog No.
1 B	18,73 – 18,80	289.00 – 290.00	**453–1**

Technische und ballistische Daten

Geschoß-∅:	12,02–12,09 mm*) 11,75–11,80 mm
Hülsen-∅ Hals:	12,28–12,34 mm
Boden:	13,31–13,33 mm
Rand:	14,60–14,65 mm
Hülsenlänge:	21,51–22,30 mm
Hülsenmaterial:	Messing
Pulverart:	Schwarz
Zündungsart:	unbekannt
Patronenlänge:	36,32–38,35 mm

*) größter Geschoßdurchmesser

Technical and Ballistic Data

Bullet dia.	.473"–.476"*) .462"–.464"
Case dia. neck:	.483"–.486"
head:	.524"–.525"
rim:	.575"–.577"
Case length:	.847"–.878"
Case material:	brass
Powder type:	black
Primer type:	unknown
Cartridge length:	1.430"–1.510"

*) maximum bullet diameter

Die Patrone Kaliber .450 No. 1 Bland hat ihren Ursprung in England und wurde für einen Revolver der Firma Thomas Bland & Söhne London/Birmingham hergestellt. Die Geschoßform und -befestigung, sowie die Fettung mit Bienenwachs im Hohlraum des Geschosses und in den Fettrillen entsprechen den Patronen Kaliber .476 Enfield Mk.III und .476 Enfield short (vergl. Katalog Nr. 470 und 471). Die Angabe .476 ist dabei das Maß des größten Geschoßdurchmessers 0.476".

Bodenstempel:
ELEY . LONDON . 450 No 1,

The cartridge caliber .450 No. 1 Bland has its origin in England and was manufactured for a revolver of the firm Thomas Bland & Sons, London/Birmingham. The bullet shape and stab crimp as well as the lubrication with bee wax in the hollow bullet and in the lubricant grooves correspond to those of the cartridges caliber .476 Enfield Mk. III and .476 Enfield short (compare catalog Nos. 470 and 471). The indication .476 refers to the measurement of the largest bullet diameter 0.476".

Headstamp:
ELEY . LONDON . 450 No. 1,

.450 Short C.F.

Synonyme/Synonyms:

454

DWM 192
GR 78
.450 C.F.
.450 Center Fire
.450 Colt
.450 English Revolver
.450 Revolver
.450 Short Revolver
.450 (12 mm) Revolver C.F.
.450-13-200 Revolver
.450-13-225 Revolver
11 × 18 – .450 kurz
11,25 × 17,75 – No. 450 (12 $^{m}/_{m}$)
11,40 × 18,40 Kal. 450 Revolver
11,5 × 18 mm – Englisch. Kal. 450
12 mm (.450) Revolver C.F.
Cal. 450 – 12 mm

	Geschoß/Bullet			Katalog
	Ausführg. Pattern	Gewicht (g)	Weight (gr.)	Catalog No.
	1 B	11,66 – 14,90	180.00 – 230.00	**454–1**
	1 B	11,66 – 14,90	180.00 – 230.00	**454–2**
	1 B	11,66 – 14,90	180.00 – 230.00	**454–3**
	1 B	11,66 – 14,90	180.00 – 230.00	**454–4**
	1 B	11,66 – 14,90	180.00 – 230.00	**454–5**
	1 B	11,66 – 14,90	180.00 – 230.00	**454–6**
	1 B	11,66 – 14,90	180.00 – 230.00	**454–7**
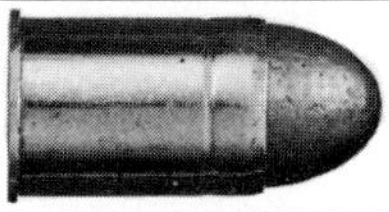	1 B	11,66 – 14,90	180.00 – 230.00	**454–8**
	1 B	11,66 – 14,90	180.00 – 230.00	**454–9**
	1 F	11,66 – 14,90	180.00 – 230.00	**454–10**

.450 Short C.F.

	Geschoß/Bullet Ausführg. Pattern	Gewicht (g)	Weight (gr.)	Katalog Catalog No.
	21 B	14,26	220.00	**454–11**
	1 P	14,26	220.00	**454–12**
	1 P	14,26	220.00	**454–13**
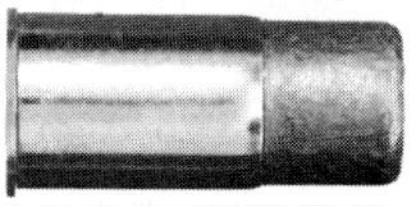	71 P	12,96	200.00	**454–14**
	90 b	–	–	**454–15**
	90 c	–	–	**454–16**
	90 d	–	–	**454–17**
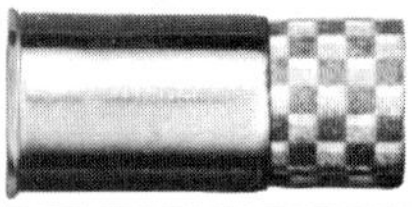	90 d	–	–	**454–18**

Technische und ballistische Daten

Geschoß-∅:	10,87–11,63 mm
Hülsen-∅ Hals:	11,60–12,15 mm
Boden:	11,68–12,20 mm
Rand:	12,60–13,55 mm
Hülsenlänge:	15,90–18,41 mm
Hülsenmaterial:	Messing
Pulverart:	Schwarz, rauchlos
Zündungsart:	Berdan, Boxer, Braun & Bloem Topf, verdeckt
Patronenlänge:	24,40–29,52 mm
V_0 (m/sec)	200ˣ) 215ˣˣ)
E_0 (J)	291ˣ) 334ˣˣ)
Lauflänge:	102 mm

ˣ) Schwarzpulver
ˣˣ) rauchloses Pulver

Technical and Ballistic Data

Bullet dia.	.428″–.458″
Case dia. neck:	.457″–.478″
head:	.460″–.480″
rim:	.496″–.533″
Case length:	.626″–.725″
Case material:	brass
Powder type:	black, smokeless
Primer type:	Berdan, Boxer, Braun & Bloem, battery cup, inside
Cartridge length:	.961″–1.162″
V_0 (ft. per sec.)	656ˣ) 705ˣˣ)
E_0 (ft. pounds)	210.4ˣ) 241.5ˣˣ)
Barrel length:	4.000″

ˣ) black powder
ˣˣ) smokeless powder

.450 Short C.F.

Bei den Patronen des Kalibers .450 short C.F. handelt es sich um eine insbesondere in Europa sehr verbreitete Patronenart. Der Ursprung ist England und geht auf das Kaliber .450 Adams 1868 zurück (vergl. Katalog Nr. 441 – 443). Diese Revolverpatrone wurde von vielen europäischen Firmen hergestellt. Sie war ursprünglich mit Schwarz- dann mit rauchlosem Pulver geladen.

Bodenstempel:
ELEY BROS,
ELEY 450,
R.W.S. 450,
450 SB,
KYNOCH . 450 .,
ELEY LONDON . 450 .,
BRAUN & BLOEM . 450 .,
FIOCCHI 450,
L.B.C. + 450 +,
GG (Monogramm) 450,
ELEY . 450 NITRO .,
KYNOCH 450 C,
LEON BEAUX & Co. MILANO .450,
W.R.A.Co. .450 C.F. (W im Zündhütchen)
GR (Monogramm) /+/+/450/

The cartridges caliber .450 short C.F. are above all in Europe widely distributed. Their country of origin is England and they date back to the caliber.450 Adams 1868 (compare catalog No. 441 – 443). This revolver cartridge was manufactured by many European companies. It was originally loaded with black powder, later with smokeless powder.

Headstamps:
ELEY BROS,
ELEY 450,
R.W.S. 450,
450 SB,
KYNOCH . 450 .,
ELEY LONDON . 450 .,
BRAUN & BLOEM . 450 .,
FIOCCHI 450,,
L.B.C. + 450 +,
GG (Monogram) 450,
ELEY . 450 NITRO .,
KYNOCH 450 C,
LEON BEAUX & Co. MILANO .450.,
W.R.A.Co. .450 C.F. (W in primer)
GR (Monogram) /+/+/450/

.454 Casull Magnum

Synonyme/Synonyms:

455

Geschoß/Bullet Ausführg. Pattern	Gewicht (g)	Weight (gr.)	Katalog Catalog No.
30 G	14,58	225.00	**455-1**

Technische und ballistische Daten

Geschoß-∅:	11,40–11,42 mm
Hülsen-∅ Hals:	12,00 mm
Boden:	12,05 mm
Rand:	12,80–12,90 mm
Hülsenlänge:	35,00–35,15 mm
Hülsenmaterial:	Messing
Pulverart:	rauchlos
Zündungsart:	Boxer
Patronenlänge:	43,15–43,20 mm
V_0	600 m/sec
E_0	ca. 3000 J
Lauflänge:	1900 mm

Die Patrone Kaliber .454 Casull Magnum wurde in Europa bekannt, als 1976 in einer deutschen Fachzeitschrift sich ein Inserat über die Waffe mit Munition befand. Es wurde in dieser Anzeige über den Revolver „mit der stärksten Faustfeuerwaffenpatrone" berichtet. Es hansich um einen Revolver .454 Casull single action, für den die Patrone Kal. .45 long Colt Pate gestanden haben soll (vergl. Katalog Nr. 430). Waffe und Munition waren bis heute (1980) in der BR Deutschland nicht im Handel erhältlich.

Bodenstempel:
454 CASULL NAA

Technical and Ballistic Data

Bullet dia.	.449"– .450"
Case dia. neck:	.473"
head:	.475"
rim:	.504"– .508"
Case length:	1.379"–1.384"
Case material:	brass
Powder type:	smokeless
Primer type:	Boxer
Cartridge length:	1.700"–1.702"
V_0	1968 ft. per sec.
E_0	2170 ft. pounds
Barrel length:	7,5"

The cartridge caliber .454 Casull Magnum became known in Europe when in 1976 an advertisement was published in a German technical magazine illustrating the weapon and its ammunition. This advertisement reported about the revolver with "the heaviest handgun cartridge". It is a revolver with the designation .454 Casull Single Action for which the cartridge caliber .45 long Colt is said to have served as a model (compare catalog No. 430). Weapon and ammunition cannot be purchased commercially up to now in the Federal Republic of Germany.

Headstamp:
454 CASULL NAA

.455 Colt

Synonyme/Synonyms:

DWM 228
.455 Revolver Mk.I
.455–18–265 Revolver
.455–18–215 Webley
11,7 × 22,0 – R.N. 455
11,70 × 22,30 Kal. 455 Revolver

456

	Geschoß/Bullet			Katalog Catalog No.
	Ausführg. Pattern	Gewicht (g)	Weight (gr.)	
	1 B	17,17 –17,62	265.00 – 272.00	**456–1**
	1 B	17,17 – 17,62	265.00 – 272.00	**456–2**
	1 B	17,00 – 17,17	262.35 – 265.00	**456–3**
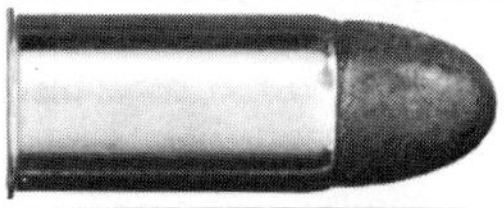	1 B	17,00 – 17,17	262.35 – 265.00	**456–4**
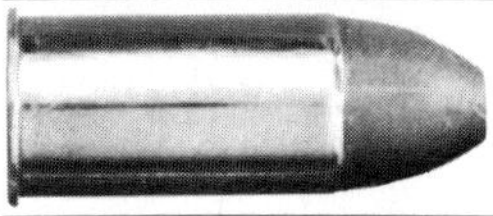	1 G	16,85	260.00	**456–4**
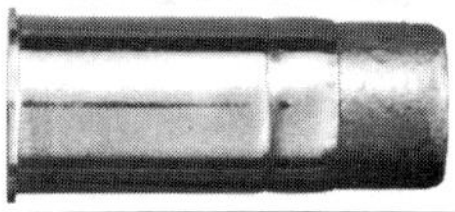	71 P	13,93	215.00	**456–6**

Technische und ballistische Daten

Geschoß-∅:	11,30–11,70 mm
Hülsen-∅ Hals:	11,99–12,18 mm
Boden:	11,99–12,20 mm
Rand:	13,33–13,59 mm
Hülsenlänge:	21,90–22,50 mm
Hülsenmaterial:	Messing
Pulverart:	Schwarz, rauchlos
Zündungsart:	Berdan, Boxer
Patronenlänge:	29,40–35,00 mm

Technical and Ballistic Data

Bullet dia.	.445″–.461″
Case dia. neck:	.472″–.479″
head:	.472″–.480″
rim:	.525″–.535″
Case length:	.862″–.886″
Case material:	brass
Powder type:	black, smokeless
Primer type:	Bedan, Boxer
Cartridge length:	1.157″–1.378″

Die Patrone Kaliber .455 Colt kann als Variante zu den Patronen Kal. .455 Webley Mk.I und den Patronen Kaliber .455 Enfield Mk.I und II angesehen weden. Die Unterschiede sind bei fast gleicher Hülsenlängen in den Patronenlängen zu suchen. Die Enfield-Patronen sind mit Schwarzpulver, die Patrone Kaliber .455 Webley und .455 Colt waren zuerst mit Schwarzpulver – dann mit rauchlosem Pulver geladen. (Vergl. Katalog Nr. 457, 458 und 460).
Die Patronen wurden von europäischen und US-Firmen hergestellt und waren bis um 1940 im Handel.

Bodenstempel:
ELEY.LONDON.,
ELEYS .455 .,
W.R.A.Co. .455 COLT
DOMINION .455 COLT

The cartridge caliber .455 Colt can be considered as a variation of the cartridges cal. .455 Webley Mk.I and caliber .455 Enfield Mk.I and II. Having an almost identical case length, these cartrigdes differ, however, as to their overall length. The Enfield rounds have a black powder charge, the cartridges caliber .455 Webley and .455 Colt were originally loaded with black powder and then with smokeless powder (compare catalog Nos. 457, 458 and 460). They were manufactured by European and US-companies and obtainable on the market until about 1940.

Headstamps:
ELEY.LONDON.,
ELEYS .455 .,
W.R.A.Co. .455 COLT
DOMINION .455 COLT

.455 Enfield Mk.I

Synonyme/Synonyms:

.455 Enfield Revolver Mk.I

457

Geschoß/Bullet			Katalog Catalog No.
Ausführg. Pattern	Gewicht (g)	Weight (gr.)	
1 B	17,17	265.00	**457-1**

Technische und ballistische Daten

Geschoß-∅:	11,55 mm
Hülsen-∅ Hals:	12,07-12,17 mm
Boden:	12,13-12,17 mm
Rand:	13,46-13,57 mm
Hülsenlänge:	21,60-22,10 mm
Hülsenmaterial:	Messing
Pulverart:	Schwarz
Zündungsart:	Boxer (englisch)

Von der sogenannten „Enfield-Patrone" sind 3 verschiedene Ausführungen (siehe auch Katalog Nr. 458 und 470) bekannt.
Mk.I: Sie gilt als Originalausführung, wovon aber, nach Berichten in offiziellen Unterlagen, nur eine geringe Stückzahl für Indien gefertigt wurde. Der erste Auftrag hierfür wurde am 8. September 1880 erteilt.
Sie hat ein kürzeres Geschoß als das der Mk.II.
Alle Enfield-Patronen (Mk.I bis Mk.III) wurden nach der Einführung der Webley-Mk.I-Patrone im Jahre 1891, am 26. September 1892 von der englischen Regierung als veraltet erklärt.

Bodenstempel: nicht bekannt

Technical and ballistic Data

Bullet dia.	.455″
Case dia. neck:	.475″-.479″
head:	.477″-.479″
rim:	.530″-534″
Case length:	.850″-.870″
Case material:	brass
Powder type:	black
Primer type:	Boxer (Englisch)

There are three versions known of the so called "Enfield Cartridge" (see also catalog Nos. 458 and 470).
Mk.I: It is considered as the original round, which, however, according to reports in official documents, was manufactured in small lots only in India. The first order was given on 8th September, 1880 for this round.
It has a shorter bullet than the version Mk.II.
After the adoption of the Webley Mk.I cartridge in 1891, all Enfield cartridges (Mk.I to Mk.III) were declared obsolete by the British Government on 26th September, 1892.

Headstamps: not known

.455 Enfield Mk.II

Synonyme/Synonyms:

.455 Enfield Revolver Mk.II
.455 Government Pattern 1881

458

	Geschoß/Bullet Ausführg. Pattern	Gewicht (g)	Weight (gr.)	Katalog Catalog No.
	1 B	17,17	265.00	**458-1**
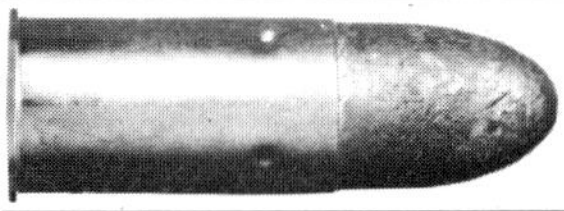	1 B	17,17	265.00	**458-2**

Technische und ballistische Daten

Geschoß-∅:	11,43-11,55 mm
Hülsen-∅ Hals:	11,94-12,17 mm
Boden:	12,09-12,19 mm
Rand:	13,38-13,56 mm
Hülsenlänge:	21,59-22,10 mm
Hülsenmaterial:	Messing
Pulverart:	Schwarz
Zündungsart:	Boxer (englisch)
Patronenlänge:	36,96-37,85 mm

Von der sogenannten „Enfield-Patrone" sind drei verschiedene Ausführungen (siehe auch Katalog Nr. 457 und 470) bekannt.
Mk.II: Die Patrone mit leicht abgeändertem Geschoß wurde bereits am 30. November 1880 von der Regierung angenommen. Das Geschoß besteht aus Weichblei. Das Verhältnis Blei:Zinn beträgt 12:1. Zur Geschoßfettung wurde reines Bienenwachs verwendet. Die ersten Fertigungen dieser Patrone weisen als Geschoßbefestigung nur einen Einzug am Hülsenmund auf. Die ab 29. 6. 1881 gefertigten Patronen erhielten eine 3-Punkt-Befestigung.
Alle Enfield-Patronen (Mk.I bis Mk.III) wurden nach der Einführung der Webley-Mk.I-Patrone im Jahre 1891, am 26. September 1892 von der englischen Regierung als veraltet erklärt.

Bodenstempel:
ELEY LONDON . 455 .
ADAMS STRAND . LONDON .

Technical and Ballistic Data

Bullet dia.	.450"-.455"
Case dia. neck:	.470"-.479"
head:	.476"-.480"
rim:	.527"-.534"
Case length:	.850"-.870"
Case material:	brass
Powder type:	black
Primer type:	Boxer (English)
Cartridge length:	1.455"-1.490"

There are three versions known of the so called "Enfield cartridge" (see also catalog Nos. 457 and 470).
Mk. II: The cartridge with the slightly modified bullet was already on 30th November 1880 adopted by the Government. The bullet consists of soft lead. The proportion lead: tin is 12:1. Pure bee wax was used to lubricate the bullet. The first cartridges of this kind ever made show merely a necked down case mouth to hold the bullet in its position. The rounds manufactured from 29-6-1881 had a 3-point stab crimp.
After the adoption of the Webley Mk.I cartridge in 1891, all Enfield cartridges (Mk. I to Mk. III) were declared obsolete by the British Government on 26th September, 1892.

Headstamps:
ELEY LONDON . 455 .
ADAMS STRAND . LONDON .

.455 Revolver C.F.

459

Synonyme/Synonyms:

GR 186
GR 288
.455 II
.455 Colt, Mk.II
.455 Eley
.455 Revolver Mk.II
.455 Target
11,5 × 19 mm – Englisch. Kal. 455 (GR 186)
11,5 × 19 mm – Englisch. Kal. 455 (GR 288)

	Geschoß/Bullet			Katalog Catalog No.
	Ausführg. Pattern	Gewicht (g)	Weight (gr.)	
	1 B	17,17	265.00	**459–1**
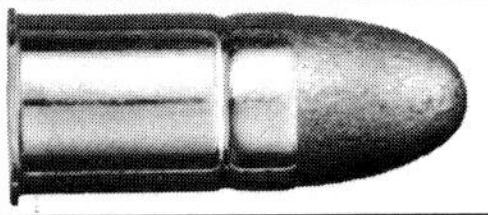	1 B	17,17	265.00	**459–2**
	1 B	17,17	265.00	**459–3**
	1 B	12,20	188.27	**459–4**
	1 P	14,26	220.00	**459–5**
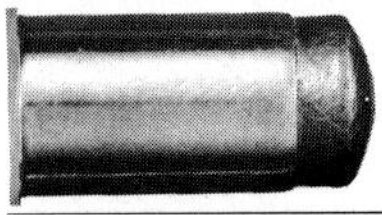	1 P			**459–6**
	1 S	11,66	180.00	**459–7**
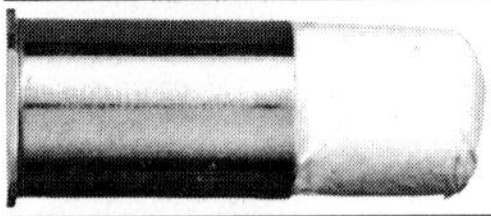	90 c	–	–	**459–8**
	90 d	–	–	**459–9**
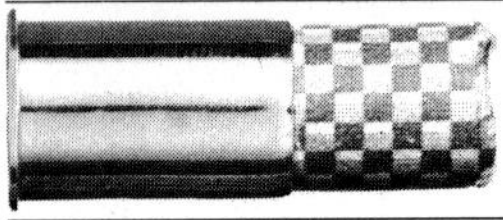	90 d	–	–	**459–10**

Technische und ballistische Daten

Geschoß-∅:	11,40–11,72 mm	
Hülsen-∅ Hals:	11,95–12,15 mm	
Boden:	12,10–12,18 mm	
Rand:	13,40–13,60 mm	
Hülsenlänge:	18,85–19,24 mm	
Hülsenmaterial:	Messing	
Pulverart:	Schwarz, rauchlos	
Zündungsart:	Berdan, Boxer	
Patronenlänge:	24,75–31,90 mm	
V_0 (m/sec)	185ˣ)	215ˣˣ)
E_0	300 Jˣ)	404 Jˣˣ)
Lauflänge:	152 mm	

Technical and Ballistic Data

Bullet dia.	.449″– .461″	
Case dia. neck:	.470″– .478″	
head:	.476″– .479″	
rim:	.527″– .535″	
Case length:	.742″– .757″	
Case material:	brass	
Powder type:	black, smokeless	
Primer type:	Berdan, Boxer	
Cartridge length:	.974″–1.256″	
V_0 (ft. per sec.)	607ˣ)	705ˣˣ)
E_0 (ft. pounds)	216.9ˣ)	292.1ˣˣ)
Barrel length:	6.000″	

Die Patrone Kaliber .455 Revolver C.F. stammt aus England und dürfte 1897 als Militärkaliber in Erscheinung getreten sein. Sie stammt aus der Reihe der englischen .455er Kaliber und war sehr verbreitet. Sie wurde in den USA bis ca. 1940 hergestellt.

The cartridge caliber .455 Revolver C.F. originates from England and it is very likely that it surfaced in 1897 as a military caliber. It pertains to the series of the English .455 calibers and was widely distributed. It was manufactured in the USA until about 1940.

ˣ) Schwarzpulver
ˣˣ) Rauchloses Pulver

ˣ) black powder
ˣˣ) smokeless powder

Bodenstempel:
ELEY . NITRO . .455,
KYNOCH .455,
E C II,
K C II,
D.C.Co. .455.

Headstamp:
ELEY . NITRO . .455,
KYNOCH .455,
E C II,
K C II,
D.C.Co. .455.

.455 Webley Mk.I

Synonyme/Synonyms:
.455 Webley Revolver Mk.I

460

	Geschoß/Bullet Ausführg. Pattern	Gewicht (g)	Weight (gr.)	Katalog Catalog No.
	1 B	17,04 - 17,30	263.00 - 267.00	**460-1**
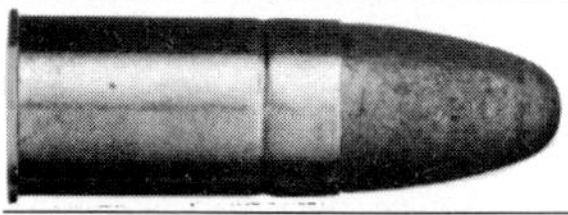	1 B	17,04 - 17,30	263.00 - 267.00	**460-2**
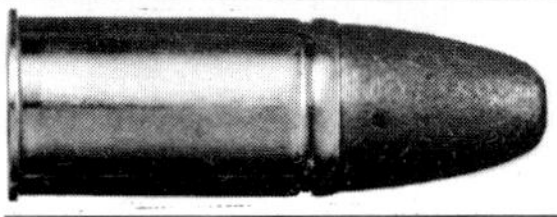	1 B	17,04 - 17,30	263.00 - 267.00	**460-3**

Technische und ballistische Daten

Geschoß-∅:	11,45-11,57 mm
Hülsen-∅ Hals:	11,52-12,17 mm
Boden:	11,90-12,17 mm
Rand:	13,40-13,67 mm
Hülsenlänge:	21,60-22,10 mm
Hülsenmaterial:	Messing
Pulverart:	Schwarz, rauchlos
Zündungsart:	Boxer
Patronenlänge:	36,30-36,78 mm
V_0	216 m/sec
E_0	408 J
Lauflänge:	152 mm

Eingeführt unter der offiziellen Bezeichnung Webley Mk. I als Ordonnanzmunition am 29. 7. 1891. Obwohl diese Patrone speziell für den Webley-Revolver entwickelt worden war, fand sie ebenfalls in dem zu dieser Zeit noch verwendeten Enfield Revolver Verwendung. Das Zündsystem bei dieser Patrone wurde von „Boxer englisch" auf „Boxer modern" abgeändert. Das Geschoß besteht aus Weichblei (Blei:Zinn = 12:1) mit Bienenwachsfettung. Es hat eine 3-Punkt-Befestigung. Die Patrone mit Schwarzpulverladung wurde offiziell am 6. August 1912 als veraltet erklärt.
Ab 14. September 1894 wurde die Patrone mit „Cordite-Pulverladung" sowohl für den Webley- als auch für den Enfield-Revolver von der englischen Armee angenommen. Die Patrone unterscheidet sich äußerlich von der mit Schwarzpulver geladenen nur durch die Art der Geschoßbefestigung (Rille in der Hülse und eingezogener Hülsenmund). Der Buchstabe C im Bodenstempel entfiel ab 9. August 1912 nachdem die Patronen nur noch mit Cordite geladen wurden. Die Patrone wurde reits am 15. 2. 1921 von der britischen Marine als veraltet erklärt, während sie bei der britischen Armee noch bis zum 19. 3. 1946 als Ordonnanz-Munition anerkannt war.

Bodenstempel:
K I
R ⩚ L CI
KYNOCH .455
ELEY . LONDON .

Technical and Ballistic Data

Bullet dia.	.451"- .455"
Case dia. neck:	.453"- .479"
head:	.468"- .479"
rim:	.527"- .538"
Case length:	.850"- .870"
Case material:	brass
Powder type:	black, smokeless
Primer type:	Boxer
Cartridge length:	1.429"-1.448"
V_0	710 ft. per sec.
E_0	295.1 ft. pounds
Barrel length:	6.000"

This cartridge was adopted with the official designation Webley, Mk. I on 29-7-1891 as ordnance ammunition. Although this cartridge had especially been developed for the Webley revolver, it also was fired in the Enfield revolver still in use at that time. The ignition system of this cartridge was changed from "Boxer English" to "Boxer modern". The bullet consists of soft lead (lead : tin = 12:1) and is lubricated with bee wax. It has a 3-point- indent to hold it in its position. The cartridge with black powder charge was officially declared obsolete on 6th August 1912. On 14th September, 1894 the cartridge with "cordite powder charge" was adopted by the British Army both for the Webley and the Enfield revolvers. Outwardly the cartridge differs from its black powder counterpart by its stab crimp only (groove in the case and a necked down case mouth). The letter C in the headstamp was omitted from 9th August 1912, when the cartridges were loaded only with cordite from that date on. Already on 15-2-1921 this cartridge was declared obsolete by the British Navy whereas it was still recognized by the British Army as ordnance ammunition until the 19-3-1946.

Headstamps:
K I
R⩚L CI
KYNOCH .455
ELEY . LONDON .

.445 Webley Mk.II

Synonyme/Synonyms:

.455 Webley Revolver Mk.II

461

Geschoß/Bullet Ausführg. Pattern	Gewicht (g)	Weight (gr.)	Katalog Catalog No.
1 B	17,04 – 17,30	263.00 – 267.00	**461-1**

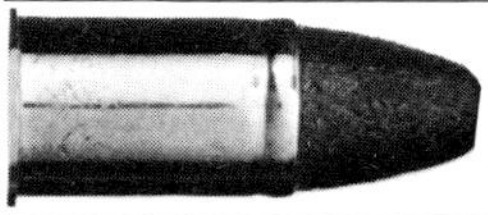

Technische und ballistische Daten

Geschoß-∅:	11,52–11,57 mm
Hülsen-∅ Hals:	12,05–12,17 mm
Boden:	12,05–12,17 mm
Rand:	13,32–13,67 mm
Hülsenlänge:	18,80–19,30 mm
Hülsenmaterial:	Messing
Pulverart:	rauchlos
Zündungsart:	Berdan
Patronenlänge:	31,52–31,92 mm
V_0	183 m/sec
E_0	293 J
Lauflänge:	152 mm

Nach amtlichen Angaben wurde diese Patrone am 21. 7. 1887 eingeführt, nachdem man mit Cordite gute Erfahrungen gemacht hatte. Der Pulverraum konnte verkleinert und dadurch die Hülse verkürzt werden. Die Patrone fand im Webley- als auch im Enfield-Revolver Verwendung. Sie wurde aber bereits 1898, nach Einführung der Patrone Mk.III als veraltet erklärt, jedoch am 14. 7. 1900 wieder offiziell eingeführt. Nach Einführung der Patrone Mk.IV im Jahre 1909 erklärte man sie zum zweiten Male als veraltet. Sie wurde jedoch im November 1914 zu dritten Male wieder eingeführt und bis zur Annahme der Ganzmantelpatrone Mk. VI im Jahre 1939 beibehalten. Der Bodenstempel, der bis 9. 8. 1912 gefertigten Patronen Mk. II trägt zusätzlich den Buchstaben C für Cordite, während die spätere Fertigung nur noch die Bezeichnung II aufweist.

Bodenstempel:
R ⩚ L C II
R ⩚ L II
KYNOCH .455

Technical and Ballistic Data

Bullet dia.	.453"– .455"
Case dia. neck:	.474"– .479"
head:	.474"– .479"
rim:	.524"– .538"
Case length:	.740"– .760"
Case material:	brass
Powder type:	smokeless
Primer type:	Berdan
Cartridge length:	1.241"–1.257"
V_0	600 ft. per sec.
E_0	212.0 ft. pounds
Barrel length:	6.000"

Official sources say that this cartridge was adopted on 21–7–1887 when good experience had been made with Cordite. The charge hole could be reduced and thus it was possible to shorten the case. The cartridge was used in both Webley and Enfield revolvers. However, already in 1898, after the adoption of the cartridge Mk.III, it was declared obsolete, but on 14–7–1900 it was officially re-adopted. After the adoption of the cartridge Mk. IV in 1909 it was a second time declared obsolete. And yet, in November 1914 it was adopted a third time and it remained in use until the round with the full jacketed bullet, type Mk.VI, was adopted in 1939. The headstamp of the cartridges Mk.II made until 9–8–1912, shows the additional letter C for Cordite whereas the later production bears only the designation II.

Headstamps:
R ⩚ L C II
R ⩚ L II
KYNOCH .455

.455 Webley Mk.III

Synonyme/Synonyms:
.455 Webley Revolver Mk.III

462

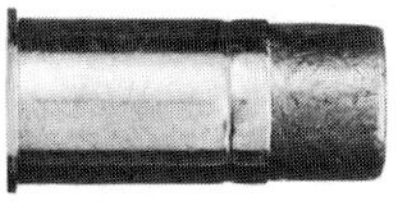

Geschoß/Bullet Ausführg. Pattern	Gewicht (g)	Weight (gr.)	Katalog Catalog No.
71 P	14,03 – 14,29	216.50 – 220.50	**462-1**

Technische und ballistische Daten

Geschoß-∅:	11,52–11,57 mm
Hülsen-∅ Hals:	12,07–12,17 mm
Boden:	12,04–12,17 mm
Rand:	13,32–13,67 mm
Hülsenlänge:	18,80–19,30 mm
Hülsenmaterial:	Messing
Pulverart:	rauchlos
Zündungsart:	Berdan
Patronenlänge:	27,20–27,22 mm
V_0	183 m/sec
E_0	242 J
Lauflänge:	152 mm

Eingeführt am 5. Februar 1898. Die Patrone besitzt ein sogenanntes „Manstopper-Geschoß" (Weichblei : Zinn = 12 : 1), gefertigt nach Webley-Patent v. 18. Juni 1897. Die Produktion war aber bereits am 14. Juli 1900 wieder eingestellt worden. Die noch vorhandenen Bestände wurden nur noch zu Übungsschießen verwendet. Offiziell als veraltet wurde sie am 18. November 1902 erklärt.

Bodenstempel:
R⋀L C III

Technical and Ballistic Data

Bullet dia.	.453″–.455″
Case dia. neck:	.475″–.479″
head:	.474″–.479″
rim:	.524″–.538″
Case length:	.740″–.760″
Case material:	brass
Powder type:	smokeless
Primer type:	Berdan
Cartridge length:	1.071″–1.072″
V_0	600 ft. per sec.
E_0	174.7 ft. pounds
Barrel length:	6.000″

Adopted on 5th February, 1898 this cartridge had a so called "man-stopper bullet" (soft lead : tin = 12 : 1) made after the Webley Patent of 18th June, 1897. However, the production was already discontinued on 14th July, 1900. The remaining stocks were exclusively used for practice shooting. The ammunition was officially declared obsolete on 18th November, 1902.

Headstamp:
R⋀L C III

.455 Webley Mk.IV

Synonyme/Synonyms:
.455 Webley Revolver Mk.IV

463

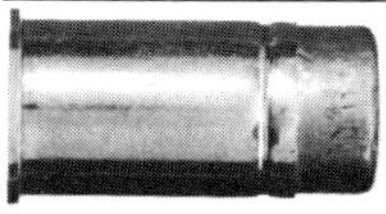

Geschoß/Bullet Ausführg. Pattern	Gewicht (g)	Weight (gr.)	Katalog Catalog No.
1 P	14,13 – 14,38	218.00 – 222.00	**463–1**

Technische und ballistische Daten

Geschoß-∅:	11,40–11,45 mm
Hülsen-∅ Hals:	12,00–12,17 mm
Boden:	12,04–12,17 mm
Rand:	13,32–13,67 mm
Hülsenlänge:	18,80–19,30 mm
Hülsenmaterial:	Messing
Pulverart:	rauchlos
Zündungsart:	Berdan
Patronenlänge:	24,55–24,60 mm
V_0	198 m/sec
E_0	285 J
Lauflänge:	152 mm

Diese Patrone wurde am 23. November 1909 von der englischen Armee offiziell als Ordonnanz-Munition angenommen, nachdem die inzwischen wieder eingeführte Patrone Mk.II in ihrer „stopping-Power" als ungenügend erschien und die Mk.III zu „gewaltig" war. Das Geschoß besteht aus Weichblei (Blei : Zinn im Verhältnis 12 : 1). Im Jahre 1914 wurde die Patrone für veraltet erklärt und nur noch für Übungszwecke verwendet.

Bodenstempel:
R∧L IV

Technical and Ballistic Data

Bullet dia.	.449"–.450"
Case dia. neck:	.472"–.479"
head:	.474"–.479"
rim:	.524"–.538"
Case length:	.740"–.760"
Case material:	brass
Powder type:	smokeless
Primer type:	Berdan
Cartridge length:	.966"–.968"
V_0	650 ft. per sec.
E_0	206.0 ft. pounds
Barrel length:	6.000"

This cartridge was officially adopted by the British Army on 23rd November, 1909 as ordnance ammunition when the Mk.II cartridge, meanwhile re-adopted, seemed to be insufficient as to its "stopping power" whereas the Mk.III was too "powerful". The bullet consists of soft lead (lead : tin = 12 : 1). In 1914 this round was declared obsolete and used for practice shooting only.

Headstamp:
R∧L IV

.455 Webley Mk.V

Synonyme/Synonyms:
.455 Webley Revolver Mk.V

464

Geschoß/Bullet Ausführg. Pattern	Gewicht (g)	Weight (gr.)	Katalog Catalog No.
1 P	14,13 - 14,38	218.00 - 222.00	**464-1**

Technische und ballistische Daten

Geschoß-∅:	11,40-11,45 mm
Hülsen-∅ Hals:	12,00-12,17 mm
Boden:	12,04-12,17 mm
Rand:	13,32-13,67 mm
Hülsenlänge:	18,80-19,30 mm
Hülsenmaterial:	Messing
Pulverart:	rauchlos
Zündungsart:	Berdan
Patronenlänge:	24,55-24,60 mm
V_0	198 m/sec
E_0	285 J
Lauflänge:	152 mm

Technical and Ballistic Data

Bullet dia.	.449"-.450"
Case dia. neck:	.472"-.479"
head:	.474"-.479"
rim:	.524"-.538"
Case length:	.740"-.760"
Case material:	brass
Powder type:	smokeless
Primer type:	Berdan
Cartridge length:	.966"-.968"
V_0	650 ft. per sec.
E_0	206.0 ft. pounds
Barrel length:	6.000"

Bei dieser Patrone, offiziell am 30. Dezember 1912 von der englischen Armee angenommen, unterscheidet sich das Geschoß von der Ausführung Mk.IV nur durch eine andere Legierung. Es besteht aus Hartblei im Verhältnis Blei : Antimon 99 : 1. Die Patrone wurde ebenfalls wie die Mk.IV nach Wiedereinführung der Mk.II im Jahre 1914 als veraltet erklärt. Die Restbestände dienten ausschließlich Übungszwecken.

Bodenstempel:
R↑L V
R.W.S. 455

This cartridge, officially adopted on 30th December, 1912 by the British Army, differs from the Mk.IV version only inasmuch as its bullet has a different alloy. It consists of hard lead in the proportion of lead - antimone = 99 : 1. The cartridge was declared obsolete, just like the Mk.IV, when the Mk.II was re-adopted in 1914. The surplus stock served practice shooting purposes only.

Headstamps:
R↑L V,
R.W.S. 455

.455 Webley Mk.VI

Synonyme/Synonyms:

.455 Revolver Mk.VI
.455 Webley Revolver Mk.VI

465

	Geschoß/Bullet Ausführg. Pattern	Gewicht (g)	Weight (gr.)	Katalog Catalog No.
	21 B	17,04 – 17,30	263.00 – 267.00	**465–1**
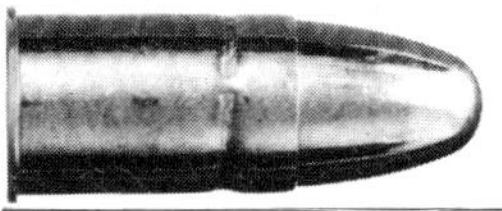	21 B	17,04 – 17,30	263.00 – 267.00	**465–2**

Technische und ballistische Daten

Geschoß-∅:	11,52 – 11,57 mm
Hülsen-∅ Hals:	12,00 – 12,17 mm
Boden:	12,04 – 12,17 mm
Rand:	13,32 – 13,67 mm
Hülsenlänge:	18,80 – 19,30 mm
Hülsenmaterial:	Messing
Pulverart:	rauchlos
Zündungsart:	Berdan
Patronenlänge:	31,18 – 31,72 mm
V_0	198 m/sec
E_0	343 J
Lauflänge:	152 mm

Technical and Ballistic Data

Bullet dia.	.453"–.455"
Case dia. neck:	.472"–.479"
head:	.474"–.479"
rim:	.524"–.538"
Case length:	.740"–.760"
Case material:	brass
Powder type:	smokeless
Primer type:	Berdan
Cartridge length:	1.227"–1.249"
V_0	650 ft. per sec.
E_0	248.1 ft. pounds
Barrel length:	6.000"

Diese Patrone, eingeführt bei der „Royal Army" am 18. September 1939, bei der „Royal Navy" am 3. November 1939 und bei der „Royal Air Force" am 1. Dezember 1939, hat ein Ganzmantel-Geschoß, das im Hinblick auf die „Haager-Konvention" entwickelt worden war. Die ersten Ausführungen waren mit Cordite geladen. Ab 22. April 1941 wurde nur noch Nitro-Zellulosepulver verwendet. Die Kennzeichnung von Nitrozellulose erfolgte durch ein Z, das der Bezeichnung VI auf dem Hülsenboden hinzugefügt war. Diese Kennzeichnung wurde bis 1. Oktober 1944 beibehalten. Die Patrone Mk.VI wurde im März 1946 von allen englischen Streitkräften als veraltet erklärt.

Bodenstempel:
K 42 VIZ,
MQ 42 VI,
K 41 VI

This cartridge, adopted on 18-9-1939 by the "Royal Army", on 3-11-1939 by the "Royal Navy" and on 1-12-1939 by the "Royal Air Force", has a full jacketed bullet which had been developed with regard to the "Hague Convention". The first versions were loaded with Cordite. From 22-4-1941 onward only nitrocellulose powder was utilized. The nitrocellulose code was the letter Z which was added to the designation VI on the case head. This marking was maintained until 1-10-1944. The cartridge Mk.VI was declared obsolete in March 1946 by all British Armed Forces.

Headstamps:
K 42 VIZ,
MQ 42 VI,
K 41 VI

.455 Webley & Scott Automatic M.1904

Synonyme/Synonyms:
.455 Webley & Scott M.1904 Auto. Pistol

466

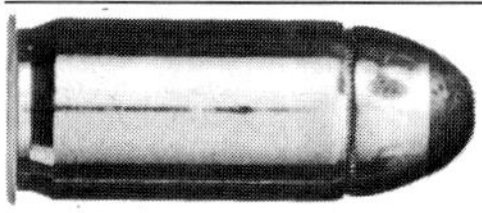

Geschoß/Bullet Ausführg. Pattern	Gewicht (g)	Weight (gr.)	Katalog Catalog No.
30 B	14,51 – 14,58	224.00 – 225.00	**466–1**

Technische und ballistische Daten

Geschoß-Ø:	11,50–11,58 mm
Hülsen-Ø Hals:	12,15–12,17 mm
Boden:	12,17–12,20 mm
Rand:	12,73–12,80 mm
Hülsenlänge:	22,35–22,53 mm
Hülsenmaterial:	Messing
Pulverart:	rauchlos
Zündungsart:	Berdan
Patronenlänge:	31,20–31,24 mm
V_0	320 m/sec
E_0	761 J
Lauflänge:	165 mm

Die Patrone .455 Webley & Scott Automatic M.1904 wurde 1904 für eine Selbstladepistole bei der Firma Webley & Scott in England entwickelt. Es handelt sich um eine Versuchspatrone die mit der entsprechenden Versuchswaffe bei der englischen Armee geprüft wurde. Nach der Bezeichnung „K" im Bodenstempel könnte die Munition bei der Firma Kynoch hergestellt worden sein.

Bodenstempel:
W&S .45 AUTO .455–K

Technical and Ballistic Data

Bullet dia.	.453"–.456"
Case dia. neck:	.478"–.479"
head:	.479"–.480"
rim:	.501"–.504"
Case length:	.880"–.887"
Case material:	brass
Powder type:	smokeless
Primer type:	Berdan
Cartridge length:	1.228"–1.230"
V_0	1050 ft. per sec.
E_0	550.2 ft. pounds
Barrel length:	6.500"

The cartridge caliber .455 Webley & Scott Automatic M. 1904 was developed in 1904 for a self-loading pistol at Webley's & Scott England. It is an experimental cartridge which was tested by the British Army in a corresponding test weapon. According to the designation "K" in the headstamp this ammunition might have been manufactured by the Kynoch Company.

Headstamp:
W&S .45 AUTO .455–K

.455 Webley Automatic, 1910

Synonyme/Synonyms:
.455 Webley Auto., 1910

467

Geschoß/Bullet Ausführg. Pattern	Gewicht (g)	Weight (gr.)	Katalog Catalog No.
21 B			**467–1**

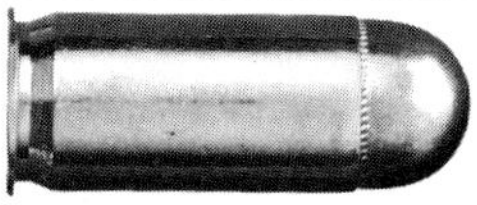

Technische und ballistische Daten

Geschoß-Ø:	11,51 – 11,54 mm
Hülsen-Ø Hals:	12,04 – 12,12 mm
Boden:	12,14 – 12,17 mm
Rand:	12,72 – 12,78 mm
Hülsenlänge:	23,39 – 23,44 mm
Hülsenmaterial:	Messing
Pulverart:	rauchlos
Zündungsart:	Berdan
Patronenlänge:	30,99 – 31,12 mm

Technical and Ballistic Data

Bullet dia.	.453″ – .454″
Case dia. neck:	.474″ – .477″
head:	.478″ – .479″
rim:	.501″ – .503″
Case length:	.921″ – .923″
Case material:	brass
Powder type:	smokeless
Primer type:	Bedan
Cartridge length:	1.220″ – 1.225″

Die Patrone Kaliber .455 Webley Automatic, 1910 liegt zeitlich zwischen den Patronen Kaliber .455 Webley Automatic M.1904 und .455 Webley Automatic Mk.I (Vergl. Katalog Nr.466 und 468). Sie hat eine ähnlich dünne Randstärke und breite Auszieherrillenbreite wie die Patrone Kaliber .455 Webley Automatic M.1904. Sie wurde nur in geringen Stückzahlen gefertigt und wurde um 1912 von der Patrone Kaliber .455 Webley Automatic Mk.I abgelöst. Ein weiteres Unterscheidungsmerkmal ist der Bodenstempel.

Bodenstempel:
W&S .AUTO 455-K

As to the period of its development, the cartridge caliber .455 Webley Automatic 1910 ranges between the rounds caliber.455 Webley Automatic M. 1904 and .455 Webley Automatic Mk.I (compare catalog Nos. 466 and 468). Its thin rim and the large extractor groove are similar to the corresponding features of the cartridge caliber .455 Webley Automatic M. 1904. It was manufactured in small lots only and superseded around 1912 by the cartridge caliber .455 Webley Automatic Mk.I Another distinctive mark is the headstamp.

Headstamp:
W&S .AUTO 455-K

.455 Webley Automatic Mk.I

Synonyme/Synonyms:

.455 Automatic Pistol
.455 Webley & Scott
.455 Webley Auto. Mk.I
455 Webley Self-Loading Pistol

468

	Geschoß/Bullet			Katalog Catalog No.
	Ausführg. Pattern	Gewicht (g)	Weight (gr.)	
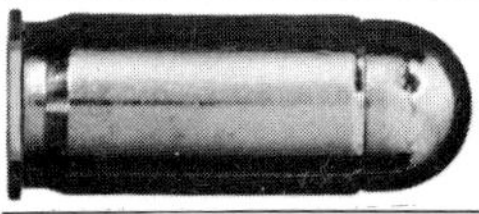	21 B	14,38–14,64	222.00–226.00	**468-1**

Technische und ballistische Daten

Geschoß-∅:	11,48–11,56 mm
Hülsen-∅ Hals:	11,96–12,09 mm
Boden:	11,94–12,12 mm
Rand:	12,67–12,80 mm
Hülsenlänge:	23,06–23,62 mm
Hülsenmaterial:	Messing
Pulverart:	rauchlos
Zündungsart:	Bedan
Patronenlänge:	31,07–31,10 mm
V_0	225 m/sec
E_0	375 J
Lauflänge:	127 mm

Technical and Ballistic Data

Bullet dia.	.452"–.455"
Case dia. neck:	.471"–.476"
head:	.470"–.477"
rim:	.499"–.504"
Case length:	.908"–.930"
Case material:	brass
Powder type:	smokeless
Primer type:	Bedan
Cartridge length:	1.223"–1.224"
Δ_0	740 ft. per sec.
E_0	270.8 ft. pounds
Barrel length:	5.000"

Die Patrone Kaliber .455 Webley Automatic Mark I war das Endprodukt der englischen Pistolenpatronen dieses Kalibers. Sie wurde 1912 für die Benutzung in Webley-Scott-Pistolen der Marine und 1915 an die Landstreitkräfte des Royal-Flying Corps, sowie 1919 bei der Luftwaffe zugelassen. 1915 wurden Colt-Pistolenmodelle für dieses Kaliber eingerichtet. Offiziel wurde die Patrone 1927 mit der Bezeichnung Mk.I versehen. Bei den Landstreitkräften wurde die Patrone 1935 als veraltet erklärt. (Vergl. Katalog Nr. 467)

Bodenstempel:
B 13 I,
R⋀L 41 I

The catridge caliber .455 Webley Automatic Mark I was the final product of the British pistol cartridges of this caliber. It was admitted in 1912 for use in Webley & Scott pistols of the Navy and in 1915 furnished to the land forces of the Royal Flying Corps and finally in 1919 to the Air Force. In 1915 COLT pistol models were chambered for this caliber. Officially the cartridge was given the designation Mk. I in 1927. In 1935, the land forces declared this cartridge obsolete. (compare catalog No. 467).

Headstamp:
B 13 I,
R⋀L 41 I

.455 Webley-Fosbery

Synonyme/Synonyms:
.455 Webley-Fosbery Revolver

469

	Geschoß/Bullet Ausführg. Pattern	Gewicht (g)	Weight (gr.)	Katalog Catalog No.
 Typ I / Type I	21 B			**469–1**
 Typ II / Type II	21 B			**469–2**

Technische und ballistische Daten

	Typ I	Typ II
Geschoß-⌀:	11,48 mm	11,54 mm
Hülsen-⌀ Hals:	12,12 mm	12,12 mm
Boden:	12,29 mm	12,17 mm
Rand:	13,44 mm	12,75 mm
Hülsenlänge:	23,47 mm	23,50 mm
Hülsenmaterial:	Messing	
Pulverart:	rauchlos	
Zündungsart:	Berdan	
Patronenlänge:	31,19 mm	31,00 mm

Technical and Ballistic Data

	Type I	Type II
Bullet dia.	.452″	.454″
Case dia. neck:	.477″	.477″
head:	.484″	.479″
rim:	.529″	.502″
Case length:	.924″	.925″
Case material:	brass	
Powder type:	smokeless	
Primer type:	Berdan	
Cartridge length:	1.228″	1.221″

Die Revolverpatrone Kaliber .455 Webley-Fosbery existiert in 2 Typen.
1. die Ursprungspatrone ohne Auszieherrille und
2. die Nachfolgepatrone mit Auszieherrille und kleinerem Randdurchmesser.
Obwohl über die Munition keine näheren Angaben bestehen, wird von dem Revolver berichtet, daß er von G. V. Fosbery in England erfunden wurde und daß für seine Entwicklungszeit 5 Jahre benötigt worden sind. Im Jahre 1902 ereignete sich beim Transport einer geladenen Waffe zu Versuchszwecken ein tödlicher Unfall. Die Ursprungspatente sollen bis in die Jahre um 1899 zurückgehen.

Bodenstempel:
W K F .455

There exist two types of the caliber .455 Webley-Fosbery revolver cartridge:
1/ the original cartridge without extractor groove and
2/ the successor cartridge with extractor groove and smaller rim diameter.
No further details are available as to this ammunition, however, it is reported that the revolver was invented by G. V. Fosbery in England and that the required developmental period lasted five years. In 1902 a fatal accident occurred when a loaded gun was transported for trials. The original patents allegedly date back to around 1899.

Headstamp:
W K F .455

.476 Enfield Mk.III

470

Synonyme/Synonyms:

.476 British
.476 Enfield Revolver, Mk.III
.476 Government Pattern 1882
.476 Revolver
.476-18-265 Revolver
11,7 × 22,25 – R. 476

Geschoß/Bullet Ausführg. Pattern	Gewicht (g)	Weight (gr.)	Katalog Catalog No.
1 B	17,17 – 17,62	265.00 – 272.00	**470-1**

Technische und ballistische Daten

Geschoß-∅:	12,04 – 12,12 mm*) 11,55 – 11,75 mm
Hülsen-∅ Hals:	12,05 – 12,17 mm
Boden:	12,13 – 12,17 mm
Rand:	13,21 – 13,57 mm
Hülsenlänge:	21,60 – 22,45 mm
Hülsenmaterial:	Messing
Pulverart:	Schwarz
Zündungsart:	Boxer (englisch)
Patronenlänge:	37,64 – 37,85 mm
V_0	220 m/sec
E_0	435 J
Lauflänge:	152 mm

*) größter Geschoßdurchmesser

Technical and Ballistic Data

Bullet dia.	.474" – .447"*) .455" – .463"
Case dia. neck:	.474" – .479"
head:	.477" – .479"
rim:	.520" – .534"
Case length:	.850" – .884"
Case material:	brass
Powder type:	black
Primer type:	Boxer (english)
Cartridge length:	1.481" – 1.490"
V_0	670 ft. per sec.
E_0	314.5 ft. pounds
Barrel length:	6.000"

*) maximum bullet diameter

Von der sogenannten „Enfield-Patrone" sind 3 verschiedene Ausführungen (siehe auch Katalog Nr. 457 und 458) bekannt.
Mk.III: Diese Patrone wurde am 10. Dezember 1881 eingeführt und als Kaliber .476 bezeichnet (bezogen auf den größten Geschoßdurchmesser). Das Besondere an dieser Geschoßkonstruktion ist die tiefe Bodenaushöhlung, die mit einem in Bienenwachs getauchten, 0,45 g schweren Tonpfropfen verschlossen ist.
Alle Enfield-Patronen (Mk.I bis Mk.III) wurden nach der Einführung der Webley Mk.I-Patrone im Jahre 1891, am 26. September 1892 von der englischen Regierung als veraltet erklärt.

Bodenstempel:
ELEY . LONDON .

There exist three versions of the so called "Enfield Cartridge" (see also catalog Nos. 457 and 458).
Mk.III: This cartridge was adopted on 10-12-1881 and designated as cal. .476 (referred to the largest bullet diameter). The peculiarity of this bullet design is a deep cavity in the base closed by a 0.45 gram clay wad dipped in wax.
After the adoption of the Mk.I cartridge in 1891, all Enfield cartridges (Mk.I to Mk.III) were declared obsolete by the British Government on 26th September, 1892.

Headstamp:
ELEY . LONDON .

.476 Enfield Short

Synonyme/Synonyms:

471

Geschoß/Bullet Ausführg. Pattern	Gewicht (g)	Weight (gr.)	Katalog Catalog No.
 1 B			**471-1**

Technische und ballistische Daten

Geschoß-∅:	11,85-11,90 mm
Hülsen-∅ Hals:	12,02-12,05 mm
Boden:	12,12 mm
Rand:	13,45mm
Hülsenlänge:	19,00-19,05 mm
Hülsenmaterial:	Messing
Pulverart:	rauchlos
Zündungsart:	Berdan
Patronenlänge:	32,10 mm

Die Patrone Kaliber .476 Enfield short stammt aus der Reihe der .476er Enfield Patronen und sollte in Revolvern des Kalibers .455 benutzt werden, für die die Patrone Kaliber .476 Enfield Mk.III zu lang war (vergl. Katalog Nr. 470). Die Hülsen stammen offensichtlich aus der Produktion der Hülsen für das Kaliber .455 Webley Mk.II bis VI (vergl. Katalog Nr. 461 bis 465).

Bodenstempel:
KYNOCH 476 C

Technical and Ballistic Data

Bullet dia.	.466"-.468"
Case dia. neck:	.473"-.474"
head:	.477"
rim:	.529"
Case length:	.748"-.750"
Case material:	brass
Powder type:	smokeless
Primer type:	Berdan
Cartridge length:	1.264"

The cartridge caliber .476 Enfield short falls into the category of the .476 Enfield series and was to be fired in .455 caliber revolvers for which the cartridge caliber .476 Enfield Mk.III was too long (compare catalog No. 470). The cases evidently originate from the production of the cases for the caliber .455 Webley Mk.II to VI (compare catalog No. 461 to 465).

Headstamp:
KYNOCH 476 C

.50 Meigs

Synonyme/Synonyms:
.492-49-295

472

Geschoß/Bullet Ausführg. Pattern	Gewicht (g)	Weight (gr.)	Katalog Catalog No.
1 G	19,12 – 19,50	295.00 – 301.00	**472–1**

Technische und ballistische Daten

Geschoß-∅:	12,34 – 12,40 mm
Hülsen-∅ Hals:	12,85 – 13,13 mm
Boden:	13,26 – 13,28 mm
Rand:	13,82 – 13,87 mm
Hülsenlänge:	32,21 – 32,46 mm
Hülsenmaterial:	Messing
Pulverart:	Schwarz
Zündungsart:	Boxer
Patronenlänge:	40,10 – 40,12 mm

Die Patrone Kaliber .50 Meigs stammt aus den USA wurde von J. V. Meigs entwickelt. Der Hinweis stammt von einer Schachtel die ansonsten nur noch mit der Bezeichnung .492-49-295 gekennzeichnet war. Es soll sich um eine Pistolenpatrone handeln.

Bodenstempel:
nicht bekannt

Technical and Ballistic Data

Bullet dia.	.486″ – .488″
Case dia. neck:	.506″ – .517″
head:	.522″ – .523″
rim:	.544″ – .546″
Case length:	1.268″ – 1.278″
Case material:	brass
Powder type:	black:
Primer type:	Boxer
Cartridge length:	1.579″ – 1.580″

The cartridge caliber .50 Meigs originates from the USA and was developed by J. V. Meigs. The hint was found on a box which, moreover, was marked .492-49-295. It is said to be a pistol cartridge.

Headstamp:
not known

.50 Remington Army

Synonyme/Synonyms:

.50 Pistol
.50 Remington Army Pistol
.50 Remington Pistol, Army M. 1871

473

	Geschoß/Bullet			Katalog Catalog No.
	Ausführg. Pattern	Gewicht (g)	Weight (gr.)	
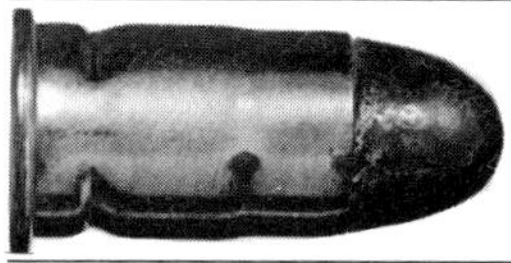	1 B	19,44	300.00	**473-1**
	1 B	19,44	300.00	**473-2**
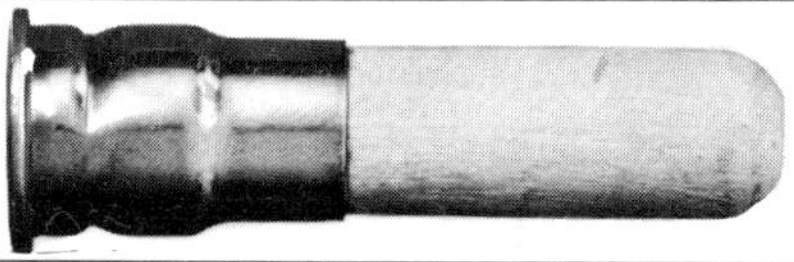	90 e	–	–	**473-3**

Technische und ballistische Daten

Geschoß-∅:	12,67 – 12,88 mm
Hülsen-∅ Hals:	13,36 – 13,72 mm
Boden:	14,30 – 14,45 mm
Rand:	16,79 – 17,02 mm
Hülsenlänge:	21,97 – 22,61 mm
Hülsenmaterial:	Kupfer
Pulverart:	Schwarz
Zündungsart:	Benet, Martin
Patronenlänge:	32,37 – 32,40 mm

Die Patrone Kaliber .50 Remington Army kann als Nachfolger der 1867 bei der US-Navy eingeführten Patrone Kal. .50 Remington Navy angesehen werden (vergl. Katalog Nr. 474). Sie wurde 1871 eingeführt nachdem das Heeresbeschaffungsamt einige Änderungen an dem Vorgänger durchgesetzt hatte. Die Waffe war wiederum eine einschüssige Remington-Pistole „Army 1871" mit Rolling-Block-Verschluß. Die Patrone unterscheidet sich von dem Kaliber .50 Rem. Navy im wesentlichen durch einen größeren Hülsenrand. Die Patrone wurde auch kommerziell bis in die 20er Jahre hergestellt (vergl. Katalog Nr. 474).

Bodenstempel:
nicht bekannt

Technical and Ballistic Data

Bullet dia.	.499″ – .507″
Case dia. neck:	.526″ – .540″
head:	.563″ – .569″
rim:	.661″ – .670″
	.865″ – .890″
Case material:	copper
Powder type:	black
Primer type:	Benet cup, Martin fold
Cartridge length:	1.274″ – 1.275″

The cartridge caliber .50 Remington Army may be considered as the successor of the cartridge caliber .50 Remington Navy adopted in 1867 by the US-Navy. It was adopted in 1871 after the Army Procurement Office's successful insistence on some modifications carried out on the precedent version. The weapon again was a single shot Remington Pistol "Army 1871" with a rolling block action. The cartridge differs essentially from the caliber .50 Remington Navy by a larger case rim. The cartridge was also commercially distributed until the twenties (compare catalog No. 474).

Headstamp:
not known

.50 Remington Navy

Synonyme/Synonyms:

.50 Pistol
.50 Remington Navy Pistol
.50 Remington Pistol, Navy M. 1867

474

	Geschoß/Bullet Ausführg. Pattern	Gewicht (g)	Weight (gr.)	Katalog Catalog No.
	1 B	19,44	300.00	**474–1**
	1 F	19,44	300.00	**474–2**
	1 H	19,44	300.00	**474–3**
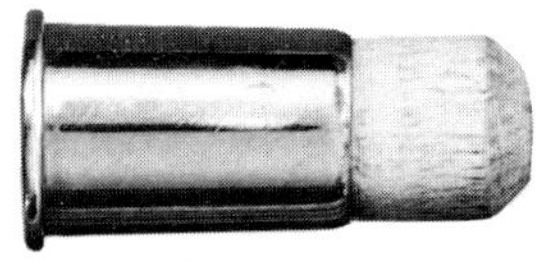	90 e	–	–	**474–4**

Technische und ballistische Daten

Geschoß-∅:	12,60–13,49 mm
Hülsen-∅ Hals:	13,38–13,77 mm
Boden:	14,25–14,40 mm
Rand:	16,13–16,64 mm
Hülsenlänge:	21,82–22,76 mm
Hülsenmaterial:	Messing, Kupfer
Pulverart:	Schwarz
Zündungsart:	Berdan, Boxer, Benet
Patronenlänge:	31,62–33,12 mm

Die Patrone Kaliber .50 Remington Navy ist der Nachfolger der 1866 bei der US-Navy eingeführten Randfeuerpatrone Kal. .50 R.F. mit der dazugehörenden einschüssigen Remington-Pistole. Sie ersetzte 1867 die vorbezeichnete Waffe mit Munition. Die Patrone unterscheidet sich von dem Kaliber .50 Remington Army im wesentlichen nur durch den kleineren Hülsenranddurchmesser (Vergl. Katalog Nr. 473). Die Patrone wurde auch kommerziell bis in die 20er Jahre hergestellt.

Bodenstempel:
W.R.A.Co. 50-PISTOL,
ohne

Technical and Ballistic Data

Bullet dia.	.496"–.531"
Case dia neck:	.527"–.542"
head:	.561"–.567"
rim:	.635"–.655"
Case length:	.859"–.896"
Case material:	brass, copper
Powder type:	black
Primer type:	Berdan, Boxer, Benet cup
Cartridge length:	1.245"–1.304"

The cartridge caliber .50 Remington Navy is the successor of the rimfire cartridge caliber .50 R.F. adopted in 1866 by the US-Navy with the single shot Remington pistol pertaining to it. In 1867 it replaced this weapon and the ammunition for it as well. The only difference between this round and the cartridge caliber .50 Remington Army is obviously the smaller case rim diameter (compare catalog No. 473). The cartridge was also manufactured for sale on the market until the twenties.

Headstamp:
W.R.A.Co. 50-PISTOL,
and without headstamp

.500 Tranter

Synonyme/Synonyms:

DWM 273
GR 754
.500 Revolver
.500 Tranter Revolver
.500-24-350 Revolver
12,6 × 20,0 – R.N. 500
12,6 × 20,5 mm – Kal. 500
12,75 × 20,80 Kal. 500 Konstabler

475

	Geschoß/Bullet			Katalog Catalog No.
	Ausführg. Pattern	Gewicht (g)	Weight (gr.)	
	1 C	23,98	370.00	**475–1**
	1 C	22,30 – 22,68	344.14 – 350.00	**475–2**
	1 C	16,52	255.00	**475–3**
	1 C	6,80	105.00	**475–4**
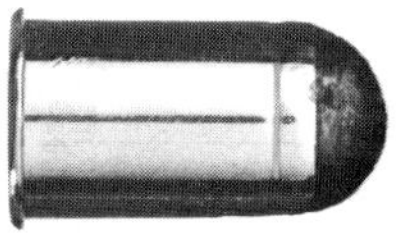	1 A	11,02	170.00	**475–5**
	90 d	–	–	**475–6**

Technische und ballistische Daten

Geschoß-∅:	12,70–13,31 mm
Hülsen-∅ Hals:	13,00–13,31 mm
Boden:	13,00–13,45 mm
Rand:	14,10–15,14 mm
Hülsenlänge:	19.30–22.20 mm
Hülsenmaterial:	Messing, Kupfer
Pulverart:	Schwarz
Zündungsart:	Berdan, Boxer, Topf
Patronenlänge:	31,10–35,05 mm 25,12–25,15 mm[x])
V_0	198 m/sec
E_0	454 J
Lauflänge:	127 mm

Technical and Ballistic Data

Bullet dia.	.500″–.524″
Case dia. neck:	.512″–.524″
head:	.512″–.529″
rim:	.555″–.596″
Case length:	.760″–.874″
Case material:	brass, copper
Powder type:	black
Primer type:	Berdan, Boxer, battery cup
Cartridge length:	1.224″–1.380″ .989″– .990″[x])
V_0	650 ft. per sec.
E_0	328.0 ft. pounds
Barrel length:	5.000″

[x]) Patrone mit Bleikugel

[x]) Cartridge with solid lead round ball

Die Patrone Kaliber .500 Tranter ist englischen Ursprungs und sie wurde um 1870 für Webley- und Tranter-Revolver hergestellt. Erstmalig ist sie im Firmenkatalog von Kynoch 1882 enthalten. Die Herstellung der Patronen dehnte sich auf den weiteren europäischen Raum aus und sie wurde 1939 eingestellt.

Bodenstempel:
ELEY BROS.,
R.W.S. 500,
KYNOCH .500 (IC im Zündhütchen),
ohne

The cartridge caliber .500 Tranter is of British origin and was manufactured about 1870 for Webley and Tranter revolvers. It was listed for the first time in the Kynoch Company Catalog of 1882. Manufacture of the cartridges spread all over the European countries and was discontinued around 1939.

Headstamps:
ELEY BROS.,
R.W.S. 500,
KYNOCH .500 (IC in primer)
and without headstamp

.577 Boxer

Synonyme/Synonyms:

.577 Boxer Pistol
.577 Coiled Pistol
.577 Pistol

476

Geschoß/Bullet Ausführg. Pattern	Gewicht (g)	Weight (gr.)	Katalog Catalog No.
1 A	18,66 - 19,70	288.00 - 304.00	**476-1**

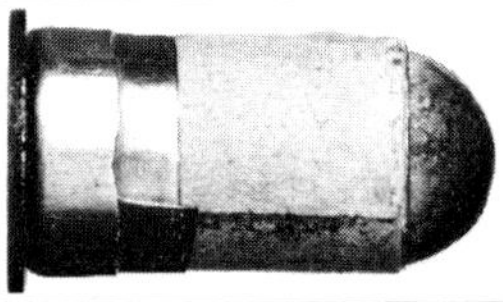

Technische und ballistische Daten

Geschoß-∅:	14,80 mm
Hülsen-∅ Hals:	15,60-16,31 mm
Boden:	16,76-16,86 mm
Rand:	18,80-18,97 mm
Hülsenlänge:	25,40-25,85 mm
Hülsenmaterial:	Pappe mit gewickeltem Messingsockel und Stahlboden
Pulverart:	Schwarz
Zündungsart:	Boxer (englisch)
Patronenlänge:	31,40 mm

Die Patrone Kaliber .577 Boxer wurde um 1868 für einen Webley-Revolver von Oberst E. M. Boxer in England entwickelt. Obwohl sie in der Folgezeit von Offizieren in Pistolen und Revolver benutzt wurde galt sie als sog. Privatpatrone. Sie sollte die Stoppkraft der damaligen Revolverpatronen verbessern, wurde allerdings ab ca. 1870 von der Patrone Kaliber .577 Revolver ersetzt (vergl. Katalog Nr. 477).

Bodenstempel:
nicht bekannt

Technical and Ballistic Data

Bullet dia.	.583″
Case dia. neck:	.614″- .642″
head:	.660″- .664″
rim:	.740″- .747″
Case length:	1.000″-1.017″
Case material:	cardboard with coiled brass base and steel head
Powder type:	black
Primer type:	Boxer (english)
Cartridge length:	1.236″

The cartridge caliber .577 Boxer was developed in England about 1868 by Colonel E. M. Boxer for a Webley Revolver. Although used in the time that followed by officers in pistols and revolvers it was considered as a so called private use cartridge. It was to improve the stopping power of the revolver cartridges of that period, however, it was replaced by the cartridge caliber .577 Revolver around 1870 (compare catalog No. 477).

Headstamp:
not known

.577 Revolver

Synonyme/Synonyms:
DWM 274
.577 Solid Pistol
.577-28-450 Revolver
14,75 × 20,90 Kal. 577 Revolver
15,4 × 20,2 – R. 577

477

	Geschoß/Bullet Ausführg. Pattern	Gewicht (g)	Weight (gr.)	Katalog Catalog No.
	1 B	29,16	450.00	**477-1**
	1 G	31,75	490.00	**477-2**
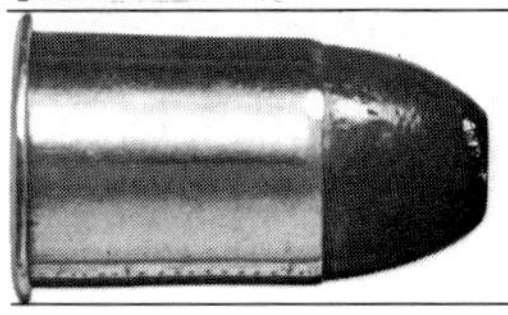	1 G	29,16	450.00	**477-3**
	1 A	19,70	304.00	**477-4**
	90 d	–	–	**477-5**

Technische und ballistische Daten

Geschoß-∅:	15,15–15,55 mm 14,80 mm[x])
Hülsen-∅ Hals:	15,95–16,26 mm
Boden:	16,66–16,80 mm
Rand:	18,52–18,97 mm
Hülsenlänge:	20,12–20,90 mm
Hülsenmaterial:	Messing
Pulverart:	Schwarz
Zündungsart:	Berdan, Boxer
Patronenlänge:	32,05–35,10 mm 27,90 mm[x])
V_0	221 m/sec
E_0	726 J
Lauflänge:	152 mm

[x]) Patrone mit Bleikugel

Technical and Ballistic Data

Bullet dia.	.596″–.612″ .583″[x])
Case dia. neck:	.628″–.640″
head:	.656″–.661″
rim:	.729″–.747″
Case length:	.792″–.823″
Case material:	brass
Powder type:	black
Primer type:	Berdan, Boxer
Cartridge length:	1.262″–1.382″ 1.098″[x])
V_0	725 ft. per sec.
E_0	525.0 ft. pounds
Barrel length:	6.000″

[x]) Cartridge with solid lead round ball

Die Patrone Kaliber .577 Revolver ist der Nachfolger, bzw. eine verbesserte Patrone des Kalibers .577 Boxer (vergl. Katalog Nr. 476)! Sie wurde um 1870 erstmalig von der Firma Eley hergestellt und ist für Pistolen und Revolver bestimmt. Die Herstellung beschränkte sich auf England und Deutschland und ist in vielen Katalogen enthalten bis mindestens 1925 (Nobel-Katalog).

Bodenstempel:
ELEY .577 . LONDON .,
ELEY .577 . S .

The cartridge caliber .577 Revolver is the successor respectively an improved cartridge of the caliber .577 Boxer (compare catalog No. 476). It was manufactured for the first time around 1870 by the Eley Company and is intended for pistols and revolvers. The production was confined to England and Germany; the cartridge is contained in many catalogs at least up to the year 1925 (Nobel Catalog).

Headstamps:
ELEY .577 . LONDON .,
ELEY .577 . S .

Exerzierpatronen

Exerzierpatronen gehören zur Gruppe der Spezialpatronen und haben sowohl im militärischen – wie auch im zivilen Bereich bestimmte Aufgaben zu erfüllen.

Die hier gezeigte Auswahl soll, wie eingangs erwähnt, nur einen allgemeinen Überblick über verschiedene gebräuchliche Ausführungen geben.

Dummy cartridges

Dummys fall into the category of special cartridges, and are employed for both military and civilian use.

As mentioned previously, the selection illustrated here gives only a general view of the usual variations.

Abb./Figure 83

1. Hülse und Geschoß verzinnt, ohne Zündhütchen
1. Case and bullet tin-plated, without primer

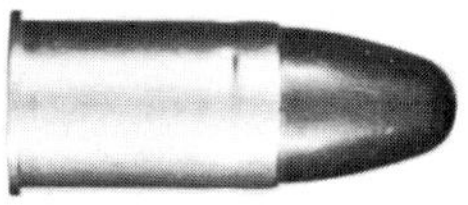

Abb./Figure 84

2. Hülse verzinnt, blindes Zündhütchen aus rotem Kunststoff.
2. Case tin-plated, inert primer of red plastic

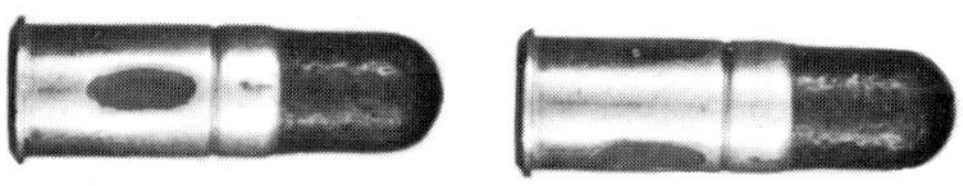

Abb./Figure 85

3. Hülse verchromt, 4 Längsrillen rot lackiert, blindes Zündhütchen aus rotem Hartgummi
3. Case chromium-plated, 4 longitudinal corrugations, red lacquered inert primer of red ebonite

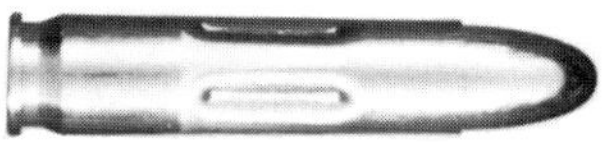

Abb./Figure 86

4. Hülse und Geschoß Messing verchromt, 4 Längsrillen, blindes Zündhütchen.
4. Case and bullet made of chromium-plated brass, 4 longitudinal corrugations, inert primer

Abb./Figure 87

5. Hülse Messing, 3 Bohrungen, blindes Zündhütchen
5. Case brass, 3 holes, inert primer

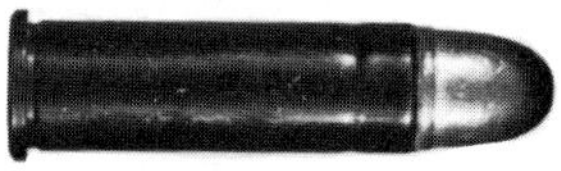

Abb./Figure 88

6. Hülse geschwärzt, blindes Zündhütchen angestochen
6. Case black, inert primer, indented

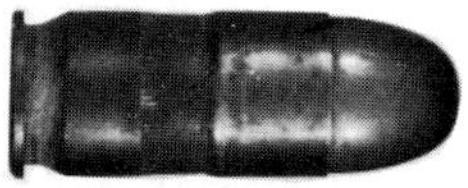

Abb./Figure 89

7. Hülse und Geschoß Messing voll, Hülse mit breiter Rändelung
7. Case and bullet full brass, case with large knurling

Abb./Figure 90

8. Hülse und Geschoß aus einem Stück Messing, 4 Längsrillen, Boden Stahl
8. Case and bullet of one solid piece of brass, 4 longitudinal corrugations, steel case head

DWM-Hülsennummern von Pistolen- und Revolverpatronen (Amerikanische und Britische Kaliber)

149 .44 Winchester C.F.
192 .450 kurz C.F.
193 .380 kurz C.F.
194 .320 kurz C.F.
202 .32 Smith & Wesson
203 .38 Smith & Wesson
204 .44 S&W amerikanisch
218 .380 lang C.F.
218A .380 lang C.F.
219 .320 lang C.F.
219A .320 lang C.F.
221 .442 Tranter
228 .445 Webley Mk.I
229 .442 lang C.F.
231 .450 lang C.F.
233 .320 kurz C.F.
242 .44 S&W russisch
260 .32 Smith & Wesson
261 .38 Smith & Wesson
261A .38 Smith & Wesson
262 .32 lang Colt (Außenfettung)
263 .38 lang Colt (Außenfettung)
273 .500 Tranter
274 .577 Revolver
284 .400 Revolver C.F.
300 .300 lang C.F.
329 .44 Winchester C.F.
513A .45 Automatik, M.1911
539 .22 Winchester C.F.
582 .38 Automatik
592 .32 lang C.F. (für Türkei gefertigt)
593 .38 kurz C.F. (für Türkei gefertigt)
595 .32 Smith & Wesson (für Türkei gefertigt)

D.W.M. case pattern numbers for American and British caliber pistol and revolver cartridges

149 .44 Winchester C.F.
192 .450 Short C.F.
193 .380 Short C.F.
194 .320 Short C.F.
202 .32 Smith & Wesson
203 .38 Smith & Wesson
204 .44 S&W American
218 .380 Long C.F.
218.A .380 Long C.F.
219 .320 Long C.F.
219A .320 Long C.F.
221 .442 Tranter
228 .445 Webley Mk.I
229 .442 Long C.F.
231 .450 Long C.F
233 .320 Short C.F.
242 .44 S&W Russian
260 .32 Smith & Wesson
261 .38 Smith & Wesson
261A .38 Smith & Wesson
262 .32 Long Colt (outs. lub.)
263 .38 Long Colt (outs. lub.)
273 .500 Tranter
274 .577 Revolver
284 .400 Revolver C.F.
300 .300 Long C.F.
329 .44 Winchester C.F.
513A .45 Automatic, M.1911
539 .22 Winchester C.F.
582 .38 Automatic
592 .32 Long C.F. (Turkish contract)
593 .38 Short C.F. (Turkish contract)
595 .32 Smith & Wesson (Turkish contract)

G. Roth-Hülsennummern von Pistolen- und Revolverpatronen (Amerikanische und Britische Kaliber)

78	.450 kurz C.F.
97	.320 kurz C.F.
98	.340 kurz C.F.
99	.360 Revolver C.F.
100	.380 kurz C.F.
101	.320 lang C.F.
102	.340 lang C.F.
103	.360 lang C.F.
104	.380 lang C.F.
186	.455 Webley Mk.II (dünner Rand)
191	.44 Winchester C.F.
288	.455 Webley Mk.II (dicker Rand)
400	.297/230 Morris lang
682	.38 S&W Spezial
754	.500 Tranter
803	.22 Winchester C.F.
909	.442 Tranter
930	.32 Smith & Wesson
931	.32 Smith & Wesson lang
932	.38 Smith & Wesson
933	.38 S&W Spezial
941	.45 Automatik Colt
943	.32 Winchester C.F.
959	.44 S&W amerikanisch
960	.44 S&W russisch
964	.44 S&W Spezial
967	.44 Winchester C.F.
971	.32 Smith & Wesson
972	.32 Smith & Wesson lang
973	.38 Smith & Wesson
974	.38 S&W Spezial
2001	.230 Revolver C.F.

G. Roth case pattern numbers for American and British caliber pistol and revolver cartridges

78	.450 Short C.F.
97	.320 Short C.F.
98	.340 Short C.F.
99	.360 Revolver C.F.
100	.380 Short C.F.
101	.320 Long C.F.
102	.340 Long C.F.
103	.360 Long C.F.
104	.380 Long C.F.
186	.455 Webley Mk.II (thin rim)
191	.44 Winchester C.F.
288	.455 Webley Mk.II (thick rim)
400	.297/230 Morris long
682	.38 S&W Special
754	.500 Tranter
803	.22 Winchester C.F.
909	.442 Tranter
930	.32 Smith & Wesson
931	.32 Smith & Wesson Long
932	.38 Smith & Wesson
933	.38 S&W Special
941	.45 Automatic Colt
943	.32 Winchester C.F.
959	.44 S&W American
960	.44 S&W Russian
964	.44 S&W Special
967	.44 Winchester C.F.
971	.32 Smith & Wesson
972	.32 Smith & Wesson Long
973	.38 Smith & Wesson
974	.38 S&W Special
2001	.230 Revolver C.F.

Bodenstempel auf Pistolen- und Revolverpatronen
Headstamps of pistol and revolver cartridges

A.R.S.: Atelier de Construction de Rennes	Frankreich
ADAMS STRAND LONDON: Adams Patent Small Arms London	England
BEAUX: Leon Beaux Mailand	Italien
BRAUN & BLOEM: Braun & Bloem Düsseldorf	Deutschland
BROWNING: Browning Arms Co. Morgan, Utah-Montreal P.Q.	Kanada
B.S.A.: Birmingham Small Arms	England
CCC: a) Creedmoor Cartridge Co. Barberton, Ohio	USA
b) Connecticut Cartridge Co.	USA
C.B.C.: Companhia Brasileira de Cartuchos S.A.	Brasilien
C D M: Cartuchos Deportivos de Mexico	Mexico
CIS: Chartered Industries Singapore	–
C R B: Cartoucherie Russo-Belge Lüttich	Belgien
D + +: G. Genschow Durlach	Deutschland
D C: Dardick Corp. New Haven Conn.	USA
DI: Defense Industries Brownsburg	Kanada
D.C.: Dominion Cartridge Co. Montreal, Quebec	Kanada
DOMINION: Dominion Cartridge Co. Montreal, Quebec	Kanada
D.C. Co.: Dominion Cartridge Co. Montreal, Quebec	Kanada
D W M: Deutsche Waffen- und Munitionsfabrik, Karlsruhe	Deutschland
E C: a) Evansville Chrysler Ordnance Plant	USA
b) Eley Brothers Ltd. London	England
E C S: Evansville Chrysler-Sunbeam Plant	USA
ELEY: Eley Cartridge Co. London	England
ELEY BROS: wie vor	England
ELEY LONDON: wie vor	England
EGESTORFF LINDEN: Egestorff Linden b. Hannover	Deutschland
F: a) Federal Cartridge Co. Minneapolis, Minn.	USA
b) Frankford Arsenal	USA
F A: Frankford Arsenal	USA
F C: Federal Cartridge Co. Minneapolis, Minn.	USA
F de M: Fábrica de Municiones	Mexico
FEDERAL: Federal Cartridge Co.	USA
F G L: G. Fiocchi Lecco	Italien
FIOCCHI: G. Fiocchi Lecco	Italien
F N C: Fábrica Nacional de Cartuchos	Mexico
F.A.M.A-P.: Fábrica Argentina Militar de Municiones de Armas Portatiles, Puerto, Borghi	Argentinien

F.A.M.M.A.P.: Fábrica Argentina Militar de Municiones de Armas Portátiles	Argentinien
F N M: Fábrica Nacional de Munições de Armas Ligeiras. Lissabon	Portugal
F.M: Fábrica Nacional de Municiones	Mexico
F M C: Fábrica Militar de Cartuchos	Argentinien
F N: Fabrique Nationale d'Armes de Guerre	Belgien
GAUPILLAT: Marcel Gaupillat Paris	Frankreich
GAUPILLAT PARIS: wie vor	Frankreich
Geco: G. Genschow, Durlach, Karlsruhe	BRD
G.EGESTORFF: G. Egestorff Linden bei Hannover	Deutschland
GEVELOT: Gevelot Paris	Frankreich
G.FIOCCI: Giulio Fiocchi, Lecco	Italien
G.F.L.: wie vor	Italien
G G (Monogramm): Gevelot & Gaupillat, Paris	Frankreich
GG & Cie: wie vor	Frankreich
G R (Monogramm): G. Roth	Österreich
H: Hirtenberger Patr., Zündhütchen u. Metallwarenfabrik Hirtenberg	Österreich
H P: wie vor	Österreich
H WIEN: wie vor	Österreich
HERTERS: Herters Inc. Waseca Minn.	USA
H X P: Griech. Pulver & Munitions Co.	Griechenland
J.A.:	
J – AO: Asahi – Seiki u. Co. Ltd.	Japan
K: Kynoch Ltd. & Co. Birmingham	England
K C: wie vor	England
KYNOCH: wie vor	England
K & C WIEN: Keller & Co. Wien	Österreich
KTW: KTW-Inc. Lorain/Ohio	USA
K & C: Keller & Co. Wien	Österreich
L.B.C.: Leon Beaúx Mailand	Italien
L.B. & C.: wie vor	Italien
L.BEAUX: wie vor	Italien
LEON BEAUX & C. MILANO: wie vor	Italien
L C: Lace City Arsenal, Miss.	USA
L.H.:	USA
MAXIM: Maxim Munitions Corp. New Haven, Conn.	USA
M.M.C.: wie vor	USA
M F: Small Arms Ammunition Factory Nr. 1	Australien
M G: wie vor Nr. 2	Australien
M MG:	Australien
M.C. & Co. Munizioni e Cartucce, Genua	Italien
METALLVERKEN: Svenska Metallwerken, Vasteras	Schweden
M.W.S. Munitionswerke Schönebeck/Elbe	BRD

Bodenstempel auf Pistolen- und Revolverpatronen
Headstamps of pistol and revolver cartridges

M Q: Small Arms Ammunitions Factory Nr. 5	Australien
norma: Norma Projektilfabrik Amotfors	Schweden
NORMA Re: wie vor	Schweden
N A A: North American Arms	USA
ORBEA: Cartucheria Orbea Buenos Aires	Argentinien
P: Fabrica National de Palencia	Spanien
P C: King Mills Ordnance Plant, Ohio	USA
P.C.Co.: Peters Cartridge Co. Cincinnati, Ohio	USA
PETERS: Peters Cartridge Co. Cincinnati, Ohio	USA
PPU: Prvi Partisan Titivo Uzice	Jugoslawien
R – A: Remington Arms Co., Conn.	USA
R.A.: Raufoss Ammunisjonsfabrikker	Norwegen
REM–UMC: Remington Arms-Union Metallic Cartr.Co.	USA
R F: Frankford Arsenal	USA
R.H.A.Co.: Robin Hood Ammunition Co. Swanton, Vermont	USA
R∧L: Royal Laboratory Woolwich	England
R – P: Remington Arms Co., Conn	USA
R.W.S.: Rheinisch-Westf. Sprengstoff A.G. Nürnberg	BRD
R Y: Etablissement Rey a Nimes	Frankreich
S.A. Corp.: Savage Arms Co.	USA
SAKO: Sako A.B. Riihimaki	Finnland
S B: a) Sellier & Bellot Prag	CSR
b) Santa Barbara Madrid	Spanien
SFI: Gevelot S.S. Paris	Frankreich
SFM: Société Française des Munitions Paris	Frankreich
S.K.D.: Selve Kronbiegel Dornheim A.G.	Deutschland
SOS: Oberschlesische Sprengstoffwerke (Patronenfabrik Lichtenwörth/ Österr.	Österreich
SPEER: Speer Inc. Lewiston/Idaho	USA
S R: Royal Ordnance Factory Spennymoore	England
SUPER-SPEED: Winchester Western Cartridge Co. New Haven, Conn.	USA
SUPER-VEL: Super Vel Cartridge Co. Shelbyville Ind.	USA
SUPER-X: Western Cartridge Co. East Alton Ill.	USA
S & W: Smith & Wesson, Fiocchi	Italien
SYI: Societá Metallurgica Italiana	Italien
T W: Twin Cities Arsenal Minneapolis/ Minn.	USA
U.S.: United States Cartr. Co. Lowell/ Mass.	USA
U.S.C.Co.: United States Cartr. Co. Lowell/Mass.	USA
U.M.C.: Union Metallic Cartridge Co. Bridgeport, Conn.	USA
V.F.M. & Cie.. Liège: V. Francotte – May & Co. Lüttich	Belgien
E S: Cartucherie de Valence	Frankreich
W: Winchester Repeating Arms Co., New Haven, Conn.	USA
W C Co: Western Cartridge Co. East Alton, Ill.	USA
W C C: Western Cartridge Co. East Alton, Ill.	USA
WESTERN: wie vor	USA
W.R.A.: Winchester Repeating Arms New Haven, Conn.	USA
W.R.A. Co.: wie vor	USA
W.R.A. SUPER: Winchester Repeating Arms New Haven, Conn.	USA
W – W: Winchester Repeating Arms Co. New Haven, Conn.	USA
W – W SUPER: Winchester Repeating Arms Co. New Haven, Conn.	USA
W & S: Webley & Scott, Birmingham (Kynoch Ldt.)	England

Arcane ist die Bezeichnung für eine neue französische Einsatzmunition. Sie wird in den Kalibern 9 mm Parabellum, .38 S&W Special und .357 Magnum hergestellt, nicht allein aus dem Grund, weil die französische nationale Polizei in diesen Kalibern einen Revolver als Dienstwaffe eingeführt hat.

Um die Leistungsfähigkeit der neuen Munition festzustellen hat man Vergleichsschüsse auf eine Aluminiumplatte mit Patronen der Kaliber 9 mm Normalausführung, 9 mm Arcane und .357 Magnum A.P. vorgenommen. Mit der „Arcane-Munition" wurden bei diesen Versuchen erheblich bessere Ergebnisse erzielt. Beim Beschuß eines Tonerdeblocks von 12 cm Stärke wurden in Vergleich ebenfalls die besseren Eigenschaften der Arcane-Munition sichtbar.

Da ausländische Fabrikate wie Produkte aus Wolframcarbid (USA) Stahl (Deutschland) oder mit teflonbeschichtete Geschosse (USA) aus vielerlei Gründen nicht infrage kamen wurde auf Kupfer zurückgegriffen. Nach Meinung der Erfinder ist ein guter Durchschlag alleine mit einem homogenen Geschoß zu erreichen. Diesen Vorzug soll reines Kupfer mit einer Härte wie sie für einen Durchschlag notwendig ist, besitzen.Außerdem soll bei Kupfer die Laufabnutzung nicht über das normale Maß hinausgehen.

Arcane-Geschosse haben eine Kegelform, die obwohl höhere Anforderungen an die Herstellung gestellt werden, die besten Resultate brachten.

Das Gewicht des 4,54 g schweren Arcane Geschosses wurde nach und nach bei Versuchen ermittelt. Es wurde dabei festgestellt, daß ein Geschoß mit einem Gewicht von 4,54 g ohne einen überhöhten Druck mit einer beträchtlichen Geschwindigkeit verschossen werden kann.

Als Treibladung wurde ein offensives Pulver gewählt, weil damit das relativ leichte Geschoß auch aus Waffen mit kurzen Läufen eine hohe Geschwindigkeit erreicht. Ein Kaliber .38 S&W Spezial-Arcane Geschoß erreicht aus dem Revolver mit einem 51 mm Lauf eine Geschwindigkeit von 510 m/s.

Aus der Literatur sind folgende Bemerkungen zusammengefaßt:
Das Gewicht des Geschosses, seine Form und Zusammensetzung in Verbindung mit der Qualität und Quantität des Pulvers zeigten folgende Eigenschaften:
- Zielenergien, die mehr als zufriedenstellend sind und über dem Durchschnitt liegen;
- ein Durchschlagvermögen, das um ca. 60% über dem der .357 Magnum-Patrone liegt;
- das Eindringvermögen in weiche Ziele ist auf Grund der geringen Masse erheblich niedriger, d.h. es besteht nicht die Gefahr der Sekundärwirkung nach dem Treffer;
- eine außergewöhnliche Aufhaltekraft infolge der hohen Geschwindigkeit des Geschosses;
- schließlich – falls ein Geschoß nicht trifft – verliert es wegen seines geringen Gewichtes sehr schnell an Geschwindigkeit und damit an Energie und es ist deshalb viel weniger gefährlich als ein schweres Geschoß.

ARCANE

ARCANE is the designation for a new French live ammunition. It is manufactured in the calibers 9 mm Parabellum, .38 S&W Special and .357 Magnum, but not only on account of the fact that the French´Police Nationalé have adopted a service revolver covering these calibers.

In order to determine the effectiveness of this new type of ammunition, tests were made by firing at an aluminium sheet with standard 9 mm cartridges, 9 mm Arcane rounds and .357 Magnum A.P. The considerably better results were obtained during these tests with the "Arcane ammunition". When conducting trials by firing at a clay block of 12 cms in diameter, the comparison showed again the better properties of the Arcane ammunition.

Since foreign brands like products made of tungsten-carbide (USA), steel (Germany) or teflon-coated bullets (USA) did not come into question for many reasons, they decided to employ copper. According to the inventors's opinion, a good piercing effect can only be achieved by means of a homogeneous bullet. Pure copper is said to have this property, with a degree of hardness as required for penetration. Moreover, copper reportedly does not cause excessive barrel abrasion.

Arcane bullets are conical; they gave the best results, although higher requirements had to be met as far as production methods are concerned.

The weight of the 70 grains Arcane bullet was found out by and by as the trials were conducted which disclosed that a 70 grains heavy bullet can be fired without excessive pressure, but with a remarkable velocity.

As a propellant an offensive powder was chosen, because a relatively light projectile will reach a high velocity, even when fired in guns with short barrels. A .38 S&W Special-Arcane bullet used in a revolver with a barrel length of 2″ reaches a speed of 1673,8 fts.

The following comments have been summarized from the pertinent literature:
The weight of the bullet, its form and composition in relation to the powder's quality and quantity showed the following caracteristic features.
- impact energy which is more than satisfactory and above the average;
- penetration power which is approximately 60% higher than that of the .357 Magnum cartridge;
- the capacity to penetrate into soft targets is considerably lower on account of the reduced mass, i.e. there is no risk of secondary effects after the bullet has hit the target;
- an extraordinary man-stopping power as a consequence of the bullet's high velocity;
- and finally – in case a bullet does not hit its target – its speed quickly decreases due to the projectile's negligible weight; thus it loses energy and therefore is considerably less dangerous than a heavy bullet.

Tabelle/Table: 3

Kaliber:	.357 Magnum	.38 S&W Spezial	9 mm Parabellum
Gesch. Gewicht:	4,54 g	4,54 g	4,54 g
Geschwindigkeit V_3:	600 m/sec	552 m/sec	545 m/sec
Energie E_3:	810 J	690 J	680 J
Lauf-Länge:	102 mm	102 mm	125 mm
Caliber:	.357 Magnum	.38 S&W Special	9 mm Luger
Bullet weight:	70 grs	70 grs	70 grs
Velocity V_3:	1968 fps	1811 fps	1788 fps
Energy E_3:	585,8 ftp	499,0 ftp	491,8 ftp
Barrel length:	4″	4″	4,9″

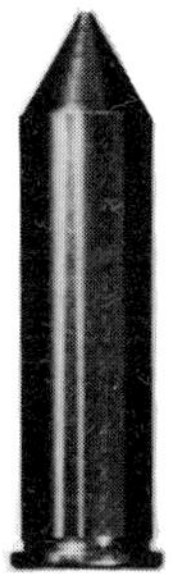
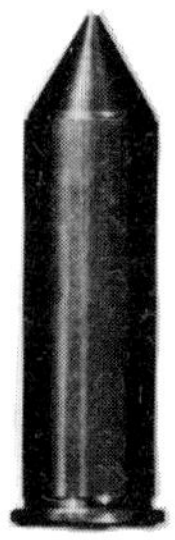

Abb./Figure 91 92 93

Dardick Corporation
Hamden Conn. USA

Dardick ist der Begriff für ein Waffensystem (Revolver), dessen Kammern über ein Magazin geladen werden und das nach dem Schuß die Hülse selbsttätig auswirft. Das Dardick-Kombigerät ist weiter eine Faustwaffe mit der unkomplizierten Umbaumöglichkeit in eine Schulterwaffe.

Die Funktion der Waffe wird durch eine besondere Form der Patronen ermöglicht, deren Hülsen aus Kunststoff hergestellt sind. Waffe und Munition wurden in den 50er Jahren entwickelt und nach dem Erfinder und Konstrukteur David Dardick benannt.

Die Waffe wird wie oben erwähnt über ein Magazin (im Griffstück) geladen. Während des Schießens können Patronen in das Magazin nachgeladen werden, ohne daß die Waffe schießunfähig wird. Über das Magazin wird die erste Patrone in die dreieckige, nach außen offene Kammer eingeführt. Durch den „Abzugsspanner-Mechanismus" (double action) wird die Trommel in Bewegung gesetzt und das erste geladene Patronenlager hinter den Lauf, und der Hahn in die hintere Position gebracht. Ein völliges Durchziehen des Abzuges führt dann zur Zündung der Patrone und der Schußauslösung. Ein erneutes Betätigen des Abzuges führt wiederum zur Trommeldrehung und damit wird die Kammer mit der abgeschossenen Patrone (Hülse) an eine Stelle bewegt, an der der Mantel, der das Herausfallen der Patronen aus den dreieckigen Patronenlagern verhindert, offen ist. Die Hülse wird an dieser Stelle ausgeworfen.

Die Waffe wurde in zwei Ausführungen, mit den Serienbezeichnungen 1100 und 1500 geliefert. Beide Modelle lassen sich mit wenigen Handgriffen und unter Benutzung von Wechselläufen von Zentralfeuer in Randfeuer umstellen. Auch läßt sich der Umbau von Faustfeuerwaffen in Schulterwaffen – und umgekehrt – mit wenigen Handgriffen problemlos durchführen.

Die Patronen aus hitzebeständigem Kunststsoff wurden in den Kalibern .38 Dardick Special und .22 Dardick gefertigt, nachdem zu den ersten Versuchen – bis 1958 – die Hülsen aus Aluminiumspritzguß hergestellt wurden. Neben den Patronen wurden Adapter für die Patronen Kaliber .38 Special, .38 ACP, .45 ACP, .22 kurz R.F., .22 lang R.F. und .22 lang für Büchsen R.F. hergestellt. Die Adapter für die handelsüblichen Patronen gleichen genau den „Dardick-Specialpatronen" nur ist hierbei der Pulverraum mit Patronenboden entsprechend der Patronenabmessung glatt durchgehend. In diese Öffnung werden die normalen Patronen hineingesteckt und sie erhalten damit die typische Dardick-Form.

Waffe und Munition fanden keine große Verbreitung.

DARDICK is the designation for a weapon system (revolver) whose chambers are loaded through a magazine and which automatically ejects the case after the shot was fired. Furthermore, the Dardick handgun may easily be transformed into a shoulder arm by a corresponding conversion unit.

The performance of the weapon is safeguarded by a particularly formed cartridge wrapped in a plastic case. Weapon and ammunition were developed in the fifties of this century and called after the inventor and technical designer David Dardick.

As already mentioned above, the weapon is loaded by using a magazine (fitted in the grip frame). While shooting the weapon, cartridges may be fed into the magazine without affecting, by doing so, the readiness to fire the gun. The first cartridge is fed from the magazine into the triangular, outwardly open chamber. By the double-action mechanism, the cylinder moves on thus placing the first cartridge into the chamber and cocking the hammer. A complete pull of the trigger will then ignite the cartridge and discharge the shot. Another trigger pull will make the cylinder turn again thus moving on the chamber, holding the fired cartridge (case), to a point where the casing that prevents the cartridges from falling out of the triangular chambers, is open. The case is ejected at this specific point.

The weapon was delivered in two versions, viz. type 1100 and type 1500. Both models can be changed by a few manipulations and by use of interchangeable barrels from a center fire to a rimfire weapon. It is, of course also possible to convert the gun with effortless ease from a handgun into a rifle – and vice versa.

The cartridges consisting of heat-resistant plastic material were manufactured in the calibers .38 Dardick Special and .22 Dardick after the first experimentals – until 1958 – had been provided with die-cast aluminium cases. Besides the cartridges there were adapters manufactured for rounds of calibers .38 Special, .38 ACP, .45 ACP, .22 short R.F., .22 long R.F. and .22 long R.F. for rifles. The adapters for the commercial cartridges look exactly like the "Dardick Special Cartridges" differing, however, insofar as the charge hole is flush with the cartridge head, according to the cartridge's measurements. The normal cartridge is inserted in the hole thus showing the typical Dardick form.

Neither weapon nor ammunition achieved wide distribution.

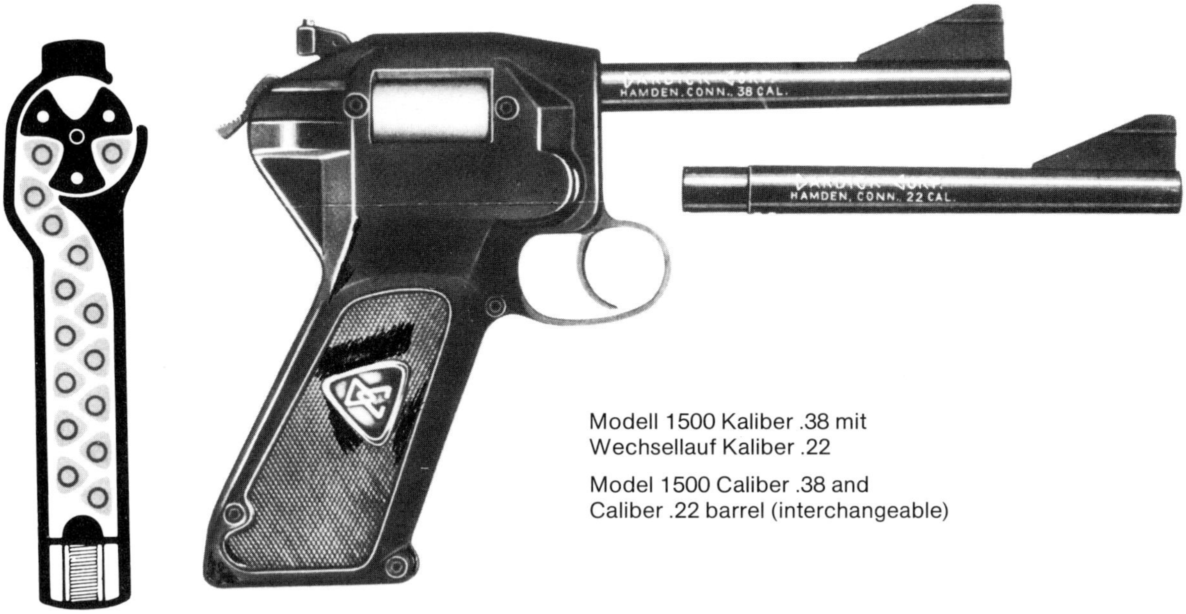

Modell 1500 Kaliber .38 mit
Wechsellauf Kaliber .22

Model 1500 Caliber .38 and
Caliber .22 barrel (interchangeable)

Abb./Figure 94

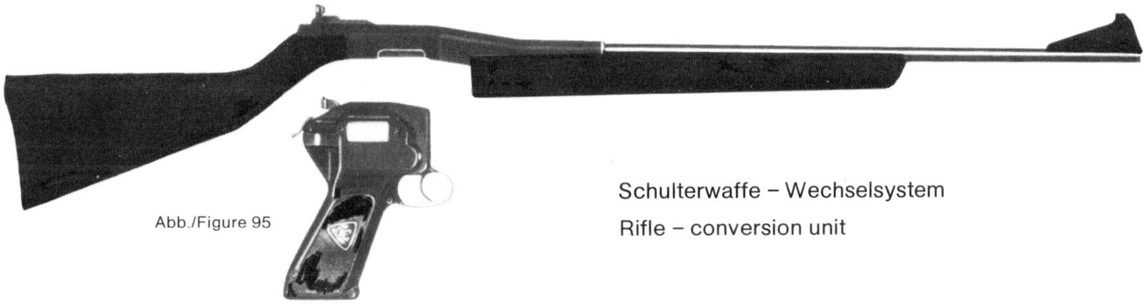

Schulterwaffe – Wechselsystem

Rifle – conversion unit

Abb./Figure 95

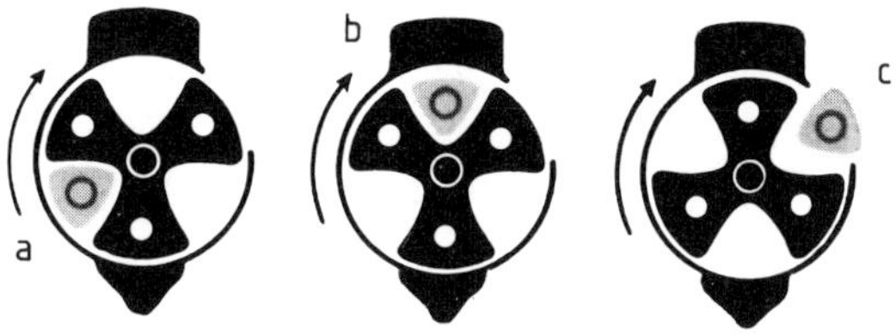

Abb./Figure 96

Abb. a: 1 Kammer ist geladen
Abb. b: Kammer steht in Feuerstellung
Abb. c: Hülse wird ausgeworfen

Fig. a: 1 chamber is loaded
Fig. b: chambe in firing position
Fig. c: case moves on for ejection

Tabelle/Table: 4

Technische Daten

	Faustfeuerwaffe	
	Modell 1100	Modell 1500
Kaliber:	.22 und .38 auswechselbar	.22 und .38 auswechselbar
Magazinkapazität:	11 TROUNDS (Spezialpatronen)	15 TROUNDS (Spezialpatronen)
Lauflänge:	76 mm und 102 mm	102 mm und 152 mm
Gewicht:	850 g	992 g
Gesamtlänge:	152 mm und 178 mm	152 mm und 203 mm
	Schulterwaffe	
Kaliber:	.22 und .38 auswechselbar	.22 und .38 auswechselbar
Magazinkapazität:	11 TROUNDS	15 TROUNDS
Lauflänge:	.22 = 597 mm	.38 = 508 mm
Gewicht:	2126 g	2268 g
Gesamtlänge:	.22 = 953 mm	.38 = 864 mm

Specifications

	Handgun	
	Model 1100	Model 1500
Caliber:	.22 and .38 interchangeable	.22 and 38 interchangeable
Capacity:	11 TROUNDS	15 TROUNDS
Barrel length:	3″ and 4″	4″ and 6″
Weight (empty):	31 oz	35 oz
Overall length:	6″ and 7″	6″ and 8″
	Rifle	
Caliber:	.22 and .38 interchangeable	.22 and .38 interchangeable
Capacity:	11 TROUNDS	15 TROUNDS
Barrel length:	.22 = 23½″	.38 = 20″
Weight (empty):	4 lbs 11 oz	5 lbs
Overall length:	.22 = 37½″	.38 = 34″

Tabelle/Table: 5

Patronen

Kaliber	Hüsenart und Farbe	Geschoß-Art	Boden-Stemp.	Katalog Nr.	Bemerkungen
.22	Kunststoff, grün	1E	DC 22	302–1	Alu-Zündglocke, verlängerte Hülse
.22	Kunststoff, grün	30E	DC 38	302–2	Mess. Zündglocke, verlängerte Hülse
.22	Kunststoff, grün	30E	DC 38	302–3	–
.22	Kunststoff, grün	30B		302–4	
.38	Alu. Druckguß	1B	–	357–1	Prototyp
.38	Kunststoff, grün	1B	DC.38	357–2	Name in Goldfarbe
.38	Kunststoff, grün	1B	DC.38	357–3	Schrift in blau
.38	Kunststoff, grün	1B	DC.38	357–4	–
.38	Kunststoff, weiß	1B	DC.38	357–5	–
.38	Kunststoff, blau	1B	DC.38	357–6	–
.38	Kunststoff, braun	1B	DC.38	357–7	–
.38	Kunststoff,schwarz	1B	DC.38	357–8	–
.38	Kunststoff, violett	1B	DC.38	357–9	–
.38	Kunststoff, schwarz	21E	DC.38	357–10	–
.38	Kunststoff, glasklar	21E	DC.38	357–11	Anschauungsmodell
.38	Kunststoff, grün	90g	DC.38	357–12	–

Beschußpatronen+)

.38	Kunststoff, weiß	1B	ohne	–	–
.38	Kunststoff, grün	1B	ohne	–	Beschriftung a. Hülse: 5.4
.38	Kunststoff, grün	1B	DC.38	–	Beschriftung a. Hülse: 6.0 (1 Ausfräsung)
.38	Kunststoff, grün	1B	DC.38	–	Beschriftung a. Hülse: 6.0 (2 Ausfräsungen)
.38	Kunststoff, grün	1B	DC.38	–	Beschriftung a. Hülse: 7.5

+) Beschußpatronen werden im Patronenkatalog nicht erfaßt.

Catridges

Caliber	Tround Type	Bullet Pattern	Headstamp	Catalog No.	Remarks
.22	green plastic	1E	DC 22	302–1	Alu-primer pocket, extended case
.22	green plastic	30E	DC 38	302–2	brass primer pocket extended case,
.22	green plastic	30E	DC 38	302–3	–
.22	green plastic	30B		302–4	
.38	aluminium impact extrusions	1B	–	357–1	prototype
.38	green plastic	1B	DC.38	357–2	with golden monogram
.38	green plastic	1B	DC.38	357–3	with dark blue monogram
.38	green plastic	1B	DC.38	357–4	–
.38	white plastic	1B	DC.38	357–5	–
.38	blue plastic	1B	DC.38	357–6	–
.38	brown plastic	1B	DC.38	357–7	–
.38	black plastic	1B	DC.38	357–8	–
.38	violet plastic	1B	DC.38	357–9	
.38	black plastic	21E	DC.38	357–10	–
.38	clear plastic	21E	DC.38	357–11	demonstrations model
.38	green plastic	90g	DC.38	357–12	–
proof cartridges+)					
.38	white plastic	1B	plain	–	
.38	green plastic	1B	plain	–	5.4 written on case
.38	green plastic	1B	DC.38	–	6.0 written on case. 1 apex milled
.38	green plastic	1B	DC.38	–	6.0 written on case. 2 apexes milled
.38	green plastic	1B	DC.38	–	7.5 written on case

+) proof cartridges are not listed in the cartridge catalog

Adapter*)

für Kaliber	Art und Farbe	Bemerkungen
.22 kurz R.F. .22 lang R.F. .22 lfB R.F.	Kunststoff, grün	
.38 Special W.C. .38 Special W.C. .38 ACP	Kunststoff, grün Kunststoff, weiß Kunststoff, grün	
.45 ACP .45 ACP	Kunststoff, schwarz Kunststoff, beige	obwohl die Adapter Kaliber .45 ACP existent sind konnte über eine Waffe nichts in Erfahrung gebracht werden.

Adapter*)

Caliber	Tround type	Remarks
.22 short R.F. .22 long R.F. .22 long rifle R.F.	green plastic	
.38 special W.C. .38 special W.C. .38 ACP	green plastic white plastic white plastic	
.45 ACP .45 ACP	black plastic beige plastic	although adapters caliber .45 ACP are existent, no information could be obtained about a corresponding weapon

*) Adapter werden im Patronenkatalog nicht erfaßt.
*) Adapters are not listed in the cartridge catalog.

Patrone Kunststoff grün und
Röntgen-Bilder Kal. .22 und .38

Cartridge green plastic and
X-ray photographs .22 and .38 caliber

Abb./Figure: 97

Patrone Kunststoff grün, Name
in Goldfarbe (Kat. 357–2)

Cartridge green plastic with
golden monogram (catalog 357–2)

Abb./Figure 98

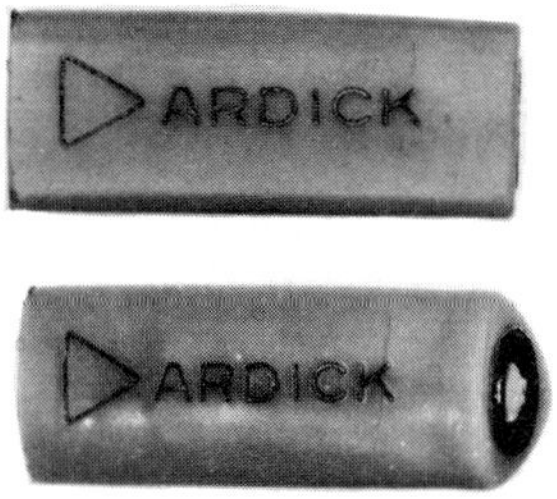

Patrone Kunststoff grün, Schrift
in blau (Kat. 357–3)

Cartridge green plastic, with
dark blue monogram (catalog 357–3)

Abb./Figure 99

Anschauungsmodell (Kat. 357–11)

Demonstrations model (catalog 357–11)

Abb./Figure 100

Aufbau einer .38-Patrone
Cartridge .38

Abb./Figure 101a

Adapter Kaliber .45 mit Patrone
Adapter cal. .45 with cartridge

Abb./Figure 101b

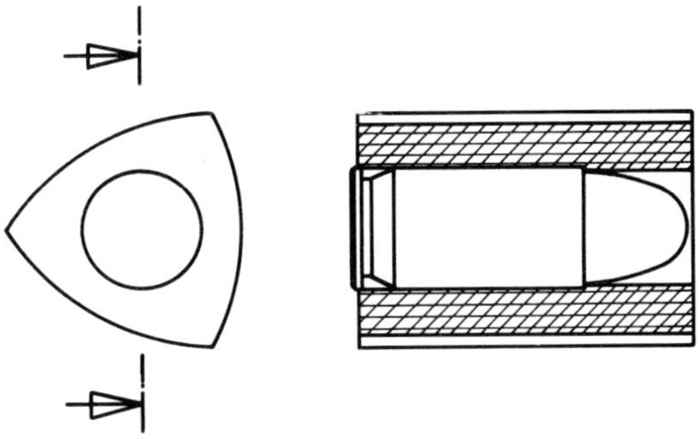

GLASER SAFETY SLUG

Glaser Safety Slug
P.O. Box 1975
Mc Allen, Texas 78501 USA

Das Glaser-Sicherheitsgeschoß als Geschoß für Faustfeuerwaffenpatronen wurde in den USA in erster Linie für die Polizei und andere Vollzugsbeamte geschaffen.

Wesentlichstes Merkmal dieser Geschoßart soll es sein, daß im Interesse der öffentlichen Sicherheit keine Querschlägerwirkung auftritt. Außerdem soll es beim Schußwechsel mehr Sicherheit bieten, d.h. der Gegner soll durch einen einzigen Treffer kampfunfähig werden. Durch eine Umfrage bei den Vollzugsbeamten in den USA wurde festgestellt, daß man allgemein mit der zum Revolver gehörenden Munition mit dem Standardgeschoß von 10,25 g nicht zufrieden war, weil sie bezüglich der Aufhaltewirkung und der Durchschlagskraft erhebliche Mängel zeige.

Es wurde ein Versuchsprogramm mit dem Ziel vorbereitet, eine Auswahl polizeitauglicher Dienstmunition zu finden. Neben 20%-iger Gelatine (zur Darstellung menschlicher Gewebe) wurde eine Hochgeschwindigkeitskamera und als Zielscheibe ein sog. Computermann eingesetzt. Während des Programms wurden 142 verschiedene handelsübliche Patronen in den Dienstwaffen der Polizei getestet. Die Glaser-Sicherheitsgeschosse erreichten aus einem Revolver mit einem 102 mm Lauf verschossen, folgende Stellenwerte zur Aufhaltewirkung:

2. 9 mm = 54,5,
4. .357 Magnum = 50,0,
15. .38 S&W Spezial = 41,8

Die am meisten gebrauchte Patrone im Kaliber .38 S&W Spezial mit einem 10,25 g schweren Bleirundkopf-Vollgeschoß erreichte einen Stellenwert von 4,2 im Durchschnitt. Die Patrone Kaliber .45 ACP erreichte einen Stellenwert von 6,5.

Die Leistung der Glaser-Patronen geht auf eine völlig neue Geschoßkonzeption zurück, bei der ein Geschoß von 6,2 g mit höherer Geschwindigkeit verschossen wird. Vom Aufbau her soll sich das Glaser-Geschoß zerlegen. Es besteht aus einem Kupfermantel in dem sich 1,25 mm Schrote befinden.Ein Querschlägerproblem soll bei dieser Geschoßart nicht mehr bestehen.

Das Glaser-Sicherheitsgeschoß soll zufriedenstellend in halbautomatischen Feuerwaffen funktionieren. Die Treffgenauigkeit soll der der Standardgeschosse nicht nachstehen, wenn es sich um Entfernungen um 15 m handelt.

Aus der Literatur wird folgende Zusammenfassung wiedergegeben:
Diese Patrone wird keine größeren Verletzungen bei Querschlägern verursachen noch wird sie den menschlichen Körper vollständig durchdringen und Unbeteiligte verletzen. Sie ist sicherer bei der Verwendung in und um durchbesiedelte Gebiete, in und um Flugzeuge und in kostspieligen Anlagen. Nach dem Eindringen gibt das Projektil seine gesamte Energie sofort innerhalb des ersten Zieles ab. Diese Munition wird nur an Vollzugsbeamte verkauft. Sie ist das Ergebnis langjähriger Erfahrung.

Die ballistischen Angaben sind der Literatur entnommen (Tabelle 6).

GLASER SAFETY SLUG

Glaser Safety Slug
P.O. Box 1975
Mc Allen, Texas 78501 USA

The Glaser Safety Slug as a bullet for handgun cartridges was developed in the USA primarily for police and other law enforcement agents. Its most essential feature is reportedly its non-ricocheting character, an effect which, no doubt, is in the interest of public safety. Moreover, it is said to offer more reliability in case of a gunfight i.e. the adversary will be immobilised by one hit.

An opinion survey carried out at law enforcement agencies in the USA showed that the officers concerned were in general not satisfied with the standard 10.25 gram projectile pertaining to the revolver ammunition, because it disclosed, according to their experience, considerable deficiencies as to man stopping power and penetration capacity.

A test program was prepared with the aim to select a variety of different types of suitable police ammunition. Besides 20% gelatin blocks (simulating human tissue), a high velocity camera and a so called computer man serving as a target, were utilised. During the test program 142 different rounds of commercially available cartridges were tested in the service weapons of the police. As to stopping power, the Glaser-Safety Slug fired in a revolver with a 102 mm barrel reached the following ratings:

2/ 9 mm = 54.5
4/ .357 Magnum = 50.0
15/ .38 S&W Special = 41.8

The most used .38 S&W Special cartridge with a 10.25 gram lead round nose projectile reached on an average a 4.2 rating.

The performance of the Glaser rounds is achieved due to an entirely new bullet design combined with a 6.2 gram bullet and a higher velocity. Considering its design the Glaser projectile is to disintegrate. It is composed of a copper jacket enclosing 1.25 mm shots. According to reports, the ricochet problem is non existent in this bullet.

The Glaser Safety Slugs function satisfactorily in semi-automatic firearms. The accuracy is not inferior to that of standard bullets up to a distance of about 15 m. The following details were compiled from pertinent literature:

This cartridge will not cause major injuries from ricochet nor will it completely penetrate a human body and injure innocent bystanders. It is safer to use in and around congested areas, in and around aircraft and expensive installations. After penetration, the projectile expends its total energy within the primary target. It is sold only to law enforcement officers. It is the result of many years of experience. The following ballistic data originate from the corresponding literature:

Tabelle/Table: 6

9 mm kurz (.380 ACP):	427 m/s	(1400 fps)
9 mm Para. (9 mm Luger):	555 m/s	(1820 fps)
.38 Spezial (.38 Special):	512 m/s	(1680 fps)
.357 Magnum (.357 Magnum):	618 m/s	(2028 fps)
.44 Spezial (.44 Special):	335 m/s	(1100 fps)
.44 Magnum (.44 Magnum):	582 m/s	(1910 fps)
.45 ACP (.45 ACP):	427 m/s	1400 fps)

	.357 Mag.	.44 S&W Spl.	.44 Mag.	.45 ACP	9 x 19 (Luger)
Abb./Figure	102	103	104	105	106

K.T.W. Incorporation
710 Copper-Forster Park Road West
Lorain, Ohio, USA

In den 60er Jahren zeigte es sich in den USA erneut, daß die 10,25 g schweren Standardgeschosse der Polizei im Kaliber .38 S&W Spezial insbesondere an bestimmten Stellen von Kraftfahrzeugen abprallten, ohne den gewünschten Erfolg zu zeigen.

Dr. Paul Kopsch, Sergeant Daniel Turcus von der Polizei Lorain und Don F. Ward als Ermittlungsbeamter des Leichenschauhauses machten sich Gedanken darüber, wie mit normalen Waffen und einer besonderen Munition eine Durchdringung von Metall und anderen gepanzerten Objekten (also auch das Stoppen von Kraftfahrzeugen durch erhebliche Beschädigung des Motorblocks) erreicht werden könnte. Die Buchstaben K.T.W. stehen für die Anfangsbuchstaben der Familiennamen KOPSCH, TURCUS und WARD. Mit ihren Erkenntnissen und ihrem Fachwissen um die Wirkungen der Munitionssorten Kaliber 9 mm, .38 und .357 Magnum gründeten sie ein K.T.W.-Versuchslabor.

Sie konnten die Behörden davon überzeugen, daß eine derartige, erfolgversprechende Munition nur aus einer besonderen Geschoßart mit einer entsprechenden Ladung bestehen könne. Es war aber auch klar, daß diese Sondermunition neben oder zusätzlich zu der normalen Munition mitgeführt werden müsse.

Daniel Turcus sah das Bedürfnis in erster Linie in einem Geschoß für das Kaliber .38 S&W Spezial für Polizei und andere Vollzugsbeamte. Sein Gedanke zielte primär darauf ab, beim ersten Schuß eine erhebliche Beschädigung des Motorblocks bei Fahrzeugen zu erreichen.

Die 3 Erfinder stellten über eine lange Zeit ausgiebige Versuche an, bei denen zuerst Stahlplatten in einem Winkel von 90° und dann in einem Winkel von 45° zur Fluglinie beschossen wurden.

Die Versuchsergebnisse zeigten, daß die auf dem Markt erhältlichen A.P. Geschosse im Kaliber .38 im allgemeinen die erste von mehreren Platten durchschlagen und dann in der zweiten hängenblieben. Im Kaliber .357 Magnum zeigten die Versuche, daß bei unbeständiger Leistung das Geschoß nur 4 Platten der gleichen Art durchschlägt. Bleikerngeschosse oder Projektile mit Stahlkappen neigten bei der Durchdringung des Metalls dazu, sich zu deformieren oder als Querschläger weiter zu fliegen, d.h. dadurch wird die Flugbahn der Geschosse beeinträchtigt und die Geschosse werden fast in jede Richtung abgelenkt.

Nach einer Reihe von Versuchen mit verschiedenen Materialien entschlossen sich die K.T.W.-Leute zu einem Geschoß im Kaliber .38 S&W Spezial, das besonders schwer, hart und teflonbeschichtet war. Es handelte sich dabei um ein Hochgeschwindigkeitsgeschoß mit niedrigem Druck und es durchschlug beständig sechs bis acht Stahlplatten, aus dem Material, wie es für den Pkw-Karosseriebau verwandt wird. Die Versuche zeigten, daß das teflonbeschichtete .38er Geschoß in der Regel seine gerade Flugbahn beim Durchschlagen des Karosseriemetalls beibehielt und wenn es einmal bei einer Platte anfing von seiner Flugbahn abzuweichen,

During the sixties of our century, it time and again happened in the United States of America, as had before, that the standard 158-grain bullets of police weapons of caliber .38 S&W Special would bounce off quite determinate areas of motor-vehicles without showing the desired success.

Doctor Paul Kopsch, Sergeant Daniel Turcus of the Lorain Police and coroner's investigator Don. F. Ward went to work on how a penetration of metal and other armored objects (also the stopping of motor-vehicles by considerable damage to the engine block) could be achieved by means of normal weapons and a particular ammunition. The letters K.T.W. stand for the initials of the surnames **K**OPSCH, **T**URCUS and **W**ARD. Putting their experience and professional knowledge about the effects of ammunition in the caliber 9 mm, .38 and .357 Magnum together, they formed the KTW Experimental Laboratory.

They succeeded in convincing the authorities of the necessity that such a promising ammunition had to consist of a special type of projectile with a corresponding load. However, it was also made clear that this special round had to be carried apart from or in addition to the normal service ammunition.

Daniel Turcus saw in the first line a genuine need for a bullet chambered for the caliber .38 S&W Special as used by police and other law enforcement officers. His idea primarily aimed at the possibility to cause with the first shot a considerable damage to the engine block of motor-vehicles.

The three inventors conducted exhaustive tests for a long period, firing at the beginning at sheets of steel held at 90 degrees to the line of flight, and later at an angle of 45 degrees. The test results revealed that metal-piercing .38 Special bullets obtainable on the market would in general penetrate the first sheet out of several ones and then get hung up in the second. The .357 Magnum load only penetrated four sheets of the same kind and its performance was not consistent. Lead core bullets or steel-capped projectiles showed a tendency to deform when penetrating the metal or would ricochet, thus having an impact on the balance and flight of the bullet, deflecting it in nearly any direction.

After a series of tests with different materials the KTW folks came up with their extra-heavy, super-hard and teflon-coated .38 S&W Special bullets. The high velocity bullet with low pressure consistently penetrated six to eight steel sheets of the auto body material. The tests disclosed that the .38 Special teflon-coated bullet stayed on a straight course through the auto body metal and, if it started to yaw in one sheet, it would straighten up by the time it passed the next sheet of steel. This implies that the hardness of the metal, the teflon-coating and the ogive shape contribute to the straight flight and penetration power of the projectile.

bekam es seine Richtung nach dem Durchdringen der nächsten Stahlplatte wieder. Dies bedeutet, das die Härte des Materials, die Teflonschicht und die Ogivalform des Geschosses zum geraden Flug und zur Durchschlagskraft beiträgt.

Auf einen Motorblock der Firma Ford waren die Versuche und Ergebnisse recht beeindruckend. Da man davon ausging, daß sich in der Regel ein Polizeibeamter ca. 13,7 m vom Fahrzeug befindet wenn er von der Schußwaffe Gebrauch machen muß, wurden für die Versuche diese Entfernung zugrunde gelegt. Bei den Versuchen stand der Motorblock vor einer Traverse aus Erde als Kugelfang auf dem Boden.

Die .38er Teflongeschosse aus einem Revolver mit einem 152 mm (6″) Lauf verfeuert, durchdrangen alle den Block, obwohl dieser an manchen Stellen eine Dikke von 9,5 mm hatte. Bei Verwendung desselben Motorblocks, derselben Waffe und der Standardmunition im Kaliber .38 Spezial, verschossen aus der gleichen Entfernung, prallten alle Geschosse vom Motorblock ab. Bei der Verwendung von Patronen Kaliber .357 Magnum drangen die Geschosse erst dann in den Motorblock ein, nachdem dreimal auf annähernd dieselbe Stelle geschossen worden war. Es handelte sich außerdem um eine Stelle, an welcher der Block besonders dünn war.

Die Versuche zeigten weiter, daß auf eine Entfernung von ca. 23 m die Treffgenauigkeit der Munition mit teflonbeschichteten Geschossen der Standardmunition mit 10,25 g schweren Geschossen nicht nach steht. Es wurden weitere Versuche mit den verschiedensten Kalibern (insbesondere im Kaliber 7,62 mm für Langwaffen) gemacht. Der gewünschte Erfolg blieb dabei mit einem 7,5 g schweren Geschoß, aus dem US Carabine Mod. 30 M1 verschossen, aus. Motorblocks, Panzerplatten und Zementwände wurden nicht wie gewollt beschädigt.

Im Rahmen der Versuche wurden zur Geschoßherstellung verschiedene Materialien wie Kennertium, Maschinenstahl u.a. benutzt. Da Maschinenstahl nicht so teuer wie Kennertium war und sich die Ergebnisse mit Geschossen aus Maschinenstahl als zufriedenstellend herausstellten, wurde von Kennertium abgegangen.

Das Geschoß aus Stahl ist massiv, d.h. es handelt sich um ein Vollgeschoß. (Ein Großteil der Nachfolgegeschosse sind aus einer Messinglegierung hergestellt. Es handelt sich dabei um reine Vollgeschosse ohne Näpfchen, d.h. die Feldereindrücke befinden sich nach dem Schuß im Geschoßmaterial). Am Geschoßboden befindet sich eine Stufe, damit an dieser Stelle ein kurzer Geschoßmantel angesetzt werden kann. Vor der Befestigung des kurzen Geschoßmantels (Näpfchens) wird das Geschoß mit einer speziellen Teflonart überzogen. Durch das Näpfchen aus einer Kupferlegierung bekommt der Teflonüberzug des Stahlgeschosses beim Schuß keine Laufberührung, d.h. die Felder des Laufes drücken sich in das Näpfchen ein.

Der Teflonüberzug auf den Geschossen bewirkt, daß diese leichter das Zielmedium durchdringen oder in es eindringen. Der Überzug macht dabei die Geschoßoberfläche gleitfähiger und vermindert den Reibungswiderstand.

Die ballisttischen Daten einiger K.T.W.-Patronen können der nachfolgenden Tabelle 7 entnommen werden.

A Ford engine block also was used as a target during the tests and the results were quite impressive. The tests were conducted from a distance of fifteen yards, assumed to be the average distance an officer would be from a passing car. The block was set on the ground in front of an earthen backstop.

The .38 teflon-coated rounds fired from a .38 Special with six inch barrel all penetrated the block, even though the thickness reached 0.37″ at some points. Using the caliber .38 Special ammunition, all bullets bounced off the engine block. Using the .357 Magnum round the bullet would penetrate the block after hitting approximately the same spot three times. This was, by the way, an area where the engine block was particularly thin.

As for accuracy, the teflon-coated rounds showed their own up to twenty-five yards in comparison tests with the standard 158-grain .38 Special loads. Other tests were conducted with quite a number of different calibers (especially with the caliber .30" for rifles). A 115.7 grain bullet fired from the US-Carbine Model 30 M 1 failed to come up to the desired expectations. Engine blocks, armored plates and cement blocks did not show the intended effects.

Within the scope of the trials various materials such as Kennertium, machine steel and others were employed. As machine steel was less expensive than Kennertium and the obtained results with bullets made of this material turned out to be satisfactory, the Kennertium metal was no longer used.

The steel projectile is solid i.e. it is a full jacketed bullet. (A great deal of bullets manufactured during the following period are of a metal alloy. They are solid jacket bullets without a cup so that the striations of the lands and grooves are to be found on the bullet material after firing the shot).

The bullet base has a step so that a short jacket can be added there. Before fixing the short jacket (cup), the bullet is coated with a particular kind of teflon. The copper alloy cup prevents touch of the teflon-coated steel bullet with the barrel when firing the shot which means that the striations of the barrel's grooves are incised on the cup.

Teflon-coated bullets penetrate the target more easily or lodge deep in it. The coating renders the projectile's surface smoother and reduces the frictional resistance.

The ballistic data of some K.T.W. cartridges may be taken from the graph hereunder.

Remark:

According to the legend on the package KTW ammunition is only available to authorized law enforcement agencies and military services.

Bemerkung:

Laut Aufschrift auf der Verpackung der Munition soll der Verkauf von K.T.W.-Munition nur auf Polizei- und Militärdienststellen beschränkt sein.

Tabelle/Table: 7

Abb./Figure	107	108	109 110	111

Kaliber:	6,35 mm	7,65 mm	9 mm Br. kz.	9 × 19
G. Gew.	2,6 g	4,6 g	6,15 g	6,5 g
Geschw. (V_0)	275 m/sec	315 m/s	305 m/sec	396 m/sec
Lauf-Länge	51 mm	102 mm	96 mm	102 mm
Caliber	.25 ACP	.32 ACP	.380 ACP	9 mm Luger
Bullet weight	40 grs	71 grs	95 grs	80 grs
Velocity	900 fps	1025 fps	1000 fps	1300 fps
Barrel length	2″	4″	3¾″	4″

	112 113	114 115	116	117 118

Kaliber:	.38 S&W Spl.	.357 Mag.	.30 Carbine	.45 ACP
G. Gew.	5,85 g	5,85 g	5,2 g	11,85 g
Geschw. (V_0)	396 m/sec	595 m/sec	663 m/sec	328 m/sec
Lauf-Länge	152 mm	222 mm	413 mm	127 mm
Caliber	.38 Special	.357 Magnum	.30 Carbine	.45 ACP
Bullet weight	90 grs	90 grs	80 grs	183 grs
Velocity	1300 fps	1950 fps	2175 fps	1075 fps
Barrel length	6″	8¾″	18¾″	5″

Erfinder:
Russel S. Robinson
Tuscon Arizona USA

Waffenhersteller:
Colt Ind. Firearms Division
Hartford, Conn. USA

Salvo Squeeze Bore (SSB) bedeutet, daß es sich um ein Waffensystem mit einem besonderen Lauf handelt. In dem SSB-Lauf bekommen mehrere Geschosse die gleichzeitig verschossen werden den üblichen Drall und sie werden dann in einem sich verengenden glatten Teil zusammengedrückt und an der Laufmündung voneinander getrennt.

Die Firma Colt hat für die Salvo Squeeze Bore-Patrone eine Selbstladepistole Colt - Modell 1971 mit double action entwickelt.

Beim Schießen mit Mehrfachgeschossen wird die Wahrscheinlichkeit mindestens einen Treffer zu erreichen wesentlich erhöht. Dies deshalb, weil mehrere (hier 3) Geschosse die gleichzeitig aus einer Waffe verschossen werden, das Ziel in einem gewissen Abstand voneinander erreichen. Es wird also der Effekt des Schrotschusses nachgeahmt. Da bei dieser Munitionsart die Anzahl der Geschosse erhöht wurde, vermindert sich die Auftreffenergie der einzelnen Geschosse, gleichzeitig verringert sich aber auch die wirkungsvolle Reichweite. Aus diesen Gründen muß eine sorgfältige Abstimmung der Wirksamkeit der einzelnen Geschosse und der zu erzielenden Treffer vorgenommen werden, zumal die Energie, die in Selbstladepistolen erzeugt werden kann, begrenzt ist. Ein Problem, welches offenbar durch das Salvo Squeeze Lauf (SSL)-System gelöst worden ist.

In dem „Salvo Squeeze"-Laufsystem werden wie schon erwähnt, mehrere Geschosse die sich in einer Patrone mit normalen Abmessungen befinden, vor dem Verlassen des Laufes voneinander getrennt. Sie erhalten die Geschwindigkeit, die sie zur Stabilität ihrer Flugbahn benötigen. Getrennt werden die Geschosse im vorderen glatten Laufteil, der sich zur Mündung hin verjüngt.

Erkennen kann man dies an der eigentümlichen Form der Geschosse, die sie beim Verlassen des Laufes bekommen haben. Die Geschoßenden werden nämlich beim Durchgang durch den konischen Lauf zusammengepreßt, wobei das jeweils nachfolgende Geschoß aus dem hohlen Boden des vorherigen Geschosses herausgedrückt wird. Durch das Zusammendrücken der Geschoßböden erhöht sich gleichzeitig die Geschwindigkeit und Energie der Geschosse.

Abgesehen von militärischen Entwicklungen wurde in der Vergangenheit neben der „Squeeze"-Lauf-Patrone im Kaliber 9 mm Parabellum eine weitere Patrone im Kaliber .45 ACP entwickelt. Sie stimmt in den Abmessungen mit der normalen Patrone Kal. .45 ACP überein und kann notfalls auch aus den normalen Waffen dieses Kalibers verfeuert werden. Die hier zu beschreibenden Patronen haben drei Mantelgeschosse mit Bleikern. Der Form nach handelt es sich um Stumpfkegelgeschosse mit ausgehöhlten Geschoßböden.

SALVO SQUEEZE BORE

Inventor:
Russel S. Robinson
Tucson, Arizona/USA

Manufacturer:
COLT Ind. Firearms Division
Hartford, Conn., USA

Salvo Squeeze Bore (SSB) is a weapon system including a particular barrel. In the Salvo Squeeze bore, several bullets fired simultaneously are given the usual spin and then squeezed in the smooth, tapering part of the bore; they separate at the muzzle.

The COLT Company have developed a self-loading double action pistol COLT Model 1971 for the Salvo Squeeze Bore cartridge. (see illustration 119).

When firing multiple bullets, the probability to achieve at least one hit is considerably increased, because several projectiles (in this case a set of three) fired at the same time in a weapon will reach the target at intervals. Thereby, the effect of a shotgun pattern is imitated. Since this type of ammunition consists of more than one bullet, the impact energy of the single projectiles decreases and also their effective range. For these reasons, the load must be meticulously chosen in proportion to the effectiveness of the single bullets and the hits to be scored, all the more since the energy that can be reached in self-loading pistols, is limited – a problem which has obviously been solved by the Salvo Squeeze Bore (SSB) System.

As already mentioned, several bullets seated in a cartridge case of standard measurements are separated in the Salvo Squeeze Bore System before leaving the barrel. They reach the velocity required for the stability of their trajectory. The projectiles are separated in the smooth front part of the bore tapering towards the muzzle. This can be seen by the peculiar form the bullets are shaped into at the instant they leave the barrel; their rear part will be squeezed when passing the conical part of the bore which presses the second and each following bullet out of the hollow base of each preceding projectile. At the same time, by squeezing the bullet bases, the velocity and the energy of the bullets are increased.

Besides military designs there was in the past developed, apart from the 9 mm Luger cartridge for "squeeze" bores, a round in caliber .45 ACP. Its dimensions correspond to those of the standard caliber .45 ACP cartridge and may incidentally be fired also in normal weapons of this caliber. The three cartridges to be described here have three jacketed bullets with lead core each. Their shape defines them as blunt coned bullets with a hollow base.

In order to stick one bullet tightly into the other, the shape of the cavity corresponds to that of the projectile's vertex. The early version of the 9 mm cartridge was provided with projectiles which were cemented together and had no wrapping. Current cartridges include three bullets wrapped in a plastic capsule thus forming a unit. Since these new cartridges with the plastic coating have the same dimensions and almost the same shape as standard cartridges, they can

Damit die Geschosse ohne Zwischenraum d.h. auf geringstem Raum untergebracht werden können, entspricht die Form der Aushöhlung der Form der Geschoßspitze. Bei der älteren Ausführung der Patrone 9 mm waren die Geschosse aneinandergeklebt und hatten keine Umhüllung. Bei den derzeitigen Patronen sind die 3 Geschosse in einer Kunststoffkapsel eingeschlossen und bilden so eine Einheit. Da die neuen Patronen mit Kunststoffmantel die gleichen Abmessungen und fast die gleiche Form haben wie die von Normalpatronen, lassen sie sich auch in der gleichen Weise verpacken und in das Magazin laden.

Wenn die Geschosse beim Schuß den gezogenen Teil des Laufes verlassen und in den konischen glatten Teil übergehen, haben sie bereits den „Drall" erhalten und sie werden nun in dem sich verengenden Teil im Durchmesser reduziert. Dadurch erhöht sich die Zahl ihrer Umdrehungen. Die gleiche Erscheinung ist bekannt von einem sich um die eigene Achse wirbelnden Schlittschuhläufer (Pirouette), dessen Umdrehungszahlen zunehmen, wenn er die Arme an den Körper anlegt.

Wenn die Geschosse dann an der Mündung des sich verengenden glatten Laufes getrennt werden, entsteht ein geringer Geschwindigkeitsunterschied zwischen den einzelnen Geschossen. Die nachfolgend angeführten Geschwindigkeiten wurden bei Geschossen ermittelt, die von 9 mm auf ca. 7,6 mm zusammengedrückt worden sind. Das erste (vordere) Geschoß verläßt den Lauf mit einer Geschwindigkeit von 389 m/s, das zweite (mittlere) folgt mit 386 m/s und das dritte (hintere) Geschoß verläßt den Lauf mit 375 m/s.

Frühere Arten der SSB-Munition wiesen verschiedene Unzulänglichkeiten auf. Diese verursachten u.a. einen erhöhten Verschleiß in dem sich verengenden Teil des des Laufes. Die Unzulänglichkeiten wurden durch verbesserte Geschosse und Änderung des konischen Teils des Laufes, sowie Fettung und andere metallurgische Zusammensetzung der Geschosse behoben. Die Lebensdauer des SSB-Systems ist jetzt dem der normalen gezogenen Läufe gleichzusetzen.

Die Tendenz der Geschosse sich zu trennen, wenn sie in einer heißgeschossenen Waffe geladen und belassen wurden, ohne daß die Patrone gezündet wurde, sind durch Änderungen an der Hülse und der Verwendung von anderen Kunststoffen behoben worden.

be packaged as well as loaded into the magazine in the usual way.

When the fired bullets leave the rifled part of the bore and pass over to the conical, smooth section, they have already reached their 'spin' and are now reduced in diameter in the tapering end of the barrel. The number of their revolutions thereby increases. This phenomenon may be compared with the performance of a skater pirouetting on the ice by folding his arms around his body and thus speeding up his rotatory motions.

When the individual projectiles separate at the muzzle, there will come up a slight difference in velocity between them. The following velocities were determined by squeezing down 9 mm bullets to about 7.6 mm in diameter. The first (front) bullet leaves the barrel with a speed of 389 m/s, the second (central) bullet follows at a speed of 386 m/s and the third (last) projectile leaves the barrel at a velocity of 375 m/s.

Former types of SSB-ammunition showed some deficiencies which caused, among other things, an increased abrasion of the smooth tapered part of the bore. By bullet improvement and the modification of the conical part of the bore as well as by lubrification and a different metallurgic composition of the projectiles, these deficiencies were overcome.

The service life of the SSB-System can now be equated with that of standard rifled barrels.

The tendency of the projectiles to separate when loaded into a hot fired weapon has been eliminated by modification of the case and the utilization of other plastic materials.

Abb./Figure: 120

Patrone Kal. .45 ACP
Cartridge Cal. .45 ACP

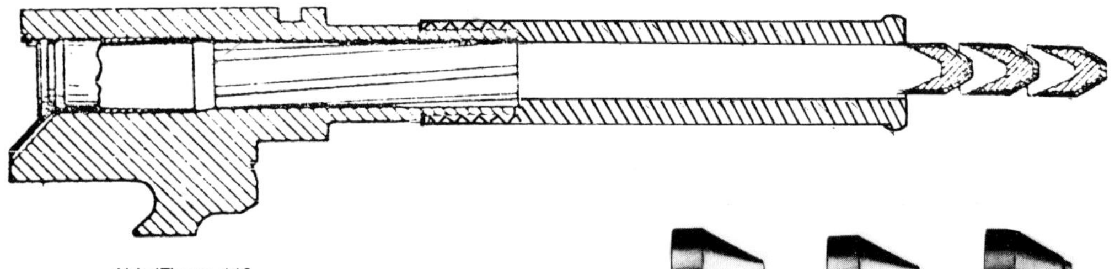

Abb./Figure 119

Abb./Figure 121

3 Geschosse .45 ACP unverschossen
3 S-Projectile .45 ACP before firing

Tabelle/table 8

Technische und ballistische Daten

Technical and ballistic data

	Kal. .45/38 SSB Cal. .45/38 SSB	Kal. 9 mm/7,62 mm SSB Cal. 9 mm/.30 SSB
Patronen-Gewicht Cartridge weight	17,24 g 266 grs	10,7 g 165 grs
Patronen-Länge Cartridge length	32,25–33,75 mm 1.270–1.329″	29,5–30,5 mm 1.16–1.20″
Geschoß-Länge Bullet length	19,8 mm gesamt- .780″ entire	17,4 mm gesamt- .685″ entire
Geschoß-Gewicht Bullet weight	10,4–10,7 g gesamt- 160–165 grs entire	6,7 g gesamt- 104 grs
Anzahl der Geschosse No. of S-bullets	3 3	3 3
Gewicht d. Geschosses S-bullet weight	3,24–3,55 g einzel- 50-55 grs single	2,13 g einzel- 33 grs single
Geschoß-Durchmesser Bullet diameter	11,43 mm vor d. Schuß .45″ before firing	9 mm vor d. Schuß .355″ before firing
Geschoß-Durchmesser Bullet diameter	9,65 mm nach d. Schuß .38″ after firing	7,62 mm nach d. Schuß .30″ after firing
Geschoßgeschwindigkeit V_8 m Velocity V_{25} ft		
1. Geschoß 1st S-bullet	344 m/s 1129 fts	389 m/s 1276 fts
2. Geschoß 2nd S-bullet	327 m/s 1073 fts	386 m/s 1266 fts
3. Geschoß 3rd S-Bullet	320 m/s 1051 fts	375 m/s 1230 fts

Mainhard and Baehl
Associates (MBA)
San Ramon, Kalifornien USA

Nachdem die Nachfrage nach einem Geschoß, das keinen Körper durchschlägt in den USA immer dringender wurde (es war die Zeit der internationalen Flugzeugentführungen), entwickelt die Firma MBA eine Munition im Kaliber .38 S&W Spezial (.357 Magnum) die sie unter der Handelsbezeichnung „Short-Stop" auf den Markt brachte. Die Munition hatte ein sich zerlegendes Geschoß, das einen Körper nicht durchschlagen sollte und das nicht das Risiko eines Querschlägers in sich barg. Außerdem sollte es über kurze Entfernung (ca. 30 m) seine Geschwindigkeit und damit auch seine Energie schnell verlieren. In einem Flugzeug sollte damit die aus vielen Schichten bestehende Wandung nicht durchschlagen werden.

Die Short-Stop Patrone besteht aus einer Patrone des Kalibers .38 Spezial/.357 Magnum mit einem roten Geschoßmantel aus Kunststoff. Ein zerlegbares Geschoß von runder, kissenartiger Struktur befindet sich zusammengefaltet in dem Geschoßmantel. In der orangefarbenen Kissenhülle befinden sich 3,5 g Schrot mit einem Durchmesser von einem Millimeter. Zwischen der Treibladung und dem Geschoß befindet sich ein Kunststoffpfropfen von 5 mm Dicke.

Im Lauf folgt das Geschoß dem Drall und nach dem Verlassen des Laufes entfaltet sich das Geschoß/Kissen auf seinen Durchmesser von 2,5 cm. Die Mündungsgeschwindigkeit V_0 liegt über 305 m/s und die Mündungsenergie E_0 bei 169 J. Nach 30 m beträgt die Geschwindigkeit V_{30} nur noch 58 m/s und die Energie liegt bei $E_{30} = 8$ J. Beim Auftreffen auf einen Körper platzt die Geschoßhülle auseinander und die Schrotkügelchen entweichen, d.h. sie dringen in den Körper ein. Bei 15 m Entfernung soll das Geschoß nicht mehr in einen Körper eindringen.

Um bei einer möglichen Flugzeugentführung den Sicherheitsfaktor zu ermitteln wurde die simulierte Wandung eines Flugzeuges (Boeing 727) aus verschiedenen Entfernungen beschossen. Bei Entfernungen bis 1,5 m durchschlug das Geschoß immer das Versuchsmaterial. Über 1,8 m wurden Beschädigungen, jedoch keine Durchschläge erreicht.

Aus der Zusammenfassung ergibt sich u.a. folgendes: Die Munition zur Verwendung auf kurze Entfernungen wurde entwickelt für den Gebrauch durch Vollzugspersonal in überfüllten, umgrenzten Bereichen und in erster Linie als ein Abschreckungsmittel zur Verhinderung von Flugzeugentführungen. Man erwartet von dieser Munition, daß sie das Risiko einer Verletzung von unschuldigen Umherstehenden heruntersetzt und Beschädigungen von Flugzeugwandungen verhindern würde.
Aufgrund der besonderen Struktur des Geschosses werden Querschlägerverletzungen vermieden.

(Siehe Tabelle 9)

When the demand for a projectile which would not pass through a body became increasingly pressing in the USA (it was the period of international hijacking of commercial airplanes), the firm MBA developed .38 Special/ .357 Magnum ammunition marketed under the trade-name SHORT STOP. The round had a collapsible bullet which was not to pass through a body and without risk of ricochet. Also, the projectile was designed to slow down at a short distance (about 33. yd. and to lose its energy quickly. In a commercial airliner, the projectile would not penetrate the multi-layered skin of the aircraft.

The SHORT-STOP round consists of a .38 Special/ .357 Magnum caliber cartridge with a red-coloured plastic cap. A collapsed projectile rests inside the cap and is composed of a circular, pillow-like structure. In the orange-coloured pillow there are contained 54 grain pellets, each pellet being 0.0394" in diameter. A plastic wad of 0.197" in diameter is placed between the propellant and the bullet.

After the cartridge has been fired, the projectile begins to spin because of the rifling in the bore. On leaving the barrel, the projectile assumes a pancake shape of 1" in diameter. Muzzle velocity is over 1000 ft/s and muzzle energy E_0 is 122.2 ft/pds. At 33 yd., the projectile's velocity is 190 ft/s and the energy $E_{33} = 5{,}8$ ft/pds. On striking the body, the "shell" of the projectile ruptures allowing the pellets to escape in the tissue. At a distance of 16.5 yd. the projectile is not to penetrate anymore into a body.

To assess the safety factor involved in the discharge of this ammunition during possible airplane hijacking attempts, a simulated wall of a Boeing 727 airplane was test-fired at from different distances. At a range of 1.37 yd. the projectile always passed through the test material. At a range of more than 1.64 yd. damages were caused, but no exiting could be achieved.

Summary:

This short-range ammunition was developed for use by law enforcement officers in congested, enclosed areas and primarily as a hijacking deterrent in commercial airliners. These rounds were expected to reduce the risk of injury to innocent bystanders and prevent damage to aircraft walls. On account of the particular structure of the projectile, injuries due to ricochet are averted.

(technical details table 9)

Tabelle/Table: 9

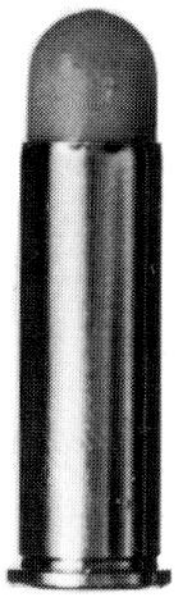

Abb./Figure: 122

Kaliber:	.38 S&W Spezial
Gesch. Gew.	3,9 g
Geschwindgk. V_0	:376 m/s
Energie E_0:	320 J
Lauf-Lg.:	127 mm
Caliber:	.38 S&W Special
Bullet weight:	60 grs
Velocity V_0	1234 fps
Energy E_0:	231 ftp
Barrel lenght:	5.0„

VELEX Weaponry Co.
N 6809 Lincoln,
Spokane, WA. USA
(Ammo Manufacturing,
Weapon Sales, Importing)

VELET Cartridge Co.
N 6809 Lincoln,
Spokane, WA USA
(Exploding bullets)

EXAMMO Research Product
Spokane Washington USA
(Division of Precision
Products of Washington Inc.)

Bei den Firmen VELEX, VELET und EXAMMO handelt es sich um Firmen, die sich mit der Entwicklung und Herstellung besonderer Munition befaßt haben, bzw. noch befassen. Im Rahmen dieses Buches soll allerdings nur Munition für Faustfeuerwaffen (Pistolen und Revolver) mit Sprenggeschossen behandelt werden.

Die „VELEX Cartridge Company" wurde von Howard Angel und Greg Loyd gegründet. Sie stellten viele Artikel des täglichen Bedarfs her, u.a. auch die nachfolgend beschriebenen Geschosse mit einer Sprengladung. Die Geschosse wurden einzeln mit einer Bohrmaschine aufgebohrt, die Bohrung mit Schwarzpulver oder einem schnellbrennbaren Pistolenpulver gefüllt und mit einem Zündhütchen von Pistolenpatronen verschlossen. Die Patronen wurden mit einem Wiederladegerät laboriert. Das geladene Bohrloch wurde dann im allgemeinen mit rotem Lack abgedeckt. Einige Exerzierpatronen, die für Händler und Ausstellungen laboriert wurden, wurden mit einer blauen Lackierung versehen.

Als Loyd nach ca. 1 Jahr aus der Firma ausschied, führte Angel die Firma unter der Bezeichnung „VELET Cartridge Company" weiter. Angel begann die Explosionsladung und das Zündhütchen durch Quecksilber zu ersetzen.

Von Greg Loyd wurde dann die Firma „EXAMMO" ins Leben gerufen. Er automatisierte die gesamte Bearbeitung der Munition unter Benutzung kommerzieller Bestandteile. Als Zünder im Geschoß wurde dabei ein Perkussionszündhütchen verwendet. Anfangs wurden nur Geschosse im Kaliber .38 hergestellt und zu Patronen verarbeitet. Die Geschosse wurden in der Spitze mit gelbem Lack abgedichtet.

Neben den vorgenannten Firmen befaßte sich noch Sidney Brigadier der „Bingham Ltd. 1775 - C Wilwat Dr. Narcross, Georgia" mit der Herstellung dieser Munitionsart. Seine Munition wurde überwiegend durch die Änderung fertiger Patronen gefertigt. Er benutzte dazu zum großen Teil „Super Vel"-Munition.

Im Geschoßaufbau könnte es sich dabei um frühe VELEX-Geschosse handeln. Es wurde bekannt. daß einige Patronen durch Fall explodiert sind.

Die Herstellerfirmen preisen ihre Munition unter folgenden Gesichtspunkten an:
„Das Sprenggeschoß wurde in dem Bemühen konstruiert, eine wirksame, querschlägerfreie und nur geringdurchschlagende Patrone für den zivilen und den Polizeigebrauch zur Verfügung zu haben. Durch diese Munition wird die Wirksamkeit beim Einsatz von Faustfeuerwaffen zur Verteidigung erhöht. Die Munition wurde bis zu diesem Punkte verbessert, daß man sie

VELEX, VELET and EXAMMO are companies which have engaged in the design and manufacture of particular ammunition and still do so today. Within the scope of this volume, however, only handgun ammunition (pistols and revolvers) being provided with explosive bullets is treated.

The VELEX Cartridge Company was founded by Howard Angel and Greg Loyd. They manufactured many articles of consumption, among others also the below-described explosive bullets. The projectiles were all bored open by means of a drilling appliance; the bore-hole was filled with black powder or a fast burning pistol powder and capped with a pistol cartridge primer. A reloading tool was used to determine the cartridge load. The loaded bore-hole was normally covered up with red lacquer. Some dummies, loaded for weapon dealers and to be shown at expositions, had a blue lacquer coating.

When Loyd left the firm about 1 year ago, Angel continued to run the company under the firm-name "VELET Cartridge Company". Angel began to replace the explosive charge and the primer by mercury.

Then, the EXAMMO Company, founded by Greg Loyd, came into existence. He automated the whole processing of the ammunition using thereby commercial components; thus a percussion cap was employed as primer in the bullet. At the beginning, only .38 caliber bullets were produced forming a component of the cartridges. The tip of the projectiles was sealed with yellow lacquer.

Besides the mentioned companies, it was Sidney Brigadier of the "Bingham Ltd.1775-C Wilwat Dr. Narcross, Georgia", who occupied himself with the production of this kind of ammunition; he manufactured it above all by modifying already fabricated rounds. He employed for this purpose to a large extent the "Super Vel" ammunition.

Looking at the bullet design it may be assumed that early VELEX projectiles have been involved in the manufacture. Some cartridges are known to have exploded when dropped by accident.

The manufacturers recommend their ammunition from the following angle:
"The explosive bullet was designed in an effort to obtain an effective, non-ricocheting cartridge with a negligibly penetrating bullet for civilian and police use. By this ammunition, the effectiveness will be increased in case of handgun use in a defense role. These rounds were improved to the point that they are real "man stoppers". Each bullet has a discriminating impact fuse in the nose with a powdered explosive charge underneath".

als tatsächliche „Man'stoppers" bezeichnen kann. Jedes Geschoß hat einen scharfen Aufschlagzünder in der Spitze und eine Pulversprengladung dahinter."

Da die Sprengladung die verfügbare Geschoßenergie sehr wirksam bringt, haben z.B. VELET-Patronen zweimal soviel „relative Aufhaltekraft" (RSP) wie Hochgeschwindigkeitspatronen mit Hohlspitzgeschossen. Im Normalfall wird angenommen, daß 50 Einheiten RSP erforderlich sind, einen nachhaltigen Effekt zu erzielen.

Die Firma VETET hat in ihren Vergleichstabellen u.a. folgende Werte angegeben: (siehe Tabelle 10).

Die Firma Velet errechnet die RSP ihrer Explosionsgeschosse aus der Messung der Geschwindigkeitsverminderung der Geschoßsplitter. Die hydrostatische Wirkung der Explosion wird nicht berücksichtigt. Daher sind die angegebenen RSP-Werte mit Vorsicht zu bewerten.

Aus den Unterlagen der Firma „VELET" sind weiter folgende Angaben zu entnehmen:

1) Da die VELET-Geschosse ihre Energie in den Zielkörper abgeben, sind sie austrittsicherer als jede andere verfügbare Munition. Was die Querschlägerwirkung anbelangt, so zerlegen sich die VELET-Geschosse besser als diejenigen einer jeglichen anderen Munitionsart.
2) Die Munition ist sehr sicher in ihrer Waffe! Sie explodiert nicht wenn sie zu Boden fällt!
3) VETET-Geschosse werden mit höchster Geschwindigkeit verschossen. Bitte diese Munition nicht mit höherer oder geringerer Geschwindigkeit wiederladen. Die Munitionsarten der Firma Velet sind sehr sicher und können wie jede Art von Munition behandelt werden, jedoch kann das Hantieren mit dem Aufschlagzünder zu Verletzungen führen.

„Außer Reichweite von Kindern Aufbewahren."

Siehe Tabelle 11

Since the explosive charge delivers the available bullet energy so violently, VELEX's cartridges, for instance have twice the Relative Stopping Power (RSP) of the High Velocity hollow point ammunition. Normally, 50 units of RSP are considered as necessary to do an effective job. The VELEX Company indicated in their comparison tables among others the following values:

(see table 10)

The VELEX Company calculate the RSP of the explosive bullets from measurements of bullet fragment deceleration. The hydrostatic effects of the explosion itself are not accounted for. As a result, the above-indicated RSP figures are conservative.

From literature of the VELET Company there are gathered, furthermore, the following comments:

1) "Because VELEX bullets deliver their energy in the objective, they are more resistant to exiting than anything available. As for ricochet, VELEX bullets fragment better than any other type of ammunition.„
2) "The ammunition is very safe in your weapon! It will not explode, if accidentally dropped!"
3) VELET bullets are driven at optimum velocity. Don't reload this ammunition to a higher or lower velocity. VELEX ammunition is very safe and can be handled as any other type of ammunition; however, tampering with the impact fuse may result in personal injury. Keep out of reach of children.

VELET ammunition is manufactured in the following calibers and with the following specifications:

see table 11

Tabelle/Table: 10

a)	Kal. 9 mm kurz HV/Hsp.	Kal. 9 × 19 HV/Hsp.	Kal. .38 HV/Hsp.
a)	Cal. .380 ACP HV/JHP	Kal. 9 mm Luger HV/JHP	Cal. .38 HV/JHP
b)	VELET	VELET	VELET
	RSP:		
a)	28	46 Austritt/Exits	35
b)	55+	98+kein Austritt/Stops	85+

a)	Kal. .357 Magn. HV/Hsp.	Kal. .45 ACP HV/Hsp.	Kal. .44 SPL. HV/Hsp.
a)	Cal. .357 Mag. HV/JHP.	Cal. .45 ACP HV/Hsp.	Cal. .44 SPL. HV/JHP
b)	VELET	VELET	VELET
	RSP:		
a)	52 Austritt/Exits	65	60Austritt/Exits
b)	115 kein Austritt/Stops	180+	175+ kein Austritt/Stops

Tabelle/table: 11

Die Velet Munition wird in folgenden Kalibern und mit den angegebenen technischen Daten hergestellt:

Abb./Figure:	123	124	125
			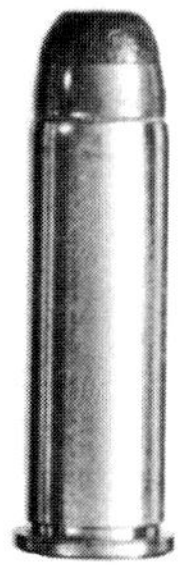
Kaliber:	9 mm Browning Kurz	9 mm Parabellum	.38 S&W Special
G. Gewicht:	6 g	6 g	6,75 g
Geschw. (V_0)	320 m/sec	410 m/sec	350 m/sec
Caliber:	.380 ACP	9 mm Luger	.38 S&W Special
Bullet weight	93 grs	93grs	104 grs
Velocity (V_0)	1050 fps	1345 fps	1148 fps

	126	127	128	129
	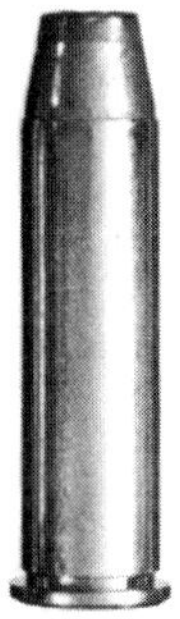	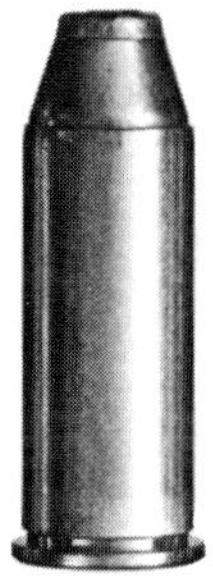		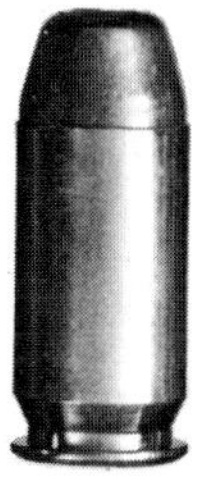
Kaliber:	.357 Magnum	.44 S&W Special	.44 Magnum	.45 ACP
G. Gewicht:	8,1 g	11,35 g	13,6 g	11,35 g
Geschw. (V_0)	410 m/sec	320 m/sec	410 m/sec	320 m/sec
Caliber:	.357 Magnum	.44 S&W Special	.44 Magnum	.45 ACP
Bullet weight	125 grs	175 grs	210 grs	175 grs
Velocity (V_0)	1345 fps	1050 fps	1345 fps	1050 fps

Tabelle/table: 12

Umwandlung von englischen Zoll in Millimeter

Conversion table inches to millimeters

Zoll				mm	Zoll				mm
	1/64	.016	(.0156)	0,3969		33/64	.516	(.5156)	13,0969
1/32	2/64	.031	(.0312)	0,7938	17/32	34/64	.531	(.5312)	13,4938
	3/64	.047	(.0469)	1,1906		35/64	.547	(.5469)	13,8906
1/16	4/64	.062	(.0625)	1,5875	9/16	36/64	.562	(.5625)	14,2875
	5/64	.078	(.0781)	1,9844		37/64	.578	(.5781)	14,6844
3/32	6/64	.094	(.0937)	2,3812	19/32	38/64	.594	(.5937)	15,0812
	7/64	.109	(.1094)	2,7781		39/64	.609	(.6094)	15,4781
1/8	8/64	.125	(.1250)	3,1750	5/8	40/64	.625	(.6250)	15,8750
	9/64	.141	(.1406)	3,5719		41/64	.641	(.6406)	16,2719
5/32	10/64	.156	(.1562)	3,9688	21/32	42/64	.656	(.6562)	16,6688
	11/64	.172	(.1719)	4,3656		43/64	.672	(.6719)	17,0656
3/16	12/64	.187	(.1875)	4,7625	11/16	44/64	.687	(.6875)	17,4625
	13/64	.203	(.2031)	5,1594		45/64	.703	(.7031)	17,8594
7/32	14/64	.219	(.2187)	5,5562	23/32	46/64	.719	(.7187)	18,2562
	15/64	.234	(.2344)	5,9531		47/64	.734	(.7344)	18,6531
1/4	16/64	.250	(.2500)	6,3500	3/4	48/64	.750	(.7500)	19,0500
	17/64	.266	(.2656)	6,7469		49/64	.766	(.7656)	19,4469
9/32	18/64	.281	(.2812)	7,1438	25/32	50/64	.781	(.7812)	19,8438
	19/64	.297	(.2969)	7,5406		51/64	.797	(.7969)	20,2406
5/16	20/64	.312	(.3125)	7,9375	13/16	52/64	.812	(.8125)	20,6375
	21/64	.328	(.3281)	8,3344		53/64	.828	(.8281)	21,0344
11/32	22/64	.344	(.3437)	8,7312	27/32	54/64	.840	(.8402)	21,3412
	23/64	.359	(.3594)	9,1281		55/64	.859	(.8594)	21,8281
3/8	24/64	.375	(.3750)	9,5250	7/8	56/64	.875	(.8750)	22,2250
	25/64	.391	(.3906)	9,9219		57/64	.891	(.8906)	22,6219
13/32	26/64	.406	(.4062)	10,3188	29/32	58/64	.906	(.9062)	23,0188
	27/64	.422	(.4219)	10,7156		59/64	.922	(.9219)	23,4156
7/16	28/64	.437	(.4375)	11,1125	15/16	60/64	.937	(.9375)	23,8125
	29/64	.453	(.4531)	11,5094		61/64	.953	(.9531)	24,2094
15/32	30/64	.469	(.4687)	11,9062	31/32	62/64	.969	(.9687)	24,6062
	31/64	.484	(.4844)	12,3031		63/64	.984	(.9844)	25,0031
1/2	32/64	.500	(.5000)	12,7000	1	64/64	1.000	(1.0000)	25,4000

Index

Inhalt	Seite	Index	Page

Literatur/Bibliography

1. BARNES	Military Handguns, Gun Digest 1964
2. BKIW	Preisliste, Karlsruhe 1928
3. BOCK, G.	Moderne Faustfeuerwaffen, 2. Aufl., Neudamm 1911
4. BOCK, G.-WEIGEL, W.	Handbuch der Faustfeuerwaffen, 2. Aufl., Melsungen 1964
4a BRANDT-HAMANN	DWJ Triplex-Geschosse 1972 - die Doppelgeschoßpatronen
5. BROWN, D.M.	The 36 Calibers of the Colt Single Action Army, Albuquerque, N.M. 1965
6. CAPITAINE, E. v. HERTLING, PH.	Die Kriegswaffen, Band I-VI, Rathenow 1885–1895
7. CHAPEL, CH.E.	Gun Collector's Handbook of Values, New York, N.Y. 1963
8. CHIEF OF ORDNANCE	Report of Board on Tests of Revolvers and Automatic Pistols, Washington, D.C. 1907
9. DARDICK CORP.	Dardick Firearms & Ammunition, Hamden, Conn. 1959
10. DATIG, F.A.	Cartridges for Collectors, Vol. I–III, Los Angeles, Calif. 1956, 1958, 1967
11. DOWELL, W.CH.	The Webley Story, Kirkgate, Leeds 1962
12. DWM	Munitions-Katalog No. 3, Karlsruhe 1904
13. DWM	Original-Hülsenbuch, Karlsruhe 1912
14. DWM	Original-Geschoßbuch, Karlsruhe 1912
15. DWM	Patrone und Schuß, Karlsruhe 1937
16. EGESTORFF, G.	Hülsen-Katalog, Linden/Hannover
17. ELEY BROS.	Munitions-Katalog, London 1898
18. ERLMEIER, H.A.	Die englische Revolverpatrone Kaliber .455, Deutsches Waffen-Journal, Mai 1968
19, FIOCCHI, G.	Munitions-Katalog, Lecco 1961
20. GENSCHOW, G.	Waffen- und Munitions-Katalog, Berlin 1937
21. GLASER, W.	Waffen- und Munitions-Katalog, Zürich 1933
22. GOODMAN, R.G.	The .455 Webley & Scott Pistol, The American Rifleman, May 1962
23. HACKLEY, F.W.– WOODIN,W.H.–SCRANTON,E.L.	History of Modern U.S. Military Small Arms Ammunition, Vol. I, 1880–1939, New York, N.Y. 1967
24. HATCH, A.	Remington Arms in American History, New York, N.Y. 1956
25. HOXIE AMMUNITION CO.	Hoxie Bullet, Chicago, I11.1907
26. JOHNSON, M.M.– HAVEN, CH.T.	Automatic Weapons of the World, New York, N.Y. 1945
27. KYNOCH, G.	Munitions-Katalog, Birmingham 1894
28. LABBETT, P.	British Automatic Pistol Trials, Guns Review, August – October 1964
29. LOGAN, H.C.	Cartridges, New York, N.Y. 1959
30. LUGS, J.	Handfeuerwaffen, Band I und II, Prag 1956
31. MATHEWS, J.H.	Firearms Identification, University of Wisconsin 1962
32. NOBEL INDUSTRIES LTD.	Munition-Katalog, London 1925
33. PETERSON, H.L.	The Remington Historical Treasury of American Guns, New York, N.Y. 1966
34. POLLARD, H.B.C.	Automatic Pistols, Old Greenwich, Conn. (Reprint of 1920 edition)
35. REMINGTON ARMS CO.	Sport-, Jagdwaffen und Munition 1970/71, Bridgeport, Conn.
36. ROTH, G.	Munitions-Katalog, Wien 1899
37. ROTH, G.	Munitions-Katalog, Wien 1910
38. ROTH, G.	Munitions-Katalog, Wien 1925
39. ROY, R.E.	.41 Colt Special, Shooting Times, March 1970
40. RWS	Hülsen-Katalog, Nürnberg 1898
41. RWS	Geschoß-Katalog, Nürnberg 1898
41. SCHMIDT, R.	Die Handfeuerwaffen, Basel 1875
43. S.F.M.	Munitions-Katalog, Paris 1900
44. SMITH, W.H.B.	Book of Pistols and Revolvers, Harrisburg, Pa. 1965

45. STERRET, L.S. — Mars Automatic Pistols, Gun Digest 1961

46. SUYDAM, CH.R. — American Pistol and Revolver Cartridges, The Gun Report, May 1965 – March 1966

47. THIERBACH, M. — Die geschichtliche Entwicklung der Handfeuerwaffen, Dresden 1886/1899

48. TREADWELL, T.J. — Metallic Cartridges, Washington, D.C. 1873

49. U.M.C. — Illustrated Catalogue of Ammunition, Bridgeport, Conn. 1905

50. U.M.C.– REMINGTON — Illustrated Catalogue, Bridgeport, Conn./Ilion, N.Y. 1910

51. U.S.C.Co. — Price List, Lowell, Mass. 1891

52. WATROUS, G.E. — The History of Winchester Firearms 1866–1966, North Haven, Conn. 1966

53. WHITE, H.P.– MUNHALL, B.D. — Centerfire Metric Pistol and Revolver Cartridges, Vol.I, Washington, D.C. 1948

54. WHITE, H.P.– MUNHALL, B.D. — Centerfire American and British Pistol and Revolver Cartridges, Vol.II, Washington, D.C. 1950

55. WHITE, H.P.– MUNHALL, B.D.– BEARSE, R. — Pistol and Revolver Cartridges, Cranbury, N.J. 1967

56. WILLE, R. — Auszug aus dem Gutachten über Bergmanns Kriegswaffen, Stuttgart 1906

57. WILSON, R.K. — Textbook of Automatic Pistols, Plantersville, S.C.1943

58. WINCHESTER — Katalog für Waffen und Munition, 1970

59. W.R.A.Co. — Catalogue and Price List No.64, New Haven, Conn.1899

60. YUST, CH.H. — Black Powder Miscellany, Gun Digest 1959

61. VELEXIVELET — Munitionsprospekte (Firma)

62. ARCANE — Bericht (Anonym)

63. K.T.W. — Munitionsprospekte u.- Berichte (Firma)

64. SHORT STOP — Bericht (v. J.E. Smialek u. W.U.Spitz)

65. GLASER SAFETY SLUG — Bericht (American Handgunner 1977)

66. SALVO SQUEEZ BORE — a) Colt-Report 850–2095
b) Bericht R.S. Robinson